THE MUTINY
OF
THE BENGAL ARMY

An Historical Narrative.

BY ONE WHO HAS SERVED UNDER
SIR CHARLES NAPIER

The Naval & Military Press Ltd

published in association with

FIREPOWER
The Royal Artillery Museum
Woolwich

Published by
The Naval & Military Press Ltd
Unit 10 Ridgewood Industrial Park,
Uckfield, East Sussex,
TN22 5QE England
Tel: +44 (0) 1825 749494
Fax: +44 (0) 1825 765701
www.naval-military-press.com

in association with

FIREPOWER
The Royal Artillery Museum, Woolwich
www.firepower.org.uk

In reprinting in facsimile from the original, any imperfections are inevitably reproduced and the quality may fall short of modern type and cartographic standards.

TO

THE LIVING AND THE DEAD—

THE LIVING EARL OF ELLENBOROUGH

AND

THE DEAD SIR CHARLES NAPIER,

WHO BOTH KNEW

HOW TO CHECK A MUTINY,

TO SELECT EFFICIENT PUBLIC SERVANTS,

AND TO GAIN THE AFFECTIONS OF THOSE OVER WHOM THEIR

SWAY EXTENDED,

These Pages are Dedicated.

India, July 2, 1857.

INTRODUCTION.

I PURPOSE to write an historical narrative of the rise, progress, and termination of the mutiny and revolt of the Bengal Army. It will be my object to expose, in the first instance, the causes of the disaffection, to state then the consequences to which that disaffection led, and to conclude by pointing out the remedies which ought to be adopted to ensure the country against a repetition of the fearful outrages that have disgraced it. As my object is simply to present to my countrymen in England a true account of this awful disaster, and of all the causes which, either directly or indirectly, have led to it, I shall be deterred by no feeling of favour or affection for any individual from speaking out as the occasion demands, awarding praise where praise has been earned, but not shrinking from denouncing those whose conduct has at all contributed to the rise and progress of the mutiny.

It will, I think, be advisable in the first instance, for the benefit of non-professional readers, to present a slight sketch of the organisation and interior economy of a Bengal Infantry Regiment, more especially as on the maintenance or entire abrogation of the existing system the future discipline and efficiency of the army will depend.

Organisation of a Bengal Regiment.—A Regiment of Infantry on the Bengal Establishment is composed of 1000 privates, 120 non-commissioned officers, and 20 native commissioned officers. It is divided into ten companies, each containing 100 privates, 2 native commissioned, and 12 non-commissioned, officers. The regiment is never quartered in barracks, but in lines—such lines consisting of ten rows of thatched huts—one being apportioned to each company. In front of each of these rows is a small circular building, in which the arms and accoutrements are stored, after having been cleaned, and the key of which is generally in the possession of the havildar (sergeant) on duty. Promotion invariably goes by seniority, and the commanding officer of a regiment has no power to pass over any man, without representing the fact to the Commander-in-Chief. A Sepoy, then, who may enter the service at the age of 16, cannot count on finding himself a naick (corporal) before he attains the age of 36, a sergeant (havildar) at 45, a jemadar (native lieutenant) at

54, and a subahdar (native captain) at 60.* By the time he has attained the age of 50, a native may generally be considered as utterly useless. The blood in his veins and the marrow in his bones have been dried up or wasted by constant exposure to the trying climate of India; his energies are relaxed, his memory impaired, and in governing and controlling the men who are especially under his surveillance in the lines, he can be of but little use to his European superior.

Caste.—But there is a principle at work, unknown to the European soldiers, which operates with tremendous force on the mind of the native, and either essentially adds to, or vitally detracts from, the authority of the native officer. This principle is *caste*. Now the predominating race in a Bengal regiment is the Hindoo; the followers of that religion, as a general rule, being to the Mahomedans in the proportion of five to one. A regiment, a thousand strong, will therefore be found to contain about eight hundred Hindoos. Of these it often happens that more than four hundred are Brahmins or priests, about two hundred Rajpoots (a high caste, but lower than the Brahminical order), and the rest of a lower caste.

The Brahmins are the most influential, as they are the most bigoted of the whole race of Hindoos. In their mythological tales the gods themselves are constantly made to do penance and propitiation to this superior order. As these tales form the only kind of literature circulated amongst the Hindoos, and as the acts they record, however absurd they may appear to the educated, are implicitly believed, it is not to be wondered at that the Brahmins are the objects of veneration to the other castes. "The feet of a holy man are like the waters of life," is a proverb which gains implicit credence from all classes, and is at the same time practically acted upon. His curse is dreaded as a fate worse than death itself, whilst his protection is earnestly sought after by means of small presents, and of what to them is more valuable, constant prostrations or salaams publicly performed, so as to show the world the extent of the belief in their mighty power. When it is considered that in each regiment of the Bengal Army there are several of these men, in many regiments from three to four hundred, the mighty influence they have in their power to exert for good or evil may be imagined.

The manner in which this influence can be brought to bear on the discipline of a regiment may be easily conceived. We will suppose that one company is composed of 20 Mahomedans, 40 Brahmins, and 40 Rajpoots and lower-caste Hindoos. The influence of the Brahmins over the 80 Hindoos is paramount, and the Mahomedans being a small minority, would not contest the palm with them. The whole company may, therefore, be said to be under Brahminical influence.

* These are the extreme ages. In the regiments engaged in the Affghanistan, Sutlej, and Punjab campaigns, promotion has been attained at much earlier ages than are here set down

If a low-caste Hindoo happened at the time to fill the responsible post of subahdar, he would be entirely under the spiritual guiding of the Brahminical clique. Were a mutiny hatching in the lines, he would not dare to divulge it, from the fear of a penalty more dreadful even than death — excommunication.

It is very evident, therefore, that by means of this pernicious system of caste, the men of a Bengal regiment, though nominally subject to the British Crown, are really under the orders and control of a Brahminical clique, formed in each regiment, constantly corresponding with one another, and acting without any sense of responsibility whatever.

European Officers.—Hitherto it has been supposed that the example of, and association with their European officers, have done more than anything else to loosen the power of caste. And it has undoubtedly been proved that on many trying occasions, especially during the Affghanistan war, when the Sepoys were exposed to more than ordinary trials, these men, generally so tenacious, have forgotten their prejudices, and have infringed many of their strictest precepts. It was in Affghanistan that the Sepoy earned the character given of him by Major D'Arcey Todd, of Herat renown, that "he would go anywhere, and do anything, if led by an officer in whom he had confidence." He earned and deserved that character in that rude country. Removed from the influences which hourly thrust themselves upon him in India, he was in Affghanistan a different and a far more useful being; but the moment he returned, he indued his prejudices at once, and became again the bigoted, relentless Brahmin. Still, even upon him then, the example of his officer had a certain influence. That is to say, he was prompt to recognise a daring, chivalrous nature, and to pay a sort of homage, not unmixed with fear, to high intellectual powers. Where an officer was at all lax in the performance of his duty, the Sepoy was certain to be lax also; and in cases where a stern strictness was unaccompanied by an occasional warmth, a good word off duty, or an inclination to patronise their sports, the officer was obeyed, but uncared for. Twenty-six officers make up the complement of a native regiment, but of these nearly half were generally absent, and there were seldom more than fifteen present at head-quarters. For the management of a regiment under Brahminical control, as all Bengal regiments are, this number is amply sufficient in times of peace. That is to say, the management is not affected by the mere number. In fact, the conduct of Irregular regiments, which possess only three officers, has always contrasted so favourably with that of Line regiments, with their fourteen or fifteen, that the natural conclusion one would arrive at is, that the latter are over-officered.

The officers live in bungalows, or thatched houses, near the lines of their regiments, but too far off to enable them to have any direct control over the movements of their men during the day; and for eight months of the year at least, the weather is too warm to allow them to ride out, except in the morning and evening. In order, however, to have the whole regiment under constant European supervision, two sergeants are allowed to each corps, who are required to live in the lines, and to report all that goes on daily to the Adjutant.

Duties of Officers.—The duties of the officers are very similar to those performed in an English regiment. There is a Commander, generally of the rank of Lieutenant-Colonel, who commands the regiment; an Adjutant, who superintends the drill, and makes daily reports to the commanding officer; an Interpreter and Quarter-Master, whose duty it is to look after the clothing of the men, and to interpret all orders: then each company is assigned to a separate officer, who is expected to settle all matters connected with his men every morning; or, should he be unable to do so, to refer them to the commanding officer.

Powers of the Commanding Officer.—The power of a commanding officer is of a very limited nature: he can make no promotions to the grade of commissioned officer; even in the ordinary rise from Sepoy to naick, should he think fit to pass over a man, his decision is liable to be upset by the Commander-in-Chief: he can make no prompt recognition of distinguished services; and, worse than all, by a recent order of Sir W. Gomm, he cannot refuse a court-martial to any Sepoy who may choose to demand it, in reference to the punishment which may have been awarded to him. The commanding officer is therefore quite powerless, and the men know it. Once it was otherwise: there was a time when the Commandant had it in his power to punish or reward, and his decision was irrevocable. But the system has been gradually changed. Commanders-in-Chief fresh from Europe, and accustomed all their lives to command Englishmen, have forgotten the inherent distinction between the European and the Asiatic, and in endeavouring to assimilate the rules for the latter to those which are suited only to the former, have broken down one of the chief barriers to Brahminical supremacy. One consequence of the present system is the gradual decline and final loss of all regard on the part of the men for their officers. As members of a Christian and converting religion they are disliked, as superiors they are no longer feared. Personal qualities may attract a short-lived admiration, but even that would shiver to atoms in the encounter with Hindoo fanaticism.

The Pension List.—But there was one resource upon which the Government relied above all others to influence their Sepoys, and this was by making it their interest to remain faithful to the British standard. The establishment of a pension list on a large and liberal scale, by the operation of which a fixed monthly stipend was secured to any soldier who might be incapacitated for further duty after a service of fifteen years, and which, moreover, provided for the heirs or nearest of kin of those who might perish in the field of battle, or from sickness whilst on foreign service, seemed well adapted to secure this end. A nobler or more liberal institution than the pension establishment for native soldiers does not exist, and it was thought by those competent to judge, that the estimation of the benefits accruing from it was fixed so firmly in the minds of the Sepoys, that that single consideration would weigh against all temptations to mutiny or revolt. The result has shown that Hindoo fanaticism, when fairly pitted against the enjoyment of present comfort, the certain prospect of rank and wealth, a sure provision for one's family, a reputation for loyalty of one hundred years' standing, will invariably carry the day in a regiment where Brahminical influence is paramount, and where the European officers do not possess absolute authority.

Yet such had been the condition of the Bengal Army for several years before the outbreak of the mutiny of which I am about to treat. The slumbering feeling first showed itself of late years during the rule of Lord Ellenborough, but the prompt and vigorous measures of that nobleman so completely repressed it, that for six years no similar symptom was anywhere apparent. A second time it rose in a still more dangerous form, and attempted to coerce the iron will of Sir Charles Napier. That gallant veteran extinguished it ere yet the spark had smouldered into a flame, and was rebuked by Lord Dalhousie for so doing. He retired, to avoid witnessing with his hands tied the catastrophe which he foresaw. A third time, in 1852, the prejudices of the Sepoys were placed in opposition to the will of Government. Lord Dalhousie requested the 38th Regiment to proceed to Burma. They refused. Lord Dalhousie succumbed. From that moment a revolt became a mere question of time and opportunity.

CHAPTER I.

THE FIRST MANIFESTATIONS OF REVOLT.

DURING the year 1854, the 38th Regiment Native Infantry, unpunished for their refusal to go to Burma, were located at the station of Cawnpore; there were two other regiments at the same station, the 63rd and 74th Native Infantry. At Lucknow, distant about fifty miles, were the 19th and 34th Regiments; at Allygurh, on the high road between Cawnpore and Meerut, was the 54th Regiment, which also supplied troops to the small civil stations of Etawah, Mynpoorie, and Bolundshuhr, the two former in the vicinity of Cawnpore and Agra, the latter close to Meerut. At Allahabad, about 125 miles from Cawnpore, the 11th and 48th Regiments were stationed. The native troops at Meerut consisted of the 3rd Cavalry, and the 36th and 46th Regiments. Considering the joint share which many of the regiments thus enumerated had in the late outbreak, it is reasonable to suppose that constant communications were going on between them all. No suspicion of it existed at the time in any quarter. Our native troops were as much trusted as Europeans; it was believed that they were not only completely satisfied, but that they regarded service in our ranks as preferable to any other mode of obtaining a livelihood. And certainly the authorities had grounds for this belief. No sound of disaffection was heard in any quarter. For every vacancy in the ranks there were more candidates than could possibly be enrolled, and the tone and bearing of the Sepoys towards their officers left nothing to be desired in that respect.

The relation of the Sepoys to the Province of Oudh.—An event, however, was about to occur, which, in the opinion of officers who had served long in India, would put to the severest test the feelings of the native soldiery towards their foreign masters. Of all the considerable native states with which we had come in contact, the province of Oudh was the only one which had maintained its independence intact. Immediately contiguous to our own possessions, inhabited by a mixed population of Hindoos and Mahomedans, from which our own army was principally recruited, the kingdom of Oudh had remained for upwards of half a century firm in its alliance to the British Government. During the height of our reverses in Affghanistan, that friendship had never wavered. So firm indeed was the attachment to, or the perception of the power of British arms, that the Kings of Oudh had more than once, in the season of our distress, accommodated our Government with loans to a considerable amount, in repayment of which we, to our shame be it said, compelled them to receive accessions of territory alike useless to both parties. We were therefore under considerable obligations to the Court of Lucknow. Undoubtedly, the Kings of Oudh regarded us in the light of a protecting rather than an absorbing power. It had been their policy for years and years to give in to every demand of the British Government, and to avoid every act which, directly or indirectly, might give a claim for interference in their internal affairs. To this end the suggestion of the Resident, whom, backed by three native regiments, we maintained at the Court of Lucknow, was always considered as law, and the intrigues for his favour amongst the candidates for places in the king's council were carried on in a manner which those who have visited Constantinople may perhaps understand.

The King of Oudh, then, believed himself secure from further interference than that which I have just related, and it was generally believed, amongst the civil and military community of India, that the Government had no serious intention of annexing any portion of his country. There seemed indeed, in a political view, to be strong objections to such a course. The King of Oudh was the sole remaining independent Mahomedan sovereign in India; as such he commanded the veneration and regard of all the members of the Mussulman persuasion. To strike him down, then, would excite a general feeling of discontent amongst a very numerous and powerful class of our subjects—men of whom the Cavalry regiments were chiefly composed, and who supplied at least two hundred bayonets to each regiment of Native Infantry. From his territories, indeed, our army was almost entirely recruited. The Hindoo and Mahomedan Sepoy alike came from Oudh; he transmitted all his savings to his relatives in that country; and it is a remarkable fact, and one that fully refutes Lord Dalhousie's assertions about the mis-government of Oudh, that not a single instance has been known of a Sepoy settling down after the completion of his service in our provinces: he has invariably proceeded to Oudh, to invest his little fortune in land. Colonel Sleeman, for many years our agent at the Court of Lucknow, and one of the ablest men who ever held that appointment, was so well aware of this fact, that he lost no opportunity of impressing upon Government his conviction that the annexation of Oudh would produce disaffection in the native army, principally because it would transfer the family of the Sepoy from the operation of the regal regulations and justice of the King of Oudh to our own civil courts.

But Colonel Sleeman died, and Sir James Outram reigned in his stead. New councillors, aware of Lord Dalhousie's mania for annexation, succeeded the tried statesmen who had hitherto so successfully administered the affairs of our empire on a contrary principle, and in an evil hour Lord Dalhousie decided upon seizing Oudh. He resolved to do it, too, in a manner the most offensive, and the most irritating to the large Mahomedan population of India, and the most prejudicial to our own character for truth and honour. He secretly collected troops, entered the kingdom of Oudh like a thief in the night, marched the British force directly upon Lucknow, and then, with the capital of Oudh virtually in his own hands, gave the first intimation to the King of his impending fate. Wajid Ali, of course, was unable to resist, and Oudh became from that moment a province of the British Empire.

It is impossible to describe the mixed feelings of indignation and hatred which pervaded the whole Mussulman population of India when they heard of this deed. Naturally treacherous themselves, they yet had an instinctive admiration for honest and truthful dealing, and they had hitherto placed implicit confidence in the word of an Englishman. When, however, they learned the story of the annexation, the juggle by which the King of Oudh had been done out of his dominions, their hearts filled with rage and a desire for revenge. Our Mahomedan Sepoys were by that act alienated at once and for ever, and the Hindoos began to reflect that the kingly power which could condescend to trick a king out of his dominions, might by a similar manœuvre cheat them out of their religion.

Such were the consequences of Lord Dalhousie's last act. He had first, in the instance of the 38th Native Infantry at Barrackpore, in 1852, sown the seed of revolt by provoking a mutiny and failing to check it. He followed this up in the early part of 1856 by the perpetration of a dark deed, calculated to raise a spirit of disaffection, dislike, and distrust throughout the native army of India, and the fruits of which I am now about to record. He did all this, I may add, in spite of, and in direct contrariety to, the warning voice of the great man whom his paltry littleness and petty jealousy had driven from the country.

Lord Dalhousie left India in the early part of 1856. So utterly ignorant was he of the real feeling of the native army, and of the effect of his ill-judged measures, that he left upon record his opinion that their position could not be improved. And yet he himself had done a great deal to affect that position most injuriously. Before Lord Dalhousie's time, the roads were free to man and beast; that nobleman imposed a tax upon all travellers. Previous to his arrival in India, a Sepoy's letters were allowed to travel free of postage all over India; under Lord Dalhousie's administration he was subjected to the same charge as his officer. These imposts were small in themselves, but they greatly restricted freedom, and told upon the pocket of the man who received only fourteen shillings monthly, with which to support his family hundreds of miles distant, and to provide himself with food and all the necessaries of life.

Lord Dalhousie left India in March 1856. It might have been supposed that the feelings of the native Indian community would have been relieved sensibly by his absence. And so, undoubtedly, they were for the moment. But it was soon found that, although he himself had quitted the country, he had left his counsellors and satellites behind him. It is a matter of necessity for a newly-arrived Governor-General, ignorant of the machinery and working of the Indian Government, to continue in office, for a time at least, the officials whom he may find installed in the several departments. Lord Canning has, therefore, been compelled since his arrival to work with Lord Dalhousie's tools. He has since, it is reported, found out their utter inefficiency. As it is important for the right understanding of my narrative that the characters and habits of thought of these men should be known and appreciated, I do not think I can do better than present in this place a sketch of each individual member of Government, for the benefit of the reader.

Characters of the Members of the Government of India on Lord Canning's arrival.—The Supreme Council of India is composed of four members, in concert with whom the Governor-General administers the affairs of the country. At the time of Lord Canning's assumption of office these members consisted of Mr. Dorin and Mr. J. P. Grant, members of the Civil Service, General Low of the Madras Army, and Mr. Peacock of the English Bar.

There were four Secretaries to Government: Mr. Lushington for the Financial, Mr. Beadon for the Home, Colonel Birch for the Military, and Mr. Edmonstone for the Foreign Department. It will suffice for the purposes of my narrative to describe the Members of Council and the Military and Home Secretaries.

Mr. Dorin.—Mr. Dorin was a man who, in a service of thirty-three years, had never been fifty miles out of Calcutta in the direction of the interior: he was, therefore, practically ignorant of the manners, and customs, and peculiar requirements of the people of India. For all practical purposes, those three-and-thirty years might as well, or even with more advantage, have been spent in England. He was verging upon sixty years of age, and in all his habits was a very Sybarite. His experience of ruling had been principally confined to the Financial Department; but even there his budgets bore a stronger resemblance in their results to those of Sir Charles Wood, than to the more perfect calculations of Sir R. Peel or Mr. Gladstone. In 1854, during Lord Dalhousie's absence in the Neelghery Hills, he had temporarily assumed the Presidency of the Council. His tenure of that office was chiefly remarkable for the outbreak of the Southal rebellion, and for the weak and inefficient measures pursued to check it. He was indolent, void of energy, deficient in mental culture and ability, and certainly, in no other country but India, and in no other service but the Civil Service, would have attained any but the most subordinate position.

Mr. J. P. Grant.—Mr. Grant was a very different character. In the prime of life, active, energetic, and possessed of a certain amount of ability, he might, had he been trained in any other school, have done good service on the occurrence of a crisis. Unfortunately, he laboured under a complete ignorance of the habits and customs of the natives of Upper India. Accustomed, during his service, to deal only with Bengalees, he had imbibed the extraordinary notion that they were a type of the Hindostanees generally. His vanity was so great, that he would not stoop to demand information even from practical men of his own service. With the supercilious manner which is so often the accompaniment of a confined understanding, he pooh-

pooh'd every suggestion which was at variance with his settled ideas. Of the Sepoys he had no knowledge whatever, although, with respect to them, he was always ready to offer a suggestion. Of military men in general he had a jealous dislike, which prompted him on every occasion to oppose any plans or suggestions offered by a member of that profession. He was an adept at intrigue, and, being possessed of a practical knowledge of revenue matters, a plausible manner, an easy address, and considerable influence at the India House, he had gained a seat in council at an earlier age than was customary. As a practical man he had always been a failure. It was his advice, given because Mr. Halliday proposed an opposite plan, which delayed for seven or eight months the proclamation of martial law in the Santhal districts; and it will be seen, that on the occasion of the mutiny at Barrackpore, his pernicious influence was always opposed to those prompt and severe measures, on the execution of which the safety of the empire depended. These faults are attributable to the evil action of the school in which he was trained, on a disposition naturally haughty and supercilious. Had he never been a civilian, had he been trained to depend on his own exertions from the moment of his entrance into life, his career would have been more useful to his country and more honourable to himself.

General Low. — General Low was the only really practical member of the council. Unfortunately he was the oldest, and age and climate had already begun to tell upon his nerves. Nevertheless, he was the only man from whom the Governor-General received any real assistance. He knew, at all events, that there ought to be no trifling with mutiny, and he advised accordingly. It is to be lamented that he was wanting in the eloquence or power of language necessary to support his views. He could record a minute, but could not make a speech. And it thus happened that he was unable to defend measures, of the propriety of which he was convinced, against the legal subtleties sometimes brought to bear on them by his colleagues.

Mr. Peacock.—Mr. Peacock was the Law member of council, and as such was not expected to be able to deal with purely military questions. When such matters were debated he generally vacillated between Mr. Grant and General Low, inclining oftener to the civilian. His intentions were always pure, and when convinced of the justice of a cause, no special pleading would alter his vote. Unfortunately, his unacquaintance with soldiers prevented him from comprehending the dangers of unchecked mutiny, and he was found, on trial, ignorant of the proper moment to disregard rule and to resort to urgent measures.

Colonel Birch.—The Secretary to the Government of India in the Military Department was a man in every way unsuited for his position. Placed early in his career in the department of the Judge-Advocate-General, his confined understanding was exerted in mastering the quirks and quibbles of the law. His intellect being essentially shallow, he was unable to take a broad view of any question; but he would argue for hours, and exhaust all his ingenuity in combating some petty detail. When Sir Charles Napier assumed the command of the Indian Army, Col. Birch was Judge-Advocate. He was rather afraid of Sir Charles's downright character, and at their first interview exerted all his powers to please him. No amount of special pleading, however, would go down with the great Conqueror of Scinde.

Sir Charles's bad opinion was, however, of this service to Colonel Birch, that it obtained for him Lord Dalhousie's patronage. That nobleman, eager to show his spite towards Sir C. Napier, took the opportunity of the first vacancy to appoint Colonel Birch Secretary to the Government of India in the Military Department; thus placing him, *de facto*, at the head of the army in India—giving him a position, indeed, exactly analogous to that of the Minister of War in France.

A worse appointment could not have been made. Colonel Birch was essentially a sycophant, always ready to give up his own opinion, if by so doing he could curry favour with his superior. He had tried this plan with Sir C. Napier, but Sir Charles found him out, and not only felt, but showed contempt towards him in consequence: he found it an easier task to ingratiate himself with Lord Dalhousie and his successor.

But he was also an ignoramus. He knew nothing of the Bengal Army. Many years had elapsed since he had even spoken to a Sepoy. He was ignorant of the composition of the army, as well as of its wants; whilst his previous training had so unfitted him for his post, that he could not even write an order without making it unintelligible by excessive quibbling.

Mr. Beadon.—Of Mr. Beadon, the Home Secretary, it will suffice to say that his great idea of policy, the one scheme which he kept constantly before him, was "India for the Civil Service." He looked, in fact, upon the country as the property of the members of the service, and he legislated accordingly. Indigo planters, merchants, in fact all Europeans who were not civilians or soldiers, were discouraged by him. He hated independent Englishmen; he hated the Press, because its motto was "India for the English:" he hated every one and every thing which interfered with his grand idea, and he never lost an opportunity of showing that hatred. Under his rule, India would have remained in our hands what it has been for the last hundred years: its resources would never have been developed, it would have continued almost like a burden on England; but as a compensation, it would have produced annually a certain sum of money as salaries for the family clique who governed the country.

Mr. Beadon had one recommendation: if he was narrow-minded and unscrupulous, he was honest: he could not "smile and smile and be a villain:" he spoke his thoughts freely and honestly, and people whilst they hated, could not help respecting him—a sentiment never entertained towards his colleague in the military department.

Lord Canning.—Such were the men by whom Lord Canning was surrounded on the outbreak of the mutiny. If they were, as a body, vain, ignorant, and incompetent, truth compels me to record that they could not have found a softer soil on which to exercise their talents than that imbedded in the nature of the Governor-General. He was a man of excellent disposition, but weak and vacillating to a degree scarcely to be imagined. It was his great misfortune to be the son of an illustrious man. Qualities were therefore expected from him which he certainly did not inherit from his sire. His abilities were essentially mediocre, and, like many weak men, he almost invariably submitted his intellect to the influence of the last counsellor who had his ear.

He possessed, however, many agreeable qualities, calculated to adorn a private station. His personal courage was undeniable, but he lacked firmness and self-reliance to a degree which quite incapacitated him for his high position. Had he been surrounded by men possessing honesty and ability, he would doubtless have taken his tone from them, and under their advice and tuition would have shown himself equal to the occasion. But the slave of intriguing and incompetent advisers, the shuttlecock of Messrs. Grant, Beadon, and Birch, he gave, as I shall now proceed to show, an impetus to a mutiny which might have been crushed in the bud.

CHAPTER II.

FROM THE OUTBREAK OF THE DISAFFECTION TO THE DISBANDING OF THE 19TH NATIVE INFANTRY.

THE King of Oudh having been, as before stated, summarily deprived of his kingdom, determined to appeal to the Parliament and people of England for redress. Accordingly, in the month of April 1856, he came down to Calcutta, and took up his abode at Garden Reach, in the outskirts of Calcutta, attended by his prime minister, Ally Nucky Khan, and several followers. The Queen-mother, his brother, and one of his sons, proceeded to England, in the month of May following, in order effectually to prosecute the schemes on which he had resolved for the recovery of his kingdom. They set out, in fact, not with any hope on their part, or on the part of the King and his advisers, that their mission would be successful, but in order to convey to the people of England the impression that he had no hope but in their justice and mercy, in order to remove attention from the vast design he had formed — to upset at one blow the British rule in India.

In fact, this plan was decided upon before the King* left Luck-

---

* It should be borne in mind that the expression, "King of Oudh," refers here to those who carried on intrigues in his name. It is probable that the king himself, an imbecile, was not trusted with the full extent of the conspiracy; but his prime minister, Ally Nucky Khan, without doubt a man of transcendant ability, was the soul of the plot. Since his confinement in Fort William he has, in private conversation, attempted to justify himself, by declaring it was a counter-stroke for the treachery by which the seizure of Oudh was consummated.

now. He had become aware, from the reports of his agents, that the Bengal Army was disaffected, and ripe to be worked upon. The Brahminical priesthood throughout the country were impatient at the proselyting efforts of the missionaries, whilst the Mahomedans, as I have shown before, were discontented at seeing the only kingdom connected with them by faith swallowed up by the paramount Power. The King found, in fact, that there never would be a time more propitious for an attempt to overthrow the British. Acting accordingly under able advice, he at once commenced a system of tampering with the native army. [Of the Mahomedans he was sure; the Hindoos, already disaffected, might be acted upon by means of their religion. The new system of administration in Oudh would, he felt satisfied, cause considerable vexation to the families of the Sepoys, and, consequently, no little discontent amongst the Sepoys themselves. His agents were accordingly directed to lay stress on this new interference of the British with the privileges of the natives. It was pointed out to them that they were the original owners of the land, the lords of the soil, but that now, gradually and insidiously, the British were depriving them of their rights, and resolved to go on until they had subverted their religion. An alliance was at the same time entered into with the King of Delhi, who entered heart and soul into the plot, and it was finally determined that throughout the Bengal Presidency, from Calcutta to Peshawur, there should be a simultaneous rising on one day, in which the life of no Christian should be spared. The month of August, 1857, by which time it was hoped the Queen-mother would have left England, was fixed upon for the outbreak.

Had the measures of the Government of India been conducted at this time with even ordinary prudence, had the Military Secretary not blundered in a manner which would have been unpardonable in an ensign of twelve months' standing, it is probable that the attempts of the King of Oudh to tamper with the native army would have altogether failed. In the absence of tangible evidence on the subject, it had been difficult to convince the Hindoo Sepoys that their religion was actually in danger, and without satisfactory proof on that point they were unwilling to rise against the Government. In fact the plot was beginning to languish, when, at this juncture, the combined ignorance and folly of Colonel Birch gave the King of Oudh the very opportunity he had been seeking for in vain.

It is well known that the chief object of a Hindoo's veneration is the cow. She is in his eyes the sacred animal, the visible presence of the Creator on earth. Her life is not only precious, but to take it the greatest crime of which man could be guilty. The slaughter of a cow in a Hindoo village would always have been the signal for a rise. So convinced, indeed, were the Governments of former days of the necessity of respecting this prejudice, that in the large towns where Europeans were stationed a paddock or compound, surrounded by high walls, was set apart for the reception of bullocks intended for their food. The Hindoos always ignored the existence of such a spot; indeed all possible means were adopted to conceal it from them.

To kill a cow openly was openly to violate their religion, and the practice was consequently forbidden throughout India.

Yet, in the face of these prejudices, of the order to respect them, and of the danger of the consequences which must result from their violation, no sooner had the Government of India resolved to introduce the Enfield rifle partially into the Indian army, than the Secretary to Government deliberately issued an order, which, by violating the caste of the Hindoo, was alone sufficient to bring about a revolt. The Enfield rifle required a particular species of cartridge, and this cartridge in England was greased with lard made from the fat either of the hog or the ox. Without reflecting, or if reflecting, ignoring the consequences of his act, Colonel Birch ordered that the cartridges for use in India should be made up similarly to the cartridges in use in England, and should be used by the native troops—that is to say, that Hindoo Sepoys should handle cartridges besmeared with the fat of their sacred animal, the cow ! The knowledge of this fact was conveyed to the Hindoos in the most casual manner. These cartridges had been made up by Lascars—men of an inferior caste. It happened that one day a Lascar requested a Brahmin Sepoy to give him a drink of water from his lotah, or brass pot. The Sepoy refused on the plea of his superior caste, and that the lotah would be defiled by the touch of the Lascar. The Lascar in reply taunted him for talking of defilement, when he every day touched cartridges besmeared with cows' fat. The Hindoo, horror-stricken, rushed to his comrades and told them the story: they inquired, and found it true to the letter. Indignant, believing themselves deceived by the Government, they wrote an account to their comrades throughout India. From that moment the work of the agents of the King of Oudh was easy.

For a man occupying the position of Military Secretary to the Government of India to make so gross a blunder was unpardonable. Equally so that, when the mistake was discovered, no disavowal was made by Government for four months, and then only in consequence of the outbreak at Meerut ! Well aware that the idea had taken possession of the Sepoys' minds, Colonel Birch made no attempt to counteract it, gave no intimation that the manufacture of greased cartridges had been stopped. He calmly surveyed the mischief his acts had caused, and—did nothing. Yet this man, whose blundering incapacity caused the revolt, is still Secretary to the Government of India in the military department !

The consequences of this gross mismanagement were quickly apparent. The agents of the native conspirators were not the men to allow such an opportunity to slip through their fingers. On the 24th of January, less than a week after the discovery of the greased cartridges, the telegraph office at Barrackpore was burned down. An idea seemed to pervade the minds of the Hindoos that the Government was resolved to Christianise them all; that as the plan of open conversion, pursued now for several years, had failed entirely, it had been resolved to resort to insidious and secret measures to bring about the same end; that Lord Canning had undertaken the government of India with that sole object in view, and that he had engaged to accomplish it in three years. Hence the greasing of the cartridges: hence the changes that were talked about in their dress and equipments. They knew our skill; they witnessed the constant scientific improvements evinced in railways, electric telegraphs, &c., and they dreaded lest some morning they should awake and find themselves, owing to some unaccountable ingenuity on our part, deprived of their religion and caste. Discontent took possession of their minds; they were in perpetual dread of something undefined, supernatural: a restless desire of showing their discontent evinced itself, and resulted, after nearly a week's hesitation, in the perpetration of the act recorded above, viz. the burning of the electric telegraph office at Barrackpore.

This station, distant about sixteen miles from Calcutta, was garrisoned entirely by native troops; at this time four regiments were quartered there, the 2nd Grenadiers, the 34th Native Infantry, the 43rd Light Infantry, and the 70th Native Infantry. Between Calcutta and Dinapore, an extent of 400 miles in length and enormous breadth, there was but one European regiment, the 53d Foot. Half of this regiment garrisoned Fort William, the other half was stationed at Dumdum, about seven miles from Calcutta. In case of any disturbance, not a single man could have been spared from the wing located in the fort, whilst the other was insufficient in strength to put down a simultaneous rising of the town and of the native army.

Such an idea, at this time, never suggested itself to a single European in the country. Although after the burning of the telegraph office on the 24th, scarcely a night passed over without the perpetration of some act of incendiarism, these acts were never traced to their source. The Government were confident and callous. Although about this time* the excited state of the minds of the Sepoys, consequent upon the discovery of the nature of the grease, was reported to them, not a single explanation was offered, not an attempt made to soothe them. It is true that an order was issued, after the interval of almost a month, to serve out no more greased cartridges, but, in the absence of any accompanying explanation, the Sepoys viewed that merely as an evidence that the Government was baffled for the time, and waited only a more convenient season for the renewal of their insidious attacks on their caste.

But, although the eyes of our Government were blinded, those of the King of Oudh and his agents were wide open to the importance of the occasion. The minds of the Sepoys at Barrackpore were hourly worked upon, and with such effect, that letters were despatched in shoals to every regiment in the service, giving full details, often amplified and exaggerated, of the cartridge business. Agents were also despatched, well supplied with money, to every station in India; these men were directed to prepare the native army for an immediate rise, and to adopt every possible means to bring about the revolt without the cognizance of the authorities.

* January and February, 1857.

The King of Oudh was well served. The whole army succumbed to his influence; a very considerable portion of the large police force came into his plans, and even where his agents were unsuccessful, in not one instance were they betrayed.

By the middle of the month of February, the discontented amongst the native regiments at Barrackpore had assumed such an appearance, and had risen to such a height, that General Hearsey commanding the Presidency division found it necessary to assemble the troops, in order to point out to them the absurdity of the fears they entertained for their religion. General Hearsey was a very gallant cavalry officer, well acquainted with the native character: he spoke the language also with rare facility. It was not in his power to do more than harangue the troops and report their state of mind to the Government: the first he did well, and at the outset with some effect; but as the second measure produced no explanation or sign from the head of the military department, the Sepoys, still secretly instigated, soon returned to their former state of murmuring against their masters.

To give one instance of the apathy of the Government at this momentous period it will suffice to state, that although disaffection had been manifested, in the most marked manner, by the Sepoys at Barrackpore and Dumdum on account of the greased cartridges, towards the end of January, it was not before the middle of the following month that Colonel Birch telegraphed to the schools of musketry at Seealkote and Umballah to prohibit the use by the Sepoys at those stations of the greased cartridge. Long before the message reached Seealkote (in the heart of the Punjab) those cartridges had been distributed to, and used by, the native troops there located.

The condition of the troops at Barrackpore, towards the latter end of February, was that of men who felt themselves aggrieved, who were resolute to revenge themselves on the supposed authors of their grievances, but who were restrained, partly by fear, partly by policy, from setting about it at once. Suddenly a spark lighted on the powder: it did not, fortunately for us, at the moment ignite, but a low rumbling noise, sufficient to enable us to make some preparation, warned us of our danger. The spark was first visible at Berhampore; it fizzed subsequently at Barrackpore; but the grand explosion took place two months later at Meerut!

On the 24th February, a small guard of the 34th Regiment N.I. arrived in the station of Berhampore; distant from Calcutta about one hundred and twenty miles. As was customary in such cases, the men of the 19th Regiment N.I., then stationed at Berhampore, feasted the men of the 34th guard, and of course inquired after the doings of their comrades at Barrackpore. The 34th men made a clean breast of it; they poured all their grievances into the sympathising ears of their entertainers: not an item in the catalogue was left out—the cartridges, the beef fat, Lord Canning's supposed mission, all were enumerated; the determination of the Barrackpore brigade to mutiny on the first convenient occasion was dwelt upon;—nothing, in short, was omitted which could possibly work upon the feelings of their listeners.

It is a remarkable fact, illustrative of the native character, that in a regiment numbering a thousand men, composed of Mahomedans and Hindoos, of high caste and low caste, not a single man after hearing the astounding stories of the 34th guard thought it worth while to go to his commanding officer or to the adjutant of the regiment and inquire into their truth. They had been associated for years with their European officers, had marched with them from station to station, had received from them the kindest treatment, and, moreover, were conscious of the pride with which they were regarded, and of the implicit confidence placed in them by all. Yet on hearing for the first time, perhaps, tales which were brought them by men of another regiment, of a vast conspiracy brewing against the state, not one of them reported the circumstance or even inquired if it were true!

The acute sensitiveness peculiar to the natives on matters affecting their caste doubtless induced them to accept all they heard as literal truth. For a whole day they brooded over it; in making the morning report to their officers on the 25th of February, their demeanour was quite respectful, there was not an outward sign of the excitement which reigned within. But their feelings had been too much worked upon to allow this passive submission a longer sway. A slight circumstance supplied the igniting spark. On the 25th February, Colonel Mitchell, commanding the 19th, ordered a parade for exercise with blank ammunition for the following morning. In the evening, the blank cartridges were served out to the men. They were of the very same description as those which for a century past had been used by the Bengal Army. These particular cartridges had, in fact, been made up before even an Enfield rifle had reached India, and had been made over to the 19th magazine by the 7th Regiment N.I., on the latter leaving the station. In ordinary circumstances no objection whatever would have been made by any Sepoy to use similar cartridges. But the passions of the men had been roused; their feelings had been so excited that they could no longer control them; they were beyond the power of reason; they felt satisfied that their caste was to be taken away by means of cartridges, and their excitement persuaded them that these were the fatal messengers. They at first refused to receive them, and it was only when their commanding officer threatened all recusants with court-martial that they took them in gloomy silence. That night they held a consultation. The "multitude of counsellors" gave new energy to their fears, and in a moment of fanatical frenzy the regiment rose as one man, and took possession of their arms, shouting defiance.

Intelligence of these facts was promptly conveyed to the commanding officer, Colonel Mitchell. Two courses were open to him. The only troops at the station besides the 19th were a detachment of native cavalry and a battery of native artillery. The night was pitch dark, and no movement could be made with any certainty. He might either, therefore, have despatched the cavalry and artillery to guard the public buildings, the treasury, &c., and await the early dawn for ulterior operations, or he might at once march down on the lines and endeavour to coerce the mutineers. The first course seemed the most prudent, and was urged upon him; however, he adopted the other, and moved as quickly as possible on his mutinous regiment. The night was so dark that he was compelled to use torches to enable him to find the way; in this manner, and with difficulty, he moved on.

In the meanwhile the 19th having seized their arms, remained drawn up in front of their lines, waiting apparently for their European officers to take the initiative. The ground near their lines was interspersed here and there with tanks, and on these, by the light of the torches, they beheld the artillery and cavalry advancing. Had they been thoroughly evil-disposed, it would have been easy for them, in darkness as they were, to have picked off their officers and the artillery-men, whilst the nature of the ground and the darkness of the night would have prevented all idea of danger from the cavalry. They were, however, more excited than ill-disposed, and with arms in their hands they waited the first movement of their officers.

On his part Colonel Mitchell could not have been insensible to the insecurity of his own position; he was marching at the head of natives against natives. Could he depend upon them? It was at all events doubtful. Were he to give the order to charge or to fire, was he certain that he would be obeyed? And if he were not obeyed, not only would there be three regiments in revolt instead of one, but the lives of the residents of that and surrounding stations would be jeopardised. Besides which he found, as had been pointed out to him, that the nature of the ground and the darkness of the night would prevent the possibility of his acting efficiently against the mutineers.

Something, however, must be done: he felt that. After deliberately weighing every circumstance of his position, he deemed it most prudent to try in the first instance the effect of conciliatory measures. He accordingly addressed the men of the 19th; he pointed out to them the absurdity of their fears and the enormity of their offence, and conjured them to give up their arms and return peaceably to their lines.

The 19th on their part were not over-anxious to push matters to extremities; their excitement was beginning to wear off, and many of them felt a little ashamed of themselves. Still they were sensible of the advantage of their position, and seemed resolved not to act under coercion. In reply, therefore, to their Colonel, they expressed their readiness to return to their lines, and to restore their arms to the proper place, provided only the artillery and cavalry were first moved away.

To this unmilitary concession Colonel Mitchell felt averse to accede. However, for the reasons above stated, he was powerless: he did not wish to provoke the 19th into a more open demonstration; he consented then to the proposal, and moved off the artillery and cavalry. The 19th gave up their arms, returned to their lines, and the *émeute* was at an end.

Reflections on Col. Mitchell's conduct.—Colonel Mitchell's conduct on this trying occasion was much criticised at the time, and he was generally condemned for not at all risks enforcing his order to the mutineers to lay down their arms. Subsequent events have proved that had he done so—had he ordered the artillery to fire, or the cavalry to charge—he would not in all probability have been obeyed. Or, even had they endeavoured to obey him, the darkness of the night would have prevented any efficient working of the guns, whilst the Sepoys could have picked off the gunners with but little risk to themselves. Had he been worsted in the encounter, the rebellion would have been precipitated two months; the regiments at Barrackpore would have risen *en masse*, and the consequences to the metropolis would have been fearful.

The writer is of opinion that if Colonel Mitchell erred, he erred in not adopting the advice said to have been tendered to him of placing guards over the treasury and public buildings till the morning, and then acting with decision. But even then, as shown above, the result would have been doubtful; and every Englishman ought to be thankful that the matter ended as it did.

The news of this outbreak reached Calcutta about the 4th of March, and first opened the eyes of the Government to a sense of their insecurity. They had but one European regiment between Calcutta and Dinapore. It would be unsafe to punish the 19th Native Infantry without having European troops at hand to overawe them, and Government had literally none. Perhaps, after securing the fort and public buildings, about two hundred men might have been available—a mere handful amongst five native regiments deeply imbued with a spirit of fanaticism. In such a crisis there was but one course for Government to pursue; and it is but justice to say that they pursued it. No intimation was conveyed to the 19th of the sense entertained of their conduct. They were allowed to do their duty as usual; but on the morning of the 6th of March the Oriental Company's steamer "Bentinck" steamed for Rangoon, with orders to bring up H.M.'s 84th Foot to Calcutta with the utmost possible dispatch.

On the account of the disturbance at Berhampore reaching Barrackpore, great excitement was manifested by the Sepoys of the regiments at that station, more especially by those of the 2d and 34th Regiments. They did their duty, it is true, but with a sullen doggedness which it was impossible to conceal: it was known that nightly meetings took place in their lines, at which the conduct of the 19th in seizing their arms was applauded, and great sympathy expressed for them. A report of these meetings was made to Government; but not having the power to interfere with effect, they wisely abstained from noticing the matter.

Reports about this time reached Calcutta of ill-feeling and disaffection evinced at the important stations of Meerut and Lucknow. The occurrence of constant incendiarisms in the neighbourhood of the

Sepoy lines cast suspicion upon them, and served to show, not only that they were dissatisfied, but were seeking opportunities to evince their feelings.

At length, on the 20th of March, to the great satisfaction of every one in Calcutta, the "Bentinck" returned from Rangoon. H.M.'s 84th were immediately conveyed to Chinsurah, a station eight miles distant from Barrackpore; and orders were immediately transmitted to the officer commanding the 19th Regiment to march his corps to Barrackpore.

Greater excitement than ever prevailed at that station in consequence of the arrival of the 84th. The native troops, feeling themselves guilty of conspiring against the state, imagined that this move was directed against them. In the 34th especially the mutineers' whispers became louder and louder; they openly expressed their sympathy with the 19th, and scarcely concealed their intention to stand by the men of that regiment in the event of their offering any resistance.

Happily for us, these feelings found a vent before the 19th reached Barrackpore.

On the 29th March it was reported to Lieut. Baugh, Adjutant of the 34th, that several of the men of his regiment were in a very excited state; and that one of them especially, Mungul Pandy by name, was traversing the lines, armed with a loaded musket, calling upon his comrades to rise, and declaring himself that he would shoot the first European he came across. On receipt of this intelligence Lieut. Baugh put on his uniform, mounted his horse, and, with a pair of loaded pistols in his holsters, rode down to the parade-ground. It must here be mentioned, that immediately in front of the Quarter-guard of the 34th Regiment the station gun was posted, from which the morning and mid-day salutes were fired. Mungul Pandy, on hearing of Lieut. Baugh's approach, concealed himself behind this gun; and as that officer drew near, he took a deliberate aim and fired. The ball wounded the horse in the flank, and brought him with his rider to the ground. Lieut. Baugh, however, quickly disengaged himself; and snatching up one of his pistols, advanced on Mungul Pandy, who, finding himself unable to load his musket a second time, had taken up a sword which he had with him. Lieut. Baugh fired and missed. Before he could draw his sword the Sepoy was on him, with one blow brought him to the ground, and but for timely assistance would have then and there killed him.

All this took place, it must be recollected, in front of the Quarter-guard of the 34th, and not thirty yards distant from the guard of a jemadar and twenty Sepoys there located. These men not only made no effort to assist their officer, but showed evident sympathy with Mungul Pandy. The Sergeant-major of the regiment, who was a short distance behind Lieut. Baugh at the time, called out to them to assist him; but their jemadar forbad them to stir. At this juncture, just as Lieut. Baugh had been struck down wounded, the Sergeant-major came up breathless, and attempted to seize Mungul Pandy; but he, too, was wounded and struck down. Upon this the jemadar advanced with the men of his guard; but these, instead of assisting their European officers, commenced striking their heads with the butt-ends of their muskets. To this treacherous conduct there was one exception. The Mahomedan orderly who had followed Lieut. Baugh from his house, arrived on the scene of action in sufficient time to seize Mungul Pandy just as he had succeeded in reloading his musket. He was quickly followed by General Hearsey and other officers, who had been roused by the firing; and by their joint aid the officers were rescued from their perilous situation. Mungul Pandy, on being seized, made an abortive effort to shoot himself. He was then taken off the ground and lodged in the Quarter-guard of the 70th Regiment. Affairs wore a very serious aspect when General Hearsey reached the ground.* That gallant officer, a friend and pupil of Sir Charles Napier, comprehended all in an instant. He felt that to give way now would be to incite a mutiny. Drawing a pistol from his belt, he rode up to the men of the guard, and ordered them back to their posts, declaring he would with his own hand shoot the first man who showed any symptoms of disaffection. This conduct had the desired effect; the men were for the moment overawed; and the dark cloud which appeared to be on the very point of bursting passed quietly away.

In order more effectually to convince the Sepoys that loyalty would always meet with a fitting reward from the British Government, General Hearsey then and there promoted Sheikh Pultoo, the Mahomedan orderly who had rescued Lieutenant Baugh and the Sergeant-major, to the rank of havildar. This had a most salutary effect: and yet it will scarcely be believed, that for this act a severe wigging was administered to the gallant officer by the Secretary to the Government of India, Military Department, Colonel Birch, whose quibbling mind and red-tape instincts could see no necessity for so grave a departure from rule!

But although the station had resumed its outward appearance of calm, within the lines all was disaffection. The jemadar and the Sepoys of the Quarter-guard, who, strange to say, had not then been, and were not for two or three days afterwards, placed in arrest, reproached their comrades for not taking advantage of so fine an opportunity of rising against and massacring the "Feringhees." The recriminations, however, were short, and the 34th, in conjunction with the 2nd Grenadiers, proceeded to mature a fresh plan, the nature of which will shortly be detailed.

On the 30th March the 19th Native Infantry arrived at Barraset, about eight miles distant from Barrackpore. It had by this time transpired that they were to march into the latter station for the purpose of being disbanded: still the behaviour of the men was respectful; and in order to avert their fancied doom, they had sent in

---

* The men of the regiment had turned out in undress in front of their lines, and had shown, by their gestures and other signs, that their sympathies were all with Mungul Pandy. They had even jeered at Lieutenant Baugh as he passed them wounded, and reproached them for not assisting him.

a petition to the Governor-General, offering, in case they were pardoned, to proceed at once to China, or to serve anywhere on land or sea. In short, they showed a repentant spirit, and were never less inclined to join in a conspiracy against the state. On arriving on the morning of the 30th at Barraset, they found a deputation from the 34th awaiting their arrival. It has since transpired that these men made them a proposal — the result of their deliberations of the previous night — which it was well for us that they did not accept. On that very morning, Her Majesty's 84th, from Chinsura, a wing of the 53d Foot from Dumdum, a couple of European batteries from the same place, and the Governor-General's body-guard (native) from Calcutta, had arrived at Barrackpore, and had been ordered to appear on parade with the native regiments at five o'clock on the following morning. The proposal made by the 34th to the 19th was to the following effect: that they should, on that same evening, kill all their officers, march at night into Barrackpore, where the 2nd and 34th were prepared to join them, fire the bungalows, surprise and overwhelm the European force, secure the guns, and then march on to and sack Calcutta.

Had the 19th been as excitable then as they had shown themselves on the 25th of February, these views might possibly have been entertained; but they were repentant, and ashamed of their former excess. That they were not thoroughly loyal is proved by the fact that the tempters were not reported: they were suffered to return unbetrayed, but their scheme was at once and definitively rejected.

On the following morning the 19th Regiment marched into Barrackpore. An order by the Governor-General in Council, in which their crime was recapitulated, their fears for their religion pronounced absurd, and their disbandment directed, was read out to them in the presence of the assembled troops before enumerated. On being ordered to lay down their arms, they obeyed without a murmur; many of them, indeed, showed signs of deep contrition. They were then paid up before their comrades, and were marched across the river without arms. They had ceased to belong to the Company's army.

CHAPTER III.

FROM THE DISBANDING OF THE 19TH REGIMENT TO THE REVOLT AT MEERUT.

THE 19th were disbanded, and in the opinion of the Government a lesson had been thereby read to the Sepoys which they would not easily forget. They argued that Lord Ellenborough, by the disbandment of a regiment in 1844 (the 34th Native Infantry), had repressed a mutiny; and that Sir Charles Napier, by a similar measure in 1849, had effected the same end; quite oblivious of the fact, that the entire circumstances were dissimilar, and that both those statesmen had followed up their disbanding orders by others. But the Indian statesmen who were at this time in power affected to sneer both at Lord Ellenborough and at Sir Charles: their pattern statesman was Lord Dalhousie (the real author of the mutiny), and they chuckled at the ease with which they had (to their own satisfaction) disproved the vaticinations of that nobleman's rival. Colonel Birch, in particular, was especially gleeful on this occasion. He — the man of whom Sir Charles had made a laughing-stock! — had he not by a single movement effected all that Sir Charles Napier had been able to bring about by twenty general orders? So at least he thought, or professed to think. All was confidence, superciliousness, and self-congratulation on the part of the Government officials! But although the Government was satisfied, the public was ill at ease. Symptoms were showing themselves throughout India, which the oldest Indian officers had never witnessed before. It was evident to them that some great movement was in progress, although they were not in a position either to fathom its causes or to avert its consequences. The bare hint of such an idea to Colonel Birch was sufficient to expose one to an outpouring of ridicule. That official's pluck at this epoch could not be questioned.

In the meantime, in April, the Sepoy, Mungul Pandy, had been brought to trial, and condemned to death. He made no confession, but stoically accepted his fate in the presence of all the troops at the station. The jemadar who commanded the guard of the 34th on the 29th March, and who had prevented that guard from assisting Lieutenant Baugh, had also been tried and condemned to death. The sentence, however, owing to some red-tape informalities originating with Colonel Birch, was deferred, most prejudicially to the public interests, to the 21st April. On that day the jemadar was brought to execution, and was hanged. Immediately before his death he harangued those around him, confessing the justice of his sentence, and warning others from following his example.

With this execution the Government appeared to rest satisfied. The atrocious conduct of the men composing the guard on the 29th March, evinced by their not only conniving at the attack upon their officer, but by themselves assaulting him and the Sergeant-major as they lay wounded on the ground, was quite overlooked. The Government appeared "satisfied of the loyalty of the 34th Regiment." Indeed, so convinced did they seem to be of the loyalty of every regiment in the Bengal Army, that at the end of the month of April they determined to send the 84th Foot back to Rangoon, and actually engaged transports for that purpose!

The Government came to this conclusion when in possession of reports from the commanding-officers of the different stations in India, which would have convinced any unprejudiced man that the whole army was ripe for revolt. At Agra the incendiarisms had been frequent, and the Sepoys had refused their aid to subdue the flames; at Seealkote, letters had been discovered from the Barrackpore Sepoys, inciting their brethren at that distant station to revolt. At Umballah, the discontent had been so marked that the Commander-in-Chief himself had been compelled to assure the Sepoys that their apprehensions regarding their caste were groundless. At Lucknow, the Sepoys of the 48th, incensed at their doctor for tasting a bottle of medicine previously to making it over to the sick man, and construing that act into an attempt against their caste (although the system had been prevalent for an hundred years), had taken their revenge by burning down his bungalow. At Benares, too, a very strong feeling of disaffection had been evinced: in fact, there was scarcely a regiment in the Bengal Army which had not shown itself ripe for revolt. Still the Government professed themselves confident, and actually issued orders to the 84th to re-embark for Rangoon.

The truth is, they were in a panic, and, like weak men in that situation, they attempted to hide it from their friends by the assumption of a bullying manner, whilst they effectually showed it to their enemies by vain attempts at conciliation. Hence the wretchedly weak measure of sparing the guard of the 34th, who had beaten their officers; they actually feared to incense them, and believed they were acting the part of statesmen by saving them from condign punishment. Little did they know the native character! That very act, miscalled an act of mercy, tended more than anything else to convince the conspirators that the Government was afraid to strike, and encouraged them still further to develope their plans.

It has since transpired, that soon after the attack upon Lieut. Baugh had been reported to the Government, it had been determined to disband the 34th, and that an order was at the time drafted in which this resolution was announced. For upwards of three weeks that order was kept back. In whose possession it remained it is impossible now to state; but this fact is certain, that for upwards of a month the men of the 34th, including those who had assaulted Lieut. Baugh, were allowed to believe themselves trusted by the Government.

The fact is, that the advisers of the Governor-General, being for the most part members of the Civil Service, refused to recognise these disloyal symptoms as overt acts of mutiny; they endeavoured to persuade Lord Canning that they were mere partial and local disturbances, which should be met rather with conciliation than with severity. In truth they were unwilling to admit, even to themselves, that their own domination, extending over an hundred years, had completely failed in attaching even one section of the population to British rule. If they had previously been called upon to declare the class upon which they would most firmly rely in case of need, they would have named Jack Sepoy; they had pampered, petted, and indulged him until they thought they had made sure of him; they had, in their love of power, wrested the control over him from their military officers, by the encouragement of appeals from their decisions, and vested an overwhelming power in the Supreme Government themselves; they had witnessed his devotion to his officer when subordinated to him alone, and they imagined that the transfer of the subordination to themselves would have ensured the transfer the devotion also. They knew that the Sepoys were the mainstay of order throughout the country, that they represented the feelings of the entire population of Oudh, of Behar, of Gwalior, the Punjab, Nagpore, and Hydrabad: that so long as they were contented, the people would remain passive, if not altogether satisfied. The Sepoy, in fact, was their barometer, and they were unwilling to believe the steady indication of a cyclone. They would not even admit to themselves that their house was founded upon sand, liable to be levelled to the ground by the first storm.

And it is certainly true that they had little other surety for the tranquillity of the country than the fidelity of the Sepoy. Attached by education, training, and hereditary policy to the principle, "India for the Civil Service," they had steadily discouraged the settlement in the land of that other element which, in a crisis like that which, in spite of themselves, they felt approaching, might have formed a countervailing barrier to Mahomedan or Hindoo rebellion. Had independent Europeans been encouraged to invest their capital in the land of India; had not the terrors of subjection to a Hindoo or Mahomedan magistracy been held over their heads to prevent such a catastrophe (to the Civil Service); had they been allowed the smallest exercise of political power, or had the way to that power been open to them, an independent body of landholders would have arisen, who would have formed the connecting link between the Government and the natives, and also have been able, from their numbers and organisation, to have checked any outbreak on the part of the people of the country. But it was very evident that such a measure could not have been accomplished without invading the exclusiveness of the Civil Service. Hence it has always been (with the brilliant exception of Lord Metcalfe, who had thoroughly at heart the interests of India,) systematically opposed by the members of that body. Their policy has ever been to shut out independent Europeans from the country. To carry out this end they have encouraged the trade in opium, whilst they have neglected purposely the cultivation of cotton; they have restricted as much as possible public enterprises which necessitated settling in the land; and although this policy has resulted in a wide-spread rebellion, it will never be lost sight of so long as the rule exists that a man, were he to possess the highest administrative abilities, would be debarred from their exercise, because he did not in the first instance come out to India as a member of the Civil Service.

True to this policy they, as stated above, affected to make light of the discontent in the native army, and persuaded Lord Canning to view matters in the same light. The determination to disband the 34th was accordingly postponed, in the hope that affairs would settle down quietly, and that no further interference on the part of Government would be needed. In pursuance of this plan the 84th were ordered to re-embark for Rangoon.

In a few days they would have started, and the long-wished-for opportunity would have been afforded to the mutineers; when, providentially, an event occurred at Lucknow which suddenly disturbed, although even that failed to rouse the Government from their apathetic attitude.

At Lucknow, the capital of Oudh, the conduct of the native troops had been for some time past in the highest degree disorderly. Nightly meetings and consequent conflagrations had been of frequent occurrence. The city had always been the hotbed of intrigue, and no efforts had been spared on the part of the agents of the King of Oudh to corrupt the native soldiery. On intelligence of the disbanding of the 19th Native Infantry reaching that city, the king's brother intimated to the native troops, that as they now saw the extent of the punishment awarded for mutiny, he was prepared to give service at a similar, or even an increased rate of pay, to all who might be discharged by the Company! The consequence was, that the troops at that station were on the verge of open revolt. Most fortunately for India, the Commissioner of Oudh, Sir Henry Lawrence, was a man who would not suffer himself to be deterred by any consideration from acting with vigour and determination. He was, without doubt, the ablest man in India. It was he who had laid the foundation of that administration in the Punjab, which had in so short a period developed the capacities of that noble province. For Oudh he was the very best ruler that India could produce. Versed in civil matters, he had to repair in the first instance the egregious errors perpetrated by his predecessor, Mr. Coverly Jackson, a redtapist of the school of Messrs. Grant and Beadon. As a military man, he found himself suddenly called upon to check a rising mutiny. In that respect he has done marvels. At the moment of my writing (29th June), although the whole province of Oudh has risen against him, — a province larger than England, — he, with a handful of Europeans (500 men), holds Lucknow, the most disaffected city in India! He has proved himself a real man, indeed! How does his conduct contrast with that of Colonel Birch, Mr. Grant, and the other advisers of the Governor-General? It will be seen that his measures were successful, because they were totally opposed to the ideas of those who administered the Supreme Government of India.

Sir Henry Lawrence had not been an idle spectator of the movements amongst the troops at Lucknow, and he resolved to visit the first overt act of mutiny with condign punishment. An opportunity was not long wanting. On the 3d of May a letter from the 7th Oudh Irregular Infantry (formerly in the service of the ex-king) was intercepted and brought to him. This letter was addressed to the men of the 48th Regiment, and its purport was as follows:—
"We are ready to obey the directions of our brothers of the 48th in the matter of the cartridges, and to resist either actively or passively." This letter was taken to a Brahmin Sepoy of the 48th. He communicated its contents to a havildar, and the latter to a subahdar. The three consulted over it, and resolved to bring the matter to the notice of the Commissioner. This was done. About the same time Sir Henry received intimation that the 7th Irregular

Infantry had proceeded to overt acts against their officers; and although none of them had been murdered, that result was more owing to their own courage than to the forbearance of the mutineers. The Adjutant, Lieut. Mecham, owed his life pre-eminently to his presence of mind. Four mutineers entered his house on the afternoon of the 3d, and told him to prepare for death; that personally they did not dislike him, but that he was a Feringhee, and must die. Lieut. Mecham was unarmed; they were armed to the teeth. Resistance was hopeless. He at once made up his mind to meet his fate with dignity and resolution. As the mutineers paused to listen to what he had to say, he replied, "It is true I am unarmed, and you can kill me; but that will do you no good. You will not ultimately prevail in this mutiny. Another Adjutant will be appointed in my place, and you will be subjected to the same treatment you have received from me." These words, delivered with coolness, without change of countenance or the movement of a muscle, seemed to strike the mutineers. They turned and left the house, leaving their Adjutant uninjured!

Tidings of these mutinous acts reached Sir Henry Lawrence on the evening of the 3d. Without a moment's delay, he ordered out Her Majesty's 32d Foot, the 13th, 48th, and 71st Native Infantry, the 7th Cavalry, and a battery of eight guns, manned by Europeans, and proceeded at once to the lines of the mutineers, distant about seven miles. Darkness had set in before he arrived there; but so prompt had been his movements, that the 7th were completely taken by surprise. They were instantly ordered to form up in front of their lines. In the presence of a force so imposing, they had no resource but to obey. The infantry and cavalry were then formed on either side of them, the guns within grape distance in front. The 7th, completely cowed, awaited their doom. They were ordered to lay down their arms: they obeyed. At this moment the artillery portfires were lighted. A sudden panic seized them, with the cry, "Do not fire! do not fire!" Mad with terror, they rushed frantically away, cowed into repentance. The ringleaders, and most of their followers, were secured that night by the native cavalry and infantry, and were confined pending trial.

Thus easily was suppressed the first mutiny at Lucknow. It has since transpired that the whole of the 71st, and very considerable portions of the 48th Native Infantry and 7th Cavalry, sympathised with the mutineers. Had Mr. Grant's and Col. Birch's plan, adopted by Lord Canning, of coquetting with mutineers, of giving in to them, of fearing to strike, of merely dismissing men for attacking their officers (an offence for which many European soldiers have suffered death); had, in fact, a delay occurred at Lucknow similar to that which occurred at Barrackpore in dealing with the 34th—a delay of three weeks—then, in all probability, that night or the following would have seen all Lucknow in revolt. It may be said that the troops subsequently did revolt. It is true; but they gave Sir Henry Lawrence nearly a month to prepare himself; and he proved that he was not the man at such a crisis to waste even an hour. When the revolt which had long been foreseen did come, every preparation which it was possible for human foresight to devise had been made. The consequence was, that the mutineers were baffled; Sir Henry kept Lucknow, and still keeps it, though the whole of Oudh, almost the whole of India, is in arms against him. Had the revolt of the 30th of May occurred on the 3rd, there could have been but one result—our European troops would have been surprised, and every European resident murdered.

On the 4th of May the electric telegraph conveyed to the Supreme Government of India at once the account of the mutiny at Lucknow and of its suppression. A new book was in that act opened for Lord Canning's perusal, and he profited by it. The conduct of the men of the 34th at Barrackpore had been characterised by a sullen doggedness which could not be misconstrued: they were evidently watching their opportunity. When called upon to name the men of the guard who had attacked Lieut. Baugh and the Sergeant-major, they had steadily refused. Their officers, with one, or, perhaps, two exceptions, had declared before a Court of Inquiry that they had lost all confidence in their men. Some, unconnected with the regiment, attributed their conduct to the ill-judged zeal for proselytism evinced by their commanding officer, Colonel Wheler; but this, although it may have acted as an additional item in the balance against us, was scarcely the main cause of their ill-feeling. They were, in fact, thoroughly corrupted—more influenced even by the agents of the King of Oudh than by fears for their religion. A bad feeling at this time prevailed amongst all the regiments at Barrackpore. A jemadar of the 70th had been caught in the lines urging his men to revolt. He was tried and sentenced by a Court, composed of native officers like himself, to simple dismissal. This sentence was approved and confirmed by the Commander-in-Chief in India. To the jemadar himself it was no punishment at all. He owed four hundred rupees; and this dismissal eased him at once of his commission and his debt! But the effect upon the Sepoys is indescribable. "This," they said, " the only punishment for mutiny! They are afraid of us—we can do what we like."

There can be no doubt that the men of the 34th and of other regiments at Barrackpore only waited the departure of Her Majesty's 48th Foot from Chinsurah. They knew that that regiment had come up from Burmah, lightly equipped ; that it would, in all probability, return thither soon; the rumour of their immediate departure was prevalent amongst them : they therefore waited, and would have waited with good purpose, but for the providential occurrence of the meeting of the 7th Irregular Infantry at Lucknow.

That mutiny, and the mode in which it was quelled by Sir Henry Lawrence, excited the admiration of Lord Canning. It also spurred him on to follow an example so nobly set. The account of the mutiny reached him by electric telegraph. It was not yet known in Calcutta or Barrackpore ; the news would, however, be widely spread by the 8th or 9th. It was most desirable to act before that time; it was, indeed, essential. A blow must be struck. Upon the

34th, as the most guilty parties, it was resolved that it should fall. The order for the 84th to re-embark for Rangoon was at once rescinded; they were directed to proceed to Barrackpore on the 5th of May; the wing of the 53rd and two batteries of Artillery were also ordered there, and a message was despatched the same evening to the officer commanding at that station, directing him to parade all the troops at the station on the following morning, to read to them an order by the Governor-General therewith enclosed, and to conclude by paying up and disbanding the whole of the 34th Native Infantry who had been present in the lines during the outrage of the 29th of March.

On the morning of the 6th of May, accordingly, the troops were paraded, the order was read, the men were paid up and disbanded. None who were on the ground that morning and heard that order read—none who, in Calcutta, read that order at the same moment that they learned the fate of the mutineers, can ever forget the lamentable effect it produced, the universal impression it infused amongst all ranks, that the Government was absolutely afraid to punish. In this order the infamous conduct of the 34th was detailed at full length; their outrage upon their officer, the sullen apathy of the whole regiment on that occasion, their unconcealed sympathy with the murderer, were all dwelt upon in forcible language; but the punishment, the retribution for mutiny and connivance at murder, what was that?—simple disbandment! Even on the men of the guard, who looked on the attack with sympathy, and even followed it up by striking the wounded men as they lay on the ground, no severer punishment was inflicted. Punishment!—it was no punishment at all. The Kings of Delhi and Oudh had offered them a national service and a higher rate of pay, and the road to these was opened to them by their disbandment.

But the Governor-General was not content even with such a demonstration of weakness. Judging him from his written proclamations, he appeared desirous to impress upon the minds of the native army that the 34th had been guilty of a very venial offence; for he wound up his order—an order which he desired to be read at the head of every regiment, troop, and company in the service—by informing the army, that if they still refused to trust in their officers and the Government, and still allowed suspicions to take root in their minds, and to grow into disaffection, insubordination, and mutiny, their punishment, too, would be "sharp and certain." Sharp and certain as what?—as the punishment awarded to the 34th? The Bengal Army proved, by their after-conduct, that they wished for nothing better!

However, the order was read, and the men was disbanded. Did they express the least contrition for their offence? Did they show the smallest regret at leaving their officers and their colours? One incident, slight but significant, will suffice to show. They were allowed to keep their Kilmarnock caps, as they had paid for them. Before crossing the river, after having been paid up, many of them were seen to take off their caps, dash them on the ground, and trample them in the mud; they would not carry away with them the smallest reminiscence of their service to the Company!

The 19th and 34th, the only two regiments of the Bengal Army who, up to this moment, had been guilty of overt acts of mutiny, had now been disbanded, and the Government fondly imagined that disaffection had been dismissed with them. Two orders of the Governor-General had distinctly intimated to the native troops, that the Governor-General had neither the desire nor the intention to interfere with their religion or their caste, and it was believed that these orders, coupled with the disbandment of the 19th and 34th, would have the best possible effect.

The men of the 34th had assaulted their officer on the 29th of March; punishment was meted out to them on the 6th of May. This interval of five weeks was not lost on the men of the Bengal Army. Throughout India every eye had been turned towards Barrackpore, to ascertain what fate would befall that regiment which had encouraged a murderous attack on one of its officers. For five weeks they looked, and looked in vain. It is true that the murderer himself and one of his sympathisers had been hanged, but less than that the Government could not do, without entirely abdicating its functions; otherwise all was quiet; the regiment had not even been rebuked for its share in the crime. The universal impression consequently prevailed amongst the Sepoys that the Government could not do without, and feared to punish them.

That these feelings would not have become modified by listening to the order published by the Governor-General, on the disbandment of the 34th, may be imagined from the fact, that when it reached Lucknow, Sir Henry Lawrence, one of the best judges of native character in India, refused to allow it to be read to the native troops, being of opinion that it would hasten rather than repress an outbreak.

At Meerut, disaffection had been more plainly manifested than in any other station in the North-western provinces. A rumour had been spread amongst the troops by means, it cannot be doubted, of the agents of the King of Oudh, that the Government had plotted to take away their caste, by mixing the grounded bones of bullocks with the flour sold in the market; that thus the Hindoo, partaking inadvertently of the substance of the deified animal, would find himself compelled to embrace Christianity. It was in vain that General Hewitt and the commanding officers of regiments attempted to combat these ideas; it was fruitless that they pointed out to the Sepoys, that during a century's occupation of India no interference with caste had ever been tried. Left to themselves, the Hindoos might possibly have been pacified by these assurances; but they were urged on by the Mahomedans, who pretended similar fears for their own religion. The disbandment of the 19th, did nothing to allay the discontent, whilst the impolitic delay which intervened between the crime of the men of the 34th and their punishment served greatly to increase it. During the latter end of April this discontent showed itself in the usual manner. Houses were burned down, officers were not saluted as usual, and whispers were heard that a resolution had been arrived at in the lines not to touch a single cartridge.

To such a height were these manifestations carried, that it appeared advisable to bring them to the test. In the presence at the station of two European regiments, the 60th Rifles and the 6th Carabineers, besides two troops of Horse Artillery and a light field battery, General Hewitt had, or thought he had, a sufficient force to repress on the instant any act of open mutiny. He was resolved, therefore, that the Sepoys should see that he was there to give orders, they to obey them. A parade of the 3d Cavalry was accordingly ordered for the morning of the 6th of May. On the evening of the 5th, cartridges, the old cartridges of the kind which they and their fathers had always used, were served out to them. Eighty-five men in the regiment at once stepped out and refused to take them. They were subsequently offered, and again indignantly refused. But one course remained to the Brigadier. The men were confined, brought to a court-martial composed of native officers, and by those native officers condemned to periods of imprisonment with hard labour, varying from six to ten years.

In the meanwhile, impressed by the consequences resulting from Sir H. Lawrence's vigour and promptitude, the Government had sent instructions by telegraph to the commandants of the principal stations in India, directing that sentences pronounced on mutineers, whatever might be their nature, should be carried out at once, that no delay might be caused by a reference to army head-quarters. General Hewitt, therefore, prepared to carry out the sentences pronounced on the mutineers of the 3d Cavalry at the earliest possible moment. The condemned mutineers were placed under an European guard, composed of two companies of the 60th Rifles and twenty-five men of the Carabineers, and a general parade was ordered for the morning of the 9th. At day-break on that morning,* all the troops in the station, leaving the guards standing, paraded on the 60th Rifle parade-ground; the Carabineers, the 60th Rifles, the 3d Light Cavalry, the 11th and 20th Regiments of Native Infantry, a light field battery, and a troop of Horse Artillery. The Carabineers and the Rifles were then ordered to load and be ready, and the Horse Artillery the same. This done, the mutineers were marched on to the ground; the European troops and Artillery guns being so placed, that the least movement of disaffection or insurrection would have been followed by instant slaughter. The mutineers were in uniform when marched on to the ground; they were then stripped of their clothes and accoutrements; and the armourers' and smiths' departments of the Horse Artillery being in readiness, every man was ironed and shackled for ten years' imprisonment on the hard roads, with the exception of five, whose period of bondage was only six years. These unfortunate wretches looked miserably crest-fallen and depressed, and many of them, putting up their hands, appealed to the General for mercy. None, of course, was

---

* I am indebted to the talented correspondent of the Calcutta *Englishman* for the graphic account of this morning's proceedings.

vouchsafed, and the work went steadily on until all had been heavily ironed. The 3d Cavalry looked very much humbled, mounted with their swords drawn and sloped, silent spectators of the doom of their comrades. When the ironing had been completed, the prisoners reproached their comrades for allowing the punishment to be carried out. It is now evident, that an understanding existed between the culprits and the native soldiery, both infantry and cavalry, at Meerut; that these latter had sworn not to allow the sentence to be carried into effect. The sight, however, of the loaded guns and the two European regiments was sufficient to chill their ardour; at all events, the prisoners were carried away, and they made no sign.

Had it been deemed advisable still to keep the prisoners under an European guard, the natives might have been overawed, and all yet have gone well; but apparently the necessity for such a deviation from the usual course of procedure did not suggest itself to the authorities, and the mutineers were made over manacled to the civil authorities. By these they were lodged in the jail—a building some two miles distant from the cantonment, and guarded entirely by native burkundazes.

Meanwhile the native troops returned to their lines, furious with pent-up indignation. There can be no doubt that on that afternoon they matured their plans for a rise; messengers were dispatched to Delhi, to inform the regiments there of the projected move, and to warn them to be ready to receive them on the 11th or 12th. They resolved to rise on the evening of the following day (Sunday), whilst the Europeans should be in church, to release their imprisoned comrades, fire the station, and to slaughter every man, woman, or child, pertaining to the Christian community. The originators of this plan were the men of the 3d Cavalry; but they found the men of the 20th Regiment as eager as themselves to join in any insurrection. Not so, however, with the 11th Native Infantry. This regiment had but recently arrived in the station, and whether sufficient opportunity had not been afforded for corrupting them, or for some other unexplained reason, they hung back, and expressed a decided disinclination to join in any attack on their officers. They did not, however, betray the secret.

All this time the authorities were unsuspicious: the havildars made the morning report to their officers; the men of the European Regiment attended morning service as usual, and there was no sign of the coming storm. The day passed away as Sundays generally pass in India, and not even the sergeants, who live in the native lines, had noticed anything to call for report, or even for remark. Evening church-time was approaching: the 60th Rifles were turning out with their side-arms to proceed thither; officers, too, were dressing either for church or for an evening ride. Sepoys! restrain your impatience for half-an-hour longer, and Meerut is your own. Providentially they cannot restrain it. Suddenly the alarm of fire is given; then there is loud shouting, as if the Sepoys were turning out to quench the flames. But, then, that volley of musketry, followed by another and another! those discordant yells! that clattering of cavalry! the bugle sound of the alarm! It is not fire only that

has caused this direful outcry—it is mutiny!—insurrection!—
THE BENGAL ARMY HAS REVOLTED!

It was nearing five o'clock on that memorable afternoon when, at a given signal, the 3rd Light Cavalry and the 20th Native Infantry rushed out of their lines, armed and furious. A detachment of the former regiment at once galloped in the direction of the jail. On reaching it, its gates were opened to them without resistance, and they at once liberated all its inmates, including their imprisoned comrades: a native smith was at hand to strike off their irons. These men, infuriated by their disgrace, ran with all possible speed to their lines, armed themselves, and mounted; they then rushed to the scene of action, yelling fearfully, and denouncing death to every European. Meanwhile the remaining portion of the 3rd Cavalry and the 20th Native Infantry had proceeded to the lines of the 11th with all possible speed. Thither also the officers of that regiment, alarmed by the shouting and noise, had gone before them. They found Col. Finnis haranguing his men, and endeavouring to keep them firm to their colours. The men were wavering when the 20th arrived. The men of this regiment, whose hands were already red with the blood of several of their own officers, seeing this hesitation and its cause, at once fired at Col. Finnis. The first shot took effect on his horse only, but almost immediately afterwards he was riddled with balls. All discipline, all better feelings, now vanished. It is true that the Sepoys of the 11th permitted their officers to escape with their lives; but having done this, the greater portion of them followed the example of the 20th. And now ensued a scene of disorder, rapine, and murder which pen cannot describe. Every house and building near the lines, except the hospital, had been fired; and the smoking and blazing barracks and houses, the yells of the mutineers, and the shouts and shrieks of the multitude gathered there, numbers of whom fell from the shots of the mutineers, made on that dark night a scene than which one cannot be imagined more horrible.* Officers galloping about, carrying orders to the European troops, were fired at, not only by the mutineers, but by the native guards placed over the public buildings for security. Ladies driving in their carriages, gentlemen in their buggies, who had left their houses unsuspicious of evil, were assaulted, and if not murdered, treated with a brutality to which death would have been a relief. Not only the Sepoys, but the released jail-birds, fifteen hundred in number—the population also, that " vile rabble" which is always available for plunder or murder, had joined the movement, and spread terror and desolation all around them. Nor were houses or public offices safe places of refuge from these assaults. Most of the houses in Meerut—all of those in the military lines—are thatched with straw, and easily inflammable: the plan of the insurgents was to set fire to the roof, and to murder the frightened residents as they quitted the burning dwelling. Many met their deaths in this way; more, providentially, escaped: yet not one of those in the latter category owed their safety to the mercy of their as-

* Correspondent *Bengal Hurkaru*.

sailants. In some instances outrages were perpetrated which the pen refuses to record. These men, whom we had pampered for a century, who had always professed the utmost devotion to us, seemed suddenly converted into demons. Nor was this a solitary example; other stations were destined to witness atrocities fouler, more brutal, and more treacherous than even those of Meerut.

Meanwhile unaccountable delay occurred in turning out the European troops, and night had set in before the Carabineers arrived on the parade-ground of the 11th Native Infantry. They found there the 60th Rifles and Artillery waiting for them. Their arrival was the signal for a move against the rebels. They found, however, that by this time their work of destruction within the station had been completed, and that they had betaken themselves to the Delhi road. Thither they followed them. The night, however, was too dark, and the movements of the insurgents too uncertain, to permit our troops to act with vigour. A portion of the rebels were, it is true, found in a wood, and shots were exchanged between them and the 60th Rifles. The Artillery, too, fired upon and dispersed them; but it was considered that nothing more effective could be done; that fifteen hundred jail-birds, maddened with the taste of blood, were at large, and might still inflict incalculable damage on the station; and that, at such a crisis, the presence of the troops was absolutely required there. These, at least, are all the reasons that can be imagined (for none have hitherto been assigned) for the languid pursuit of that evening. One fact is clear, that the rebels were not followed up with any vigour, and that, after seeing them clear of the station, the troops returned to the scene of the outbreak of the mutiny, and there bivouacked. The night was spent " in taking precautions against attack, and in measures preliminary to strengthening the place, so as to secure it, if the troops should be compelled to leave it."*

The horrors of that fearful night could scarcely have been surpassed. The rebels, it is true, had been driven away, but the liberated prisoners and the rabble continued their fearful work. It is true that European sentries were posted, with all possible celerity, in the different parts of Meerut; and the constant fire of their rifles showed that their presence was necessary. Still, in spite of all precautions, foul deeds were even then perpetrated. To every one it was a night of agonising suspense. Husbands had missed their wives, and wives their husbands; infants had been separated from their mothers, and mothers from their children. Many passed the night, depending entirely on the fidelity of their native servants; and it is gratifying to state that, in more than one instance, that fidelity was proof. To this source Mr. Greathed, the commissioner, and his wife, owed their safety. Their house—a flat-roofed one, fortunately—was one of the first attacked by the Sepoys. On the first alarm they fled to the roof; thither, on the least intimation from the servants, the Sepoys would have followed them: but these persisted in

* Correspondent *Bengal Hurkaru.*

the story that they had left the house; and the mutineers, after searching every room, at last believed them and went away. The courageous action of the ayah, or female servant, in the service of Captain and Mrs. Macdonald of the 20th Regiment, must here be recorded. She had heard the alarm, and had perceived the blood-stained mutineers advancing towards her master's house. Unable to save him or her mistress, she seized their two children, and concealing them as well as possible, carried them to a place of safety. They never saw their parents again. Subsequent experience has shown that the "brave and loyal Sepoy" does not disdain treating children of one and two years of age with the most cruel barbarity.

How that night passed with those poor sufferers, they alone can tell. The day at length dawned, and the sun shone on dismantled Meerut. Their worst sufferings were over; the houseless were sheltered, and order was in some degree restored. Thenceforth they were safe from further attack, and could watch the progress of the avalanche by which they had been almost overwhelmed.

As soon as it was ascertained that the mutineers had taken the road to Delhi, only forty miles distant from Meerut, messengers were despatched to intimate the fact to Brigadier Graves, commanding at that station. The situation of this officer was full of peril. Besides the officers and sergeants of the native corps, he had not a single European under his command. The garrison consisted of the 38th, 54th, and 74th Regiments, Native Infantry, and a battery of Native Artillery. The men of these regiments had hitherto shown no symptoms of disaffection; but the 38th was the corps which had so successfully defied Lord Dalhousie in 1852, and the men of it had ever since been impressed with the idea that the Government was afraid of them. The British rule in India seemed to be staked on their fidelity, and Brigadier Graves must have felt that the issue would at least be doubtful. But he was not the man to give way to despair under any circumstances; and he at once resolved to make the most of the means at his disposal.

The approach to Delhi from Meerut is defended by the little river Hindun, which is traversed by a small bridge. On receiving intimation of the movements of the rebels, the Brigadier's first idea was to cut away the bridge and defend the river. But there were two objections to this plan. The first was, that at the season of the year, the height of the hot weather, the river was easily fordable, and his position on the other bank might be turned. The second, that in case of their attempting that manœuvre, he would be compelled to fight (even if his men continued stanch) with the rebels on his front and flank, and the most disaffected city in India, the residence of the descendant of the Mogul, in his rear. This plan, therefore, was abandoned almost as soon as conceived, and he determined to content himself with defending the city and cantonments as best he could. As this might endanger the lives of the non-military residents, intimation was conveyed to them to repair to the Flagstaff Tower, a round building of solid brickwork, well capable of defence, and at some distance from the city. In many instances that intimation never reached those for whom it was intended, by some it was received too late, but by none was it wilfully disregarded.

Meanwhile the regiments were ordered out, the guns loaded, and every possible preparation made. The Brigadier harangued the troops in a manly style; told them that now was the opportunity to show their fidelity to the Company to whom they had sworn fidelity, and by whom they had never been deceived. His brief, pithy address, was received with cheers. The 54th, especially, seemed eager to exterminate the mutineers, and loudly demanded to be led against them.* The Brigadier, responding to their seeming enthusiasm, put himself at their head, and led them out of the Cashmere Gate to meet the rebels, whose near approach had been announced. As they marched out in gallant order, to all appearance proud and confident, a tumultuous array appeared advancing from the Hindun. In front, and in full uniform, with medals on their breasts gained in fighting for British supremacy, confidence in their manner, and fury in their gestures, galloped on about two hundred and fifty troopers of the 3rd Calvary: behind them, at no great distance, and almost running in their efforts to reach the golden minarets of Delhi, appeared a vast mass of Infantry, their red coats soiled with dust, and their bayonets glittering in the sun. No hesitation was visible in all that advancing mass; they came on, as if confident of the result. Now the Cavalry approach nearer and nearer! At this headlong pace they will soon be on the bayonets of the 54th. These latter are ordered to fire; the fate of India hangs on their reply. They do fire, but alas! into the air; not one saddle is emptied by that vain discharge. And now the Cavalry are amongst them; they fraternise with them; they leave the officers to their fate; and these are remorselessly cut down wherever they can be found!

It was too true, indeed! The bold and confident bearing of the rebels was thus accounted for; the Delhi troops, too, had been corrupted. In shouting to be led against the mutineers, they had acted a part which to Asiatics is familiar from their youth, but which Englishmen accustomed to them all their lives have never been able to comprehend. All was now over with Delhi. The enraged troopers, accompanied by the greater part of the 54th, the other arrivals from Meerut, and gaining fresh recruits at every step from the 38th and 74th, dashed into the city, shooting in their progress all the Europeans they met with. Many of them pointed to the marks eft by the manacles on their legs, as if to justify their atrocities. Not a Christian whom they could lay hold of was spared, and on the women death was the smallest of the barbarities inflicted. The Governor-General's agent, Mr. Simon Frazer, and Captain Douglas commanding the palace guards of the titular King of Delhi, were cut down in the very precincts of the palace. Mr. Jennings, the chaplain, and his daughter, were seized when making their way to

* Private account.

the king for his protection. They were brought before the monarch—a man the descendant of the house of Timour, born our pensioner and ever treated by the English Government with marked liberality. "What shall we do with them?" inquired the enraged troopers of the king. "What you like; I give them to you!" was the reply. This man and the King of Oudh were at the bottom of the conspiracy: it was thus that the former repaid British generosity.

Meanwhile Brigadier Graves, rallying a few men who had remained faithful, retreated to the Flagstaff Tower. Here he found a vast assemblage of ladies and gentlemen—all, in fact, who had received or who had been able to comply with his intimation. Here also were stationed a company of the 38th and two guns; and so great was the strength of the tower that it was imagined that these men, if they remained faithful, might hold it against the enemy. But when the Brigadier addressed them, it became evident that their hearts were with the rebels, and that they only waited an opportunity to join them.

A remarkable occurrence, a feat of gallant devotion, unsurpassed in any age or country, brought the matter quickly to a crisis.

The Delhi magazine, situated in the very heart of the city, contained at this time immense stores of ammunition;* it was in charge of Lieut. Willoughby, a young Artillery officer. Of him, as the writer had the pleasure of a slight acquaintance with him, he may be allowed to say a few words. He was a young man of modest unpretending worth; his mother, if I may be pardoned for mentioning her, (for she still lives), is a lady possessing very superior accomplishments, a refined taste, and a generous disposition. All these young Willoughby had inherited. Those who met him in society might pronounce him shy and reserved, for so he appeared to strangers; to appreciate him, it was necessary that he should be known intimately; and by those to whom that gratification was extended, his generous sentiments and steadfast principles were rated at their real value. There was nothing showy about him, all was sterling gold. He sought on every occasion the path of duty, and he followed it careless of the consequences. I am fully sensible of the feebleness of my pen when endeavouring to render homage to his merits; the deed I am about to chronicle speaks for itself, and will, I am certain, ensure for him at least the enthusiastic recollection of his countrymen to never-ending time.

Young Willoughby, in common with others, had heard of the approach of the rebels, of the insurrection of the troops sent out to check them, and of their rush upon the city. In the heart of the city was the magazine, and that building contained stores which would enable their possessors to arm all the extent of the wall of Delhi against an enemy. This consideration decided him; his duty was clear—that magazine should not fall into the hands of the

* The official account of the blowing of the Delhi magazine differs somewhat from that given above, which was necessarily compiled from accounts written by people who were in another part of the station when the event happened. It is given in this edition in an Appendix.

rebels. The consequences to himself he little recked; they would most likely be fatal. There was, it is true, a subterranean passage, of which he might avail himself; but even there the effects of an explosion would probably be felt. He was convinced, that after the first desire for blood was glutted, there would be a rush to secure the stores in the magazine; there he could await the insurgents, and there should they find their doom.

It turned out as he predicted: on they came, red with gore, infuriated with slaughter: in the meanwhile he had laid the train and stood ready to fire it. Not for an instant did his coolness desert him; not for a second, when he placed in the balance his own life against theirs, did he hesitate; he thought only of the consequences to the rebels and to his countrymen hereafter. Gradually the place was filling, and yet the portfire was not applied. Now, now it is full—they are struggling for admittance, it will contain no more; and now he stoops, the steady hand is applied, the slow-match burns,—a few seconds, then a puff of white smoke,—an immense cloud of red dust—an explosion—and the bodies of two thousand* rebels are hurled into the air!

And he! where was he, the gallant author of the deed? Scorched, maimed, bruised, almost insensible, he still had life. How he escaped, how he afterwards got away, I cannot tell; but I read in the paper of this morning (1st July) that he had died of his injuries at Meerut. Let us hope that his death,—the death of one so young,—so gallant, so devoted to his country, will be still more terribly avenged. Will it be so? I cannot say. The proclamation of Mr. John Colvin, the Lieutenant-Governor of the North-west Provinces, offering pardon to these villains, is yet unrepealed!

To those assembled at the Flagstaff Tower this explosion could have but one meaning: it plainly told, or seemed to tell, that the rebels had penetrated into the heart of the city, and would be upon them before long: it had, at all events, the effect of deciding the movements of the company of the 38th. The men, previously hesitating, now became actually hostile, and, taking possession of two guns which had been sent up to increase the defences of that position, they prepared to point them against the tower. It was now evident that nothing more could be effected: the troops, almost to a man, had revolted; the jail-birds, as at Meerut, had been released; the Delhi population, composed principally of ignorant and bigoted Mahomedans, were up in arms: this intelligence would shortly be conveyed to the surrounding inhabitants, who were chiefly Googiers, a race of savage marauders, and by them escape would be cut off. Not an instant was to be lost. Brigadier Graves perceived this, and advised every one to escape as best he could: his own conscience was clear: he had done his duty, and now that the inevitable hour of departure had arrived, he remained, the last to leave the ancient capital of the Mogul. Some on foot, others crowded in carriages, a few riding, the remnants of the Europeans left Delhi: their fate has yet

* The numbers are variously stated from 1500 to 3000.

to be related: some who were for six weeks afterwards despaired of have since turned up living; their adventures have to be told: the great proportion of them, we know, met with all but insurmountable difficulties and dangers, and the escapes of many remind one of the supernatural. Up to the date of writing but few authentic accounts have been received, but sufficient is known to make us long for the time when the story of each individual's adventures can be published.

Meanwhile the rebels reigned supreme in Delhi. Undismayed by the loss incurred at the magazine, perhaps thereby rendered more furious, they ruthlessly pursued every Christian. The officers' bungalows were all entered and searched: they were not, in a single instance, pillaged *by the Sepoys:* they significantly remarked that they wanted only life. Their deeds, too, have yet to be recorded and revenged. Language cannot describe the bitter animosity or the savage cruelty evinced by those who, up to a recent period, had been the chief pillar of British supremacy!

It will be sufficient to add, that from the first moment the King of Delhi showed sympathy with the revolters: the Europeans, who fled to him for refuge, he handed over to their tender mercies: their several regiments he called after the names of his sons; he proclaimed himself Emperor of India; and, after the first few days of disorder he appointed Lall Khan, a subahdar of the 3d Cavalry, commander-in-chief of his army. He threw for a great stake, and has more than once been within an ace of winning it.

To show how the revolt at Meerut gave the signal for a general rise over India; how successively the troops at Ferozpore, at Benares, at Allahabad, and at Cawnpore, in the provinces of Oudh and Rohilcund, rose against us, and for a time achieved success; how the atrocities of Meerut and Delhi were surpassed by those of Oudh and Allahabad, will be my task on a future occasion. I shall then be able to prove, if indeed proof be required, (for I hope and believe that the people of England will have already judged and decided), how, up to the very last moment, the members of the Government, true to their principle of "India for the Civil Service," refused to open their eyes to the magnitude of the danger, and endeavoured as much as possible to conceal its extent from Lord Canning; how, in pursuance of this policy, they rudely declined to take precautions against a rising of the troops at Barrackpore, until an accident disclosed a plan which was to have been executed on the following day for murdering every European; how, in spite of their miserable policy, Calcutta has three times been providentially preserved when on the very brink apparently of destruction; how, notwithstanding their assumed blindness to the public danger, the principal civil servants of Government took most extensive precautions for their own security. I shall also show how precisely the same policy was pursued in the North-west provinces; how Mr. John Colvin, when the massacres of Meerut and Delhi were fresh in the recollection of all, offered free pardon to the rebels on the sole condition of their laying down their arms; how, up to this hour, no official proclamation has been published disavowing that act; how by its operation many mutineers, laden with plunder and red with the blood of our countrymen, have found their way to their homes.

I shall then ask if the people of England will permit this policy to be further carried out; whether they will allow India still to remain an appanage of the Civil Service? This noble country has been under the rule of that service for a century: the present insurrection is the inevitable result of that domination. They have had no root in the land; their interests have not been the interests of the people of India. We have lately seen how, in many parts of the country, the Indigo planters, men like Mr. Venables, Mr. Saunders, Mr. Chapman, have actually not only held their own factories, but have rescued the magistrates and others from the insurgents: in some instances the Commissioners have been compelled to invest them with magisterial powers. Whence was their authority derived? In what lay the secret of their immunity from outrage? The answer is plain: they are owners of the soil; their interests are the same as those of the population. These, then, are the men who ought to be made magistrates, in place of unfledged boys, ignorant of the people and imperfectly acquainted with the language of the country.

The last act of the Government has, as much as any other, exposed the "courage and capacity" of our civil administrators. So long as there was real danger they pretended to ignore it; but no sooner had the crisis passed away, than, looking back at it, appalled at its magnitude, they fell into a panic. They determined on a vigorous demonstration, one which should strike terror into the hearts of all. The question was, Whom they should attack? The rebels, unfortunately, were beyond their reach; Barrackpore was quiet. But a demonstration was necessary. They could not attack the national enemy, so they resolved to assault the declared antagonists of the principle, "India for the Civil Service;" and in pursuance of this plan, they actually persuaded Lord Canning to go down to the Legislative Council, suspend all the standing orders, and in the course of forty minutes to abolish the freedom of the Press!!!

Take the present members of the Government of India, the Members of Council, and the Secretaries; try their powers, analyse their abilities, and with the single exception of Mr. Edmonstone, there is not one of them whose capacity can be rated higher than that of an average lawyer's clerk; had their lot not been cast in "the pleasant places" of an exclusive service, few of them would have been able to earn an independent livelihood!

It is easy, therefore, to imagine why they should have been jealous of a Press which did not recognise their pretensions to an exclusive possession of intellect, but that such men should have subordinated Lord Canning to their views appertains to the marvellous. Lord Ellenborough would have used them to his own purposes; they have moulded Lord Canning to theirs!

With terrible anxiety do the independent Europeans wait the decision of the people of England regarding the future government of India. It is a most momentous question, fraught with all-important results for good or evil, not only to the independent Europeans, but to the millions of native inhabitants! For the good of all, it is *essential* that the exclusive Civil Service should be abolished!

I cannot, however, conclude this part of my narrative without paying the homage which is due to those civil and military servants who have in every respect deserved well of their country. Sir Henry Lawrence at Lucknow, and his brother Sir John Lawrence in the Punjab, have, in this crisis, not only nobly sustained their great reputation, but have risen to a height in public estimation beyond which it is impossible to ascend. Sir Henry especially has, with the smallest means at his disposal, effected the greatest marvels. With five hundred Europeans he has held the most disaffected city in Asia, and kept at bay the inhabitants of a province larger than England! Sir Hugh Massey Wheeler, at Cawnpore, has successfully defended a barrack containing two hundred Europeans against thousands of natives thirsting for their blood. Messrs. Gubbins and Lind, and Colonel Neil, at Benares, have done all that men could do in their circumstances. I mention the names of these illustrious men in this place, not with the vain hope of doing them justice here, but to show that my pen is not entirely dipped in gall—that I wish to speak impartially of all, irrespective of the service to which they belong.

At a future and not very distant occasion I hope to produce a fully detailed narrative of their deeds.

One word on the subject of Army Reform. That subject is now under the consideration of the Government of India, but as their plans must be primarily submitted to the Court of Directors and the Board of Control, they will doubtless be subjected to alteration according to the expressed sentiments of the people of England. I will only say on this occasion, that the Brahmins have proved that they cannot be trusted with arms: the Mahomedans, too, have shown that they cherish in their hearts the proselyting doctrines of their religion, and that us Christians they will ever detest, and take advantage of every opportunity of destroying Europeans.

We shall therefore be compelled to adopt an entirely new system; of this, one necessary feature must be a large increase to the purely European force: this is indispensable. Then the whole of the Bengal Army—at least the regiments which have not mutinied—should be disbanded, and re-organised on a new footing: the rank of native officer should be abolished; promotion by merit directed; the pension establishment, which has failed in its purpose, should be done away with.

Those regiments which, few in number, have not mutinied or been disarmed, might be allowed to retain their arms; their numbers be reduced to 800 men, and they should always be quartered with Europeans. The practice of living in lines should be forbidden, but barracks similar to those of the European troops should be provided. To each company, in lieu of native officers, who have proved themselves either mutinous or incompetent, two steady European non-commissioned officers should be attached. They should live in the barracks with the men, though separated from them, and should keep the keys of the bells of arms.

Supposing twenty more European regiments to be added to Bengal, there might be twenty native regiments of the nature I describe. Not a Brahmin should be admitted; they should be composed chiefly of low-caste Hindoos and Sikhs. The Goorkhas should remain as they are, unmixed.

The men of the regiments thus re-formed should never be sent on escort duty; they should remain cantoned with Europeans, and should be constantly brigaded and exercised with them.

To carry on other duties, mere police duties, such as escorting treasure and commissariat stores, other regiments should be raised, under the denomination of Police Corps. To these fire-arms should not be entrusted. A short sword and an iron-bound club should be their weapons; they should be paid at a lower rate than the others, and should not be allowed to rank as soldiers.

As a preliminary measure it will be necessary, merciless as it may sound to English ears, to hunt down every mutineer. India will not be secure so long as a single man remains alive. Since I commenced this page, details have been received of the merciless slaughter of upwards of an hundred unarmed ladies—women and children flying for a place of refuge. These are our sisters and your sisters, people of England! And ought their murderers to be spared, perhaps pensioned? Yet, canvass Calcutta at this moment—inquire from civilians, merchants, and military men, and the all but universal answer will arise, that at the hands of our Government—a Government comprehending such men as Messrs. Dorin, J. P. Grant, Beadon, and Birch, there will be the same shrinking from severe punishment, the same paltering with mutineers, the same truckling to rebels, by which their measures, up to the present moment, have been fatally marked.

DII AVERTANT OMEN!

END OF PART I.

APPENDIX.

From LIEUTENANT G. FORREST, *Assistant-Commissary of Ordnance, to* COLONEL A. ABBOTT, C.B., *Inspector-General of Ordnance and Magazines, Fort William.*

SIR,—I have the honour to report for the information of Government, and in the absence of my commanding officer, Lieutenant Willoughby, Artillery, supposed to be killed on his retreat from Delhi to this station, the following facts as regards the capture of the Delhi magazine by the mutineers and insurgents on the 11th instant. On the morning of that date, between seven and eight A.M., Sir Theophilus Metcalfe came to my house, and requested that I would accompany him to the magazine for the purpose of having two guns placed on the bridge, so as to prevent the mutineers from passing over. On our arrival at the magazine we found present Lieutenants Willoughby and Raynor, with Conductors Buckley, Shaw, Scully, and Acting Sub-conductor Crow, and Serjeants Edwards and Stewart, with the Native Establishment. On Sir Theophilus Metcalfe alighting from his buggy, Lieutenant Willoughby and I accompanied him to the small bastion on the river face, which commanded a full view of the bridge, from which we could distinctly see the mutineers marching in open column, headed by the cavalry; and the Delhi side of the bridge was already in the possession of a body of Cavalry. On Sir Theophilus Metcalfe observing this, he proceeded with Lieutenant Willoughby to see if the city gate was closed against the mutineers. However, this step was needless, as the mutineers were admitted directly to the Palace, through which they passed cheering. On Lieutenant Willoughby's return to the magazine, the gates of the magazine were closed and barricaded, and every possible arrangement that could be made was at once commenced on. Inside the gate leading to the Park were placed two six-pounders, double-charged with grape, one under Acting Sub-conductor Crow and Serjeant Stewart, with the lighted matches in their hands, and with orders that if any attempt was made to force that gate, both guns were to be fired at once, and they were to fall back on that part of the magazine in which Lieutenant Willoughby and I were posted. The principal gate of the magazine was similarly defended by two guns, with the chevaux-de-frise laid down on the inside. For the further defence of this gate and the magazine in its vicinity, there were two six-pounders so placed as either to command the gate and a small bastion in its vicinity. Within sixty yards of the gate and in front of the office, and commanding two cross-roads, were three six-pounders and one twenty-four pounder howitzer, which could be so managed as to act upon any part of the magazine in that neighbourhood. After all these guns and howitzers had been placed in the several positions above-named, they were loaded with double charges of grape. The next step taken was to place arms in the hands of the Native Establishment, which they most reluctantly received, and appeared to be in a state not only of excitement, but also of insubordination, as they refused to obey any orders issued by the Europeans, particularly the Mussulman portion of the establishment. After the above arrangements had been made, a train was laid by Conductors Buckley, Scully, and Serjeant Stewart, ready to be fired by a preconcerted signal, which was that of Conductor Buckley raising his hat from his head, on the order being given by Lieutenant Willoughby. The train was fired by Conductor Scully, but not until such time as the last round from the howitzers had been fired. So soon as the above arrangements had been made, guards from the Palace came and demanded the possession of the magazine in the name of the King of Delhi, to which no reply was given.

Immediately after this the subadar of the guard on duty at the magazine informed Lieutenant Willoughby and me, that the King of Delhi had sent down word to the mutineers that he would without delay send scaling-ladders from the Palace for the purpose of scaling the walls, and which shortly after arrived. On the ladders being erected against the wall, the whole of our Native Establishment deserted us by climbing up the sloped sheds on the inside of the magazine, and descending the ladders on the outside, after which the enemy appeared in great number on the top of the walls, and on whom we kept up an incessant fire of grape, every round of which told well, as long as a single round remained. Previous to the natives deserting us they hid the priming pouches; and one man in particular, Kurreembuksh, a durwan, appeared to keep up a constant communication with the enemy on the outside, and to keep them informed of our situation. Lieutenant Willoughby was so annoyed at this man's conduct, that he gave me an order to shoot him, should he again approach the gate.

Lieutenant Raynor, with the other Europeans, did everything that possibly could be done for the defence of the magazine; and where all have behaved so bravely, it is almost impossible for me to point out any particular individual. However, I am in duty bound to bring to the notice of Government the gallantry of Conductors Buckley and Scully on this trying occasion. The former, assisted only by myself, loaded and fired in rapid succession the several guns above detailed, firing at least four rounds from each gun, and with the same steadiness as if standing on parade, although the enemy were then some hundreds in number, and kept up a continual fire of musketry on us, within forty or fifty yards. After firing the last round, Conductor Buckley received a musket-ball in his arm, above the elbow, which has since been extracted here. I, at the same time, was struck in the left hand by two musket-balls, which disabled me for the time. It was at this critical moment that Lieutenant Willoughby gave the order for firing the magazine, which was at once responded to by Conductor Scully firing the several trains. Indeed, from the very commencement, he evinced his gallantry by volunteering his services for blowing up the magazine, and remained true to his trust to the last moment. As soon as the explosion took place, such as escaped from beneath the ruins, and none escaped unhurt, retreated through the sallyport on the river face. Lieutenant Willoughby and I succeeded in reaching the Cashmere Gate. What became of the other parties it is impossible for me to say. Lieutenant Raynor and Conductor Buckley have escaped to this station. Severe indisposition prevented my sending in this Report sooner.

I have, &c.
(Signed)   G. FORREST, Lieut.
Asst. Commy. of Ordnance.

Meerut, May 27th, 1857.

N. B.—After crossing the river, on the night of the 11th, I observed the whole of the magazine to be on fire, so that I am in hopes that little of the property fell into the hands of the enemy. Park-Serjeant Hoyle was shot about 11 A.M., by the mutineers, in attempting to reach the magazine to aid in its defence.

(True Copy)   A. ABBOTT, Colonel,
Inspector-General of Ordnance and Magazines.

THE MUTINY

OF

THE BENGAL ARMY.

An Historical Narrative.

BY ONE WHO HAS SERVED UNDER
SIR CHARLES NAPIER.

PART II.

LONDON:
BOSWORTH AND HARRISON, 215 REGENT STREET.
MDCCCLVIII.

LONDON:
PRINTED BY SPOTTISWOODE AND CO.
NEW-STREET SQUARE.

TO

THE LIVING AND THE DEAD;—

TO

THE STATESMAN

WHOSE PRESCIENT POLICY SAVED A MIGHTY EMPIRE FROM RUIN,—

TO

THE HERO,

WHOSE VOICE EVEN FROM THE TOMB FORETOLD THE ADVENT
OF THE
NEMESIS OF MISRULE;—

TO

THE LIVING EARL OF ELLENBOROUGH,

AND

THE DEAD SIR CHARLES NAPIER,

These Pages are Dedicated.

ADVERTISEMENT.

In presenting the second part of his narrative of the great national insurrection in India to the public, the writer is anxious to avow the reasons which primarily induced him to adopt a step so foreign to his previous habits, as that involved in publication.

Having, in India, been precluded from offering warning or advice, the writer, in common with many others, foresaw at an early stage that the system adopted by the Supreme Council of Calcutta, so far back as March 1857, of coquetting with mutiny and with mutineers, would inevitably lead to disaster. There was not an officer in Bengal, living out of the charmed circle of official red-tapeism, that did not scent from afar the stormy blast; and although the revolt in all its magnitude was anticipated, probably, by none, still there was a deep conviction on the minds of many, that something dangerous was impending.

The crisis came. At first, apparently, a mere military mutiny, it speedily changed its character, and became a national insurrection. The Rajpoot villages in Behar, those in the districts of Benares, Azimgurh, Goruckpore, in the entire Doab, comprising the divisions of Allahabad, Cawnpore, Meerut, and Agra, in the provinces of Rohilcund and Oudh, shook off our rule and declared against us. But the men who administered the affairs of India refused to admit the existence of events which were clear to all around them; they persisted in governing as though there were no disorder in the civil districts, and feigned to believe that the cultivators of the soil — the class from which the Sepoys are selected — were, to a man, in our favour. Their tactics were at once detected; but no sooner had their exposure been threatened by the local press, than the fourth estate was summarily silenced by the authoritative application of a Press Act.

In the midst of the unparalleled disaster by which the country had at this period been overwhelmed, with a Government whose measures, always tardy, were often ill-advised, whose policy was a hand-to-mouth policy, in whose eyes the suppression of the mutiny seemed to be of less importance than the maintenance of an exclusive service, and with the ordinary vehicles of information virtually suppressed, it appeared to the writer to be the duty of every Englishman, to the best of his abilities, to enlighten his countrymen on the rise and progress of an insurrection which, if not misunderstood, had certainly been mismanaged.

The first part of the narrative, therefore, was the offspring of the Gagging Act.

In the second part, now offered to the public, the writer has endeavoured, still maintaining the narrative form, to trace the consequences of a still-existing adherence to principles inaugurated upwards of a century ago. The natural tendency of those principles has been, to place all the power and patronage of the country in the hands of a class who have no stake in its prosperity beyond the salary they draw, who have been educated in an implicit belief in Leadenhall Street, who are jealous of every other class of Europeans, and who therefore cast every obstacle in the way of their settling in the country — a policy advocated by Lord Metcalfe, Mr. Shore, and others of the Civil Service, whose combined integrity and capacity had elevated them above the prejudices of their education.

These civilians, thus forming an oligarchy and possessing power so great that by their means one Governor-General, who saw through and defeated their designs, was recalled, are now intrusted with the task of re-organising a system on the ruins of that internal administration which has broken down under their misrule. They have already commenced their work in a manner that plainly indicates the mere re-erection of the ancient edifice.

It is because the writer is convinced that the selfish nature of their policy needs only exposure to meet with the indignant reprobation of the people of England, that he has ventured in the course of this narrative to exemplify some of its results. He would humbly suggest to his countrymen, that in any future scheme for the government of India the "exclusiveness" which has been the bane of the present system be abolished, and that it be made lawful for the supreme power to appoint any man of talent and ability, beyond the pale of the Civil Service, to the highest places of trust and confidence under the Government.

It would appear also most essential that the Legislative Council be either remodelled, or abolished altogether. Constituted as it now is, of paid nominees, it commands neither respect nor consideration.

This work is dedicated to Lord Ellenborough, and to the lamented Sir Charles Napier, partly because those two great men, each in his turn, suppressed mutinies which, in their development, only became less dangerous than the present one because, instead of wasting their time in discussing milk-and-water theories, in writing minutes on abstruse legal technicalities, or in debating the distinction between treachery and treason, they acted not to excite, but to crush them, and succeeded accordingly;—because also they not only detected the sore spot in the Indian system, but likewise applied to it "the incision-knife and the caustic;"—because they adopted justice as the basis of their systems of government; and because, finally, their wise policy in Scinde, on one side, and in Gwalior, on the other, have assured the safety of India in this as in preceding crises.

Of personal admiration, shared in as it is by all around them, this is not the place to speak.

It had been the intention of the writer to have included a notice of the able administration of the Punjab in the narrative now submitted to the public; but its insertion would have increased the bulk, and have delayed the publication of the present part, already too long postponed: it shall assume a prominent position in the third part.

With respect to the facts which are adduced in this work, there is not one which is not based upon authority. To those kind friends who have sympathised with his undertaking, and who share his sentiments, the best acknowledgments of the writer are offered; something more is due to those who have aided him by their assistance and advice.

The writer cannot but be sensible that he has rendered but scant justice to many of the gallant officers and soldiers who have fought so nobly for their country. In common with his countrymen, he is at a loss to pronounce whether the daring energy of Havelock's soldiers, the patient and determined fortitude of those who for four months sat before Delhi, or the undaunted resolution of the heroes who defended Lucknow, is most worthy of admiration. Should this work reach a second edition, it will be his pleasing duty to endeavour to portray at greater length the deeds of those who have the greatest claims on the gratitude of England.

To that portion of the English press which noticed so favourably the first instalment of this narrative, the writer desires to convey his warmest acknowledgments. Composed without access to a single official document, its details have been found singularly correct; but one or two trivial errors occur. The whole part is now under revision, and will, it is hoped, be shortly again presented to the public in a slightly enlarged form.

INDIA: 10th Dec. 1857.

CONTENTS.

CHAPTER I.
The Effects of the Revolt at Delhi in Calcutta and Agra. — The Mutinies at Ferozpore, Allygurh, Etawah, and Mynpoorie. — Mr. Colvin's Proclamation - - - - - - - - - - 57

CHAPTER II.
Calcutta to 31st May. — Oudh to 2nd June - - - - - 72

CHAPTER III.
Insurrections at Azimgurh, Juanpore, Benares, and Allahabad - - 83

CHAPTER IV.
Calcutta to 30th June. — Massacres at Futtehpore, Jhansie, Nowgong, and Rohnee - - - - - - - - - - 98

CHAPTER V.
Allahabad to 4th July - - - - - - - - 118

CHAPTER VI.
Cawnpore - - - - - - - - - - 123

CHAPTER VII.
Havelock's Advance to Cawnpore. — Futtehgurh. — Attempts to relieve Lucknow - - - - - - - - - - 143

CHAPTER VIII.
Calcutta to 5th August. — Dinapore, Patna, Arrah, Gya. — The Clemency Act. — Mr. J. P. Grant - - - - - - - - 171

CHAPTER IX.
Gwalior. — Central India. — Agra. — Rohilcund - - - - 191

CHAPTER X.
Delhi - - - - - - - - - - 200

PART II.

CHAPTER I.

THE EFFECTS OF THE REVOLT AT DELHI IN CALCUTTA AND AGRA. — THE MUTINIES AT FEROZPORE, ALLYGURH, ELAWAH AND MYNPOOREE. — MR. COLVIN'S PROCLAMATION.

WHILST the terrible events recorded in the last chapter were being enacted at Meerut and Delhi, Lord Canning and the Supreme Council were congratulating themselves on the success and facility with which they had eradicated the spirit of mutiny from the Bengal Army. It is true that a written report from Sir Henry Lawrence of the *émeute* at Lucknow on the 3rd of May, a telegraphic notification of which had been received on the 4th, arrived on the 9th of May, but it caused the members of Government no uneasiness whatever. Sir H. Lawrence's vigorous measures had suppressed the mutiny, and to the majority of the Council there appeared no necessity for any precautions for the future. Mr. Grant, indeed, who was considered to carry the brains of the Council, in a minute which he recorded on that date, expressed his marked approval of the dilatory policy which had been pursued with reference to the 34th Native Infantry, and hoped that the Government would not depart from it on this or on any future occasion. He, therefore, advised that the punishment of the 7th Oudh Infantry should neither be prompt nor sudden, and that it should be prepared by all those tedious forms under shelter of which the guilty parties in the 34th Native Infantry escaped punishment. Both he and Mr. Dorin were evidently desirous to make the European officers the scapegoats: the latter recorded his opinion that no regiment which was properly commanded would mutiny, and both expressed a desire that before punishment should be meted out to those men who had mutinied with arms in their hands, a strict and searching investigation should be made into the conduct of the European officers, and a proportionate punishment awarded to them — to those very men who were at the time risking their lives and the lives of their wives and children by remaining at their solitary posts, and by endeavouring to preserve order and discipline — many of whom, not long after, paid for their zeal and confidence in their men by a lingering and cruel death.

The Governor-General himself was apparently quite satisfied with the aspect of affairs; on the 12th of May, whilst our countrywomen at Delhi were being massacred, he recorded his belief that the measures taken with reference to the mutineers had not been "too mild," and he was evidently of opinion that the spark of mutiny, though it might glow for a time, was fast dying out.

It was in consequence of these feelings that he and his Council at this period acted a part which very nearly, for a time, lost to England the possession of India — to which many of the horrors which were afterwards perpetrated may be traced.

The long agitation about the cartridges, the mutiny of the 19th, the continued smouldering of the native regiments at Barrackpore, the murderous attack on Lieut. Baugh, the incendiarisms committed at all the principal stations in India, and lastly, this outbreak in the heart of Oudh, a newly annexed country, had made a very deep impression on the minds of all thinking men in India. The want of decision on the part of Government, the long interval of five weeks which had been suffered to intervene between the crime of the 34th Native Infantry and its punishment, if punishment it can be called, had too evidently impressed the natives with the idea that we were afraid of them; and it was apparent to a vast number of our military commandants, that unless our policy underwent a total change, unless a system of repression of mutiny were substituted for the existing plan of coquetting with and succumbing to it, it would be impossible to maintain the discipline of the army. The Sepoy now felt that his commanding officer was a cypher; the Government, his real master, was at a distance, and, moreover, had showed that it feared him. What was there to deter him from making himself master of the situation? All who had studied the Asiatic character, who from constant intercourse had become acquainted with its peculiarities, felt assured that a further system of conciliation would but impress the Sepoys with an idea of their own power; that instead of becoming more reconciled to us by our constant and slavish acknowledgment of their religion, and by our system of entirely ignoring our own, they would the rather despise us. Already in their eyes we were on a par with their lowest caste. A Christian was one who drank brandy and eat pork and beef. Was not the idea that we wished to reduce them by trick to the same degrading position sufficient to excite every deep-seated prejudice against us? Yet we knew that they entertained that idea. We knew, or we ought to have known, that such an idea once imbibed by an Asiatic, once thoroughly taking possession of his prejudiced and uneducated mind, was ineradicable, that every attempt to remove would only confirm it, and be regarded as a part of the process by which he was to be suddenly converted.

But the men who ruled India in 1857 knew little of Asiatic character. The two civilians had seen only that specimen of it of which the educated Bengalee is a type: the legal member and Lord Canning had seen no more, and General Low was a Madras officer. How could a Council so constituted comprehend the crisis through which they were passing, — a crisis the result of which depended on their treatment of a proud, bigoted, relentless race, of whose national character and peculiarities they were one and all ignorant? The manner in which they did treat it, in which they are now treating it, proves that up to the present moment even they have not comprehended it.

The many signs and warnings which had been given them from the end of January up to the beginning of May, might have convinced even intellects of no extraordinary power that an occasion might arise for the employment of an European force, larger than that at the time of their disposal. The measure therefore adopted by Lord Canning of ordering up the 84th from Rangoon so early as March, met with universal approval. It was fondly believed that he foresaw the danger, that he was providing against it by anticipation. Alas! for the imputation of good motives! No sooner had the 34th Native Infantry been disbanded than, in the face of all that had passed, of the smothered mutinies at Barrackpore, of the *émeute* at Lucknow, he resolved to send back the 84th Foot to Rangoon. This was decided upon on the 8th May, 1857. Had that measure been carried out, there would have been but one weak European regiment to guard the arsenal of Fort William, and the entire country between Calcutta and Dinapore. What would have been the consequences if the 84th had left before the insurrection at Meerut had become known? Lord Canning, at least, would have paid dearly for his incapacity, and India would have been temporarily lost to us. Providentially the account of that insurrection arrived on the 14th, before the arrangements for the departure of the 84th had been completed, and the order was recalled.

If Lord Canning, finding that, notwithstanding his conciliatory policy towards the 19th and 34th Native Infantry, the bad feeling was gaining ground, was showing itself by incendiarisms at Agra, Meerut, Umballa, and throughout the North-west, by actual mutiny at Lucknow, had acted on the 4th May as he acted subsequently to the 16th May, and, instead of resolving to send away one regiment, had written to Madras, Ceylon, Rangoon and Moulmein for three or four others, what should we not have escaped? The fearful massacres of Cawnpore, Futtehgurh, and Allahabad would not have occurred: Oudh and Rohilcund would have been preserved from the contagion, and Delhi might have fallen in a fortnight. When he did send for them, it was "too late;" the plague had spread throughout India, and there required, not staying, but extirpation.

But up to the 14th of May, the Government believed that their "not too mild" measures had overcome the spirit of mutiny. From the enjoyment of that pleasing dream they were somewhat rudely disturbed by receiving an account of the Meerut outbreak. The telegraph had flashed it to them on the 11th, but it was not till the 14th that they became acquainted with the main fact, that our troops were in open revolt and had murdered their officers. On that date, then, a Council assembled. Its first measure was to countermand the departure of the 84th; its second showed how little our statesmen were able to appreciate the crisis, to comprehend the scene that was acting before their eyes.

The system which allowed to each native regiment a certain

number of native officers, about twenty-two to every corps, also granted to these native officers the privilege of sitting on courts-martial. By them alone could a Sepoy be tried; the verdict at which they might arrive could be disturbed by no superior power. The Commander-in-Chief might return their "finding" and "sentence" for revision, but they possessed the power, and not unfrequently exercised it, of adhering to their original decisions. Their sentences in general courts-martial, whatever they might be, were invariably sent for the approval of the Commander-in-Chief; no lesser power could confirm, and even he had no power to increase, the punishment awarded: he might indeed withhold his approval and confirmation, but in that case the prisoner would escape scot-free. It will be evident then to all, that in this important matter of courts-martial, the discipline of the army was in the hands of the native officers, and they had it in their power, so long as this system might be upheld, to abet treason by inflicting only a nominal punishment on traitors.

A notable instance of this had but lately occurred at Barrackpore, where a native officer brought to trial for trying to incite the men of his own regiment to mutiny, by going about the lines and imploring them in the name and for the sake of their religion to rise, was sentenced only to dismissal from the service, which to him was no punishment at all.

This circumstance of the discipline of the army being, in its most important particular, in the hands of native officers, could not have escaped the notice of the members of Council or of the Military Secretary, for the court-martial above alluded to had only recently been published, and the subject had been commented upon by the Press. It is not surprising, therefore, that it was the second subject to which the members of the Government turned their attention at the meeting of Council on the 14th of May. But how did they treat it? With the Bengal Army "drifting" into revolt, how did they meet together to strike a deadly blow at mutiny?—how did they settle this question? They actually feared to touch it; they still left that part of the order existing in which it was laid down that native soldiers must be tried by native officers, that is, mutineers by mutineers, and their solitary remedial measure was to transfer the appointing confirming and approving power from the Commander-in-Chief to commanding officers of divisions and stations!*

This was on the 14th; on the 15th or 16th, the news of the Delhi massacre arrived. Still assuming it to be a mere affair of greased cartridges, regarding the instrument as the cause of the revolt, the Government on the latter date issued a proclamation in which the native army and the native population were assured that the Government never had and never would interfere with their religion; at the same time the mischief having been completed, the anomaly regarding courts-martial was rectified, and it was left optional with commanding officers to appoint either European or native officers

* Vide Calcutta Gazette Extraordinary, 14th May, 1857.

upon them. On the same day Lord Canning telegraphed to Bombay for the troops of the Persian expedition, whom the treaty with the Shah would place at the disposal of that Government.* It may fairly be presumed that to Sir Henry Lawrence belongs the credit of this measure; his critical eye had discerned the coming storm, and on the 16th he telegraphed to Lord Canning to send for troops from China, Ceylon, and elsewhere, wherever they might be available. That message reached Calcutta the same day, and was acted upon at once both in letter and spirit, for expresses were sent to Moulmein and Madras, and not long after to Ceylon and Singapore for every available man.

It has been the fashion to bestow all the credit of this measure upon Lord Canning, but the Blue Book abounds with proofs that it is a credit which must be shared with many others; not only Sir Henry Lawrence, but his brother Sir John, General Anson, Sir P. Grant, and Mr. Colvin made it the subject of their earliest messages. It was, in fact, an idea which must have struck every one; to have neglected it, would have shown the grossest incompetency. It was indeed our only hope of safety — the sheet anchor which was left us wherewith to ride out the storm. In acting upon it Lord Canning was animated by the instinct of self-preservation. It was the rope at which he clutched when overset by this mutiny: none but a madman, or one utterly careless of life, would have neglected it. The fault which posterity will find with Lord Canning is, that he did not avail himself of these resources earlier. During the month of April, whilst all India was fermenting, a prudent statesman would have employed himself in strengthening his hands; he might without risk or danger to any part of our Indian possessions, have brought up one regiment from Moulmein, in addition to the 84th from Rangoon, and another from Madras. When the mutiny broke out, these two regiments might have been at Cawnpore; they would have preserved that most important station, and probably Oudh, from outbreak; they would have kept up our communications with the North-west, and the revolt would probably have been confined to the very district of Delhi.

In acting after the event as it would have been prudent to act before, Lord Canning earned but small claims to our admiration; especially if it be remembered that on the 8th May he was actually contemplating the return of the 84th to Rangoon. It is but justice to him, however, to state, that on the 16th May, when the full force of the storm became apparent, he took all ordinary precautions to meet it. He sent everywhere for troops, he telegraphed to the Commander-in-Chief " to make short work of Delhi," he gave full powers to Sir John Lawrence in the Punjab, and on the 19th he issued an order promising rewards to all who might distinguish themselves by conspicuous acts of gallantry and devotion to the state. All these arrangements were excellent as far as they went, but they did not go far enough. The Governor of Bombay, Lord Elphinstone, with a

* Blue Book.

keener instinct of the danger, offered to despatch an extra steamer to Suez on the 17th May, which would forestall by a fortnight the ordinary Calcutta mail, and have enabled the authorities in England to make prompt arrangements for sending out reinforcements. But Lord Canning, full of hope that we should gain some countervailing advantage before the next ensuing mail should leave Bombay, would not avail himself of the offer. He was, at this time, probably, the only * man in Calcutta who looked for a speedy issue to the revolt. He alone would not believe that the whole army was pledged to insurrection. He ignored the fact that even in Calcutta we were a handful of Christians living in the midst of a fierce, bigoted, intractable race, who knew no law but that inspired by fear, and on whom the intelligence of the revolt of Delhi was likely to have the worst possible effect. Yet so keen was the sense of this amongst the merchants, the shopkeepers, and others, whom long residence and constant intercourse had made well acquainted with the temper of the natives, that although the use of arms was foreign to their habits, they came forward between the 20th and 31st May, and tendered their services to Government in any manner in which they could be most usefully employed for the preservation of the peace. An enrolment on a large scale at this time, would have enabled the Governor-General to dispense with the services of one European regiment at least; but so bent was he on ignoring the danger, that he not only declined the offers of the Trades' Association, the Masonic Fraternity, the Native Converts, the Americans, the French inhabitants and others, but he declined them in terms calculated to deaden rather than to excite a spirit of loyalty, for whilst he seemed to refer the cause of their petitions to a "passing and groundless panic"† on their part, he snubbed them for supposing for an instant that the whole Army of Bengal was infected with the spirit of revolt! At the same time, as if in mockery, he invited those who wished to enrol themselves to apply to the Commissioner of Police, to whom, it transpired, orders had been issued to furnish applicants with clubs!

On the 23rd May the Madras Fusiliers, under their gallant commanding officer, Colonel Neill, arrived in Calcutta, and were at once despatched in the most expeditious manner possible to the Northwest. Up to this moment, no account of any fresh mutiny had been received, and Mr. Colvin, Governor of the North-west Provinces, was beginning to believe that "the worst of the storm was passed, and that the aspect of affairs was brightening."‡ Neither Sir Henry Lawrence nor Sir Hugh Wheeler was so confident; but Mr. Colvin, being a civilian, was supposed to be far better acquainted with the character of the people, and to possess better opportunities for judging them than were open to military men. He was not only of opinion that severity in dealing with mutineers was a mistake§, but he was anxious to fetter the Commander-in-Chief by placing a civilian at his elbow. This principle, introduced by Lord Auckland, when Mr.

---

* The members of Council of course excepted.
† Vide letters to the French inhabitants.
‡ 16th May.   § 19th May.

Colvin was his private secretary, had been wisely abolished by Lord Ellenborough. Like many of that great nobleman's alterations, it had been effaced immediately by his successors, and the application of the system was now, not unnaturally, advocated by one who had all along been its warmest supporter. Up to this moment, indeed, the opinions of Mr. Colvin had been entirely in accord with those of the Governor-General.

Thus did matters progress up to the 25th May — the day on which Her Majesty's birthday was celebrated. The Governor-General and the Lieutenant-Governor very confident in the future; Sir Henry Lawrence and Sir Hugh Wheeler, at Lucknow and Cawnpore, making every preparation to meet the coming storm; the European society, military men and civilians throughout India, anxious, yet not desponding. The crisis was about to take a turn.

The 25th May must be ranked as one of the memorable days connected with the mutiny. In the morning, the 70th Native Infantry, one of the regiments stationed at Barrackpore, volunteered to a man to march against their countrymen in Delhi; Mr. Colvin issued his famous proclamation, in which he announced that "soldiers engaged in the late disturbances," *i. e.*, in the massacres of Delhi and Meerut, who might give up their arms at the nearest Government post, should be "permitted to go to their homes unmolested," and in the evening intelligence arrived of the mutiny of the native troops at Ferozpore, on the border of the Punjab, on the 13th and 14th of the month.

Before commenting upon the two first-named occurrences, it may be as well to give a detailed account of that ill-managed affair. On the 12th May, an account of the occurrences at Meerut reached Ferozpore. The troops in that station consisted of Her Majesty's 61st Foot, the 45th and 57th Native Infantry, the 10th Light Cavalry (Native) and about 150 European Artillery; they were commanded by Brigadier Innes*, certainly an active, and up to that time considered an intelligent officer. He had arrived only the day before, and had had but little opportunity of testing the temper of the native troops. The value of Ferozpore must be estimated not only from its having been, up to the period of the Sutlej campaign, the frontier station in the North-west, and of its consequent importance with reference to the Punjaub, but from its possessing an entrenched magazine of the largest class, and containing military stores almost equal in amount to those in the arsenal at Fort William. Ferozpore is only seventy-three miles from Delhi, and it may be easily imagined that the rebels, already possessed of the Delhi Arsenal, and aware alike of the contiguity and importance of that at Ferozpore, would spare no efforts to make themselves masters of it also. Had they been capable of acting in concert with their brethren at Meerut, they might have succeeded; but the sound of that explosion was sufficient to put the commanding officers all over India on the alert.

---

* Not James, as erroneously named in the Blue Book.

On the 12th, the report of it reached Ferozpore. On the following day, the Brigadier ordered out the troops to judge of their disposition. Trained amongst natives himself, he might have been supposed to be a competent authority on such a point. He looked at them, and believed their bearing, especially that of the 57th, to be "haughty:" the 10th Cavalry he considered loyal. The commanding officers of all three regiments pronounced the state of their corps to be satisfactory.

At noon on the same day information of the occurrences at Delhi reached the station. At that time the entrenched magazine, the most important position in Ferozpore, was held by a company of the 57th Native Infantry. Immediate arrangements were made for relieving them by a company of Her Majesty's 61st, and one of European Artillery. This was not done completely, for the company of the 57th was allowed to remain in the magazine. At the same time the 10th Cavalry, in whom every confidence was placed, were stationed under the walls of the new arsenal, and the 61st, under Colonel Jones, were held in readiness to move on any point. These arrangements having been completed, the 45th and 57th were ordered to parade at 5 P. M. with the view of being marched out of cantonments. The Brigadier went at that hour to the parade ground, formed them up in quarter-distance columns, and addressed them. They were then ordered to move off in opposite directions. They obeyed unhesitatingly. The road by which the 45th were ordered to march took them close to the entrenched magazine. Arriving there they halted and refused to advance a step. They then loaded their muskets, and, heedless of the entreaties of their officers, ran to the north-west bastion of the magazine, and stood there, apparently hesitating what to do next. At this moment scaling ladders were thrown out to them by the Sepoys who had been allowed to remain inside. They immediately commenced climbing over the parapet, and three hundred of their number having succeeded in finding their way inside, made an attack on the company of the 61st, who were hurriedly drawn up to receive them. They were repulsed with the loss of about half a dozen of their number, but not despairing of success, made a detour and attempted to take our men in the rear, but were again unsuccessful. At this moment two more companies of the 61st arrived, and the mutineers fled in all directions — many of them being killed. The company of the 57th, which had not apparently joined actively in the *émeute*, was disarmed and turned out of the magazine. So far the arrangements of the Brigadier had been apparently defective: he had suffered the entrenchment to be escaladed to the great peril of the arsenal, and he had no troops at hand to keep the mutineers in check. Still he had been successful in repelling their attack : the movements that followed proved that success to have resulted rather from accident than from skilful organisation on his part.

It must be remembered that in Ferozpore there were the 61st regiment and about 150 artillerymen supplied with all the munitions of war, to combat against two native infantry regiments. They could have beaten a dozen of them, deprived as these were of their European officers. There was also a regiment of cavalry, which was supposed to be, and which proved loyal. But admitting that the Brigadier was justified in looking upon these as doubtful, or even as hostile, he still should not have feared the issue with the force at his disposal. It was his duty to have attacked and followed up the 45th immediately he heard of their outbreak. What did he do? Believing, he says in his report, that the 57th would follow the example of the 45th, he determined to maintain the barrack and the entrenchment. Fatal policy! to shrink before Asiatics! The movement of two companies of the 61st, with the horse-battery of artillery, would have completely dispersed the 45th, and in all probability have deterred the 57th from following their example. He remained, however, on the defensive; the consequence was that the 45th took the initiative against him!

The men of that regiment, on being repulsed from the entrenchment, retreated towards the ice-pits, carrying their dead with them. These they left in the Mahomedan burial-ground, and, returning in small bodies to the cantonment, set fire to and burned the church, Roman Catholic chapel, two vacant hospitals, the 61st mess-house, and several bungalows. In doing this, strange to record, they were not even molested except at the chapel, where one of them was shot. They even made several fresh attempts upon the entrenchment, but were foiled on every occasion. Hitherto, panic had reigned throughout Ferozpore: one part of the 61st remained in the barracks, the other part in the entrenchments: not a single man was brought to act against the mutineers. To such an extent was the defensive principle carried, that hearing that the mutineers intended seizing their own regimental magazine on the following morning, instead of choosing that moment for attacking and dispersing them, the Brigadier actually preferred as it were abandoning his position by causing the magazines of the 45th and 57th to be blown up. The great body of the former regiment, having done all the mischief they could, then set off for Delhi. On this intelligence reaching the Brigadier, he, for the first time, began to act with vigour, for he despatched three troops of cavalry and two guns in pursuit of them, whilst he caused at the same time the 57th to be disarmed. Both these measures were fairly successful. The 45th the moment the initiative was taken against them were panic-stricken, and fled in confusion; they lost a number of men, and several of those who escaped threw away their arms to accelerate their flight. The greater part of the 57th were disarmed quietly, a few only preferring to follow the fortunes of the 45th. The 10th Cavalry throughout the affair behaved with the most perfect loyalty and emulated the conduct of the Europeans.

Such was the mutiny of Ferozpore,—a mutiny which affords painful evidence of the evil action of the government of India on characters not more than ordinarily distinguished by firmness. It has been noticeable throughout the insurrection that only on rare occasions, and when a Lawrence, a Neill, or a Wilson have been invested with supreme authority, have commanding officers dared to cast regulations to the winds and act on their own responsibility.

Men of average capacity even have felt the conviction that, act as they might, they would be judged only by the result, and they have therefore felt compelled, in self-defence, to adhere as much as possible to the letter of the regulations. The burden of red tape has weighed them down. It was so with Colonel Mitchell at Berhampore, with General Hewitt at Meerut, and on this occasion with Brigadier Innes at Ferozpore. That officer, on hearing of the sad events at Meerut and Delhi, must have felt that all middle courses were insecure ; that there was but one road to be pursued consistently with safety. If he had, for instance, especially after noticing the "haughty" bearing of the Native Infantry, ordered a general parade of all the troops, taking care by previous arrangement and skilful disposition to place the guns, manned as they were by Europeans, on both flanks of the Native Infantry, the 61st in their front between them and the entrenched magazine, — if he had at the same time directed the actual, not the nominal, relief of the company of the 57th inside the magazine ; — if he had then ordered the native regiments to lay down their arms, and, on their failure to do so, had been prepared to open out on them with grape and small arms, — all would have been well : there would have been no attempt on the magazine, no burning of churches and houses, no panic, no loss of property. Why did he not do it then ? He feared the responsibility of disarming them in the first place, of mowing them down in case of refusal in the second. But had he no reason for his fear ? Had he not seen the Government of India allow itself to be insulted for three months with all but impunity by its native troops ? Had he not read in the public prints the uncontradicted statement that Lord Canning had affirmed that if Colonel Mitchell at Berhampore had opened fire on the 19th the Government would not have supported him ? Was he justified, he probably asked himself, in taking this responsibility upon himself, — in doing more than the Government, with all its appliances and means at hand, had thought it necessary to do ? The truth is, Brigadier Innes was neither a Neill nor a Lawrence : he could not see that to succeed in such times as were coming, he must be ready to brave every responsibility. He could not look beyond the Book of Regulations, and to it he adhered with a zeal worthy of a better cause.

Had his measures been successful, identical as they were in spirit with those of the Government of India, he would doubtless have been held up as a pattern Brigadier. Unfortunately for himself, the regulations led him to failure, and his failure cost him his command. He failed, — and was summarily removed from the list of brigadiers.

The account of the Ferozpore mutiny reached Calcutta simultaneously with Mr. Colvin's proclamation and the report of the volunteering of the 70th Native Infantry. Lord Canning dealt promptly with both. He telegraphed to the Lieutenant-Governor his disapproval of the spirit and wording of his proclamation, and he rode down on the following morning to Barrackpore, personally accepted the services of the 70th, and promised them that they should start for Delhi as soon as arrangements could be made for sending them up-country. This promise was never fulfilled, and it seems a pity that it was ever made. Subsequent events convinced even the

Governor-General that the whole army was tainted; and the 70th were eventually disarmed along with the other regiments of the Barrackpore Brigade, on the 14th June. Still the fact of their having volunteered, and of their example in that respect being followed by many other regiments stationed at or near Calcutta (of whom those which have not mutinied have been since disarmed), made a deep impression at the time on the minds of Lord Canning and the members of his Council, and probably induced them to reply so discourteously to the patriotic offers of the Trades' Association and others. They perhaps acted in his mind as incidents counterbalancing the disaster of Ferozpore and the proclamation of Agra.

This latter document was yet unrepealed. Up to the hour I am writing * it has never been recalled from circulation, and it is even supposed to have influenced our authorities at Delhi in sparing the life of the blood-steeped king, of his youngest and favourite son, and of many of those chiefs who were most forward in the rebellion against us. On the 26th May Lord Canning expressed his disapproval of it, and begged that it might be recalled. Mr. Colvin replied that it was too late to recall it, that it had been circulated all over the country (in the interval between the 25th and 27th), that it was perfectly understood by all, and that it was hoped and believed that it would have the best possible effect. He concluded by pleading earnestly that it might stand.

But Lord Canning had not, at this epoch, entirely enslaved himself to the policy of "India for the Civil Service." On the same day (the 27th), he replied to Mr. Colvin, pointed out the necessary inference which the mutineers must draw from the terms of his proclamation, and requested that, as it could not be withdrawn, another which he forwarded, extraordinarily mild, but not open to the objections which were fatal to Mr. Colvin's, might be substituted for it, and sent up forthwith to the Commander-in-Chief. Still the Lieutenant-Governor hesitated: he felt disinclined to stultify himself; and instead of obeying the orders of his superior, he ventured (the 28th May) on another remonstrance. This was too much for a nobleman wielding the authority of Governor-General of India. Every moment that this miserable document was allowed to circulate was big with ruin to our interests: it betrayed weakness in every line, it was conveying to mutineers the fact that we feared them, that they might murder our women and children and go to their homes unpunished. And yet, although issued on the 25th of May, up to the 29th it had not only been cancelled, but the Lieutenant-Governor was still pleading for it, and in substance refusing to obey the instructions of the Governor-General. The latter had submitted to this treatment for four days, but when he saw this continued trifling with his instructions, he could bear it no longer. He forthwith sent a copy of his own proclamation to Major-General Sir Hugh Wheeler, commanding at Cawnpore, with instructions that it might be forwarded *viâ* Futtehgurh to the Commander-in-Chief. Sir Hugh, with a

* 21st November.

soldier's promptitude, obeyed at once, but the message never reached General Anson, and it is the prevailing belief that Mr. Colvin's proclamation is still in force. That gentleman certainly made another, and a final attempt (31st May) to retain his own ideas, and to be spared the pain of transmitting to the Commander-in-Chief the opinion of the Governor-General, that he had offered life to the murderers of his countrymen; but Lord Canning was obdurate, and on the same day transmitted very peremptory instructions that his own proclamation should be sent on, uncurtailed, to the Commander-in-Chief.

This was all very well, but, like so many of Lord Canning's acts, it was only a half-measure. Mr. Colvin's proclamation had been published in the Agra Government Gazette, marked with all the official emblems of authority. Lord Canning's counter-stroke was smuggled into the North-west, was circulated perhaps by the Commander-in-Chief, but necessarily in a very limited degree, and never appeared in the Agra Gazette at all. The Commander-in-Chief has no civil power whatever: the people therefore who read one proclamation published under authority — the authority under which they were placed, that of the Lieutenant-Governor — would naturally pay more obedience to it than to a written document, circulated by a military man of whose connexion with themselves they had never heard. So indeed it has proved. Every letter from the north-west induces the belief that Mr. Colvin's proclamation of the 25th May, securing pardon to bloody-handed mutineers, is still considered by the authorities, as well as by the people, to be the law of the land!

In reflecting upon this ill-advised proclamation, the first thing that strikes us is, the fact of its having been promulgated at Agra, without previous reference to the Governor-General. The telegraph line between Agra and Calcutta was complete. From the Meerut outbreak up to the 4th June daily messages passed between the two high functionaries. If Mr. Colvin had telegraphed the proclamation for approval on the morning of the 25th, he would have obtained a reply the same day. Up to that moment he had received the cordial support of the Governor-General: he had done well: he had shown nerve in addressing the native regiments at Agra, in maintaining a bold front, and his position outside the Fort. All his previous intentions had been communicated to Calcutta; why was not this one? It is a point which, if Mr. Colvin were living, might be worth investigating: but Mr. Colvin is no more, and it is now far more pleasurable to dwell on the fact that to the last he never left his post, than on the causes of that important error which cost him the confidence of his countrymen.

Meanwhile affairs were not progressing favourably in the North-west. On the 20th of May four companies of the 9th Regiment Native Infantry, considered the pattern regiment of the Bengal army, mutinied: two companies of the same regiment stationed at Mynpoorie followed their example on the 22nd; two more at Etawah on the 23rd; and the remainder at Bolandshuhr on the 24th. About the same time information reached Calcutta that a company of Sappers which had been ordered from Roorkee to Meerut after the outbreak, had mutinied at that station on the 16th, and, after killing their forming officer, Captain Fraser, had set out for Delhi. Our men were, however, fortunately on the alert, and followed them up so quickly, that fifty-six of their number were killed. About two hundred and eighty managed to reach Delhi with their arms. A hundred and fifty of them, who had been on duty when the main body mutinied, were promptly disarmed.

The mutiny of the 9th Regiment at Allygurh was caused by a circumstance which places in a strong light the bigotry of the Hindoos, and demonstrates most clearly the ease with which they can be acted upon by the lever of their religion. Allygurh lies about eighty miles south of Meerut on the Grand Trunk Road. It possesses a bastioned fort, well capable of defence, and memorable in Anglo-Indian history as having been stormed by Lord Lake in 1803. In May 1857 it was garrisoned only by four companies of the 9th Native Infantry. This detachment had not apparently been shaken by the events at Meerut and Delhi. The corps had always been a good one, well behaved and well drilled. The officers felt the utmost confidence in their men, and this feeling was apparently reciprocated. Up to the morning of the 20th, their behaviour had been most exemplary, and the men had made over to their officers several spies who had entered their lines with the avowed object of seducing them from their allegiance. One of these villains, caught in the very act, had been condemned to suffer death that morning. Accordingly he was brought out, the Sepoys were drawn up, and his sentence was read to him in their presence. He had in fact been convicted by a court-martial composed of native officers. He was then led to the gallows, the rope was adjusted, the drop taken away. In a few minutes he had ceased to breathe. All this time the Sepoys were looking on in silent approbation. But just as they were about to be moved off the ground, a small detachment of their own corps, which had been absent on command, marched in. They too beheld the dangling corpse, and they too seemed to think that the miscreant had received his deserts. At this critical moment, one of their number more bigoted than the rest stepped forth from their ranks, and pointing to the gallows exclaimed, "Behold a martyr to our religion." By that simple exclamation he touched a chord which had till then lain dormant. Instantly these men, who had passed the sentence and assisted at the execution, overcome by a sudden frenzy, broke out into open mutiny. They did not, it is true, assault their officers, they simply dismissed them: but they plundered the treasury, opened the jail doors, and then went off bodily to Delhi. The detachments of the same regiment at Bolundshuhr *, Etawah †, and Mynpoorie ‡, followed the example of their comrades. The outbreak at Bolandshuhr was accompanied by no violence: that at Mynpoorie was principally remarkable for the

---

* Forty miles from Allygurh.   † Seventy-three miles from Agra.
‡ Seventy-one miles from Agra.

courage, coolness, and presence of mind displayed, under trying and most perilous circumstances, by Lieutenant De Kantzow of the 9th Native Infantry.

The mutiny broke out very suddenly on the morning of the 22nd, by the men of the 9th rising upon their officers.* Lieutenant De Kantzow, instead of leaving them, as he might have done, stood up before them, urged them to reflect on the lawlessness of their acts, and evinced the utmost indifference of his own life in his zeal to make them return to their duty. But the Sepoys would not listen; many muskets were levelled at him, and his life was in the greatest danger: they commenced plundering in every direction; and finally, dragging their officers with them, proceeded to the treasury, and endeavoured to force open the iron gates. A fearful scene here ensued: the jail-guard, about thirty in number, and some of the jail officials, rallied round the Lieutenant. He did not desist a moment from his efforts to quiet his men: though jostled and buffeted by them, he stood up manfully, and for three dreary hours in turns threatened and implored them to return to their duty.

His efforts were not altogether in vain: aided latterly by a trustworthy native, who had been sent down by the magistrate, he at length persuaded the Sepoys to retire from the treasury. They returned to their lines, and, after plundering the regimental treasure chest, took the road to Delhi. It must in justice be added that the conduct of Mr. Power, the collector, and his brother, in remaining at their posts, is worthy of praise.

This victory—for that surely is a victory in which one European officer, standing alone against 200 armed native soldiery, causes them finally to quit the station, leaving the treasury unplundered—had the effect of restoring confidence in the city and district of Mynpoorie. The gallantry of Lieutenant De Kantzow was acknowledged in the most handsome manner by Lord Canning, and he was at once placed in command of a special body of police. On the following day (the 23rd) the mutiny broke out at Etawah: this too was a bloodless affair, but the Sepoys succeeded in plundering the treasury and private houses. Mr. Hume, the magistrate, escaped in the dress of a native woman. On the 25th the station was re-occupied by a Gwalior regiment, and British authority was temporarily re-established. The news of these events reached the Lieutenant-Governor of the Northwest Provinces at Agra before he had issued his famous proclamation. Up to this time Mr. Colvin had been very successful in maintaining tranquillity in his neighbourhood. As soon as possible after the Meerut and Delhi massacres he had paraded the two native regiments, which with one English corps (the Company's 3rd Europeans) and some artillery formed the garrison of Agra, and had succeeded apparently in pacifying them. He felt confident that "all would be put to rights in a few days," if a "simple proclamation were issued to quiet the minds of the troops." He evidently had no conception of the magnitude of the crisis, and on the 20th May, two

* Magistrates' report.

days before the outbreaks at Mynpoorie and Etawah in his own immediate neighbourhood, he telegraphed to the Governor-General that "a very few days would see the end of this daring mutiny." He had previously, with the assent of the Supreme Government, proclaimed martial law throughout the districts under his rule.

On the 21st May the intelligence of the disaster at Allygurh reached him. He immediately organised an expedition for its recapture: this expedition consisted of about 230 cavalry under Lieutenant Cockburn of the Gwalior Contingent and fifty volunteers. This small party reached Allygurh on the 26th, and effected its recapture without difficulty. Six or seven Europeans who were besieged in a neighbouring factory were released, a large amount of treasure recovered, and the whole brought back to Hattrass, a walled town about twenty-two miles from Allygurh on the Agra road. Here a portion of Lieutenant Cockburn's cavalry, about 100 in number, who had up to this moment performed excellent service, suddenly rebelled. After vainly attempting to seduce their comrades, who were mostly Mahomedans, the rebels rode off to plunder the country. But Lieutenant Cockburn was resolved to pay them out, if possible, for their treachery. Hearing that, increased in number to 500, they were plundering and murdering in the vicinity of Hattrass, be resolved to attack them. And, to do so with the more certainty as to the result, he hit upon a stratagem. He procured a covered cart of the description in which native women were in the habit of travelling, and, placing in it four of his troopers with loaded carbines, he followed himself with the main body at a distance of about fifty paces, under the shade of some trees. The rebels, attracted by the cart, rushed out to seize the supposed inmates, but the foremost of them was saluted by a bullet, and at this signal Lieutenant Cockburn's party dashed amongst them, and not only defeated and dispersed them, but killed forty-eight of their number.

The history of the mutiny abounds with similar instances of individual tact and courage.

But the recapture of Allygurh, the preservation of Mynpoorie, the re-occupation of Etawah, and the gallantry of individuals, could not check the progress of the mutiny. From this moment, indeed, it began to assume a popular character. The zumindars and the ryots joined in it. From Agra to Delhi, to Meerut, to Cawnpore, to Allahabad, from Allahabad downwards, and throughout Central India, the entire country made a tremendous effort to shake off our sway. On the 30th of May two companies, both belonging to the regiments stationed at Agra, but themselves located at Muttra, thirty-five miles to the north of that station, mutinied, plundered the treasury, committed a few murders, and went off to Delhi. In the face of this, and of the disorganisation prevailing all around him, Mr. Colvin could no longer hesitate. On the following morning (31st), the two native regiments, the 44th and 67th, were disarmed, and allowed two months' leave to visit their homes.

The atmosphere was indeed thickening, and it was impossible even to guess the quarters in which the storm would next break out.

CHAPTER II.

CALCUTTA TO 31ST MAY. — OUDH TO 2ND JUNE.

Accounts of the occurrences detailed in the last chapter were all promptly conveyed by the electric wire to Calcutta, in the order in which they became known to the Lieutenant-Governor at Agra. Darker and more unfavourable reports reached the Governor-General about the same time from Cawnpore and Lucknow, and so impressed was he with the danger that he actually telegraphed to General Anson his opinion (31st May), that " his force of artillery would enable him to dispose of Delhi with certainty ; " he therefore begged that he would " detach European infantry and cavalry to the south of Delhi." The movements of General Anson, and of the force which undertook the siege of Delhi, will be recorded in a separate chapter. It may suffice here to state that the measure proposed by the Governor-General — like all his measures, a half-measure— was impracticable. It might have been a question whether the Commander-in-Chief's force should not have been concentrated on the lower provinces, leaving Delhi for a time to its fate. This plan would have had the advantage of securing Cawnpore, Oudh, Agra, Goruckpore, and the country south-east of these places ; but, on the other hand, it would have permitted the conspirators to raise the semblance of an empire at the imperial seat of Government : it would have allowed an unchecked communication with Central India and with the armies of Madras and Bombay. It would have been in the highest degree unwise to have allowed treason and treachery to remain unchecked or unmenaced. Our retirement on the Lower Provinces would have been attributed to fear. It is even possible that the Punjaubees, a warlike race, seeing rebellion raising its victorious head so near their frontier, would have been tempted to endeavour to shake off our yoke also. It cannot then be doubted that General Anson and his successors in command acted wisely in going to Delhi, in preferring to risk everything rather than forego the capture of the stronghold of the murderers. They persevered in this undertaking, despite of difficulties hardly surmountable, and they well deserved that glorious success which was finally vouchsafed to their arms.

If Delhi had been the defenceless place, which some represented it to be, there would even then have been little force in the Governor-General's suggestion : for we knew it to possess a large arsenal, and at least ten thousand insurgent troops. Had we despatched our infantry and cavalry to the southward, the result would have been, that the enemy would have captured our siege train !

About this time (May 29th), when the mutinies at Meerut, Delhi, Allygurh, Mynpoorie, and Etawah, were known to the Governor-General, when it must have been perceived that the insurrection must now be put down, not by words, but by bayonets; the military secretary, Colonel Birch, issued the first and only proclamation to the army on the subject of the greased cartridges. Before this circular reached the upper provinces, the whole of Oudh, the important districts of Benares, Allahabad, and Cawnpore, were in open insurrection. It therefore fell to the ground, a blunted weapon. Far different, in all probability, would have been its effect had it been issued in the month of January, when suspicion regarding greased cartridges was first mooted. But Colonel Birch and the Government were dumb at that time. The Sepoys murmured, yet no explanation was offered. They were suffered then to "drift" into the belief that the Government was endeavouring to impose upon them. But now, when the time for explanations had passed away, when every word falling from Government was liable to be misconstrued, a full and complete explanation was offered regarding the substitution of the Enfield rifle for Brown Bess, and the whole question of greased cartridges! Alas for that terrible "Too late" which attaches itself as the motto of statesmen without prescience or genius,—of little men in great positions!

Meanwhile fearful events were enacting at Lucknow. As it was that city which set the example to the surrounding districts, it may be as well to give a *résumé* of the doings of Sir Henry Lawrence, subsequent to the revolt of the 7th Infantry*, so promptly quelled on the 3rd of May.

Lucknow.—It has been already mentioned † that on the 3rd May a treasonable letter had been sent by the Sepoys of the 7th Native Infantry to the 48th Native Infantry, but that it had fortunately fallen into the hands of a faithful Sepoy, who, after consulting with the havildar and subadar of his company, in conjunction with them, reported the matter to Sir Henry Lawrence. This able officer having already struck terror into the minds of all by his prompt and vigorous treatment of the mutineers, was justly of opinion that to openly reward these men, who, in spite of the temptations of caste, had done their duty, would impress upon the minds of the natives that the British Government was equally prompt to reward as to punish, and that whilst it had no mercy for mutineers, it had honours and emoluments for those who did their duty faithfully and honestly. With this view he summoned all the civil and military residents, the officers and men of the native regiments, and other native officials, to a grand durbar on the evening of the 12th May. The lawn in front of the Residency was carpeted, and chairs were arranged forming three sides of a square. At 6 P.M. Sir Henry Lawrence entered, followed by his staff and a large body of officers, and took his seat at the head of the assembly. Beside him were deposited in trays the presents intended for the native soldiers. Before, however, he distributed them, he addressed the assembled company in the Hindustani language. He commenced by alluding to the fear of the Hindoos for their religion: he pointed out how, under the rule of the Mahomedan emperors of Delhi, that religion had never been respected: how Hindoos were

---

* Recorded in Part I.   † Part I.

forcibly converted by having the flesh of the cow forced down their throats. To the Mahomedans he showed how Runjeet Singh would never tolerate their religion at Lahore. Then turning to the assembled crowd, he asked them to reflect on the toleration which the Government of India had for a century always afforded to both religions. He next noticed our power, our exploits in the Russian war, our ships, our resources, how in a few months the British Government could, if necessary, concentrate a large army on that very spot. Finally, he alluded to the inseparable connexion between the Sepoys and their officers; he dwelt long and eloquently on this subject, on the dangers they had shared, on the services they had performed together; on the feeling instinctive in the breast of every officer that the regiment was his home, that the glory of the regiment was his glory, its disgrace his shame. He then impressed upon his listeners to think upon what he had told them, to place firm reliance on the assurances of Government, warning them that if, the dupes of fools and knaves, any of them were to attempt to follow in the footsteps of the 19th and 34th, the Government would inflict such a punishment as would not easily pass away from the memory of man. Sir Henry then called forward the Subadar and the Sepoys, and shaking hands with them bestowed upon them, in the name of the government of India, substantial testimonials of its appreciation of their fidelity.

The speech of Sir Henry Lawrence, truthful, solemn, and striking, had an immense effect. The entire scene was particularly calculated to impress those to whom it was addressed. The vast assemblage of all the representatives of British authority, the congregated natives, and this simple-minded Christian addressing them in their own language, and swaying them not less by the eloquence than by the truthful force of his harangue, presented indeed a picture which could only have been realised in the East. Bigoted as were those men, prejudiced against us, the dupes of vile intriguers, they left that durbar the most loyal subjects of the British Government, anxious only to have an opportunity of showing their zeal. But Sir Henry was not deceived by transient impressions: he felt that the time could not be far distant, unless Delhi should unexpectedly fall, before these loyal soldiers would become bloodthirsty mutineers, and he commenced taking every precaution in anticipation of an outbreak.

On the 16th of May, he became fully acquainted with the events of Meerut and Delhi. Precluded as he was by his situation from forcing advice upon a Governor-General with whom he had no personal acquaintance, he at once felt that the present was not a time for ceremony, and he telegraphed a strong recommendation to send for Europeans from China, Ceylon, and elsewhere, as well as for Goorkhas from the hills. Feeling also the anomaly of his own position, a military man invested with the chief civil authority, and yet subordinate in a military capacity to many of those who were about him, he applied for plenary military power in Oudh. On the 19th, he received a notification of his appointment as Brigadier-General. Assuming command at once, he without delay made an entirely new disposition of the troops. Before entering upon this subject, it may be convenient to give an outline of the city and cantonment of Lucknow.

The city of Lucknow, built on the right of the river Goomtee, and extending for four miles along its banks, lies about fifty miles to the north-east of Cawnpore. All the principal buildings, including the Imambarrah, the King's palace, and the adjoining gardens, are between the city and the river bank. Here also is the Residency, a large walled enclosure, comprising not only the palace of the Resident, but other houses and outhouses, as well as underground buildings, or vaults on a large scale. It is situated on higher ground than the rest of the town, which it may be said to command. Near this, and higher up the river, almost on its bank, is a strong, turreted, castellated building, called the Muchee Bawun, very well adapted for defence against native troops. To the south, and covering an immense space, lies the town, intersected by a canal, which falls into the Goomtee close to the Martinière, about three miles south-east of the Residency. A little to the south of this is the Dilkoosha, a hunting-box, or palace, within an enclosed park. To the north-east of the Residency and on the left bank of the Goomtee is the cantonment, communicating with the right bank by means of two bridges, one of stone near the Muchee Bawun, the other of iron close to the Residency. Recrossing by these to the right bank, we come to the space between the Residency and the Martinière. This is filled up principally by native palaces, amongst which the Motee Mahal, Shah-munzil, Secundrabagh, and Furrahbuksh-ke-kotee, are the most conspicuous. To the south of the town, about four miles from the Residency on the Cawnpore road, is the Alum-bagh, a very strong, defensible position. The troops at Lucknow, in the month of May, 1857, consisted of H. M.'s 32nd Foot, about 570 strong, between fifty and sixty European Artillerymen, a native battery of artillery, the 13th, 48th, and 71st Regiments, and the 7th Light Cavalry. They had previously been disposed in the ordinary manner, the Europeans being preserved as much as possible from exposure, and the natives entrusted with the charge of several important buildings.

Sir Henry's first object was to remedy this error. He commenced by reducing the number of posts from eight to four; three of these he greatly strengthened, and so arranged their composition that none of the natives on duty could effect anything against the buildings, of which, conjointly with the Europeans, they were in charge. All the magazine stores hitherto under the charge of Sepoys, he caused to be removed into the Muchee Bawun, and entrusted that building to a company of Europeans: thirty guns were also placed in position there, and supplies for European troops rapidly stored in. At the Treasury, within the Residency Compound, he stationed 200 Sepoys, 130 Europeans, and six guns; the Treasury tent was actually under the charge of the Sepoys, but the guns were so disposed that at the first alarm they could be brought to bear upon them.

In the centre, and between these two positions, was a strong post of four hundred men with twenty guns, some of them eighteen-pounders, commanding the two bridges leading to cantonments.

The fourth post was at the dâk bungalow, between the cantonment and the Residency, and consisted of six guns and two squadrons of the 2nd Oudh Cavalry.

In the cantonment, on the left bank of the Goomtee, were the head quarters of the three native regiments, 340 of the 32nd Foot, fifty artillerymen (European), and six guns, and a battery of native artillery.

In consequence of a pressing requisition from Sir H. Wheeler, on the 21st May, the European force in cantonments was reduced by about fifty men. The 7th Cavalry were stationed at Moodkeepore, seven miles distant from the infantry cantonment.

That the precautions above detailed were necessary was proved by the fact, that during the night, papers were constantly posted up in prominent positions in the town, in which all good Mahomedans were called upon to rise *en masse*, and massacre the Frank infidels. The city police, from their inability to discover the perpetrators of these insurrectionary invitations, showed either that they connived at them, or that they were incapable. From their subsequent conduct, it may be assumed that they were at this time in league with the conspirators.

About the 24th, in consequence of a report that the Regiments would rise that night between 8 and 9 o'clock, all the ladies were moved into the Residency Compound; here also the sick and families of the 32nd were placed, and it was appointed the general rendezvous in the event of a rise. At the same time, the uncovenanted assistants, comprising clerks, copyists, section-writers, &c., were embodied as special constables, and took night duty. One great source of strength was the entire confidence which Sir Henry Lawrence inspired in all around him. He never for a moment underrated the danger, but, beholding its approach, he did not fear to look it in the face. Every precaution that man could take, he adopted. He improvised a fortress in the Muchee Bawun, seized and held the bridges, strengthened the Residency, conveyed into it all the ladies and invalids, and then, having his European force well in hand, prepared for any alternative. All this time, so far from betraying any of the anxieties which he felt, he went freely amongst the people, rode constantly about the city, endeavoured to calm men's minds, to reason with them, to show them their folly, their fool-hardiness. The designs of the men who were duping them he laid bare. But all was in vain. There was the same servility of manner on the part of the natives; but their hearts were shut to reason and argument. They thought they had caught us in a trap, and should find us isolated and unable to afford assistance to one another. They felt, in fact, sure of their game, and no persuasions or reasoning would, at that hour, have induced them to forego the attempt to win it.

At length, after nightly alarms, on the night of the 30th May, at 9 o'clock, the insurrection broke out. At that hour, suddenly a few shots were heard from the lines of the 71st Native Infantry; the men of this Regiment had been told off in parties, to fire the bungalows and murder their officers, and these shots were the signal. They were joined at first by only a few of the 13th and 48th; but, nothing daunted, they commenced at once their murderous work. Brigadier Handscombe, a meritorious and much respected officer, who commanded under Sir Henry, and who lived in the cantonment close to them, had hastened to their lines on the first sound of the firing: he was received with a volley, and shot dead. Lieut. Grant, who was out on picket duty, was wounded by a random shot. Unable to stir, the subadar of his guard concealed him under a charpoy*, and told the mutineers that he had escaped. But a havildar of the same guard, merciless in his intense bigotry, pointed to the charpoy, whence Lieut. Grant was at once dragged, and brutally murdered. All this, and the firing of every bungalow they came near, lasted only a few seconds,—less time than I have taken to describe it. Sir Henry Lawrence had, on the first sound, ridden to the scene of action. It was his great object to prevent all communication between the insurgents and the mutinously disposed in the city. Accordingly, he at once moved off two guns and a company of Europeans to the corner of the only road by which the mutineers could approach the bridges, and disposed the rest to meet the attack of the enemy. This was not long waited for: the insurgents came on, infuriated with bang, and excited by their own deeds; but, as they neared the guns, they were received with such a volley of grape, that they at once retreated into their lines, whence they continued for a short time to carry on a desultory fire. As, however, the Europeans and the guns moved on, although only for a few hundred yards, they abandoned even these defences, and as they moved off, the Irregular Cavalry were sent in to cut them up. But their hearts were not in the contest, and although they followed their gallant commandant, Lieut. Hardinge, who greatly distinguished himself, it was but with little effect. Still pursuing their retreat, the insurgents reached the cavalry lines at Moodkepore, about 4 A.M. on the 31st. Finding they were not pursued, they determined to return, persuaded that they would be joined by others of their creed and colour. Firing the cavalry lines to encourage themselves, they started back for Lucknow. But Sir Henry was ready to meet them. Having secured the safety of the Residency, he marched forward with two hundred Europeans, two guns, the 7th Light Cavalry, and a handful of Daly's, Gall's, and Hardinge's Irregular regiments. As he passed the native lines, he was joined by the men of the three native regiments who had not joined the insurgents, about five hundred in number. The 7th Light Cavalry were sent in advance; but, on nearing the enemy, two troops went bodily over and joined them. Seeing our force still advancing, the enemy then turned and fled, although still about a thousand yards distant. Our artillery at once opened upon them, and quickened their flight; they were pursued by the Europeans as far as Moodkepore, and by the Native Cavalry for twenty miles further, in the direction of Seetapore. Their loss in killed, however, was only two or three; but sixty were taken prisoners. At Moodkepore was found the body

* A low native bedstead, with four legs.

of a young officer, Raleigh, quite a boy, who had but lately arrived. Left from ill-health at Moodkepore, he had been surprised and murdered by these assassins.

Unable, with a city full of men plotting our destruction, to pursue the mutineers further with his Europeans, Sir Henry returned to cantonments, and leaving there two hundred of the 32nd Foot, and four guns, he moved the remainder of his force into the Muchee Bawun and the Residency, distributing two of the battery guns to each. He at once proclaimed martial law. The city guards he strengthened with a hundred Europeans and four guns. The city, indeed, was surging with excitement; an insurrection was threatened that night, and but for the bold attitude assumed by Sir Henry (who, with Colonel Inglis, H. M.'s 33rd, slept in the town), and the hold which his character had obtained on the minds of all with whom he had been brought much in contact, it would have undoubtedly broken out. As it was, a good deal of firing took place between the more riotous of the city people and our police. The latter, however, aided by the Europeans, beat them off on each occasion. It is gratifying to add that the havildar who so basely betrayed the place of Lieut. Grant's concealment was caught and hanged; six or seven of the mutineers shared the same fate. Amid the all but universal disaffection, it is also pleasing to record that the officers of the 48th owed their lives to the fidelity of their men. They were at mess when the insurrection broke out, and were consequently in very great risk from detached parties of the mutineers. But about an hundred of their own men rallied round them, and escorted them in safety to the Muchee Bawun. Of the three thousand five hundred comprising the four native regiments, less than one fourth remained true to their colours, and these gradually dropped off as the rebellion progressed.

The spark which on the 30th May was fired at Lucknow, lit up the whole of Oudh. But before carrying the reader in the steps of the mutineers, it will be as well to trace the proceedings of a party of cavalry, which had left Lucknow for a specific purpose before the mutiny broke out.

Towards the end of May, in consequence of communications between Mr. Colvin, Sir Hugh Wheeler, and Sir H. Lawrence, it was resolved that a party of Gall's horse, upon whom it was believed every reliance could be placed, should be detached to clear the road between Cawnpore and Mynpoorie, and thence re-open communications with Allygurh. As this was a service of an important and delicate nature, Sir Henry Lawrence selected his military secretary, Captain Fletcher Hayes, an officer of great abilities, to perform it. He took with him two troops of Irregular Cavalry, and was accompanied by Lieut. Barbor, Adjutant of the regiment, Captain Carey, and Mr. Fayrer. The party reached Cawnpore safely, and on the evening of the 31st of May, had progressed by forced marches as far as Bowgong, about a hundred miles north of Cawnpore. Here they heard that Mynpoorie had been re-occupied by our troops, but that a Rajah in the neighbourhood had set our rule at defiance. As Mynpoorie was only eight miles distant, Captains Hayes and Carey cantered in to consult the magistrate about attacking this miscreant. They remained there the entire day (1st June), the cavalry being halted at Bowgong. Orders, however, were transmitted to them to march on the following morning to Kurrowlie, sixteen miles on the road to Allygurh, at which place Captain Hayes would join them by a cross road. On the evening of the 1st, one of the native officials came in from Bowgong with the intelligence that the men were bent on mutiny. But as the small detachment which formed Captain Hayes' escort, and which arrived very soon after, merely complained regarding the length of the marches, no importance was attached to the previous information. In the morning, the two officers started by the cross-road, and after riding eleven miles, came in sight of their men proceeding in an orderly manner towards Kurrowlie. They crossed the plain to meet them, but as they approached, a native officer rode up and bade them fly for their lives. The words were scarcely out of his mouth before the two troops, yelling like demons and discharging their carbines, made at them. They had nothing for it but to wheel their horses round and make off. Captain Carey was fortunately untouched, but Captain Hayes, who was riding next the troopers, had not gone many yards before a native officer rode up to his side and cut him down. They then made after the other, but by judicious riding and being a light weight, he escaped after a two miles' chase, and eventually arrived safely at Mynpoorie.

It subsequently transpired that Lieutenant Barbor and Mr. Fayrer had been murdered about ten minutes before Captain Hayes came up. Mr. Fayrer was drinking at a well, when a dastardly sowar came up behind him and nearly cut off his head. Lieutenant Barbor seeing this, fled up the road, pursued by the whole body; he shot one horse and two of the sowars, when he was himself hit; the mutineers almost immediately afterwards came up with him and cut him down. The sowars, after plundering the property of their officers and securing all that they wore on their persons, went off to Delhi.*

Meanwhile the Lucknow rebels, baffled by the vigilance and promptitude shown by Sir Henry Lawrence, had taken the road to Delhi, viâ Seetapore. At this station were the head-quarters of the 41st regiment Native Infantry commanded by Lieut. Colonel Birch, a brother of the Military Secretary, and two regiments of Oudh Local Infantry. This officer, hearing of the approach of the mutineers, and justly feeling that in such times as the present boldness was the greatest safety, drew up his regiment to oppose their passage. As they approached, Colonel Birch gave the order to fire and was obeyed. The mutineers were so much discouraged by this reception, that they desisted from the attack, and continued their route to Delhi.

It must not be supposed that the conduct of the 41st, gratifying as it might appear on a mere superficial examination, was to be attributed in any degree to a spirit of loyalty. It was indeed supposed so at the time, and the "loyal 41st" was held up as a pattern to the

* Captain Carey's Letter, published in the "Times."

Bengal Army. But their conduct is capable of another and a more facile solution. There was a treasury at Seetapore. The 41st felt that if they delayed their revolt until the other regiments had passed away, the treasure would be theirs and theirs only. There would be none to share it with their brigade. Hence their apparent "loyalty" in repulsing the Lucknow mutineers. On the following morning, the 4th June, this regiment rose in revolt, murdered Colonel Birch, and many, if not all of the officers present, civil and military, and plundered the treasury.* It did not then, like so many of the other regiments, take the road to Delhi, but proceeded, committing fearful atrocities on the road, as will be recounted hereafter, to Futtehgurh, and aided in the capture of that place.

The whole country was now in flames. Not only the province of Oudh, but our own districts, had felt the force of the contagion and had risen on every side. On the 3rd, 4th, and 5th, the troops at the stations of Azimgurh, Benares, Allahabad, and Cawnpore rose in revolt. The entire province of Rohilcund, on the north-west frontier of Oudh, had even previously pronounced against our rule. In few of these districts did our countrymen escape massacre; in some they were put to death with every exaggeration of torture. But before detailing these events it will be necessary to follow the progress of the revolt throughout Oudh.

Sultanpore, ninety miles to the south-east, and Fyzabad, about the same distance to the eastward of Lucknow, felt the shock of the insurrection about the same time. At the former place were the 15th Irregular Cavalry and the 8th Oudh Locals. The cavalry regiment had been raised eleven years before by Colonel S. Fisher, an officer of H.M.'s service, a first-rate soldier, and the kindest-hearted man in existence. He was very proud of his men, felt entire confidence in them, always associated with them as much as possible, and being a great sportsman, was in the habit of taking his native officers with him to share his sport. He had felt the insecurity of his position, but he did not doubt his own men. In order, however, to remove one great incentive to revolt, the desire of plunder, from their minds, he resolved on the 8th June on emptying the treasury. He ascertained that this process might be effected by issuing three months' pay in advance to officers and men. This plan was accordingly carried out on the same evening. The following morning, as he was riding down to his regiment, he was shot in the back by a native policeman; his men — the men he had commanded for so many years — saw it but did not stir: the adjutant, Lieut. Tucker, however, went up to them and persuaded some of them to get a dooly †; in this he was placed; Lieut. Tucker then took out the ball and gave him some water; but he felt he was dying. Just at this moment, and as the second in command, Captain Gibbings, was coming up, a party of men, headed by a favourite orderly of Colonel Fisher's — a man who had accompanied him throughout that shooting season, rode up, first speared and then cut

---

* Account of a Bengalee, who escaped in the disguise of a Fakir.

† A covered conveyance for sick people.

him down. Lieutenant Tucker, finding it was all over, rode off, and, although pursued for three miles, escaped.

Fyzabad was the head-quarters of the 22nd Regiment Native Infantry, a local regiment, a detachment of Irregular Cavalry, and a battery of Native Artillery. Intelligence was received early in June that the 17th Native Infantry, who had mutinied at Azimgurh on the 3rd, would pass through Fyzabad *en route* to Delhi. The native officers and men of the 22nd were at once sounded; they swore that they were loyal and " of one heart " with their European officers. On the morning of the 8th it was ascertained that the 17th were within one march of the place. Colonel Lennox, commanding the 22nd, proposed moving out to give them battle; but the native officers of his regiment seemed much averse to it, as they said their families were with them, and they would prefer fighting on the spot for the lives of those dear to them. Whether the Colonel saw the force of this reasoning or not, he was compelled to succumb to it; but from that moment he must have felt that the game was up with them. But no distrust was shown. On the evening of the same day the troops were ordered to be drawn up against the anticipated attack, the guns being placed in the centre, supported by infantry on both flanks. Thus they remained till 11 P.M., when, on a signal from the lines of the local regiment, the artillerymen loaded their guns with grape. At this moment the two companies of the 22nd rushed amongst them, followed by the main body from the lines and the detachment of cavalry, and formally appointing Dhuleep Singh, a Subadar of the 22nd, as their colonel, and a Repaldar of the cavalry their general, took possession of the guns. In his new capacity the Subadar procured boats for the officers and let them go off uninjured: information of their departure was, however, conveyed to the 17th Native Infantry, who were encamped lower down the banks of the Gogra, and many of them were intercepted and massacred; those who escaped were wonderfully preserved through all but insurmountable dangers. The conduct of the 22nd, in sparing the lives of their officers, was much lauded at the time; but there appears to be but little real difference between men who actually commit murder and those who invite others to perpetrate the deed.

The regiments at Secrora, Pertahgurh, Pershadipore, Durriabad, Baraitch, and Gouda mutinied about the same time. Everywhere the treatment was the same, death to the "Feringhee" was the warcry; and those who escaped that fate, escaped in the face of dangers and difficulties which few of them would care to encounter again.

There was one case showing so strongly the fickleness of the native character, that it will well bear insertion in this place.

In the months of February and March, a rebel chieftain, Fuzl Alli, had made himself notorious by the murder of Mr. Boileau, a civilian, and the commission of other atrocities. In pursuit of him a detachment of the 3rd Oudh Infantry, under Lieutenant Clarke, had been especially active, and that officer had finally succeeded in executing justice upon him. His own men were the instruments of British vengeance; they had followed him unhesitatingly, unmurmuringly, and had striven equally with their commander in pursuit of the murderer: but in the month of June they revolted. Lieutenant Clarke, their former leader, and another officer, were powerless in their hands. The 17th Regiment Native Infantry were close at hand. To them these men, the accomplices of Lieutenant Clarke in the pursuit and death of Fuzl Alli, sent this message: "We have the murderer of Fuzl Alli; what shall we do with him?" "Behead him," was the reply. The injunction was at once executed upon the unfortunate officer and his companion.

From that day to the present all Oudh has been up in arms against us. Not only the regular troops whom we poured into that province, but the sixty thousand men who formed the army of the ex-king, the zumindars with their retainers, the two hundred and fifty forts, most of them heavily armed with guns, have been working against us. Here and there a petty raja has been found ready to spare the lives of our fugitives, and even in his heart wishing us success; but these exceptions have been very rare. The great body of the landowners, the mass of the people, have declared against us: they have balanced the rule of the Company and the sovereignty of their own kings, and have pronounced almost unanimously in favour of the latter. The very pensioners who had served in the ranks of our army, and who now derive their support solely from our bounty, have declared definitively against us; not only have they to a man joined in the insurrection, but it is a well-authenticated fact that they have been foremost in the commission of atrocities.*

Such is the political aspect of the question. In a military point of view, Oudh has been the great stumbling-block in our course, the ulcer that has swallowed up and paralysed all our resources. Granting that we should have had the rebellion, if Oudh had not been annexed, there would still have been one European regiment available for Cawnpore. There would have been no occasion to keep all our reinforcements between that place and Calcutta, or to pour them into Oudh in long-fruitless attempts to succour our countrymen. In all probability, Oudh would have remained to us what it was in the Mahratta, Sikh, and Burman wars, not only a harmless but a friendly country. Our troops would have been able to reinforce the army before Delhi and to re-conquer Rohilcund. As it is, they have been reduced by exposure, by disease, and by the sword, in the endeavour to rescue from the clutches of the enemy those of our countrymen who had been sent, in defiance of the most solemn treaties, to usurp the place and dignity of the native sovereigns of the country.

Seldom indeed has retribution so quickly followed crime as in the case of Oudh. The nearest approach to it in history is the seizure of Spain by Napoleon, under circumstances infinitely less revolting than those which accompanied the spoliation of Oudh. And yet Spain was Napoleon's ruin. In the agony of his mighty heart he

---

* I am unwilling to publish my authority for this statement; but my publishers will receive, privately, the name of my informant.

exclaimed, "This great Spanish ulcer has ruined me!" It swallowed up his armies as Oudh swallowed up our reinforcements, and his power from that moment received a death-blow not inferior to that which the immoral and illegal annexation of Oudh has dealt to the Court of Directors. In both cases justice was violated: in the first, happening long ago, she was speedily, in the second we will hope she will be as quickly, avenged. Already the accents of despair, significant of the death-bed of the unrighteous, have been heard from Leadenhall Street. It is fit that man should be taught that there are certain fixed laws which cannot be violated without bringing upon the head of the violator, even in this life, dishonour, confusion, and disgrace.

CHAPTER III.

INSURRECTIONS AT AZIMGURH, JUANPORE, BENARES, AND ALLAHABAD.

THE little stations of Azimgurh and Juanpore, forty miles apart, constituted our advanced posts on the south frontier of Oudh. With the larger towns of Benares and Ghazeepore, they formed a square based upon the Ganges. Thus the natural action of a detachment beaten at Juanpore would be to retreat on its main station, Benares, of a force overwhelmed at Azimgurh to retire on Ghazeepore. This latter station and Benares, likewise forty miles apart, and based on the Ganges, constituted thus the heart on which the smaller arteries of Juanpore and Azimgurh depended for a constant supply of vitality.

To the north again of Azimgurh, sixty miles from it, and abutting on the Oudh and Nepal frontiers at the extreme front of our territory, was the station of Goruckpore: this was held merely by two companies of the 17th Native Infantry, and a small party of Irregular Horse. The remainder of the 17th Native Infantry, and a detail of Native Artillery guarded Azimgurh. Juanpore was defended by a detachment of Sikhs.

As soon as the events of Meerut and Delhi became known at Azimgurh, the demeanour of the Sepoys of the 17th assumed a form not to be mistaken. They had always been a most indifferent regiment, and it was now their misfortune to be commanded by a man totally unfit to have charge even of a company. The consequence was that disorder reigned rampant; the Sepoys behaved exactly as they chose, and became the terror, instead of being the safeguard, of the European inhabitants.

Such was the state of affairs at the end of May. It was known that every station in India was "shaky," that no native troops could be depended upon. Yet at this epoch, the Accountant of the North-West Provinces, a civilian, wiser in his own conceit than his neighbours', issued an order for the removal of ten lakhs of treasure from

Goruckpore and seven from Azimgurh to Allahabad: that is to say, at a time that native troops were known to be disaffected, he placed the entire treasure of the Azimgurh and Goruckpore districts under their charge, directed them to march with it through a country surging as it were against us, and to convey it to another station where only native troops were posted. It was, in fact, to give the insurgents the very opportunity they were seeking for, of plundering the whole.

However, the orders of the Accountant must be obeyed. The ten lakhs of treasure were therefore brought from Goruckpore to Azimgurh by an escort, under the command of Lieutenant Palisser of the Irregular Cavalry: here they took charge of the seven lakhs. But the 17th Native Infantry were not going to lose this money without a struggle. On the 2nd of June they made a desperate effort to prevent the party leaving Azimgurh; but the tact and coolness of Lieutenant Palisser, and the staunchness of the troopers of the cavalry, quite paralysed them, and they were compelled for the moment to forego their intentions. But, though baffled, they were not defeated. On the night of the 3rd the treasure party started: it consisted of two companies of the 17th and Palisser's Horse. They had scarcely marched three hours when the six companies left behind rose in revolt, killed Lieutenant Hutchinson, their quarter-master, and, letting loose the prisoners from the jail, accompanied by them and by all the police, set off after the treasure.

It had been Lieutenant Palisser's intention to disarm the two companies of the 17th with him; but on his intimating his resolve, they went down upon their knees and swore that they would stand by him to the last. At that time we were not so well acquainted with the value of native oaths and with the estimation to be placed on native honour as experience has subsequently made us, and Palisser believed them. They were, therefore, not disarmed. The consequence was that when the excited crowd, pouring out from the station, came near him, all armed to the teeth and thirsting for blood, Palisser was helpless. His troopers stood by him so far as to defend him and the officers with him (Lieutenant Simpson and Mr. Turner), but no more. They would not act against their countrymen. He was compelled, therefore, to draw off, and abandon the treasure: his troopers retired with him.

But it did not suit the object of the mutineers to permit these officers to retire unmolested. Their avarice was even surpassed by their desire for blood. They therefore did all in their power to persuade the sowars to give up their officers; they appealed to religion, nationality, love of money; even offered 5000*l*. for each head: but all in vain. The sowars were negatively faithful: they would neither act for us or against us, and, resisting all temptation, safely escorted their officers into Benares. The very next day they deserted. Sensible perhaps that they had done but half their duty, and secretly sympathising with the rebels, they had gone, probably after having seen their officers safely disposed of, to swell their forces.

On the mutiny breaking out at Azimgurh, the lives of the residents were in great danger, and had it not been that the Sepoys were primarily intent on securing the treasure, but few of them would have escaped. As it was, one only who went amongst them was killed; the others barricaded themselves till the mutineers had started after the treasure party, and then set out for Ghazeepore,— Mr. Astell, the judge, leading the way in his carriage, most of the others following as best they might. However, all who started reached in safety. On arriving at Ghazeepore it was discovered that some of the indigo-planters and the poorer class of Christians had been left behind. As it was known that the 17th Native Infantry would return to plunder the place, great anxiety was felt on their behalf by one, at least, of those who had escaped. This was Mr. Venables, an indigo-planter residing in the neighbourhood of Azimgurh, a gentleman of large property and of a very high character. Fearing for the unfortunates who had been left behind, Mr. Venables endeavoured to persuade Mr. Astell, Mr. Horne, and others, to return with him. They were most unwilling, and pleaded fear of the Commissioner's anger, if they should return without his sanction. A message was instantly despatched for that sanction. But the Commissioner, Mr. Tucker, comprehending in an instant the feelings of his subordinates, sent back a reply to the effect that "he had no objection to Mr. Venables' going, but the civilians were on no account to risk their lives."

Thus privately and officially left to himself, this noble-hearted man determined to go alone. He started the next day, went direct to his estate at Doorie Ghat, some two and twenty miles on the Goruckpore side of Azimgurh, assembled his ryots *, armed them, marched at their head, and recovered Azimgurh. He did more; he held it; and whilst the apathetic civilians had retired into Benares, and were allowed to continue to draw their immense salaries — Mr. Astell alone 250l. per mensem — Mr. Venables, the indigo-planter, remained at their proper station, did all their work, even collected the revenue which they ought to have collected, restored order where all was chaos: and whilst these men were whining over the loss of their own private property, he employed himself in restoring the power and re-asserting the prestige of Government.

And yet he was one of those *" adventurers" whom the Government of India takes every opportunity of insulting. Mr. Venables held this district, reinforced only by a small detachment of native troops, for about six weeks. At the end of that time the civilians were most unwillingly compelled to return. The events which subsequently happened will be related in their proper place. It is time now to notice the effect which the events at Azimgurh produced on Benares and its out-stations.

The city of Benares, distant four hundred and twenty miles northwest of Calcutta, and nearly eighty east of Allahabad, is on the left bank of the river Ganges. It is the metropolis of Hinduism, sacred to the votaries of that religion. Thither do they proceed, that, by

* Tenantry.

presents to the Brahmins and bathing in the holy water of the Ganges, they may be purified from their sins. Thither they are taken to die, convinced that the departure of the soul in the stronghold of Brahminism ensures a certainty of eternal bliss. The population may be estimated at 300,000, of whom four-fifths are Hindoos. These, it may easily be imagined, are almost entirely under the influence of the priests: by them the poorer class are kept in rigid subjection, whilst the richer are permitted to atone for defalcations and indulgences by offerings of no mean value in the various temples. The cantonment of Benares, denominated Jeccole, is three miles inland. Here were stationed in May, 1857, the 37th Regiment Native Infantry, the Sikh Regiment of Loodhiana, an irregular Cavalry regiment, and half a company of European Artillery, or about thirty men. Thus, notwithstanding the warnings that had been given, the Government of India, in the early part of May, considered that thirty European gunners were sufficient to hold in check three native regiments, and a city — the hot-bed of Brahminism — containing 300,000 inhabitants.

There were other considerations which ought to have inspired a far different arrangement.

Benares, in addition to its sacred character, might be styled the city of dethroned monarchs. Hither came the despoiled princes of Sattara, the ex-royal family of Nepal, a branch of the royal family of Delhi, boorg rajahs and Sikh chieftains, to seek an asylum in their misfortunes. All these were elements of mischief. Some of them were princes whom we had dethroned, or grand seigneurs whom we had deprived of their estates. Intrigue was their delight, they could not live without it; treachery had been familiar to them from their childhood, and it might have been surmised, without any great stretch of imagination, that no opportunity would be lost by them of exercising their talents with effect against us.

The inhabitants of Benares were a proud turbulent race, fond of ancient ways, and very impatient of innovation. Previous to 1851 they had successfully resisted all attempts to trench upon any of their customs. Thus they would prefer that filth should lie in their streets rather than that the novel system of draining should be introduced; that the highways should remain unlighted at nights, their roads encroached upon by filthy huts, than that a clear thoroughfare should be made. Many magistrates had endeavoured to remedy these evils; but, after several trials, the population, or rather the bourgeoisie backed up by the priests, who looked upon improvement as the first step to undermine their religion, were too much for them: the magistrates were baffled, and receded from their orders.

But in 1851 a gentleman was appointed to the post of magistrate, who did not like to be baffled. He too ordered improvements after the manner of his predecessors: unlike them, he carried them out. This was Frederic Gubbins of the Civil Service.

His first attempt had been unpromising: the inhabitants, according to custom, resisted his innovations, and, finding that he did not succumb, the very next time he came into the city, they pelted him out of it. He had in fact to fly for his life. But he still persisted in his plan. The bourgeoisie, not to be beaten, resolved to starve him out; they shut all their shops and sent to stop their supplies of grain from all quarters. As the troops were dependent upon their regimental bazars, and these again dependent on the city of Benares for grain, it was supposed that, on the failure of the three or four days' supply laid up in the bazars, the magistrate would be glad to give in. But Mr. Gubbins resolved to fight them with their own weapons: he sent to Mirzapore and other places for grain; and finally, hearing that the leading members of the insurrection were about to hold a meeting to concoct a further scheme of opposition, he sent down two companies of Sepoys, caught them in the act, and lodged them in jail.*

The next morning he rode through the city and opened all the shops. From that moment, not only was the insurrection at an end, but Mr. Gubbins was lord of Benares. He had inspired a conviction of his power, his earnestness, his energy, such as if a native once imbibes he exaggerates,—he never loses the feeling. From that time forth, the idea reigned supreme in the minds of the people of Benares that it was impossible to organise a successful opposition against Mr. Gubbins.

It is necessary to mention this, because in every phase of the insurrection at Benares, this influence is visible, not only preventing the townsmen from joining the insurgent troops, but overawing them subsequently, when all the surrounding districts had risen. At the time of which I am writing, Mr. Gubbins was judge, Mr. Lind, an able active zealous officer, was magistrate; the troops were temporarily commanded by Brevet Lieut.-Colonel Gordon of the Sikhs corps, a very steady capable commandant; the commissioner or civil ruler of the district was Mr. H. C. Tucker, a most amiable good man, but ill adapted to rule in the emergency which was now approaching. Very soon after the news of Delhi and Meerut reached Benares, it became visible that, of the troops, the 37th were "gone;" the Sikhs mostly faithful, but some of them even wavering; the Irregular Cavalry doubtful. How to maintain order amongst these, and in the city, with the aid and by the sole means of thirty European artillerymen with three guns, was a problem which required solution.† With this view, a meeting of the principal members of the society was held. There one gentleman proposed to abandon the station, and to retreat upon Chunar, a fortress thirteen miles distant, and on the opposite bank of the river: he was supported at first by two others; but the idea was so strongly combated by Messrs. Gubbins and Lind, to whom it appeared in the light of a shameful abandonment of the most important city between Calcutta and Lucknow, that it was given up, and a resolution adopted to make a stand where they were, taking every precaution against an emergency.

---

* I received all these particulars from a gentleman who was at Benares at the time.

† On the authority of an officer who was at Benares at the time.

The first of these precautions was to despatch an urgent requisition to Dinapore, 130 miles distant, for troops. This was attended to, and two companies of Her Majesty's 10th foot, about 150 strong, were at once sent up by steamer.

There was unfortunately no defensible position in Benares; but arrangements were made that in the event of an outbreak, the ladies and others should repair on the first alarm to the Mint, a very large oblong brick building, proof against fire, and capable of being defended against men unprovided with artillery.

Towards the end of May the symptoms of disaffection amongst the native troops became even more strongly marked; the agents of the king of Delhi were found to be busy amongst the Mahomedan Sepoys; the Hindoos went openly to their temples, and prayed for the time to arrive when they might murder us; placards were posted up calling on the people to rise, and every thing indicated the approach of a crisis.

On the 3rd and 4th June, reinforcements of the Madras Fusiliers, sixty men in all, arrived, and it appeared that the time had now come when stronger measures might be adopted. It was felt that an insurrection was imminent, that it could not be deferred much longer; it was therefore thought that with 240 Europeans at their disposal, with the Sikhs believed to be staunch, and with the 13th Irregulars in whom their officers had every confidence, the measure might be adopted of disarming the 37th Native Infantry. About a fortnight before, Colonel Gordon had been superseded in command of the station by Brigadier Ponsonby, a cavalry officer. Both these officers, Mr. Tucker and Mr. Gubbins, debated these questions on the afternoon of the 4th June. In the height of the discussion, suddenly the brigade-major rushed in with the startling intelligence that the 17th Native Infantry at Azimgurh, sixty miles distant, had risen in revolt, and plundered the treasure. This decided them. It was unanimously resolved to disarm the 37th Native Infantry the following morning, and a plan of operations was arranged by which that measure could be effected, it was believed, without the effusion of blood.

All was settled. Brigadier Ponsonby had gone to his own house to issue the necessary orders, when the sudden arrival of one man changed the whole aspect of affairs. This man was Lieutenant-Colonel Neill, commanding the Madras Fusiliers.

As Colonel Neill is one of the characters figuring in the suppression of this mutiny, who rose at once to the surface, and never sank below it, it may be as well to give some brief outline of his character.

It is told in a very few words, and may be illustrated by one example. Colonel Neill was the type of a resolute, determined, energetic Englishman — a man of very quick observation and an iron will. He saw the true bearings of a question in an inconceivably brief space of time, and acted always at once: he was not to be trifled with when he gave orders: he always knew that he would be obeyed. His character was quickly appreciated by those with whom he came in contact.

The illustration is as follows:—When he arrived in Calcutta at the head of the Madras Fusiliers, he was ordered up with a detachment by railway. The train was to start at a certain hour; but, owing to some delay on the part of the authorities in procuring boats, a portion of the detachment seemed likely to be a few seconds behind time. Colonel Neill had already arrived. The station-master, addressing him, stated that he was behind time, and could not wait for his men, and that the train should go without them. As he rose to execute this threat, Colonel Neill ordered his men to seize and detain him till the rest of the detachment should arrive. When they came up, the station-master was let go, the men got into the carriages, and the train started. A military man who could thus brave the civil power, was not likely to shrink before mutineers. When, therefore, Brigadier Ponsonby detailed to Colonel Neill his plan for the following morning, and the grounds upon which it had been formed, the latter inquired the reason for delaying the measure even so long. "Why," said he, "give the 37th, who will hear, or have heard, of the Azimgurh mutiny, the opportunity of rising to-night?" He strongly urged that the measure should be carried out at once. Convinced by his arguments, the Brigadier yielded, then and there altered all his arrangements, and sent orders to the regiments to parade that same evening.

The lines of the 37th were in the centre of the parade, about midway between those occupied by the Sikhs and by the artillery. At the hour appointed, and before the 37th had come out in front of their lines, the artillery advanced from the left, the Sikhs and Irregular Cavalry from the right. As they came near, the Sepoys of the 37th were directed to place their muskets in the bells of arms appointed to receive them: some obeyed, but as the Europeans still continued to advance, they appeared to repent, for, rushing forward, they recovered their muskets, many of which were loaded, and commenced a brisk fire from the whole line on their officers and the advancing Europeans. Some of their officers, confident of their loyalty even then, went amongst them to smooth them down; but upon these also they fired, and even went at them with their bayonets.

The Sikhs and Irregular Cavalry were now approaching. The commanding officer of the former, Captain Guise, riding in front of them near the lines of the 37th, was shot dead. Captain Dodgson, the brigade major, seeing the catastrophe, rode up to them, and intimating that he had been sent by the Brigadier to take the command, called on them to follow him. They flashed their swords in reply, giving vent to a low equivocal murmur. At the same moment, one of them drew his pistol and fired at Captain Dodgson; the shot took effect in his sword arm, paralysing it for the moment. The sowar then rode up and was about to cut him down, when another interfered, and both were lost in the *mêlée*.

The sound of that pistol-shot had not yet been borne away on the winds, when the Sikhs, hitherto standing firm, brought up their muskets to the shoulder, and opened an indiscriminate fire on their own officers and the Europeans. Our guns, which, up to this time, had been blazing away at the 37th, then turned upon the Sikhs: these latter dashed forward to charge them, but were repulsed and broken. The Irregular Cavalry, most of whom had joined the mutineers, were also put to flight and dispersed. The 37th likewise fled in terror and confusion. Brigadier Ponsonby, in an early part of the day, had fallen, stricken apparently by the sun, on the ground, and the command had been assumed by Neill, who directed the arrangements which ensured the defeat and flight of the rebels.

Whilst this was going on on the parade ground, the civilians, with their wives and families, had, according to previous arrangement, assembled on the roof of the treasury, distant about two miles, and there abided the fortunes of the day. Just before the firing commenced, Soorut Singh, a Sikh *détenu*, had left Mr. Gubbins; but on the booming of the first gun, he returned to the place where he and the others were collected; and, taking a double-barrelled gun from the hands of that gentleman, announced his intention to share his fate. His arrival was most opportune. A quarter of an hour had not elapsed before it was announced to the Sikh guard stationed over the treasury, on the roof of which the civilians were standing, that our guns had been turned on their countrymen, who were being slaughtered in every direction. Already the Sikhs began to feel that they at least were capable of avenging their comrades, when Soorut Singh, going amongst them, pointed out to them that the attack must at all events have been unpremeditated, or the civilians would not have placed themselves and their families in their power. He stated his firm belief in the sincerity and good faith of the English, and announced his intention to stand by them. These arguments, proceeding from one of their own countrymen, himself a *détenu*, had the desired effect, and the men never afterwards attempted to swerve from their duty.

The presence of Messrs. Gubbins and Lind on the roof of the treasury that evening, undoubtedly saved the building from plunder. Had they not been there, the Sikh guard, hearing of the massacre of their comrades, would at once have made the best of their time, and have helped themselves, previous to making off. There would have been no one to prevent them. But the presence of Mr. Gubbins primarily, and of Soorut Singh secondarily, saved the station from that catastrophe — a catastrophe which might have been the prelude of a greater.

In the cantonment, meanwhile, the ladies and non-combatants, on the first sound of fire, had hurried into the mint, which had been prepared for their reception: here also congregated, after the mutiny had been crushed, the officers and civilians. Every bungalow was deserted; but it is a fact that speaks decisively as to the effective manner in which the *émeute* had been suppressed, that, though all the houses were deserted and every door left wide open, not a single robbery took place that evening.

The revolt of the Sepoys had, indeed, been effectually put down; but no sooner had it become known in the districts around that there had been an insurrection, than the whole country rose as one man: communication was cut off with the neighbouring military stations, and it appeared as if the ryots and zumindars were about to attempt the execution of the project in which the Sepoys had failed. All depended on the deportment of the city. It was at this epoch that the character and influence of Mr. Gubbins came fully into play. The memory of the fruitless revolt of 1852, and of the punishment meted out to the ringleaders, had its full effect. The powers with which, in their eyes, Mr. Gubbins was endued, were sufficient to discover and overturn any cabal; and what was really the effect of untiring zeal, undaunted energy, and clear-headedness unmatched, was attributed by them to the supernatural.

They saw, indeed, that Mr. Gubbins exposed himself as much or more than any one else. One shot would have brought him low; and on his death the insurrection of the city would have followed as a matter of course: but the shopkeepers and the *canaille* had fired at him in 1852; he had laughed at their miserable attempts; he had baffled, he had punished them. They feared the same result now.

So argued the commonalty. With the superior class his influence was of a higher order. There were two native noblemen in Benares at that time, both of them of great wealth and immense influence, and one of them possessing, in addition, strong sense and ability of no common order. This was the Rao Deo Narain Singh; the other was the Rajah of Benares. Everything that the former possessed he placed at the service of Government. After the mutiny he and the Sikh Sirdar Soorut Singh, actually lived in the same house with Mr. Gubbins. The former procured for us excellent spies, first-rate information, and placed all his resources, and they were great, whatever he possessed in the world in fact, at the service of our Government. Soorut Singh almost gave his life, at least he offered it; but, as will be subsequently shown, the rebels were content with paralysing a limb. As for the Rajah of Benares, he behaved throughout like a loyal subject. Although not so personally active as the Rao, he was equally liberal with his resources, which were even greater, and never, in our darkest hour, did he hang back from assisting us.

It has been stated that the entire district rose at the sound of the cannon at Lecrole. But in this emergency our countrymen were not wanting to themselves. A small number of the Irregular Cavalry, under the command of Lieutenant Palisser, had remained faithful; but they were suspected by every one. At this crisis Mr. Chapman, an indigo-planter, came forward and offered to accompany them anywhere; he even proposed to take a portion of them under his command, and surprise and attack the Azimgurh mutineers. But this proposal, after due consideration, was rejected by Colonel Neill, who had arrived at a very correct appreciation of native troops. But this gallant volunteer's services were not refused. He was endowed with the powers of a magistrate, and sent first with the Irregulars, and afterwards with detachments of Europeans, against the surrounding districts, and with marked success. Three gibbets were erected at Benares. Again the name of Mr. Gubbins became a proverb for swift stern justice. Neither rank nor caste protected any man; and by this means, and the success of the flying parties who were sent out, order was temporarily restored in the Benares division. Meanwhile Colonel Neill, having driven away the rebels, and in the short space of three days made every department as efficient as possible, set out for Allahabad, making over his command to Brevet-Lieutenant Colonel Gordon.

Before we follow him in his travels, or relate the cause of his prompt departure, we may refer to the occurrences at the little station of Juanpore.

Juanpore lies, as I have already stated, forty miles from Benares, in the direction of Oudh, and was at the time of the outbreak garrisoned by a detachment of the Loodhiana Regiment of Sikhs under Lieutenant Mara. The station had remained tolerably quiet up to the 5th June. But on the morning of that day some indigo-planters, who lived three miles from the station, galloped in with the information that the 37th mutineers had attacked their factory. All the residents at once assembled in the treasury, over which was a Sikh guard. The men of this guard shook hands with our countrymen, and swore to protect them. Soon, however, information reached them how their comrades had been shot down on the Benares parade ground. They forthwith mutinied, commencing by shooting their own officer, Lieutenant Mara, and progressing by pillaging the treasury. At this crisis Mr. Guppage, a young civilian, going outside in the direction of the jail, was shot dead by the Sikh sentry on duty. The other residents remained in the enclosure of the magistrate's cutcherry*, until the Sikhs had gone off, when, at the instigation of Mr. Fane, the magistrate, they gave up their arms, and started in the direction of Benares. Had they retained their arms, and pushed on like Englishmen, little opposition would have been offered. As it was, they were reduced to the most humiliating straits, being compelled to give up their watches and personal ornaments to natives, who but the day before had crouched before them. They were finally compelled to take refuge with one Hingun Lall, a native of some power and influence. In this pitiful state they remained, until, intelligence of their situation having reached the Benares authorities, a party was organised to go out and bring them in—a movement which was effected without loss.

But we must turn from this incident to notice the events which in the interim had occurred at Allahabad. The important station of Allahabad, its fort and arsenal, were in the month of May 1857 garrisoned entirely by natives,—the 6th regiment Native Infantry, a battery of Native Artillery, and five companies of the regiment of Ferozpore (Sikhs). The military value of Allahabad cannot be over estimated. Situated at the juncture of the rivers Ganges and Jumna it commands both, and the troops who possess it can therefore prevent all river navigation. It also commands the road. Indeed it is only approachable on the Benares side by a bridge of boats thrown across the Jumna,

---

* Office.

and this is completely within range of the guns of the fort. The Ganges separates it from Oudh; there are or were no defences on either bank, and that river also is spanned by a bridge of boats. The fort itself is stored with immense quantities of arms and ammunition: it is of great natural strength, resting absolutely on the Jumna on one side, and commanding on the other the entire station of Allahabad, the city, and the road to Cawnpore.

To have left so strong a position and such immense stores under the guardianship of natives, so soon after the acquisition of Oudh, its nearest neighbour, was an inexcusable fault. If we had lost Allahabad, we should have lost all power of communicating with the north-west, — the whole aspect of the campaign would have been changed; and our enemies at Cawnpore and Lucknow, after massacring our garrisons at those places, would probably have marched 50,000 in number to overwhelm our troops at Delhi. Lord Ellenborough, when Governor-General of India, was so impressed with the importance of Allahabad, that he would never allow less than three companies of Europeans to be stationed there. He built for them magnificent barracks inside the fort, and made every possible arrangement for their comfort. Sir Charles Napier also took care that European troops should always garrison the fort. But what were Lord Ellenborough and Sir Charles Napier to Lord Dalhousie, Lord Canning, and Colonel Birch? Why, it had been the practice of the two former not only to give orders direct to the parties concerned, but invariably to see them obeyed, — an unpardonable offence in the eyes of those illustrious red-tapists! Hence all they did was undone by their successors; and, amongst other "reforms," the Europeans were moved away from Allahabad.

In no scene of the drama was the action of Providence more conspicuous than in the events by which the Allahabad mutiny was characterised. The news from Delhi and Meerut arriving about the 14th May, had a visible effect on the 6th Regiment: they looked round and saw no one to interfere with their plans: they were, or might become, without even the semblance of a struggle, the masters of all they surveyed. They took duty over the treasury, in which there were 170,000l. in silver; they guarded, alternately with the Sikhs, the arsenal, the fort gates, the magazine; they had only to rise and say, "these are ours;" there were none or few to share it with them: the population of Allahabad are bigoted Mahomedans; their sympathies would ever be with those, of whatever religion, caste, or tribe, who would fight against the British. Why, then, did they not mutiny at once? A question to which but one reply can be given. They were Asiatics: they could not comprehend the advantages of time, circumstance, position, promptitude: they saw that they could seize these places and this treasure when they chose; therefore they did not seize them at once: they had, in fact, all the wickedness and all the irresolution of Macbeth. In their manner and tone they allowed, even at this time, something to appear which alarmed, not the authorities or their own officers, but the European residents at Allahabad. These latter wrote their fears to the Indian newspapers, and the press, then unfettered, inserted their letters. The consequence was that, having no other Europeans to spare, the Government ordered up a portion of the European invalids from Chunar: sixty-five of these arrived on the 23rd May, and were at once placed in the fort. To their presence, and the presence of the few Europeans who followed them, the subsequent safety of the fort may be attributed. About the same time a detachment of the 3rd Regiment Oudh Irregular Cavalry, under Captain Alexander, was brought over from Oudh. All this time the officers of the 6th had the most perfect confidence in their men. There was not a regiment in the service in which the Sepoys were so looked after, so cared for, as in this one.* The officers' feelings seemed to be entirely one with theirs. They encouraged them in their wrestling and in all their sports, and contributed largely towards their maintenance from their own private funds. They had battled on their behalf with the civil authorities, and had exposed themselves to contumely by the pertinacity with which they held out for the character of their men. They were proud of them: the regiment was truly their home: they would have gone anywhere with it, and, had the entire Bengal army risen before their eyes in revolt, they would still have placed implicit confidence in the 6th. Men like Mr. Mangles, who passed their career in India, in the luxurious ease of a civilian's life, may, if they chose, libel the officers, whose character and interest they are bound to protect; they may endeavour to make those officers the scape-goats for a rebellion, which their own lust of territory and mis-government have caused; but who that studies these events will believe them? We have seen how the officers of the 6th had behaved for years past toward their men; it has now to be related how they were requited.

On the 22nd May, Colonel Simpson, who commanded the 6th, wrote a letter to the newspapers, in which he denounced the statement that the 6th had evinced symptoms of discontent and insubordination as "false and malicious." This assertion was apparently borne out on the 1st June by the 6th volunteering *en masse* to march against Delhi, — a demonstration which had the effect of inducing the utmost confidence in their loyalty. About this time, too, they made over to public justice two spies, who had come into their lines for the purpose of tampering with their fidelity: this circumstance combined with their volunteering seemed to stamp them as proof against every temptation.

Yet throughout this period they were bent on mutiny: the man in the regiment most trusted by them was the very soul of the plot: but he and the others maintained to the last every appearance of respect and loyalty, and not one Sepoy out of the thousand who composed the regiment warned their officers of their impending fate.

On the 27th May the first detachment of Europeans sent up by Government from Calcutta arrived at Allahabad: they were not detained there, but were sent on at once to Cawnpore. Daily batches of them arrived, and were forwarded with all despatch. The danger appeared to have passed: the very sight of the Europeans would, it

---

* Personal experience.

was thought, scare the evil-disposed from their designs. Grave error! It had an effect the very opposite: the Sepoys of the 6th saw those men arrive, and they felt that the prize was slipping from their grasp: a few more Europeans, and their chance of the treasure would be *nil*. It was resolved to strike at once, and strike boldly. In order, however, completely to deceive their officers, they, on the 1st, as already stated, volunteered for Delhi.

On the 5th Colonel Simpson received a telegraphic message from the Governor-General requesting him to inform the regiment that the thanks of the Governor-General in Council were due to them, and would appear in the next Gazette. The officers were delighted at this manifestation, and were in raptures with their men for having, by volunteering, caused so great a distinction to be bestowed upon the corps.

All was quiet till the 5th June: on that day accounts of the mutiny at Benares reached the station, accompanied by reports that the mutineers were in full march upon Allahabad. On the same day a message was received from Sir Hugh Wheeler, commanding at Cawnpore, to "man the fort with every available European and make a good stand." Preparations were consequently made: all the ladies and non-combatants were advised to go into the fort. Many of the latter obeyed, and formed themselves into a volunteer company about a hundred strong; but a great number, confiding in the loyalty of the 6th, preferred remaining outside. Two guns and two companies of the 6th were ordered down to the bridge of boats which crosses the Jumna underneath the fort, in order to be ready to play upon the Benares insurgents: the guns of the fort were at the same time pointed on to the Benares road. Captain Alexander, with two squadrons of cavalry, was posted in the Alopee bagh, a large encamping ground under the lee of the fort, and commanding all the roads to the station: the main body of the 6th were not taken from their lines,—distant from the fort about three miles,—but were kept in readiness to move anywhere at the shortest notice.

The fort itself was garrisoned by sixty-five invalid artillery-men, four hundred Sikhs, and one company of the 6th. In addition to these were the civilians and other non-military men, who might have numbered about one hundred.

The removal of the ladies into the fort did not appear to satisfy the men of the 6th, who, it may be inferred, were bent even then on bloodshed; for they remonstrated with one of their officers for sending his wife into the fort, and begged him to allow her to return to cantonments, as they were one and all determined and able to defend her. The officer hesitated; but his better genius prevailed: he did not bring back his wife. Still he had no distrust of his men, and showed his feeling of confidence by himself remaining in the lines.

On the afternoon of that day (the 6th) Colonel Simpson ordered a parade of the regiment, in order to communicate the Governor-General's message. Great was the real enthusiasm of the officers, as great the apparent heartiness of the men. After the message had been announced, they cheered like Europeans; and when the order to fall out was given, the European shook hands with the native officers, and congratulated them on their all being of one mind on their regiment having thus come forward. Little did they dream at that moment that their death-warrant had been signed by the very men whom they were congratulating!

That night almost all the officers in the station dined at the 6th Mess, Colonel Simpson presiding. Every one was in the highest good humour; the officers, proud of their regiment, congratulating themselves and one another that, placed in the midst of mutineers, their regiment—a word comprehending home, honour, glory, reputation, to zealous officers—had remained loyal. The cloth was removed; it was half-past nine o'clock; already some were thinking of going home, when suddenly the alarm was sounded. Jumping to the not unnatural conclusion that the Benares insurgents were advancing, or that there was an inroad from Oudh, the officers started up, buckled on their swords, and, those that had them ready, mounting their horses, rode down to their lines to call out their men. They were still in the highest spirits, rejoicing in the prospect of an encounter and proving the loyalty of their men. As they rode on to the parade, they perceived one of their companies drawn up. They called out to them: the answer was a volley. Yes: those men they had mingled with, trusted, encouraged, shown every kindness to, thus deliberately murdered them! Most of the officers were shot dead. Colonel Simpson managed to escape to the fort. Captain Gordon was miraculously saved by some of his men. All the others upon whom they could lay hands were remorselessly butchered. Those even that had remained in the mess-house, for the most part boys lately arrived from England, were treacherously assaulted by the mess-guard, and, though defending themselves with desperation, were one and all murdered.

Rebellion was now in full swing. Houses were plundered and burnt, their inmates chopped to pieces, some roasted, almost all cruelly tortured, the children tossed on bayonets. Foremost in the commission of these atrocities were the pensioners,—a body of men retired from military service, entirely dependent on Government, and receiving from it half-yearly a handsome sum for their maintenance. These men, unable from their infirmities to fight, were not thereby precluded from inflicting tortures of the most diabolical nature: they even took the lead in those villanies, and encouraged the Sepoys and others to follow their example.* And yet these men still draw, they still receive, their pensions from the merciful Government of India!

To plunder the treasury, let loose the prisoners, raise the townspeople, to hunt after Europeans, to destroy all property useless to themselves, was the work of that night and the following day. Meanwhile, on the first sound of musketry, the two companies of the 6th and the native artillerymen who had been stationed on the bridge,

---

* I have these particulars from an undoubted source. My informant received them from the lips of an eye-witness.

turned against their officers. These latter, however, preferred trusting the waters of the Jumna to the tender mercies of the 6th; and finally, after a swim for it, succeeded in gaining the fort, quite naked: there they were at once taken in and cared for. Captain Alexander, of the cavalry, was not so fortunate. Warned, by the firing, of some impending catastrophe, he jumped on his horse and rode towards the lines, followed by several of his men: but the Sepoys were waiting for him in ambush, and as he passed they fired at him, at so close a distance that they blew out his heart. He was a fine, noble, dashing soldier, beloved by all.

In the fort, all this time, a scene was going on which almost baffles description. Our countrymen there too heard the "alarm" sounded: they rushed to the ramparts, in expectation of an enemy; then came the sound of a volley, then another, then steady file-firing, constant, without intermission. Never doubting the loyalty of the 6th, they believed that they were in action with some insurgents. This belief was confirmed as the firing grew fainter and fainter: they congratulated one another that the gallant 6th had been so successful in beating off the foe. But these pleasing impressions did not remain very long: the sight of the flaming cantonment first suggested a doubt, and immediately afterwards an officer who had escaped the massacre brought in the fatal tidings.

Their situation was a very precarious one: not 200 Europeans in the fort,—of these 65 invalids, a hundred non-military, the remainder officers, conductors, sergeants, &c., to meet 400 Sikhs and a company of the 6th, the latter now known to be hostile, the former, since the conduct of their brethren at Benares, scarcely to be trusted. It was necessary to act boldly, and, as the only chance of safety, to take the initiative. Fortunately there was a man on the spot, who comprehended all this at once, and acted accordingly. This was Captain Brazier, who commanded the Sikhs, an officer who had risen from the ranks, having been promoted for daring and cool courage displayed during the Sutlej campaign. He had been originally posted to the Sikh regiment as quarter-master, and had risen through the grades of adjutant and second in command to the post of commandant, which he still holds.

The first thing was to disarm the 6th, who had loaded their muskets. This was difficult on account of the temper of the Sikhs, amongst whom some little hesitation was visible. Thanks to the coolness of their commandant, who went amongst them and almost forcibly kept them firm in their loyalty, the operation was successfully accomplished. The muskets were then taken from the 6th, and the men of that corps were turned out of the fort. The Sikhs then quietly resumed their posts on the ramparts.

That night passed in painful anxiety. Nor was this feeling sensibly diminished the next day. The conduct of the Sikhs alone was sufficient to give cause for alarm. They were permitted to plunder in every direction; the stores of the European merchants and others, containing wines of every description, private packages from Calcutta, and provisions were sacked, wholesale — the commandant of the fortress, Colonel Simpson, looking on, and fearing by checking to exasperate them. But in another point this officer was even more culpable.

The greater portion of the 6th, after their successful mutiny, despairing of gaining the fort, and eager probably to secure their plunder, had made off, some for their houses, others for Oudh. There remained then at Allahabad only a few Sepoys, the inhabitants of the neighbouring villages, untrained to arms, and possessing only the two guns which had been abandoned on the bridge on the night of the mutiny. And yet Colonel Simpson allowed himself and the fort to be invested by this rabble; nay more, to such an extent did his amiability stretch, that on some few Sepoys being pointed out to him passing in and out of the village of Deragunj, the inhabitants of which also had rebelled, he refused to permit the guns of the fort to be turned upon them, for fear of destroying the innocent with the guilty.

Such a state of things could not last very long without producing most disastrous consequences. Fortunately it was not permitted to last. On the 11th June, Colonel Neill arrived, and from that moment affairs took a turn.

How he raised the investment, and dispersed the enemy, how he restored order out of chaos, and, infusing his own energy into all around him, equipped an army out of an exhausted country, will be recounted in another chapter. For the present we must unwillingly leave him to survey the effect which these events produced on the magnates of Calcutta.

CHAPTER IV.

CALCUTTA TO 30TH JUNE. — MASSACRES AT FUTTEHPORE, JHANSIE, NOWGONG, AND ROHNEE.

THE latter end of May and the beginning of June witnessed the arrival of strong reinforcements to our European garrison in India. In quick succession the Madras Fusiliers from Madras, the 64th Foot and 78th Highlanders from Persia, the 35th from Moulmein, a wing of the 37th, and a company of Royal Artillery from Ceylon, were poured into Calcutta. It would have been imagined that the Government, aware as they must have been at this time of the universal disaffection, would have been glad to display their troops, to notify to the mutinously disposed the arrival of such strong reinforcements, to show them that they had means at their disposal wherewith, if necessary, to strike home. But they acted on a contrary principle. The European troops were smuggled in like contraband goods; the Government even went out of the way to conceal their arrival. If, for instance, it were known that the "Auckland," or some other war steamer, was bringing troops, and the public were in consequence naturally on the tiptoe of excitement expecting her, orders would be transmitted by the Home Secretary, that on the arrival of the "Auckland," the telegraph should announce the "Sarah Sands," or a similar *nom-de-guerre*. The ship thus came up unnoticed, the troops generally landed in the dark, and were smuggled into the fort.* Had they landed with all the pomp and circumstance of war, in broad daylight, in martial array, with crowds of Englishmen looking on and cheering them, the insolent demeanour of the natives would have been checked, the Sepoys at Barrackpore have been cowed, the Government have been spared some very anxious moments, and Calcutta might possibly have escaped the imminent peril to which it was subsequently exposed.

But even the safety of an empire must give way to the importance of an individual. When clerks occupy the position of statesmen, they are specially impressed with the necessity of parading their power in the face of their former associates; they will do anything to attract notice, and in the dread of being despised, will often exert themselves unnecessarily to gain popular hatred.

It must be remembered, too, that in the beginning of June, the prospects of the Government were looking up. They believed that Delhi would fall in a very few days; they had called upon General Anson to send down his infantry and cavalry to Cawnpore, and to take Delhi with his artillery †; they were sending up infantry as fast as they arrived; all was *couleur de rose*.

But their dreams of restored tranquillity were destined to be somewhat rudely broken. Thick as hail, post by post, came tidings of disaster. The mutiny at Lucknow, followed by the defection of the whole of Oudh, the revolts at Azungurh, Benares, and Allahabad, already related, the fearful massacre of Jhansie, yet to be told, burst on their astonished ears. To counterbalance these, there was only the victory of Ghazee-ood-deen-Nuggur, gained by Brigadier Wilson over a portion of the rebel force on the 31st May. About this time, also, intelligence was received of the death of the Commander-in-Chief, on the 27th May. But little communication had passed between General Anson and the Government since the revolt at Delhi. He had gone to the Upper Provinces early in the year, with the assent of the Government and the Court of Directors, and when the Meerut disaster occurred he was in the hills. The tidings reached him on the 12th of May, and he at once made every preparation which man could make to meet the coming storm. His operations will be detailed in a future chapter. It is necessary to make a cursory allusion to him here, because a great outcry was made against him on account of the delay in reducing Delhi; on his shoulders was laid all the blame, and men connected with the Government were anxious to single him out as the scape-goat. The rash schemes proposed by the Government at this time have been commented upon in a previous page; had they been adopted, ruin must have overtaken us. The plan pro-

---

* My authority for this statement is as follows: 1st, Personal observation: 2nd, the telegraphic reports: 3rd, the notice of the circumstance by the local press.

† Blue Book.

posed and followed by General Anson up to his death, and subsequently adopted by his successor, was the only practicable one ; and yet, because it involved a little delay, the gallant General became the *bête noir* of vice-regal circles and of the Secretary's walk.*

The fact is, General Anson was no favourite in Council: his abilities were far superior to those of his colleagues, and in clearheadedness not one of them came near him. His ways too were not their ways. If there was one thing more than another against which he had set his face, it was the Calcutta-prevailing system of jobbing. He would have none of it: he would not touch the unclean thing.

It was a common practice to sneer at General Anson as a mere Horse-Guards' General, as one who had gained his honours at Newmarket. But it is nevertheless a fact, that this Horse-Guards' General, by dint of application and perseverance, made himself so thoroughly master of his profession, that when the mutiny broke out, he drew up a plan of operations, which his successor, a Crimean warrior, carried out in all its details, rejecting as crude and ridiculous the suggestions sent up by the collective wisdom of Calcutta. It cannot be denied that this man, who "gained his honours at Newmarket," when brought in both the Councils face to face with men who had made legislation for India the study of their lives, "distanced" them all: that, whatever the subject, he always mastered it, and showed in reasoning a strong good sense, which was more than a match for the special pleadings by which he was frequently met; whilst in facility of expression, and power of laying down an argument clearly and forcibly, not one of them came near him.

It is not to be wondered at that they disliked him. A Commander-in-Chief is always a bugbear to civilians, who, in India at least, have an innate jealousy of military men, of which very few can divest themselves. And when the Commander-in-Chief, in addition to his superior position, is a man who is beyond them in every other respect, they invariably manœuvre to get rid of him. They like an easy, impressionable man, who will be ready on all occasions to see with their eyes, and hear only what they tell him. The Napier school is their abhorrence.

When, therefore, the intelligence of General Anson's demise reached the members of Government, whatever they might have felt for the man, they certainly did not sorrow for the Commander-in-Chief. Lord Canning instantly telegraphed to Madras for Sir Patrick Grant; and he appointed General Barnard to succeed to the command of the Delhi force. Sir Henry Somerset became, by virtue of seniority, Commander-in-Chief in India. Sir Patrick Grant, who was now about to proceed to Calcutta, was an officer of the Bengal army. He had always been "lucky." He had, when a comparatively young officer, raised the Hurrianah Light Infantry, a local battalion which he commanded for many years, with the character of being unsurpassed

---

* A public pathway in Calcutta, in which secretaries of Government and their toadies meet every evening to discuss the gossip of the day.

as a commandant. A vacancy occurring in the department of the Adjutant-General, Grant was selected to fill it. Whilst in this position, he married a daughter of Lord Gough, and from that moment his rise was assured. He became Adjutant-General, served in that capacity under his father-in-law and Sir Charles Napier, and finally obtained the command of the Madras army, — the first officer of the Company's service to whom that honour had been vouchsafed.

Sir P. Grant was not altogether undeserving of his fortune. Without being a general, he was a fine soldier under fire, possessing great coolness and imperturbable presence of mind; his general capacity was good, though not great: he had a clear knowledge of the details of his profession, and an intimate acquaintance with the natives of India. On the other hand, he was ill-informed, had received an inferior education, was destitute of imagination, and had not been endowed with the slightest spark of genius. He was better fitted to carry out the details of a campaign than to plan one; he adopted favouritism rather than merit as his principle of dealing out the rewards in his gift; was at the same time a subtle courtier, and ever ready to give up his own opinion at the proper time, and with the best possible grace.

He was just suited for the officials of Government House, but, with a true instinct, the people of England divined that he was not the man to command the army which they were sending out to crush the mutiny.

Sir Patrick Grant was telegraphed for on the 3rd of June: he arrived on the 19th. In the interim events of great importance had occurred.

The disastrous tidings from Azimgurh, Benares, Allahabad, and Oudh—the rumours afloat respecting Jhansie, Cawnpore, Rohilcund, and Central India—made a deep impression on the Government. They appeared at last to have an idea of the magnitude of the crisis. But what could they do? They had, as it were, anticipated all their resources. Not three weeks had elapsed since they had refused the volunteering offers of the British and French merchants, with the rude and baseless insinuation that they were the result of "a passing and groundless panic." Had they accepted those offers in May, they would, in June, have had at their disposal a militia ready to take the place of the regiment of the Line, which might have been despatched to the scene of action. But again they were "too late." All their anticipations had failed them; and, to add to their troubles, they at this time received intelligence of the mutinous disposition of the troops at Barrackpore, and the certain proof of the connection of the King of Oudh with the revolt. Strong measures were, indeed, necessary. What could they do?

In the beginning of June, it had been brought to the notice of the Governor-General that the native newspapers were primed with incendiary articles, abetting and encouraging the insurrection. It was then strongly urged upon his lordship that the native press, being the organ of the enemy, it would be politic, convenient, and justifiable to suppress it. The reply of Lord Canning was, "The remedy is worse than the disease."

He was wrong. The native newspapers were the organs of the enemy; they disseminated treason throughout the country; they were read by all natives who could read; they advocated the cause of the King of Delhi. It was the bounden duty of Lord Canning to suppress them.

But Lord Canning was in the hands of his secretaries. The Indian Press, that is, the English portion of it, had been, as every press must be, the organ of the European society in India. Formerly, a portion of that press had advocated more especially the interests of the Civil Service. But as India became more closely connected with England, as the interests of both countries became more closely involved, the conductors of that portion of the newspaper press favourable to the Civil Service perceived, that in advocating the peculiar interests of that service, they were running counter to the interest both of England and India — that an exclusive service was, in fact, the bar, the most effectual bar, to all improvement in the latter country. Hence all the old established and respectable journals had dropped their cause, and none other of any character had risen to advocate it.

It may be imagined, then, that the hostility of the leading members of the Civil Service to the Indian Press was not light. That Press had already in fact commenced the exposure of their shortcomings in this insurrection: it had discriminated between Lord Canning and his advisers, knowing that the avowed opinions of the former at the outset of the mutiny were very different from those which he afterwards adopted—knowing also that he was dependent on the advisers whom he had inherited from Lord Dalhousie. The leaders of the Civil Service had, too, at this time, prepared an outline of the policy to be carried out at all risks, as the only policy which could save their service — the policy of ignoring, as much as possible, the magnitude of the insurrection; of treating it as a mere revolt of the Sepoys, caused by the incapacity of commanding officers; a policy of conciliating the natives, of pardoning the mutineers — even those red with the blood of our countrymen; and they dreaded nothing more than the exposure by the Press, not only of this line of action, but of their previous neglect of warnings, of their false security, of their design of implanting a native magistracy with power over all Europeans, of their discouragement of European settlers, of their betrayal of the great trust confided to them by treating India, not as a country to be improved, but solely as an appanage of their own exclusive service. When, therefore, the incendiary articles appeared in the native newspapers, openly advocating the cause of the King of Delhi, they jumped at the opportunity of making a crusade against the entire Press, of shutting the mouths of those who alone could expose their shortcomings, of triumphing over the great domestic enemy of their interests. It was necessary, in the first instance, to gain over Lord Canning to their views.

That nobleman, prompted by his English instincts, and true to the principles he had inherited from his great father, had only a fortnight before declared, with reference to any restriction even on the Native Press, that the "remedy was worse than the disease." But the leaders of the Civil Service knew Lord Canning.* The great man of their party, the Lieutenant-Governor of Bengal, had just arrived from his retreat at Darjeeling, to give his counsel in the crisis. He was the head of the family clique, whose policy is comprehended in the words "India for the Civil Service." He entered cordially into the views of his colleagues, and the thing was done. Mr. Halliday had an interview with Lord Canning; Mr. Beadon had an interview; Mr. Grant had an interview. The result was, that without consulting those whose English instincts would have made them invaluable counsellors in such a crisis, Lord Canning went down to the Legislative Council, suspended all standing orders, and in the course of forty minutes abolished the Freedom of the Press.

The Legislative Council is a council of nominees: it comprehends, besides the members of the Supreme Council, and the judges of the Supreme Court, four civilians—a member for Bengal, one for the North-west Provinces, one for Madras, and a fourth for Bombay. They are generally selected on account of their great interest, and because, from physical or mental incapacity, they are unfit for the heavier duties of a Judge's Court.

There were present when the Gagging Act was read three times in forty minutes, and passed, Lord Canning, Mr. Dorin, General Low, Mr. J. P. Grant, Mr. Peacock, to all of whom the reader has been introduced; the two Judges, Sir James Colville (a painstaking, industrious Judge, but, as regards the Vice-Regal Court, the most obsequious Chief-Justice that ever occupied a seat on the bench), Sir Arthur Buller (brother of the lamented Charles Buller, and himself possessing more abilities than were contained in all the Council besides, but indolent to a degree that made him one of the drones of life), Messrs. Currie and Le Geyt—the former a most amiable gentleman, but of no capacity whatever, the latter well known at Bombay under Lord Falkland's administration. Lord Canning, in introducing the measure, took the whole responsibility upon himself: he said it had been caused by the seditious tone of the Native Press; that it was not "specially levelled at the European Press, but that he had found it impossible to draw a line of demarcation between the two, and that therefore he must place the gag upon both." His Lordship's argument amounted to this: that because in a conquered country, the natives of which had risen in revolt against our rule, the Native Press had sided with them, therefore a law should be passed placing restrictions upon the European Press as well as on the native, notwithstanding the loyalty of the former, and the support it had given to Government. It was not a logical argument, but in a case in which his Lordship was arguing against the convictions of a life-time, the tool, though he knew it not, of a corrupt party, logic was scarcely to be expected.

The motion was seconded by Mr. Dorin, and carried without a

* I received these details from one of the rank and file of the party.

division. Sir James Colville went so far as to profess his readiness to take his share of the responsibility, and Mr. Grant moved an augmentation of some of the penalties that had been proposed.

The only man, in fact, in that Council from whom a generous opposition to this truly Austrian measure (as the *Examiner* well terms it), might have been expected, was the brother of Charles Buller. He possessed all the ability, all the readiness necessary for the purpose. A few sentences such as he was capable of pouring forth would have utterly discomfited his assailants: there was not a man amongst them (Lord Canning having already spoken) who possessed sufficient ability to reply to him. Had he done so, had he obeyed the whisperings of his heart, his name would have been enshrined for ever in the grateful recollection of his countrymen. He would have gone down to posterity as the one Englishman who in that Council of nominees had had the courage and the honesty to withstand tyranny to its face. He might have so acted without any personal risk, for, as a Puisne Judge of the Supreme Court, he was entirely independent of the Company.

But he was dumb, and spake not. He afterwards stated that he believed the assertion of the Governor-General, that the measure was not to be directed against the English Press.

Unopposed, therefore, it became law.

It has been said that strong measures were earnestly required. This was one of them. With the whole country up in arms, with station after station rising in revolt, the opportunity was chosen to insult the entire European community, to place them before the law on a level with the natives who had revolted, to show contempt for the rights and privileges which they had inherited from their ancestors, and to intimate to them, in a manner that could not be misunderstood, that they were living under a despotic Government. This treatment was the better appreciated by the inhabitants of Calcutta, as they had but just given the best proofs in their power of their earnest desire to assist the Government to strengthen its hands in the crisis.

It will be recollected that in May, the offers of the inhabitants of Calcutta to serve as volunteers had been contemptuously refused. In June the Government found that had those offers been then accepted, they would have been in a position to detach a reinforcement of at least one European Regiment to assist our countrymen at Cawnpore. Rendered wise by experience, they now desired the aid which they had before declined. But there was one difficulty; the Calcutta residents were not likely to proffer their services again, and the Government did not wish to place itself in the "humiliating position" of having to ask for them. In this emergency negotiations were opened between some of the officials of Government House and the leading merchants. The latter were assured that if they would offer their services again, the Government would accept them. This compromise was arranged, and on the 12th of June Lord Canning announced, that having received many offers from the inhabitants to enrol themselves, he had much pleasure in accepting them, and directed the formation of a corps of Cavalry and Infantry. Such was the origin of the Volunteer Guards of Calcutta,— a body of men comprehending the leading lawyers, merchants, and tradesmen of the place, who, foregoing their customary pleasures, gave themselves up ungrudgingly to all the fatigues of drill and discipline; who, through the long nights of the hot weather, and the inclement rainy season, took all the duties of a corps of the line; who, by their very formation, gave the first check to the insolent demeanour of the natives of Calcutta; who were instrumental in saving that city from the horrors of an insurrection; who, raised in June, were thoroughly organised in July, and who, when brigaded with crack Highland Regiments in November, were halted by Sir Robert Garrett, in order that he might compliment them upon the unsurpassed manner in which they went through their duties. It cannot be denied that but for the Calcutta Guards, Horse and Foot, this city, in the suburbs of which were 60,000 fanatical Mahomedans, ready and waiting the opportunity for a rise, would, in all probability, have been exposed to the most imminent peril.

On the 12th June, Lord Canning accepted their services; on the 13th he rewarded them by gagging the Press, of which they were the principal supporters.

It cannot be denied that the Gagging Act of the 13th June, 1857, was a very bold measure, but the Calcutta public had not many hours to wait before they had ocular demonstration that it was the work of very timid men.

On the evening of the same day an express arrived from Major-General (now Sir John) Hearsey, commanding at Barrackpore, to the effect that the native troops there contemplated rising that night, that he was about to send for the 78th Highlanders from Chinsura, and he proposed disarming them all, to prevent the outbreak which must otherwise ensue. The Government, terribly alarmed, at once authorised General Hearsey to carry out his views.

It has been said by a great writer, that "there is scarcely a less dignified entity than a patrician in a panic." The veriest sceptic as to the truth of this aphorism could have doubted no longer, had he witnessed the living panorama of Calcutta on the 14th June. All was panic, disorder, and dismay. The wildest reports were in circulation. It was all but universally credited that the Barrackpore brigade was in full march on Calcutta, that the people in the suburbs had already risen, that the King of Oudh, with his followers, were plundering Garden Reach. Those highest in office were the first to give the alarm. There were Secretaries to Government running over to Members of Council, loading their pistols, barricading the doors, sleeping on sofas; Members of Council abandoning their houses with their families, and taking refuge on board ship: crowds of lesser celebrities, impelled by these examples, having hastily collected their valuables, were rushing to the Fort, only too happy to be permitted to sleep under the Fort guns. Horses, carriages, palanquins, vehicles of every sort and kind, were put into requisition to convey panic-stricken fugitives out of the reach of imaginary cut-throats. In the suburbs, almost every house belonging to the Christian population was abandoned. Half-a-dozen determined fanatics could have burned down three parts of the town. A score of London thieves would have made their fortunes by plundering the houses in the neighbourhood of Chowringhee * which had been abandoned by their inmates.

It must in fairness be admitted, that whilst his advisers—the patricians of Leadenhall Street—were hiding under sofas, and secreting themselves in the holds of the vessels in port, Lord Canning himself maintained a dignified attitude: his palace remained guarded by armed Sepoys: he might have provoked the danger, but he did not flinch when it was at hand. Meanwhile General Hearsey, at Barrackpore, had quietly disarmed the Sepoys: they had been deterred, probably by the extra precautions which were taken, from rising in the night, and when morning came, and they saw the 78th Highlanders march into the station, they felt that the game was up. But there can be little doubt but that some of the bolder spirits amongst them had been anxious to hasten an *émeute* before the arrival of the 78th. But whatever their intentions, their hearts failed them when the hour for action arrived. It passed, and they saw themselves overmatched. The entire brigade, comprising the 2nd Grenadiers, 43rd Light Infantry, 70th Native Infantry, and a portion of the 34th, was disarmed successfully in the afternoon of the 14th. This result having been telegraphed up to Calcutta, the native troops on duty there were marched into the Fort, and were disarmed without resistance.

On the following morning, the King of Oudh and his Prime Minister, Ally Nucky Khan, were arrested. Every precaution had been taken to prevent resistance: a detachment of the 37th Foot and a company of Royal Artillery were posted in the vicinity of the house occupied by the ex-king, every outlet was secured, and every salient point commanded by our guns. Mr. Edmonstone, the Foreign Secretary, then went forward to the residence of the Prime Minister, and asked for him. "He is at his prayers," was the reply. Mr. Edmonstone signified his intention of waiting, and at the end of half an hour, Ally Nucky Khan appeared. He seemed a little startled at the sight of the soldiers, but quickly regained his composure, and when it was signified to him that his presence was required in the Fort, he simply acquiesced. His house was then searched, and himself and his papers were secured. The party then proceeded to the king's apartments: after some little delay they were admitted. Mr. Edmonstone almost immediately broached the subject of his visit. He plainly told the ex-king that the Governor-General had reason to believe that he had connected himself with the disaffected in the Bengal army, and that he wished to see him. Wajid Ally, taking off his jewelled turban and placing it before the Foreign Secretary, replied, "If I have by word, by deed, or in any way whatever encouraged the mutineers, I am worthy of any punishment that can be devised: I am ready to go wherever the Governor-General thinks fit." The public apartments, but not the zenana, were searched for

---

* The patrician quarter of Calcutta.

papers, but, as might have been anticipated, none of any importance were found. As the king was being carried off, a ludicrous incident happened. The inmates of the zenana had been spectators, behind a lattice, of the scene: as the king was departing, one of them, tall, dark, and ill-favoured, stepped into the room, and forbad his removal. "What will the king do without us?" was the burden of her song, accompanied by protestations of his innocence. They were of no avail; the king and his minister were both taken off and lodged in the Fort; the former in the Government House there, the latter in the Royal Barracks, both guarded by Europeans.

The demeanour of both prisoners since their incarceration has been strikingly characteristic of their respective characters. Whilst the King has relapsed into the state of idiotcy which is natural to him, Ally Nucky Khan has omitted no plan, has left no stone unturned, with the view of communicating with his friends outside. He has admitted, in the course of conversation, that he considered the insurrection as a just measure of retaliation for the seizure of Oudh; that we, leaving the high road of justice, had condescended to fight them with the weapons of trickery and expediency, and that we ought not to be surprised at their meeting our attacks with the weapons we had selected.

That he was the soul of the plot, that that plot was organised and arranged at Garden Reach, is beyond a doubt. The Government of India have, or had, in their possession, proofs sufficient to convict the King of Oudh and his minister of complicity in the plan of insurrection. Whether they will use them is another question. The lives of their enemies seem to have a far greater value in their eyes than the lives of those English troops who have been sent out to subdue them.

The King of Oudh was arrested on the 15th June: on the 17th Sir Patrick Grant arrived from Madras. He brought with him the account of General Barnard's first victory at Delhi — the victory of the 8th June. Great was the delight; it was even announced by vice-regal lips that evening that Delhi had fallen. Intense was the gratification of every one; the Gagging Act was for the moment forgotten, until it was discovered that instead of the city it was only the cantonment of Delhi of which we had obtained possession. Still Sir Patrick Grant had arrived; and at first many men believed in Sir Patrick. It was thought that he would give a tone to the proceedings of Government, that he would infuse a little energy into their counsels, and induce them to feel that the Sepoy Army, and not the European population, was the enemy most to be feared. Such were the feelings with which Sir Patrick Grant's arrival was greeted. He held the command for nearly two months. What he did during that interval has not been made public. Ensconced in his comfortable quarters in Government House he may have performed wonders — upon paper; but one thing is certain, that the public mind was sensibly relieved, when it was announced, in the month of August, that Sir Colin Campbell had arrived to relieve him. Simultaneously, in the same steamer in fact with Sir Patrick Grant, arrived General

Havelock, Adjutant-General of H.M. forces in India. This officer, on the breaking out of hostilities with Persia, had been sent to Bushire to assume the command of a division; he had commanded the troops at the attack of Mohumrah, and was preparing to give further proofs of his capacity for command, when the preliminaries of peace were signed. Havelock then returned to Bombay, and, unaware of the state of the country between Meerut and Calcutta, sailed for the latter place before even he had heard of General Anson's demise. Had the intelligence of that melancholy event reached him before leaving Bombay, he would not have come on to Calcutta, as his proper place as Adjutant-General of H.M. forces would have been with the temporary Commander-in-Chief, General Somerset.

Providentially he did not hear of it until he had too far progressed in his voyage to be able to return. General Havelock had seen perhaps more Indian service than any living man. He had served throughout the first Burmese war, of which he wrote a clear and graphic history. In 1838-9 he went into Affghanistan, and only left it in 1842 in company with the avenging armies of Pollock and Nott: he had in fact remained one of the illustrious garrison of Jellalabad, throughout our terrible disasters in that country. In the campaign of Gwalior, in 1843, and in the Sutlej campaigns of 1845-6, he took a distinguished part, having in one action had two horses, in another a third horse, shot under him. It was after this that he became first Quarter-Master-General, and subsequently Adjutant-General of H.M. forces in India. In his private life, and in manner, Havelock was the most quiet and retiring of men. He ate and drank little — sufficient only for the purposes of life, and devoted his whole time to his profession and to his God. Religion was not with him a mere outward sign; it was a part, and by far the most important part of his daily exercises. He had mourned over the idolatry-encouraging system of the Government of India, but he was powerless to prevent it. Nevertheless, he was one of those men who, in olden days, would have led the Crusaders to Ascalon, and whose deep enthusiasm would have inspired all around him with equal fervour in the cause.

Who indeed that saw that spare figure, below the middle height, that pale, thoughtful face, seldom showing any interest in the general conversation, but often lighted up by the latent fire within, would have thought him capable of mighty deeds? He would sit silent and meditative. He might be thinking of the yet possible destiny of India under a bold and God-fearing policy. The smile would gleam on his face, but as quickly die away, for what chance seemed there then of action for him? He was approaching the term of life, the end of his days, and all India lay before him calm and still, not a breath agitating her bosom, not even a ripple indicating the quarter from which a storm might be approaching. The faith of our rulers in Hinduism was never stronger.

Who that saw him then would have believed that that pale, thin, spare man, studiously avoiding all fare but the plainest, was the hero who would place his heel on the neck of this terrible rebellion?—was the man who, under a July, August, and September sun,— deadly to the strongest,—would march without tents against twenty times his number, would baffle all their attempts to overwhelm him ? Who would ever make a retreat the prelude of a further step in advance ; and finally, after three months' encounters with a persevering foe, would succeed in forcing his way, at the head of 2,500 British troops, through 50,000 fanatics, holding the largest and most defensible city in Asia, and be the first to bring relief to our countrymen?

And yet Havelock did all this.

This day, 27th November, intelligence has reached Calcutta that he is dead. Mourn not for him, my countrymen, for a nobler and a purer spirit never winged its way to its God. Mourn rather for India, that at such a crisis as this, a God-fearing soldier, a Christian warrior, as yet unsurpassed—in the present crisis unequalled by any —should have been removed from the head of her armies!

An officer of far inferior rank to General Havelock, Captain Stuart Beatson of the 1st Bengal Cavalry, came round to Calcutta about the same time. He was an officer of great promise, of very considerable talent, and of a very manly nature. He, too, on the outbreak of the war with Persia, had been sent to that country to raise a regiment of Arab Horse. But peace was concluded too soon for his ambition, and he returned to Bombay. Arriving there, he heard of this mutiny, and that his own regiment, the 1st Cavalry, had broken out into insurrection at Mhow. It had previously been his intention to proceed to England to recruit his failing health, but on hearing this intelligence, he came round to Calcutta, determined to place his services at the disposal of the Government, in the hope that he might be useful in some way. He had scarcely arrived before he was struck with the fact, that all or the greater part of our native cavalry having mutinied, we should experience the greatest difficulties from our deficiencies in that arm. Looking about him and making inquiries, it appeared to him, that it would be feasible to raise a corps of Eurasian Cavalry on the spot, provided the Government would sanction the arrangement. He accordingly drew up a scheme, the bases of which were, forty rupees per mensem nett pay to each trooper, the Government furnishing horse, arms, and accoutrements. But the eyes of the Government were not even yet opened to the necessities of the times. The scheme was of a novel character; Captain Beatson had no personal acquaintance with any of the Secretaries or Members of Council: his scheme was rejected, and he was himself informed that the Government had no need of his services.*

One month later, when Havelock was advancing towards Cawnpore, when the fiend Nana Sahib was escaping for want of cavalry to pursue him, when the prices of horses had risen enormously, the Government which had rejected Captain Beatson's plan of forty rupees per mensem, was compelled to raise a corps on the infinitely more expensive basis of 100 rupees per mensem for each trooper, with horse, arms, accoutrements, and camp equipage supplied by Government.

* My informant received this account from Captain Beatson himself.

But although Captain Beatson's offers were not appreciated by the members of Government, he received shortly after the offer of the highest appointment in his gift from one second to none in his capability of judging men — General Havelock.

Before, however, alluding to this officer's nomination to high command, it will be as well to give a brief detail of the events which had been occurring in different parts of the country, and accounts of which reached Calcutta about this time.

Of the places or districts which had been especially distinguished by deeds of atrocity, and intelligence of which reached Calcutta at the end of June, Central India and Rohilcund demand separate chapters; Futtehpore, Jhansie, Nowgong and Rohnee may be treated of here.

Futtehpore is a small civil station, distant about two-thirds of the road from Allahabad to Cawnpore. It is the centre of a Mahomedan district, and indeed furnishes many of the recruits for the Cavalry. The native troops there consisted of a detachment of fifty men from the 6th Regiment, stationed at Allahabad. Besides these were only the usual hangers-on of a civil station, consisting of burkundazes, chuprasses, deeroghas, moonsips, and others. The residents comprehended the judge, the magistrate and collector, the assistant-magistrate, the opium agent, salt agent, the doctor, and three or four gentlemen connected with the railway; in addition to these, amongst the officials, was the deputy-magistrate, a native and a Mahomedan.*

Although the district had been tolerably quiet during May, yet in anticipation of possible evil the residents had adopted the wise precaution of sending their wives and families to Allahabad. At the same time they made arrangements for all to assemble in the house occupied by the magistrate in case of need. On the 4th they received an account of the events of the 30th May at Lucknow, and an intimation from Cawnpore that the troopers of the 2nd Cavalry would certainly rise in insurrection that evening. On the following day (5th June) heavy firing was heard in the direction of Cawnpore, only forty miles distant; the residents accordingly adopted the precaution of all sleeping on the flat roof of their house, with their weapons by their sides, to guard against surprise. On the following day, expecting a party of the 2nd Cavalry and 56th Native Infantry in progress to Cawnpore, they deemed it advisable to make a permanent lodgment on the roof, conveying thither tents, water, provisions, ammunition, &c. On the 7th this detachment arrived, and shortly after, in confirmation of the worst fears of the residents, made an attempt on the treasury. The "loyalty," however, of the 6th repulsed them — this loyalty consisting in an earnest desire to appropriate the treasure to themselves, and to permit none to share it with them. The troopers shortly after went on towards Cawnpore.

Thus far they were delivered, but they were still in a hostile

---

* The name of this man was Hikmut-oolla Khan: on the arrival of Havelock's victorious force at Futtehpore six weeks subsequently, he went out to congratulate him, was recognised, and hanged.

country, and in a dangerous position. That same day they received intelligence of the Allahabad catastrophe ; they learned that the deputy-collector and all their subordinates had turned against them, and that some mutinous troopers, accompanied by some released prisoners, were in full march for the place. Still, unable to devise a feasible plan of escape, they determined on remaining; they barricaded the house, and waited the issue.

On the 9th the ruffians came on, and, burning every bungalow, threatened to attack them. But they showed a determined front, and the natives, with their instinctive dread of Europeans, feared to make the assault. During the day they heard that the 6th from Allahabad, and some mutineers from Cawnpore, were marching upon them. In the afternoon, the recreant deputy-collector, attended by a large body of armed men, made his way towards them, apparently on a friendly errand, but our countrymen, suspecting him, made the best of their way to the roof. That night, environed by dangers, they held a council of war, in which it was resolved to fly. Accordingly, at 10 P.M., they mounted their horses, and attended by four sowars who were faithful, all started for Banda, which, after many difficulties and hair-breadth escapes, they reached in safety.

All started—all save one—the judge, Robert Tucker of the Civil Service; he steadily and manfully refused to desert his post. He remained as usual in his own house. But the natives who had been deterred from attacking eleven armed Englishmen, felt themselves not unequal to the murder of one. They could not appreciate the sublime rashness which prompted Mr. Tucker to remain alone at Futtehpore; nay, so confident did they feel of "victory" over him, and so determined were they on his death, that, at the suggestion of the deputy-collector, who now openly avowed himself their leader, they resolved upon making him undergo the mockery of a trial, with all the forms of the Civil Court. Full of this idea they marched against him.

But Mr. Tucker, enthusiast as he was, was not the man to give away his life. The native Christian who witnessed the attack upon him asserts, that he killed sixteen men with his own hand before he was secured. Secured, however, he was at last. He was, in mockery, tried; of course condemned; and, as naturally, executed. His hands, head, and feet were cut off, and held up for the inspection of the rabble—the deputy-collector being present, and directing the proceedings.

It is a noticeable fact that, under the *régime* of the exclusive Civil Service, those men only have been chosen for the appointment of deputy-collector who, in the opinion of the civilians, were the *élite* of the natives of India. It is also to be observed that, in the month of February, 1857, a project of law had been read a second time in the Legislative Council, without opposition from any of the Civil members, by which it was proposed to place the persons and property of Europeans under the jurisdiction of natives of even a lower class than those who, like the Futtehpore assassin, filled the office of deputy-collector. Had the mutiny been unhappily postponed one year, our civilian legislators, labouring for their exclusive system, would have organised a system by which men devoid of honour, without conscience or self-respect, and gifted only with a smattering of education, would have been placed as arbiters over the lives and fortunes of our countrymen in India.

Can we wonder that the isolated mutiny of one regiment drifted into a wide-spread insurrection in the hands of puling theorists such as these?

We must turn for a moment to another horrible incident, the details of which made Calcutta mad for vengeance about this time,—the massacre of Jhansie.

The town of Jhansie, in Bundelcund, lies in the direct route from Agra to Saugor, about 140 miles south of the former. It is surrounded by a wall, and this again is overlooked by the fort, a lofty stone building, surmounted by a round tower. In the cantonments, which were outside and a little distance from the town, was a smaller fortified building, denominated the Star Fort, in which the guns and treasure were deposited.

The garrison of Jhansie was composed entirely of natives. There were a detail of Foot Artillery, the left wing of the 12th Regiment, the head quarters and right wing of the 14th Irregular Cavalry. Towards the end of May, apprehensions of an outbreak were entertained, as some of the agents of the dewan of the Ranee of the district were discovered plotting to seduce the Sepoys: but there was nothing in the demeanour of the latter to sanction the belief that they had been in any way successful. Still, as a precautionary measure, the authorities stored the Star Fort with provisions and ammunition.

To their dismay, on the afternoon of the 4th June, a company of the 12th Regiment marched into this fort, and announced their intention of holding it on their own account. The greater part of the residents then retired to the town fort; but the regimental officers went among their men, and, encouraged by their demeanour, which was quiet and respectful, ordered a parade for the following morning. The parade was held, and the native officers and men of infantry, cavalry, and artillery solemnly declared that it was their intention to stand by their officers to the last. That very afternoon they all rose in revolt. The Irregular Cavalry, scouring across the plain, came upon two officers of the 12th: these they shot dead with their carbines. They then made a rush at their own commanding officer, who, well mounted, was making for the fort; but though they managed to wound him, he reached the fort in safety, and our countrymen on the ramparts, opening fire on his pursuers, killed some five or six of them. There was only one officer now remaining outside, and he was on foot—Lieutenant Turnbull of the Artillery—a young man of great promise, and of a fine, generous disposition. Despairing of escape, and believing himself unseen, he climbed a large leafy tree, about midway between the fort and the cantonment. But a miserable townsman had seen him, and this wretch, in his fanatic zeal, or, perhaps, in a true spirit of Asiatic servility, could not rest till he had pointed him out to the sowars. He was at once shot down.

With loud shouts the mutineers then proceeded against the fort, and, on the second day, the Ranee sent her guns and elephants to assist them. But there was not only force without, there was treachery within. The Europeans numbered only fifty-five, including women and children: the natives who were with them were numerically superior. Two of these, brothers, were discovered in the act of opening one of the gates to the enemy. Lieutenant Powys, who saw them, instantly shot one dead, and was himself cut down by the brother. Captain Burgess avenged him in a second, and the assassins lay side by side in the ditch.

But provisions were failing them; two attempts to communicate with Nagode and Gwalior had been abortive; some Eurasians who had tried to escape over the parapet had been caught and killed; all appeared hopeless. At this crisis, the Ranee sent to say that, if they would surrender, their lives should be spared, and they should be sent safely to some other station. She swore, the troopers of the cavalry swore, the Sepoys swore, the native gunners swore, to adhere to these terms. Seizing this as the only chance of life, unable indeed to hold out for twenty-four hours longer, the garrison surrendered.

They came out two and two; as they advanced through the line of cavalry and infantry they saw none but hostile faces, but there was no movement against them. At last, every Christian had quitted the fort: then was commenced a deed of ruthless treachery, unsurpassed even by the Nana Sahib. The gates were shut behind them; they were seized, the men and women separated, and tied together in two rows, facing one another; the children standing by their mothers. The men were then decapitated; the children were seized, and cut in halves before their mothers' eyes; and last of all, the ladies found what, under those circumstances, they must have felt to be a happy release in death.

The natives, upon whose authority it is alone possible to give any details of this terrible massacre, assert that the lives of the quartermaster sergeant and his wife were spared: nothing has since been heard of them; but it has been ascertained that his name was John Newton, that his wife was a country-born woman, or Eurasian, and that they had four daughters, all of whom were with them in Jhansie when the troops mutinied.

Such was the massacre at Jhansie, a deed unsurpassed in fiendish cruelty by any in the world. In reflecting upon it, we are struck with the impolicy of allowing native troops to be thus congregated in close vicinity to a native power beyond the influence of a European force; with the folly, in any case or under any circumstances, of trusting to the oaths of natives; with the preferable alternative of perishing of starvation or of running all the chances of war, to trusting to the tender mercies of the natives of India.

It may be as well, for the sake of connection, to follow the movements of the other wings of the same regiments in Nowgong, the sister station to Jhansie, in Bundelkund. At Nowgong were quartered a company of Artillery, the head quarters and right wing 12th Regiment Native Infantry, and the left wing 14th Irregular Cavalry, the whole under the command of Major Kirke of the 12th. On the 5th of June, the wing of 12th Regiment volunteered to march against the Delhi mutineers: the men of that wing and the native gunners professed the most enthusiastic loyalty, whilst the sowars* of the 14th stood aloof, and acted as if they believed it was impossible to doubt them. On the 8th, the account of the terrible events of that morning at Jhansie reached them: on the following day the Artillery volunteered to go against Delhi. But something in the deportment of the men having excited suspicion, four of their number, notoriously disaffected, were seized, and, it being dangerous in the temper of the men to try them by court-martial, were sent off to the Fort of Chutterpore. This bold demonstration had a wonderful effect for the moment, and that day and the next morning all appeared quiet. But on the evening of the 10th, as the guards were being relieved, three Sepoys of the 12th, all of them Sikhs, and one a large and very powerful man, stepped forward with loaded muskets, went up to the havildar-major, and shot him dead. They then made a dash at the guns: these the Artillery sergeant made an effort to defend; but, deserted by his own men, he was compelled to fly, and, though fired at, he succeeded in getting off. Almost immediately, a discharge of musketry was heard from the lines — a sure sign that the revolt was universal.

But the officers did not flinch from their duty. Careless of the consequences to themselves, they rushed to the parade, and endeavoured by every argument in their power to induce the men not to swerve from their allegiance. But their efforts were not very successful: about a hundred rallied round them, out of five times that number, and accompanied them to the appointed rendezvous at the mess-house.

Here also all the residents were assembled. It being evident that the efforts of the mutineers would not stop at this point, Major Kirke endeavoured to persuade the hundred "staunch" Sepoys to go out and attack the enemy before their preparations were completed. But not a man would stir. At this moment, before any definite plan of action had been settled, the mutineers brought up the guns to bear upon the mess-house: intelligence also reached them that the sowars were going from house to house thirsting for their blood. Unless they were prepared to undergo the fate of their friends at Jhansie, there was left them but the resource of flight. On flight then they determined; and mounting horses, buggies, and a carriage drawn by three camels, and accompanied by about eighty Sepoys, they started.

It does not belong to this history to follow them in their flight. It will suffice to say, that after suffering incredible hardships, after enduring in fifteen days privations more than sufficient to be allotted to an ordinary existence, a few of them arrived in safety at Banda: of the rest many were killed by the natives, others struck down by the sun. Those that were saved bore up with the most unflinching fortitude, with the most unselfish heroism,— the men guarding the women with the utmost solicitude,— caring not for the ladies only,

---

* Troopers.

but for the sergeant's wife, evincing in the trying circumstances under which they were placed a firm reliance on a Higher Power.* They did not abandon one another, neither did He desert them.

It is necessary that one more tragical event should be recorded — the murderous assault at Rohnee. Rohnee is a new station in the Sonthal district, distant about 300 miles from Calcutta. It was the head-quarters of the 5th Irregular Cavalry: there were present of that regiment Major Macdonald, commanding; Sir Norman Leslie, the Adjutant; and Dr. Grant. On the 8th June these three officers were seated outside the bungalow of the first-named, engaged in friendly conversation. During a pause, Dr. Grant rose, with the intention of entering the bungalow. In the very act of rising he noticed the stealthy approach of three men, apparently strangers. As he turned to point them out to his companions, the intruders, drawing their swords, rushed upon them. Our party were without weapons of any sort, and had not time to fly. Sir Norman Leslie indeed turned to enter the house in search of his sword, but his foot slipping at the threshold, he was cut down at once. The other two seized the chairs on which they had been sitting, and with them endeavoured to ward off the blows aimed at them. Both, however, were wounded, Major Macdonald receiving three severe cuts on the head; and the affair would probably have terminated unfavourably for both of them, when unaccountably their assailants lost heart and fled. It was not known who they were; there was a guard close to the house, but the troopers composing it declared that they had neither seen nor heard anything of the intruders.

The news of this dastardly attack was quickly conveyed to the lines; all the men were instantly collected, and their swords drawn for inspection: all, however, were found clean: not a speck of blood was apparent on any of them. All was mystery: no suspicion attached to the men of the regiment, who had up to that time behaved well; and from the fact of the murderers having worn dhotees †, they were believed to be disbanded Sepoys, many of whom had been seen in the neighbourhood.

Such were the first impressions, but time brings to light every evil deed. It was ascertained, by the confession of a comrade, that these men belonged to Major Macdonald's own corps. They were at once seized, brought to a drum-head court-martial, and sentenced to be hanged. Now came the trying moment, it was impossible to say whether these men had or had not any accomplices in the regiment; whether the entire corps was not infected. They might refuse to allow the sentence of death to be carried out; they might turn against their officers, only two in number, one of them deprived of his scalp. These contingencies appeared not only possible but probable: more unlikely events had happened before, and have occurred since. In this emergency Major Macdonald showed the undaunted

---

* Mrs. Mawe's narrative, sent by Lady Canning to the Queen. Captain Scott's letter, published in the *Times*.

† A cloth wrapped round the loins.

pluck of a Briton. Let him tell his own story; it is worth recording: " One of the prisoners was of very high caste and influence, and this man I determined to treat with the greatest ignominy by getting a low caste man to hang him. To tell the truth, I never for a moment expected to leave the hanging scene alive; but I determined to do my duty, and well knew the effect that pluck and decision had on the natives. The regiment was drawn out; wounded cruelly as I was, I had to see everything done myself, even to the adjusting of the ropes, and saw them looped to run easy. Two of the culprits were paralysed with fear and astonishment, never dreaming that I should dare to hang them without an order from Government. The third said he would not be hanged, and called on the Prophet and on his comrades to rescue him. This was an awful moment; an instant's hesitation on my part, and probably I should have had a dozen balls through me; so I seized a pistol, clapped it to the man's ear, and said, with a look there was no mistake about, ' Another word out of your mouth and your brains shall be scattered on the ground.' He trembled and held his tongue. The elephant came up, he was put on his back, the rope adjusted, the elephant moved, and he was left dangling. I then had the others up and off in the same way. And after some time, when I dismissed the men of the regiment to their lines, and still found my head on my shoulders, I really could scarcely believe it."

In another letter, in reply to a brother officer who advised him to go away on account of his wounds, he replied : " Certainly not : leave any strange officer with the men ! I'd rather stay and die first."

Such is the stuff of which British officers are composed! Who can wonder that, in spite of divided counsels, or orders and counter-orders, of procrastination unheard of before, of the weakest, the most selfish, and most incapable Government that ever ruled in any crisis, the mutiny should have been put down? Had Captain Macdonald gone away for the cure of his wounds, had he flinched on the day of, execution, had he feared to take upon himself the responsibility of ordering that execution, the 5th Irregulars would then and there have risen in revolt. Subsequent events have proved, that there was at that time an organised conspiracy in the regiment; that many knew of the plot to assassinate their three officers; that they waited its fulfilment to rise *en masse.*

They were cowed first by the ill-success of the plot, secondly by the determined spirit and truly English pluck displayed by Major Macdonald. At the execution, everything depended upon his spirit. Another call from the condemned trooper to his comrades to save him, and Major Macdonald's life would not have been worth five minutes' purchase. The regiment would have risen; and in the middle of June an insurrection in that part of the country would have endangered Calcutta, Patna, and the whole of Bengal.

And yet although Major Macdonald's firmness undoubtedly saved us at that time from a great calamity, we fail to trace in the papers published by authority any signification to him of the approval of the Supreme Government. There are glorifications *in extenso* of civilians, an occasional notice of military men, but in praise of Major Macdonald, the Government of Lord Canning is silent.* Does any one inquire the reason? Major Macdonald was a nominee of the late Sir Charles Napier. For a deed of unflinching daring and ready presence of mind in shutting the gates of the fortress of Umritsur against the whole body of the mutinous 66th in 1849-50, Sir Charles Napier gave him the command of the 5th Irregulars. To the army at large the bestowal of an appointment by that great man was a proof that it had been deserved; from the clique that ruled at Calcutta, it insured coldness, neglect, often insolence. The account of these massacres arriving towards the end of June simultaneously with rumours of butcheries at Hansi and Hipar, with telegraphic messages from Sir Henry Lawrence, intimating that he was closely besieged and could afford no help to Sir Hugh Wheeler, who was worse off than himself, at length aroused Government from its lethargy. It was resolved to assemble a considerable force at Allahabad, and to make an onward movement towards Cawnpore. General Havelock was selected to command it. He appointed Captain Stuart Beatson, before referred to, as his Adjutant-General; and, accompanied by him, on the centenary of Plassey, left Calcutta to assume his command.

That day too was another panic day in Calcutta. The "patricians" had imbibed the idea that there was to be an universal rising. The scene of the 14th was therefore repeated, although on a scale not quite so large; that is to say, the wives and daughters were sent on board ship, but there was less personal apprehension. In the interval ridicule had done her work, and fears, if entertained at all, were less loudly expressed. There is little pleasure in dwelling upon such a topic; it has been introduced to show that the men who advised and passed the Gagging Act were bolder in the Council Chamber than they cared to be on other occasions, and to demonstrate the truth of the axiom, that there can be no more dangerous legislators than those who in every respect of life must be regarded as little men.

From the contemplation of their characters, let us turn to a far nobler and more inspiring theme; let us survey the actions of those who restored victory to our standards, and dwell, while we may, on the unsurpassed achievements of real men — men inspired by an earnestness of purpose, by a depth of zeal, by a determination to avenge the murder of our countrywomen, which those who guided our counsels in Calcutta could neither understand nor appreciate.

* There is an expression of approval from the Commander-in-Chief, but it is not endorsed by the Governor-General.

CHAPTER V.

ALLAHABAD TO 4TH JULY.

COLONEL NEILL left Benares on the night of the 9th of June, and proceeded by post, in company with forty-three men of his own regiment, to Allahabad, to the command of which post, in supersession of Colonel Simpson, he had been appointed. The road between the two stations was deserted; the post-horses had been carried off; the country round about was infested with plunderers; and it was with the utmost difficulty and by intense labour, that a journey ordinarily occupying from eight to ten hours was performed by our troops in twenty-four. However, on the afternoon of the 11th, the Colonel and his party found themselves at Jhoosie, a village on the high bank overlooking the junction of the Jumna and the Ganges, and the point where the road from Benares merges into the bridge of boats across the former river. This bridge, however, was partly destroyed and in the hands of the enemy: the village, or rather the suburb of Deragunj, which commands it, was also in their possession: not a boat was visible on the right bank: the men were prostrated by fatigue. But Colonel Neill was not the man to be overcome by any difficulties. Descending the Ganges below the junction, he obtained possession of a solitary boat, having bribed a native to bring it over from the right bank: in this he embarked a portion of his men, intending to wait for its return to cross over with the remainder; but at this juncture he was seen by the guards in the fort, and boats were sent over for the whole detachment: by their means they all arrived safely in the fort, though completely exhausted by the long journey and the intense heat.

His first act on arriving was to assume command. It was indeed time. He found the fort invested; the Sikhs, coaxed into the appearance only of subordination; confusion and disorder in every direction; — an unchecked enemy without, vacillation within.

He did not lose an hour. Notwithstanding his fatigue and consequent exhaustion, he did not sleep until he had arranged his plans for the early morrow. Day had scarcely dawned when the guns of the fort opened on the suburb of Deragunj, the head-quarters of the most bigoted Brahmins. After eighteen or twenty rounds had been fired, three companies of Sikhs, sixty Madras Fusiliers, and forty Irregular Cavalry, — the sole loyal remnant of the Oudh corps, — advanced from the fort, attacked the suburb, drove the enemy out, bayoneting all that came within their reach, burnt a great part of the village, and secured the bridge of boats. This he instantly caused to be repaired, and, placing at its head a company of Sikhs, re-opened the communications with the Benares road.

The movement was opportune. The very next morning, 13th, Major Stephenson, at the head of a hundred Fusiliers, arrived at

Jhoosie: instead of being compelled to hunt for boats, and to expose himself and his men to the deadly fury of a June sun, he was able, thanks to Colonel Neill's vigour and forethought, to cross by the bridge of boats.

On the same day an attack was made on the village of Kydgunj, situated midway between the fort and the city. The attacking party consisted of the Sikhs, the remnant of the Irregular Cavalry, and a small party of European Volunteer Cavalry, composed of railway engineers and others, whom Colonel Neill, even in this short space of time, had succeeded in organising. The Sikhs went in advance, the cavalry on their flanks. The enemy attempted a mere nominal resistance, and were driven out with loss. Our troops then returned to the fort.

All this time, since the hour of Colonel Neill's arrival in fact, a very sharp cannonade had been kept up day and night on the city. The enemy, headed by a fanatic Moulvie or priest, had taken up their head-quarters at the gardens of Sultan Khoosroo at the other extremity of the city, about three miles distant from the fort. They had few regular troops with them, but the whole country had risen, and arms were plentiful. They had also possession of the two guns which we had lost on the bridge on the night of the 6th: they also occupied the cantonment and the villages in its vicinity.

It was incumbent to drive them out of these positions. Colonel Neill having obtained an accurate plan of the station, and received reports from the residents of the bearings of the several villages, came to the conclusion that by marching from the fort directly on to the jail,— about three miles, and situated midway between the gardens of Sultan Khoosroo and the cantonments, — the enemy's position would be cut in two, and he could destroy them at a blow.

He was not, however, yet strong enough to attempt it: he had no carriage for his guns, and the Sikhs were daily becoming more troublesome and more unmanageable. It was necessary, in the first instance, to deal with these men.

It has been already related how, after the events of the 6th of June, Colonel Simpson permitted the most disgraceful pillage on the part of the Sikhs. The go-downs of the European merchants, of the agents of the steam companies, and of others, were plundered of all their contents: the Sikhs were actually allowed to bring the property they had thus obtained into the fort, and to guard it as their own. There was, indeed, much more than sufficient for their own consumption, — and they are a money-loving race; consequently, upon the arrival of the Europeans, they opened a store on their own account, and sold the liquor,— comprehending everything from brandy to champagne,— at four anas (sixpence) a bottle. The result was, that facilities to drunkenness were afforded to Europeans; and experience has shown that that is a temptation that they are seldom able to resist.

Colonel Neill's object, then, was to deprive the Sikhs of this liquor, and to locate them outside the fort, away from our magazine; for he did not quite trust them. But it was quite evident that they would not give up their plunder; and it was doubtful whether they would leave the fort without a struggle. Under these circumstances,

Colonel Neill's conduct was singularly judicious. He wished to avoid embroiling himself with these men: he was anxious, indeed, that their sympathies should remain with us; but he was as resolved to maintain discipline. He accomplished his purpose in this way:—he ordered the Commissariat to purchase from the Sikhs all the liquor in their possession: he then paraded the regiment, and, by dint of a little management, in which he was ably abetted by Major Brasyer, the Commandant, he succeeded in marching them out and in locating them outside the fort and under its guns, in some old storehouses on the banks of the Jumna. The Sikhs had scarcely reached their new position before they were attacked by the enemy, and were, at first, compelled to retire; but they soon regained their lost ground, and never after receded from it.

Secure in this important particular, Neill again turned to the enemy. Unable yet, from the causes before stated, to execute his plan of cutting them in two, he resolved to clear the suburbs, which had been re-occupied in the night. Accordingly, early on the 15th, he commenced pounding Kydgunj with round-shot; he sent a steamer up the Jumna with twenty picked men and a howitzer-gun; at the same time the Sikhs, supported by fifty Fusiliers and the cavalry, were directed to scour Kydgunj and penetrate beyond it.

The plan succeeded admirably. The villages on the banks of the Jumna suffered very severely from the firing of the party on board the steamer, to which they were unable to reply with any effect. The land-party were opposed, the Europeans especially, very obstinately; nevertheless, the rebels were so completely beaten, were followed up with such vigour, and lost so many men, that the chiefs of the insurrection were completely panic-stricken, and that very night the Moolvie himself, with three thousand of his followers, evacuated his quarters in the gardens of Sultan Khoosroo, and fled with precipitation across the Ganges into Oudh.

This result was not known to Neill till the next morning. He had proposed sending a steamer up the Ganges, with the view of procuring bullocks for his guns. The steamer, indeed, had already started, when the news of the evacuation of the city reached him: his wants, in the way of bullocks, were at once supplied. It was fortunate; as the small depth of water in the Ganges effectually prevented the progress of the steamer.

On the 18th, his force having been augmented by successive reinforcements to 360 Europeans, he resolved to move out, and sweep the enemy altogether away.

On that morning, therefore, while a steamer containing eighty Fusiliers and a hundred Sikhs steamed up the river to attack the villages of Durgabad, Sydabad, and Russoolpore, on its banks, Neill, with the remainder of the Sikhs, 200 Fusiliers, and the cavalry, marched on the jail. Interposed thus between the city and the insurgent villages, he turned on the latter and destroyed them,—the enemy making no opposition. Finding the work of destruction so easy, he did not proceed with the European portion of his force beyond the parade of the 6th, leaving the Sikhs and the cavalry to complete what he had so well begun. It was his intention to have permanently occupied the cantonments; but cholera had broken out among his men. He therefore deemed it advisable to return with the Europeans to the fort, leaving the church to be occupied by the detachment of the 84th, then daily expected.

That morning another party of one hundred and fifty Fusiliers, under Captain Fraser, reached Allahabad. This officer had been detached, in company with eighty sowars, under Lieut. Palliser and Mr. Chapman, an indigo planter, but to whom the necessities of the times had given the appointment of magistrate, to clear the country between Benares and Allahabad. Right well had the task been performed. Not long before, Mr. Moore, the Magistrate of Mirzapore, had been murdered, in company with two friends, whilst bathing at Gopeegunj, midway between the two stations on the Grand Trunk Road. Terribly was their death avenged: everywhere our authority was re-asserted. One man in the neighbourhood of Sydabad, who had set himself up as Raja, having been caught and condemned to death, threatened to appeal to the Sudder.* In twenty minutes he was dangling from a tree! Large quantities of plunder and treasure, to the extent of twelve thousand rupees, were recovered by this party; and not only this, but communication with Benares was rendered facile and safe. From this day (the 18th) all opposition from the villages in the Allahabad district having ceased, the town having been coerced by a very heavy contribution — the native merchants having evinced the strongest feelings against us throughout — and the constant arrival of troops having been regulated, Colonel Neill turned his attention to procuring carriage and stores for an onward movement. Indefatigable himself, he infused his own energy into all around him, and he received the most willing and effectual assistance from Messrs. Chester and Court, the Commissioner and Magistrate of the district, whose local knowledge and experience were invaluable. In a very few days affairs began to assume an improved aspect. The cantonment was occupied, carts and camels were brought in, and the natives, ready to run from one extreme to another, from crowing over our downfall became as cringing and as suppliant as before. On the 24th everything was getting on famously; Captain Russell at the Ordnance, Captain Davidson in the Commissariat, and Captain Brown of the Artillery, and others, working well, and with effect. Neill superintending all, and encouraging them in their up-hill work. Throughout this period, the gallows were well at work. Daily some three or four scoundrels were brought in, who, on being convicted of being concerned in the massacre of our countrymen and women, were strung up without hesitation. Extraordinary was the effect of this promptitude. The natives, accustomed to our civil courts, to the long delays, the appeals, and all the trickery of native subordinates, could not comprehend this sharp and severe justice — this necessary retaliation on them for their misdeeds.

* The highest court of appeal in India, presided over by civilians. Its natural action is to render the prompt execution of justice impossible.

It was on this day, 24th June, that Neill, having surmounted all the difficulties in his path, having organized a force, ready to start in a few days for Cawnpore, learned that another was to reap the fruit of his labours — that he was superseded.

It is true that he was superseded by Havelock: but to replace him at all was an injustice to him. He was the first man who had turned the tide of the mutiny; his arrival at Benares had converted what might have been a massacre into a victory; his presence at Allahabad had produced order out of chaos; he had proved himself a real man; he had gained the confidence of the troops under his command; he had organised all the arrangements for the advance. It was unfair to deprive him of the opportunity of reaping the fruit. It is true, I repeat, that he was superseded by a good man; but it is a fact, that it was not because he was a good man that Havelock was appointed. They gave him the command because he wanted active employment. To prove that it was a mere hap-hazard selection, it is only necessary to point to the supersession of Havelock himself, after he had reached Cawnpore, by Sir James Outram.

Nevertheless, disappointed as he doubtless felt, as he must have felt, the true-hearted Neill never relaxed a single energy. He was now working for another; but he worked with as much heart and vigour as before: the preparations for the march of the column progressed every day, and on the afternoon of the 30th June, a force, consisting of 300 Sikhs, 400 Europeans, and 120 native horse, under the command of Major Renaud, a gallant and most intelligent officer, started for Cawnpore. The same day, General Havelock arrived and assumed command of the station.

It had not been merely on the organisation of this advanced body under Renaud that the attention of Neill had been fixed. He had made arrangements also to follow them up, at the expiration of two or three days, by a much larger force. When, therefore, Havelock assumed command, it was with the determination to follow out this plan, to leave with the main body on the 4th, if possible, and to detach a steamer up the Ganges with provisions and stores for Cawnpore. This latter arrangement was very speedily carried out, and, on the morning of the 3rd, a vessel having on board 100 Fusiliers and two guns steamed from Allahabad.

But before she started, terrible rumours had reached Havelock as to the fate of the Cawnpore garrison. On the 2nd, a message came from Sir Henry Lawrence informing him that they had one and all been massacred. Neill disbelieved it. Havelock doubted. To provide against accidents, the two guns were placed on board the steamer. On the following day the intelligence was confirmed; time, place, dates, all were given. Havelock no longer hesitated. He sent up orders to Renaud to halt till he could join him himself, and he delayed his own departure until he could make arrangements for the transport of his guns.

It was not till the morning of the 7th that all his preparations were complete. On that evening, at 4 o'clock, he gave orders to his column to march, and bent his steps resolutely towards Cawnpore.

But before we follow him in his heroic achievements, it will be necessary to record the actual occurrences at that ill-fated station.

CHAPTER VI.

CAWNPORE.

The news of the outbreak at Meerut reached Cawnpore on the 13th May. The force at that station consisted at that time almost entirely of natives. So unsuspicious were our rulers of intrigue on the part of the late sovereign of Oudh, so confident in their policy of annexation, so sure of the loyalty even of those whom their recent measures had reduced from wealth to poverty, from a state of seigneur-ship to a condition of vassalage, that although Oudh had been occupied by our troops so recently as 1856, they did not deem it expedient in 1857 to add a single European soldier to the sixty artillerymen who were the representatives of our army at Cawnpore. They even went further: at the end of 1856, they ordered the wing of the 1st Bengal Fusiliers, which had been temporarily detained at Cawnpore at the request of the Chief Commissioner of Oudh, to proceed to Umballa!

The departure of the wing of the Fusiliers left Cawnpore garrisoned as follows. There were the 1st, 53rd, and 56th Regiments of Native Infantry: the 2nd Regiment Light Cavalry, and sixty one European artillerymen with six guns — five of which were nine-pounders, and the sixth, a twenty-four pound howitzer. In case of a revolt of the native troops, there were therefore at the disposal of the General only sixty-one Europeans, besides the officers, to oppose to, in round numbers, three thousand five hundred trained soldiers, backed by a rabble of at least equal numerical strength.

It can easily be imagined that the intelligence of the events at Meerut, following, as they did, an agitation in the minds of the men of the Native army of more than four months' duration — an agitation which the weak and vacillating measures of the Government had served but to increase, must have been received with no slight anxiety by the Commander of a force so almost wholly native as was this at Cawnpore. It is true that the officer who in May, 1857, held the command of the Cawnpore Division, was one of the most distinguished generals of the Company's army. Sir Hugh Massy Wheeler had spent nearly fifty-four years in India, and throughout that period he had served only with natives. He had had peculiar facilities of studying their character; he had served with them under Lord Lake, against their countrymen; he had led them in Affghanistan against foreigners: they had achieved victory under him in both Sikh campaigns, in the second of which he held an independent command. By Lord Gough, under whom he gained his brightest laurels, he was most highly esteemed. He had proved himself on so many occasions so fertile in resources, so ready to overcome difficulties, so prompt, active, and energetic, that it was thought he was the man of all others most competent to deal with an insurrection of this character, most fitted to unravel the web of mystery in which its origin was then clouded, and to open the minds of the Sepoys to the insensate folly of their proceedings. And if this had been a mere military outbreak, as some have imagined, if the dispossessed princes and people of the land, farmers, villagers, ryots, had not made common cause with the Sepoys, there is every reason to believe, as will be shown hereafter, that but a portion of the force would have revolted: the certainty exists that not a single officer would have been injured.

The outbreak at Meerut was not wanted to open Sir H. Wheeler's eyes to the magnitude of the crisis. He had, from the first sign of disaffection at Berhampore, been watching with an anxious eye the progress of events, and, in common with many others, he had been deeply struck with the fatal delay which occurred in dealing out punishment to the 34th Native Infantry; and with the immunity granted to those who attacked Lieutenant Baugh. Still, the Government of India, having announced that their "forcibly feeble" acts had restored discipline to the Bengal army, Sir Hugh was bound to strengthen their hands as much as possible, by endeavouring to maintain and to justify the confidence they felt. He was powerless to do more without exciting the suspicions of those whom the Government had proclaimed well-affected and loyal.

The news of the Meerut outbreak, which reached Cawnpore on the 13th May, left him freer scope to act. Although the Government even then professed to look upon that outbreak as a mere local revolt, although they ignored the possibility of its being part and parcel of a plan for a general rising, it was not so with Sir Hugh Massy Wheeler. That experienced officer felt that the army was gone; that, incapable of acting in concert, every regiment would take its own time and opportunity; but that all would go he felt morally certain. Surveying then his own position, he found himself the commander of a large native force, separated by the river only from Oudh, and in the heart of a native population, with but sixty-one Europeans at his disposal: his cantonment was an open one, no semblance of fortification existing in any portion of it; the magazine, which bore the nearest approach to anything of the sort, being seven miles distant. It was, in truth, a perilous position.

The minds of all in Cawnpore were naturally much excited by the accounts of the Meerut insurrection, full details of which reached the station on the 15th. It was felt that, composed as their own force was, a revolt might break out any day; and as there were many ladies in the station, and all the families of H.M. 32nd Regiment then quartered at Lucknow, as too there was a large mercantile community, it was deemed desirable to select and to fortify some place of refuge to which the entire European community could retire in case of need. The magazine, a very large building on the banks of the river, surrounded by a high wall, was first proposed for this purpose: but the fatal objection existed that it was seven miles from the native lines, and on the Delhi road. It was argued that, in case of a rising, the native troops, as at Meerut, would, after massacring every European who might come in their way, march as quickly as possible towards Delhi, and that it would only be necessary to provide a place of refuge at the opposite end of the station, sufficiently fortified to resist a sudden attack, and provisioned for a few days, in which the whole of the residents might remain until the first fury of the mutineers had been spent, and they had left Cawnpore for Delhi. These views prevailed, and two large barracks, formerly the hospital barracks of the European Regiment *once* stationed at Cawnpore, were selected, and earth-works were commenced upon without any further delay.

These barracks were situated in the centre of a very large plain, with a tolerably clear space all round them. In front was the cricket-ground, a very clear space, bounded on its left and left-front by unfinished barracks, then in the course of construction; on its right was the road, and beyond it another level plain of smaller extent terminating in a row of houses; beyond these another road, another row of houses, and then the river. To the left and left-rear of the barracks was an extensive plain, upon which the European Regiments, on passing through the station, were wont to encamp: to the right and right-rear the description I have already given of the country to the right of the cricket-ground applies. It has, since the catastrophe, been regretted by some that the magazine had not been selected as the place of refuge. As one who knows the locality well, I cannot coincide with those who are of this opinion. The magazine was seven miles distant from the new native lines, and on the Delhi road; it was next door to the jail. Unless Sir Hugh Wheeler had chosen to abandon the station before any signs of mutiny were apparent, he, the officers, and ladies would have found it impossible to get there. The Government of India had loudly proclaimed their trust in the Native army. Could Sir Hugh Wheeler have told the portion of that army stationed at Cawnpore, "I have no trust in you; I resign command of you: your officers I take from you into the magazine, and bid you defiance," — this too before a single overt act of mutiny had been committed? Had he acted so, he would at once have been made the scape-goat for all that has since followed. Had he, on the other hand, waited for a movement on the part of the native troops, and then endeavoured to reach the magazine with the ladies and children, not one-third the number would have arrived there.

There is more plausibility in the expression of regret which I have also heard, that Sir Hugh did not entrench himself on the river, still not abandoning his position in the native lines. To this I can only reply, that an officer of General Wheeler's judgment and experience must have perceived the advantages resulting from such a course, but that under the circumstances he must have perceived also that it was not feasible. There were no barracks on the immediate banks of the river, and therefore there would have been no cover for the women and children. He had the terrific heat of the months of May, June, and July to calculate upon, as well as the enemy; besides which, it was not then a question of standing a siege. The object was to provide a temporary refuge for the European residents till the mutineers had left the station. The barracks afforded this better than any other place he could have selected, and he was justified, both by his innate knowledge of the Sepoys and by events which had occurred elsewhere, in making that selection.

That position was therefore chosen, and it was commenced to fortify it, and to furnish it with supplies. At the same time everything was done which could be done to keep the Sepoys firm in their allegiance. At this time, and to the very day of the outbreak, the regimental officers had perfect confidence in their men. They had associated with them, had joined in their sports, and had in every way identified themselves with them; the name of their regiment was to them all in all; its glory, its honour were their pride. They refused to entertain the slightest suspicion of those with whom they had for years past mixed so freely and unreservedly; who had followed them through the swamps of Burma, and the snows of Cabool; who, in the Sutlej campaign, had withstood all the seductions of the Sikh soldiery. They believed them faithful, and they showed their belief; every night the officers slept in tents in the lines, each officer at the head of his own troop or company, liable to be murdered in their sleep, but they flinched not. Most of them rejoiced in the opportunity of showing their confidence in their men. So much, and to such an extent, can the wily Asiatic deceive the open-hearted, too credulous Englishman!

At this epoch another character appeared on the scene — one whose powers of duplicity exceed the bounds of imagination, and whose treachery and cruelty stand out in bloody relief, far surpassing the crimes that have been recorded under the same headings in the annals of the world.

Dhoondoopunt Nanajee, quasi Raja of Bithoor, was the son of the late Peishwa's Subahdar, Ramchundur Punt. Although never legally adopted by Bajee Rao, for adoption requires the performance of many ceremonies, commencing in the lying-in room, Dhoondoopunt was yet as a boy received into his family, and was treated as a member of it. He received a tolerable education, and can both read and write English. On the death of the Peishwa without issue, either actual or adopted, his widow became, according to Hindoo law, his legal heiress, Dhoondoopunt still continuing in the position of a dependant. But his grasping ambition was ill-content with so subordinate a position. He forged a will, and on its authority claimed posession of the personal property of the Peishwa. That chieftain's widow having unsuccessfully contested the claim, fled to Benares, determined to appeal to the British Government. She was, however, inveigled thence by the arts of Dhoondoopunt, and persuaded to proceed to Bithoor, where she had ever since remained, her claims having been abandoned from that date. Emboldened by the success of his measures against the personal property of his deceased benefactor, Dhoondoopunt laid claim to his title and possessions, on the ground of his being the adopted son, and he sent an agent to England to push his appeal. He was not, as I have already shown, the adopted son, but his claims were refused on other grounds by the British Government—the principle of inheritance by adoption having been disallowed. He was, however, allowed to keep six guns, to maintain as many followers as he chose, and to live in almost regal state at Bithoor—a castellated palace about six miles north of Cawnpore. In his social relations he much affected European society, and appeared fond of joining those pursuits in which Englishmen in all climates delight. He was hospitable, too, after his fashion, gave entertainments on a large scale, and was always ready to lend his elephants to any of the more exalted *employés* of Government.

Between this man and the Collector of Revenue at Cawnpore, Mr. Hillersdon, there had been considerable intercourse on official subjects, and the latter had been greatly impressed by his suave and courteous manner of transacting business. This intercourse had increased since the commencement of the agitation in the Sepoy mind, and the Nana Sahib (as I shall call him in future—that being the name by which he is now best known to the world) had more than once commented on the folly of the Sepoys in believing that any plan was being hatched against their religion. Very soon after the news of the Meerut outbreak had arrived, he again met Mr. Hillersdon, and advised him to send his wife and other ladies to Bithoor, assuring him that they would be quite safe there, as he would protect them against any number of Sepoys. Although Mr. Hillersdon did not act upon this offer at once, yet so confident was he in the loyalty of the Nana Sahib, that he made arrangements for carrying it into effect on the first symptoms of insurrection. He further arranged a plan with the Nana, that the latter should organise 1500 fighting men, who should be ready to surprise the Sepoys on their showing a disposition to rise, and to put them all to the sword.

This plan had been arranged in consequence of the successful insurrection at Delhi, an account of which reached Cawnpore on the 17th May. This information redoubled the anxiety of General Wheeler; the works at the barracks were hastened, and the preparations for the supply of provisions hurried on, for it was felt that no time was to be lost. On any night the signal might be given, and the women and children massacred in their beds. It was felt on all sides that the speedy recapture of Delhi could alone avert a great catastrophe. The General had learned from his spies that meetings of an insurrectionary character were held nightly in the lines of the 1st Regiment of Native Infantry and the 2nd Light Cavalry; that these latter especially were bent on revolt, that they knew their power and our weakness. Fatal knowledge for all parties! Lamentable want of foresight in the Government that sanctioned such a disposition of troops!

On the night of the 21st matters were very nearly coming to a crisis. The 2nd Cavalry had completed their arrangements, the examples of their comrades at Meerut and Delhi had fired them, and they were determined to revolt. Sir Hugh Wheeler had received early information of the probability of such an event; he had, therefore, sent to all the European residents, advising them to repair towards evening to the barracks, and he had dispatched an express to Sir Henry Lawrence at Lucknow, begging him to lend him two or three companies of H.M. 32nd, or as many as could be spared. He made at the same time an attempt to move the treasure, which was seven miles distant from the station, into the barracks; but, as the Sepoy guard at the treasury showed a disinclination to part with it, loudly protesting that they were able to defend it where it was, and Sir Hugh being powerless to coerce them, he preferred accepting the offer of the Nana Sahib, made through Mr. Hillersdon, and strongly recommended by that gentleman. It was to the effect that the Nana's troops should guard the treasury. Accordingly, that night, 200 Mahrattas, armed with matchlocks and fully equipped, accompanied by two guns, moved from Bithoor and took up their quarters at the treasury, close to the jail, and within a stone's throw of the magazine in which were all our military stores.

That night all the European residents, with the exception of Sir George Parker, the cantonment magistrate, who at that time disbelieved the excess of danger, slept in the barracks: the ladies had scarcely arrived there ere the arrival of the Mahratta troops caused an alarm, and the guns were sent for; they arrived about 11 P.M. Meanwhile, four native officers of the 2nd Cavalry, either finding that the other regiments would not join them, or that the pear was quite ripe, and unable of their own authority to control some of their younger and more excitable privates, had made a virtue of the emergency, and reported to their commanding officer, Major Vibart, that the regiment was ready to rise. He instantly went down to the lines, turned out the men, and addressed them in a manly style, appealing to the number of years he had passed with them, the dangers and vicissitudes they had encountered together, and imploring them to remain true to their colours, and to maintain the glory of their regiment unsullied. How they were affected by this address it is impossible to say, but they returned to their lines apparently contented.

Of the scene in the barrack that night descriptions have appeared from the pens of some of the actors in it. One of them, a gentle lady, wrote: "There were an immense number of ladies and gentlemen assembled there, and oh! what an anxious night it was. The children added much to our distress and anxiety; it was some hours before I could get them to sleep. I did not lie down the whole night." Another, a high-spirited and promising young officer: "Nearly all the ladies in the station were, however, turned out of their houses, and hurried off to the barracks. The scene in the morning you can imagine. They were all huddled together in a small building, just as they had left their houses; on each side of this the guns were drawn up." It seems strange now to read what follows: "I still put all trust in our Sepoys, and shall do so until I see that they are unworthy of it." Such was the confidence engendered by long association and constant intercourse with their men, that even these sad events could not shake it.

Early on the morning of the 22nd, eighty-four men of H.M. 32nd Foot, under the command of Captain Moore of that regiment, a most able and energetic officer, cheered the hearts of the residents by their arrival; they were all that Sir Henry Lawrence could spare — he himself being in a most precarious situation. Indeed, most men in his position would have declined General Wheeler's request; but Sir Henry had an enlarged and sympathising soul, and he did not hesitate to reduce his garrison to the smallest possible number, in order to render assistance to his imperilled countrymen at Cawnpore. They were accompanied by two squadrons of Oudh Cavalry, who were at that time believed to be staunch: their fidelity, however, being shortly afterwards questioned, they were sent back again.

For an entire week, from the 24th to the 31st of May, the state of suspense was awful, in some instances, more than could be borne. One lady lost her reason in consequence, and almost all suffered in a manner defying description. They were daily, hourly, expecting an insurrection,— in fact almost praying that it might come, in order that the too terrible suspense might pass away. Every precaution was taken to avoid giving the natives the slightest cause for revolt. Even the customary salute in honour of the Queen's birthday was forbidden, lest the sound of the guns should afford a pretence to the Sepoys to revolt. Still the officers slept in the lines of their men: in the most heroic manner they passively placed themselves in the power of those who had shown but too clearly their ultimate intentions against them. They did it, it is true, by order; but they went without hesitation to what some of their number at least must have considered certain death: but they looked that fate boldly in the face, and not in one single instance did they shrink from encountering it.

At length on the morning of the 31st, after a terrible night, in which rumours of the rising of the 1st Native Infantry were rife, the joyful intelligence spread through the station that the first instalment of the European reinforcements had arrived. It was quite true; on that day and the two following, fifteen men of the Madras Fusiliers and 150 of the 84th Foot joined the garrison, and cheered their hearts by the information that they were but the forerunners of several regiments; that troops had poured into Calcutta from Madras, Burma, and Ceylon, and were being sent up with all possible speed. A letter also arrived from Lord Canning to General Wheeler, in which it was stated that all the available troops should be sent up; that many were on their way, some coming by steamers, some by bullock-train, some by dâk carriages.

All might yet have been well, and all would have been well, but for the stoppage of these reinforcements by the mutiny of the 6th Regiment of Native Infantry at Allahabad. The Government had permitted this, the most important military post in India, a strong fortress and immense magazine, to remain, after this crisis had commenced, under the charge of a native regiment. The result was, that all Bengal very narrowly escaped destruction,—Cawnpore and the adjoining stations were swept away.

So confident were the authorities at Cawnpore that the crisis had passed, that the daily arrival of European troops would render our force more than a match for the natives, that on the morning of the 8th of June Sir Hugh Wheeler ordered one company of the 84th and a portion of the 32nd Foot back to Lucknow.* There then remained at Cawnpore:—

1st comp. 6 batt. Artillery	61
H.M. 32nd Foot	84
1st Madras Fusiliers	15
H.M. 84th Foot†	50

Total 210 men.

In addition to these were about a hundred officers, the same number of merchants, and about forty drummers; making a total of 450 Europeans, with six guns. These, had they been alone, could have fought their way either to Agra or Allahabad; but there were besides about 330 women and children, many of them reared tenderly, and unaccustomed to hardships. Their lot, indeed, was the hardest of all, and his heart must be hardened who can think of their protracted sufferings without a pang.

It was on the morning of the 3rd of June that the Europeans left for Lucknow. On the evening of the same day, half of the 3rd Oudh Horse Battery, under Lieutenant Ashe, which had been sent towards Futtehgurh to quell a disturbance in that quarter, but had been compelled to retreat on account of the mutiny of the troops which accompanied it, arrived at Cawnpore. They had with them two 9-pounders and a 24-pounder howitzer, which were at once placed in the entrenchment. The men had behaved well on the road, had refused to join the mutineers, and it was hoped and believed that they would continue proof against the inducements to revolt which seemed to loom in the future.

On the morning of the 4th June, Sir Hugh Wheeler received positive information that the 2nd Cavalry, the 1st and 56th Regiments, were determined in the course of the next four and twenty hours to rise and murder their officers: these latter were therefore directed to discontinue sleeping in their lines. Orders had been previously issued to Mr. Reily, in charge of the magazine, to blow it up, in the event of an outbreak. He was prevented carrying out these directions by the Sepoys on guard at the magazine: consequently, when the mutiny did break out, immense stores of ammunition, guns, and small-arms, fell into the hands of the insurgents.

Meanwhile the Nana Sahib, in order, as it was imagined, to testify his sincerity, had moved, with a very large number of his followers, from Bithoor to the civil station, and had taken up his residence in a house not far from that belonging to the collector. He was here for

---

* Lieut. Delafosse's Narrative. † Mr. Shepherd's Narrative.

a double purpose, to excite the Sepoys to revolt, and to guard the treasure for himself. Nevertheless, he was not once suspected; every one, even after the outbreak of the mutiny, placed implicit confidence in him. It was believed that it was his interest to remain true to us, not only on account of his vast territorial possessions, but because he had invested upwards of 500,000*l*. in Government securities. It was not known until afterwards that ever since the annexation of Oudh he had been gradually disposing of these securities, until in the month of June, 1857, only 30,000*l*. worth remained.*
This is one of those incontestable facts which prove that it was the spoliation of Oudh which decided the large chieftains and landowners to rise against us. It was the last feather on the camel's back; they thenceforth saw no security for themselves in passive submission; they had no hope remaining but the sword.

By the 4th of June nearly a month's provisions had been stored in the entrenchment, the guns placed in position, and every possible arrangement to secure the lives of the European residents had been completed. Dire suspense reigned in every mind: the arrival of reinforcements from Calcutta had ceased, and there appeared no hope from any quarter. They all felt, as had been the case during that last long fortnight in May, that any day they might be attacked and massacred. Nevertheless, no hearts quailed: there was but one feeling amongst the men—an indomitable resolution to defend the British flag and the lives of the ladies and children committed to their charge to the very last.

At length, on the night of the 4th, the 2nd Cavalry, on the pretence that they felt themselves suspected, and could not bear it, rose in revolt with a great shout, mounted their horses, and set fire to their sergeants' bungalows. Thence proceeding to the commissariat cattle yard, they took thirty-six elephants, the property of Government, and went direct to the treasury, some seven miles distant: here, assisted by the Mahratta troops of the Nana Sahib, they plundered the treasury (about eight lakhs and a half of rupees), and packed it on the elephants and carts. They had hitherto been unsuccessful in persuading the 1st Native Infantry to join them; but these latter being informed of the process going on at the treasury, also left their lines with a loud shout, and joined the 2nd Cavalry. Their officers attempted, but in vain, to persuade them to be loyal. Command and entreaty were alike ineffectual: the Sepoys begged and even forced them to return to the entrenchment, intimating at the same time that they were no longer under their orders. They then took the road to the treasury, burning and plundering all the bungalows, and seizing all the property on which they could lay hands.

This had been a night of horror in the entrenchment: the mutinous shouts, the discharge of pistols, the blazes of fire in every direction must have struck terror into the hearts of the ladies and children. The men were, however, not at all dismayed. No attack had been made upon them; there had been no disposition to shed blood:

* Vide Government Gazette, published by authority.

accordingly, about seven o'clock next morning, three or four officers sallied forth and proceeded on horseback toward the assembly-rooms, with the intention, it is stated*, of blowing up the magazine. But when they reached the canal, less than one-third of the distance, the Sepoys fired upon them, and killed one officer; the remainder returned to the entrenchment. On their arrival, the 3rd Oudh Horse Battery (natives), with a company of Europeans, were ordered to pursue the rebels. On reaching the canal they were recalled, as symptoms had in the meanwhile manifested themselves in the 53rd and 56th Native Infantry, which rendered it highly undesirable that the barrack should be left unprotected.†

These symptoms were soon changed for actions. The native officers had reported that the men were no longer to be depended upon; and very soon after, about 9 A.M., a bugle was sounded, and the two regiments were seen drawn up in columns on their parade ground, showing a defying front: they were, however, dispersed immediately, on hearing the booming of cannon from the entrenchment, and, making a circuit, they joined their rebellious brethren at Nawabgunj (the place where the treasury, magazine, and jail were situated). The native artillerymen (belonging to the Oudh Battery) went off about the same time, to swell the ranks of the rebels.

The station was now clear of insurgents, and yet Sir Hugh Wheeler had no choice but to remain where he was. The road to Allahabad was the only one open to him, had he been inclined to make a move; but, independently of his being unprovided with carriage, it was clear to him, from the non-arrival of further reinforcements, that something had gone wrong there also. He could do nothing, then, but remain where he was, and strengthen his fortifications as much as possible. Some muskets had been left in the native lines; these were brought in and distributed to the merchants, clerks, drummers, and others. These latter were told off in sections, placed under the command of officers, and assigned distinct duties.

Hopes were entertained at this time that they would be allowed to remain in the barracks unmolested, for information reached them early on the 6th of June, that the mutineers, having cleaned out the magazine, and loaded as much as they could carry upon carts, had marched to Kullianpore, the first stage on the road to Delhi, leaving a small body of cavalry behind as a rear-guard. That they would have gone on, that they were then innocent of any bloody intentions against our garrison, is more than probable. They were themselves inclined to push on to Delhi: it was in their eyes the principal seat of war; there they thought the struggle for the empire of India would be fought and decided, and they were emulous to join those comrades and relations who were so fiercely combating under the green flag in the city of the Mogul. Their intentions were, in fact, pronounced by

---

* Deposition of Marian ayah.

† The narrative that follows is compiled from the following sources: viz. Mr. Shepherd's and Lieut. Delafosse's Accounts, Marian's Deposition, Statement of the Writer in the Pay Office, Statement of an Eye-witness, Nujoor Tewarree's Account.

their march on Kullianpore. DELHI was the cry which burst from every lip as they marched forth from Cawnpore. And it must be a strong temptation to induce them to forego that resolution; nevertheless, that temptation was held out, and by one whom our party even at that moment believed to be their friend—by the treacherous friend—the Nana Sahib.

This man in fact saw that, if the troops were to go to Delhi, all the advantages he had promised himself from the revolt would slip from his hands. The shadowy dream of a Mahratta Empire reconstructed on the ruins of the British power was already passing away: the march to Delhi would dissipate it for ever. He knew the extent of the conspiracy, and there can be no doubt but that he firmly believed that the British authority was about to receive a death-blow. His object then was to lay the foundation of his future sovereignty at Cawnpore; his influence would thence be spread into the surrounding districts; it would penetrate to Delhi itself. The mighty power once exercised by the Peishwas would be restored, and to himself, the architect of his own fortunes, would belong the glory of replacing their vanished sceptre. There can be little doubt that some such thoughts influenced him, when, as he accompanied the insurgents to Kullianpore, he used every argument to persuade their leaders to place themselves under his orders, and to return and destroy the band of Feringhees whom they had left behind. He, in all probability, pointed out to them, that, so long as their officers lived, their lives would not be safe; they would always be marked men, and, should their insurrection prove unsuccessful, they would be hunted to death all over India. These considerations, and the reports brought out by the Oudh Artillery-men of the large quantity of treasure in the entrenchment, and of the facilities existing for attack, in consequence of the quantity of powder and guns still remaining in the magazine, besides about forty boat-loads of shot and shell lying in the canal, decided the mutineers to place themselves under the orders of the Nana Sahib.

Accordingly, about 8 o'clock on the morning of the 6th, the whole force returned to Cawnpore, with the Nana at their head. He pitched his camp in the centre of the station; and, although a high-caste Brahmin himself, he hoisted two standards, one to the honour of Mahomed, the other of Hunaman (the Hindoo Deity); and to these he bade all the faithful repair. He then sent about fifty sowars into the town, to kill any Europeans who might be found there, as well as the native converts to Christianity; at the same time the houses of the Cawnpore Nawab and other influential native gentlemen were attacked and gutted, on the pretence that their owners had harboured Europeans: he himself spent the greater part of the day in mounting some heavy guns, of which he had obtained possession, and of making preparations for the attack.

On the following morning, the 7th of June, a letter was received by General Wheeler from the Nana Sahib. Up to that moment, his fidelity had not been questioned, but now the mask was thrown off. The letter merely intimated the Nana's intention to attack the garrison. It very soon appeared that this was by no means an idle threat, for two guns opened upon them from the north-west, and musketry from all directions. On the 8th three more guns were brought against them, and on the 11th the enemy had in position, and playing upon the garrison night and day, three mortars, two 24-pounders, three 18-pounders, two 12-pounders, the same number of 9-pounders, and one 6-pounder. Their numbers had in the same interval greatly increased. The 6th from Allahabad, red with the blood of our countrymen there, irregular corps from Oudh, and *budmashes*, *i.e.* armed rabble from all parts of the country, had poured in to make common cause against us. All the bungalows in the neighbourhood of the barracks were occupied by rebel infantry, and these poured an incessant fire day and night upon our unhappy countrymen. A small church, situated to the south-east of the entrenchment, was strongly occupied, and the fire from it was most galling. The unfinished barracks, to which I have already referred as lying on the left front of the entrenchment, were also constantly threatened and attacked; but fortunately the enemy were never able to obtain a permanent lodgment in them.

Meanwhile, the sufferings of the garrison were such as no description can adequately portray.* The heat was very great; and what with the fright, want of room, want of proper food and care, several ladies and soldiers' wives, as also children, died with great distress: many officers and soldiers also were sunstruck from exposure to the hot-winds. The dead bodies were thrown into a well outside the entrenchment near the unfinished barracks; and this work was generally done at the close of each day, as nobody could venture out in the daytime, on account of the shot and shell flying in all directions like hail-stones. The distress was so great, that no one could offer a word of consolation to his friend, or attempt to administer to the wants of another. The dead bodies of young ladies tenderly brought up, were placed outside the verandah amongst the ruins to await the time for the fatigue party to carry them to the well. For there was scarcely room to shelter the living, the buildings were so riddled; and every available corner was considered a great object.

They began too to be badly off for water. There was but one water-well, in the middle of the entrenchment, and the enemy kept up their fire so incessantly both day and night, that it was as much as giving a man's life-blood to go and draw a bucket of water. So great did the demand become, even after the second day's siege, that five rupees were paid for a leathern bag full, and one rupee for a small bucket of water: it became finally a matter of necessity for every one to procure it for himself, and as, after the first three days' incessant firing, there was generally a cessation for two hours about candle-light, the well was then crowded by gentlemen and others endeavouring to fill their pitchers and buckets.

As the siege went on, as the weary night succeeded the never-ending day, each fraught with new horrors, their sufferings increased

* Mr. Shepherd, an eye-witness.

tenfold. Although after the first few days the barracks became so riddled as to afford little or no shelter, yet the greater portion of the garrison preferred remaining in them to exposure to the heat of the sun outside. A great many had made holes under the walls of the entrenchment, covered over with boxes, cots, &c. In these they were safe from the shot and shell of the enemy, but not from the effects of heat; and the mortality from apoplexy was considerable. At night every person had to sleep out and take watch in turn: the women and children then slept under the walls of the entrenchment, near their respective relatives. Here the bomb-shells kept them in perpetual dread, for nearly all night they were seen coming through the air and bursting in different places, often doing mischief. To add to their miseries, the stench from the dead bodies of horses and other animals was not only horrible in itself, but the means of their being annoyed by myriads of flies, who never left them. Nevertheless, if their sufferings were great, their fortitude was greater. Sir Hugh Wheeler himself, an old man and worn with anxiety, was physically unable to take an active part in the defence of the entrenchment, but his subordinates rivalled one another in their exertions and contempt of danger. Prominent* amongst these was Captain Moore of H.M. 32nd Foot, who, though severely wounded in the arm, never gave himself the least rest, but wherever there appeared most danger, he was sure to be foremost, his arm in a sling and a revolver in his belt, directing the men or leading them to the fight. It was his custom to place scouts on the top of one of the unfinished barracks, who were able to direct the fire of our artillery. Occasionally the Sepoys would endeavour to take possession of these buildings; but Moore was always on the alert, and whenever they came on in large numbers he would call for volunteers, who, sallying out under cover of a line of carts which connected the unfinished barracks with the entrenchment, would quickly put the enemy to the rout. On such occasions our men generally escaped unhurt, whilst the loss of the enemy was invariably great. They could never stand a British cheer and a British charge. On two occasions this gallant officer sallied forth at night, with about twenty-five Europeans, and succeeded in spiking the nearest guns of the enemy. On every occasion the immense superiority of the British soldier was apparent,—even the enemy's cavalry, though their numbers were very great, never daring to attack our small party.

Meanwhile events were progressing in the rebel camp, which plainly showed that the soul of the Nana was open to no compunctions, that his primary object was the extirpation of the European race, and that he would allow no consideration to interfere with that object.† On the 10th June, a lady with four children, travelling by post from the north-west to Calcutta, arrived, unsuspicious of evil, at Cawnpore. She was taken before the Nana, who, at once, ordered that she and her babes should be slaughtered. The innocent children, exposed to the sun, and unable to comprehend the scene, were crying

* Mr. Shepherd's Narrative.   † Journal of a Native.

to their mamma to take them into the bungalow and give them food; but no one listened, and in a few minutes, tied hand to hand, and made to stand up in the plain, they were shot down by pistol bullets. On the following day another lady fell into the hands of these fiends, and experienced a like fate, her head being subsequently offered as a "nuzzur," or royal gift, to the Nana Sahib.

On the 12th, intelligence reached them that a large party of Europeans were coming from the north-west. Some cavalry and infantry were at once despatched to reconnoitre; and it was found that the advancing party were fugitives from Futtehgurh, about 136 in number, most of them females. They had left Futtehgurh with the intention of proceeding to Allahabad, thence to Calcutta by water, when, on passing Cawnpore, they were pounced upon by these rebels. Being brought before the Nana and sentenced to death, one of them, disdaining to sue for life, reproached him with his cruelty and the insensate folly of his proceedings; showing how futile it was to imagine that by the slaughter of a few hundred women he could exterminate the English. She also warned him of the fate which, sooner or later, must inevitably overtake him. In reply to this spirited remonstrance, the ruffian ordered that her two hands should be filled with powder, and the powder exploded: the rest were ruthlessly shot down. At the same time an order was issued that all boats should be secured, in order to prevent the escape of even a solitary individual. The story of these atrocities never reached the garrison, and some of them still believed that the Nana was an unwilling instrument in the hands of others.

Flushed by this easy conquest over unarmed women, the Nana prepared on the following day a tremendous assault on the entrenchment. For some days past he had been firing shells, with the intention of firing the barrack; but it was not till 5 P.M. on the evening of the 13th of June that he succeeded in setting fire to the hospital barrack: it contained not only the sick but the families of the European soldiers, and the flames spread so rapidly that many of the former unfortunates (about forty in number) were consumed. Nearly the whole of the medicines and surgical instruments shared the same fate. No sooner was the fire visible to the enemy, than they came down, 4000 in number, to attack our half-starved, dispirited countrymen; but not even on such an occasion, with such odds, could they muster up courage to dare a hand-to-hand encounter with Englishmen. The fire of our artillery was sufficient to keep them at bay, and, although they prevented our men from offering effectual succour to the wounded in the blazing hospital, they finally slunk back discomfited to their lines.

From the 13th to the 21st similar attacks were made, and with a similar result. Although the enemy succeeded in disabling six out of our eight guns, they never could get beyond the fire of those that were left. But on the 21st, having been largely reinforced from Oudh and other districts, a tremendous attack was made on all sides of the entrenchment. To counteract the effect of our fire, the enemy had provided themselves with large bales of cotton, which they used as a flying sap. On the north-west they took possession of three of the empty barracks, and endeavoured to drive our picket out of the rest: on the south-east they advanced under cover of the cotton bales. On the former, Captain Moore advanced with twenty-five men under the cover of a fire of grape, and, after a very brief conflict, succeeded in driving them entirely out of the barracks. The latter party were equally unsuccessful; for, having advanced behind the bales within 150 yards of the entrenchment, they suddenly made an attempt to charge, but a few rounds of canister and perpetual file-firing speedily caused them to change their determination; and they dispersed with a loss of about 200 men, including their leader. An attack was made at the same time by about 200 men on the north-east; but the fire of the enemy, after having been kept up for an hour and a half, was silenced by our musketry.

Among the deeds of daring performed on this day, the following, related by Mr. Shepherd, deserves a place, not in the history of this revolt only, but in the annals of national prowess. About mid-day one of the ammunition waggons in the north-east corner was blown up by the enemy's shot, and whilst it was blazing the batteries of the rebels directed all their guns towards it. Our soldiers, being much exhausted with the morning's work, and almost every artillery-man being killed or wounded, it was a difficult matter to put out the fire, which endangered the other waggons near it. However, in the midst of all this cannonading, a young officer, Lieutenant Delafosse, 53rd Native Infantry (one of the survivors), with unusual courage, went up, and, laying himself down under the burning waggon, pulled away from it what loose splinters he could get hold of, all the while throwing earth upon the flames. He was soon joined by two soldiers, who brought with them a couple of buckets of water, which were very dexterously thrown about by the Lieutenant; and whilst the buckets were taken away to be replenished, the process of pitching earth was carried on amidst a fearful cannonade of about six guns, all firing upon the burning waggon. Thus at last the fire was put out, and the officer and men escaped unhurt.

A deed like this tells its own story. It betokens that calm, cool, determined courage which is rarely bestowed except upon those who are capable of even greater things. It is, as a simple act of courage, without a parallel in history. The chief performer, Lieutenant Delafosse, still lives: it will be a consolation to him to know that he has earned the lasting admiration of his countrymen: I will hope that he has gained more—the highest reward for valour which it is in the power of the Crown to bestow. Of his comrades, let him speak: if they still live, let them share with him the gifts of the Crown; should they not have escaped the fearful ordeal, let their families reap some portion of the benefit derivable for matchless courage.

From the 21st to the 24th June our unhappy countrymen were subjected to an incessant bombardment: the barracks were now riddled with balls and shot, and afforded but little protection. The season, too, for the commencement of the rains had arrived, and it was evident that at the first heavy shower not only would the whole

K

edifice come down, but the holes which, as mentioned before, had been made in the ground, would be filled up. Added to this, since the first five or six days of the siege, the supplies of fresh water had failed entirely, and the garrison had subsisted on otta (ground wheat) dak, and gram (two species of grain peculiar to India). In order to make this supply last the longer, they had lived for some days on half rations. They were now in great straits, and all felt that affairs could not last as they were much longer. With insufficient food, the prospect of the barracks, their only place of refuge, tumbling about their ears, with no hope of relief, and with the agonising sight before them of gentle ladies perishing before their eyes, it was the conviction of all that something must be done. A great many of the officers and men were of opinion that it would be best to sally out in a body at night and take the guns, or perish in the attempt — and this course, if adopted, would probably have succeeded; but it was felt that, if unsuccessful, the women and children would be left a prey to their infuriated antagonists. Although often considered, and earnestly advocated by many, it was never put into execution. The fact is, the character of the Nana Sahib was not rightly appreciated in our entrenchment: he had mixed so much with Europeans, his prime minister, Azimoollah, a Mahomedan, had actually been to England, and been received in society there, and he had been apparently so earnest in our behalf before the outbreak occurred, that some believed that he was secretly in our favour, that at all events he would, if he had the power, protect the lives of our countrymen. Had a contrary belief prevailed, had the massacre of the 12th of June been known in the camp, there can be little doubt that the first alternative would have been tried, and as little (from information subsequently obtained, whereby it appeared that the enemy's guns were almost abandoned at night) that it would have been successful.

However, under the impression which unfortunately prevailed, it had been almost determined to treat with the Nana, when, on the afternoon of the 24th, a note arrived from that individual, brought by Mrs. Greenway (a member of the family of Greenway Brothers, merchants of Cawnpore), to the effect that all the Europeans in the entrenchment who had nothing to do with Lord Dalhousie's Government[*], and would lay down their arms, should be sent to Allahabad. The preliminaries were agreed to, and the following day Azimoollah, on the part of the Nana, and Captain Moore, deputed by General Wheeler and armed with full powers, met in one of the unfinished barracks. Azimoollah attempted to open the conversation in English, but was prevented by the sowars who accompanied him. It was, therefore, carried on in the Hindustani language. An agreement was concluded to the effect that the Government money, the magazine, and the guns, should be made over to the Nana, who on his part bound himself to provide tonnage and permit every individual in the entrenchment to proceed to Allahabad unmolested. This agreement

---

[*] It will be recollected that it was Lord Dalhousie who annexed Oudh and deviated from the previously recognised practice of acknowledging the principle of adoption.

was drawn up in writing, signed, sealed, and ratified by a solemn oath by the Nana. On the morning of the 26th a committee of officers went down to examine the boats; they found them serviceable and in good order: they were molested neither in going nor in returning. On their report every preparation was made to start on the morrow.

That fatal day at length arrived, and on the morning of the 27th, carriage for the women, children, and wounded having arrived, the whole party started,—our men taking with them their muskets and ammunition, and being escorted by nearly the entire rebel force. They arrived at the river about 8 A.M. without being at all molested. There were no signs of any preparation for a breach of faith; they were even allowed to seat themselves in the boats, and some of these actually pushed off. But no sooner had our unfortunate countrymen laid down their muskets than, at a signal given by the Nana, two guns were run out, and opened upon them immediately, whilst the Sepoys, running from every direction, kept up a strong musketry fire. The boats' crews (natives) immediately deserted them; some of the boats were set on fire, whilst volley after volley was poured on the unhappy fugitives, numbers of whom as they attempted to get away were followed into the water breast-deep by the Sepoys. A few boats managed to get over to the opposite bank; but there they were met by the Sepoys of the 17th Native Infantry and by a regiment of Oudh Cavalry, who effectually prevented their escape. The boats, with one exception, were finally all secured, and all the males they contained were at once massacred: the women, reserved for a worse fate, were brought to the Nana's camp and placed in a brick building, where for the first three days no attention was paid them, beyond supplying them with food of the coarsest description.

But one boat had managed to run the terrible gauntlet, and on this many of the wounded and the refugees from other boats had crowded. The bloodthirsty Sepoys, not content with the massacre of the others, were resolved that our countrymen in this boat also should fall into their hands, that not one, in fact, should escape. For the first day and night she was followed by the two guns and by crowds of Sepoys along the bank.* On the 28th there was still one gun on the Cawnpore side, and the infantry on both sides blazing away. Still they pushed on. But on the morning of the third day their strength was gone, the boat had stuck on a sandbank; and there she lay, a mark for the enemy's fire. Directly any of our men jumped into the water to try and move her, they were fired upon by thirty or forty men at a time. In this emergency, it was resolved again to try the efficacy of a British charge, and fourteen of the wearied band were deputed to drive over the persevering fiends. Amongst them were Lieutenant Mowbray, Thomson, and Delafosse, 53rd Native Infantry, private Murphy of the 84th, and gunner Sullivan of the Artillery. Amongst those in the boat severely wounded was Captain Moore of H.M. 32nd, whose exertions in defence of the entrenchment had been the theme of

* Lieut. Delafosse's Narrative.

universal admiration: many other gallant spirits were there, stiff with their wounnds, or lying in the agony of death, unable to strike a blow for their own lives and those of their countrywomen. Of many tender beings the success of these fourteen was the last hope, the only chance of life. It was but a glimmering, and was destined soon to be extinguished. They saw them, however, advance boldly and rapidly, and drive the enemy before them. A bend of the river soon hid them from their sight: the sound of the firing grew fainter and fainter, and presently a boat filled with Sepoys was discerned advancing from the direction of Cawnpore.* They still, however, had sufficient strength to repulse these new assailants, and, a flood coming on in the night, they were carried off the sandbank and floated down a short distance. Meanwhile the Nana hearing of their position, had sent off a force of three companies of Sepoys to secure them: these, placing themselves on board boats propelled by men accustomed to the work, soon came up with our unfortunate countrymen, after a short struggle overpowered them, and, lifting them from their boat, took them back to Cawnpore in carts. On arriving there they were at once taken out of the carts and seated on the ground. There were sixty men, twenty-five women, and four children. The Nana in person ordered the men to be shot; but the Sepoys of the 1st Regiment, of which General Wheeler's son had been Quarter-master, making some demur, an Oudh regiment was brought up for the purpose. The order was then given to separate the wives from the husbands; but to this last indignity the poor captives refused to submit, and it was finally accomplished by force. In one instance husband and wife were so firmly locked together that they were unable to separate them, and finally desisted from the attempt. The Sepoys were then making every preparation to fire, when the Chaplain of Cawnpore, the Rev. E. Moncrieff, formerly Curate of Tooting, requested leave to read prayers. Permission being accorded, the whole party read and prayed together; they then shook hands all around. The signal was then given, and the Sepoys fired. Many were killed, others only wounded; but these latter were quickly despatched with swords. This bloody work having been completed, the women were conveyed to the place in which those previously captured were confined, whence the whole party, about 150 in number, were taken to the house in which they were finally slaughtered.

There yet remain to be accounted for the fourteen heroic Englishmen who left the boat on the sandbank to drive off their persevering assailants.† Wading to the shore, musket in hand, they charged the enemy: these did not wait their attack, but fled before them. Our party, however, having followed them up too far, were cut off from the river, and were compelled, for fear of being surrounded, to retire. Unable to make direct for the river, they took a road parallel to it, and came upon it a mile lower down. But as they approached, they found they had been cut off by a large body of men, whilst another party on the opposite bank was ready to receive them in case they

---

* Nujoor Tewarree's Account. † Lieut. Delafosse's Narrative.

should attempt to cross. There appeared indeed no hope of safety. But even at this moment they did not despair. Close to the river, and very near the force in front of them, was a small temple. They fired a volley at the enemy and made for this temple, losing in the attempt one man killed and one wounded. However, they gained it, and, secure themselves, they fired on every insurgent who showed himself. The enemy finding that they could effect nothing so long as our party remained inside, determined to smoke them out. They accordingly heaped wood all around it, and then set it on fire. Our gallant countrymen, unable to stand the smoke and heat, took off their clothes, and, musket in hand, charged through the fire and the enemy. Seven out of the twelve remaining reached the river, and began to swim for their lives, followed by the insurgents along both banks, wading and firing as fast as they could. Before they had gone far, two of their number were shot, leaving five only remaining. After swimming about three miles down the stream, one of these, an artillery-man, to rest himself, began swimming on his back, and not knowing in what direction he was going, got on shore and was killed. The other four, Lieutenants Thomson and Delafosse (the same whose heroism is recorded at page 137), private Murphy 84th, and gunner Sullivan of the Artillery, succeeded in out-swimming the mutineers, and finally gave themselves up to an Oudh raja who was friendly to the English. They eventually succeeded in rejoining a party of our troops.

It remains * only to add that, on the evening of the 27th June, the day on which his deed of treachery was consummated, the Nana celebrated his "victory" by a grand parade of his troops, at least ten thousand in number, on the plain of Subada to the north of our entrenchment. Three salutes were fired: one of twenty-one guns for the Nana as sovereign, nineteen guns for his brother Balla Sahib as Governor-General, and seventeen guns for Jowalla Pershad (a Brahmin) as Commander-in-Chief. He then caused to be proclaimed by beat of drum throughout the district that he had entirely conquered the British, whose period of rule in India had come to an end; that they were defeated at Delhi, and dared not set foot in Cawnpore; that he himself was prepared to drive them all out of India. A few days after, he broke up his camp and proceeded to his seat at Bithoor, where he ordered one hundred guns to be fired in honour of the King of Delhi, eighty in honour of his self-styled adopted father, the ex-Peishwa Bajee Rao, sixty in honour of himself, and twenty-one each for his mother and his wife. He evidently thought that he had laid the first stone of the Mahratta sovereignty, and made it firm with a bloody cement.

Such was the termination of the Cawnpore insurrection. If, on the one hand, it resulted in the defeat of our arms, in the massacre of our soldiers and our countrywomen, it formed, on the other, a scene for the display of those qualities which pre-eminently belong to the national character. We see here Englishmen, originally only three hundred and fifty strong, of whom two-thirds only had been bred to

* Mr. Shepherd's Narrative.

arms, their numbers daily decreasing, successfully defending a barrack situation on a level plain, against ten thousand trained soldiers,—for although the rebels numbered only four thousand when they made the first attack, yet, by reinforcements from Allahabad, Oudh, Agra, and other districts, they gradually increased to more than double that force. We see them deprived of animal food, living for days on half rations of grain, performing feats of individual heroism unsurpassed, eager to make a dash at the enemy with their full strength to the cry of victory or death, yet restrained solely by the thought that failure would leave three hundred and thirty women and children the prey of men who knew neither mercy nor pity, who neither feared God, nor regarded man. We see them again, on their own accounts unwillingly, and animated solely by a hope of saving the women and children, giving themselves up to a faithless enemy, who, despite of oaths the most binding, condemned them all to the most ruthless massacre. We see them finally in the hour of death, forcibly separated from their wives and daughters, still comforting themselves as Christians, devoutly appealing to their Creator for pardon, and, incapable of resistance, submitting, in firm reliance on Him, to the fire of the enemy.

But we may conjecture, Did they not, in that last hour, when they prayed to their God for pardon, look to their country also for retaliation on those who had so treacherously murdered them? Could they have imagined it possible that, within a few days of the account of their fate reaching Calcutta, an order would be issued by which immunity to their assassins would be virtually secured? by which evidence would be required as to the actual presence of every individual at this massacre before he could be convicted? Evidence! when the Sepoys had ruthlessly murdered all who could witness against them! Evidence! when the four native regiments at Cawnpore had for three weeks been attacking our countrymen in that all but defenceless barrack! Evidence! when it could be proved from the muster-rolls that there was scarcely a man belonging to those regiments * who was not a partner in the revolt, a consenter to the massacres that had been perpetrated from the very commencement! The names of the few who had remained staunch were known to Government; the rest had revolted *en masse!* But the members of the Government of India could not nerve themselves to summary proceedings. Instead of expressing sympathy for the dead, in place of acknowledging their devotion and their valour, they issued an edict, promising immunity to their murderers! Why should it have been otherwise? There are some natures so cold-blooded as to be incapable of feeling sympathy with suffering humanity. Lord Canning was safe: his kith and kin were far away in England: what were the lives of three or four hundred unknown English women and children to him? Was it worth while further perilling the ancient and anti-Christian system of Government, which had lasted a century, on such an account? The answer may be found in the Home Secretary's circular of the 30th July!

* The 1st, 6th, 17th, 53rd, 56th, Native Infantry; the 2nd Cavalry.

But the shades of our brave countrymen and the surviving relatives of our countrywomen appeal from the selfish and cold-blooded Government of Lord Canning to the People of England. Our generous-hearted countrymen at home have answered by anticipation. They have sent out their thousands of warriors; they have testified by public meetings, by subscriptions, by letters in the newspapers, how they sympathise with those who to the last never despaired of the fortunes of England, who, perishing in her cause with their latest breath testified to their belief in her ability to reassert her sway, who died, I must believe, in the fullest confidence that she would avenge them. And she will yet avenge them. The soldiers she has sent forth have no sympathy with the *doctrinaires* who govern India: no special pleading will restrain them; they will view with their own eyes the charnel-house in which our sisters were murdered, and the cry of all will be :—

> "Front to front
> Set thou these fiendlike Sepoys and ourselves;
> Within our swords' length set them; if they 'scape,
> Heaven forgive them too!"

CHAPTER VII.

HAVELOCK'S ADVANCE TO CAWNPORE. — FUTTEHGURH. — ATTEMPTS TO RELIEVE LUCKNOW.

It is now time to return to Havelock's movements. That gallant officer left Allahabad at 4 P.M. on the 7th July. His force was composed as follows: —

3rd company, 8th battalion Royal Artillery	76 men
H. M. 64th Regiment	435 ,,
,, 78th Highlanders	284 ,,
,, 84th Regiment	190 ,,
Volunteer Cavalry	20 ,,
Natives.	
Sikhs	150 ,,
Irregular Cavalry	30 ,,

His staff consisted of an assistant adjutant-general, an assistant quarter-master-general, and an aid-de-camp. In the selection of officers for these posts he had been particularly happy. Captain Beatson, of whom mention has already been made, filled the first-named office; Colonel Tytler, a dashing Irregular Cavalry officer, acted as quarter-master-general, and the General's son had been taken from the adjutancy of the 10th Foot to perform the duties of aid-de-camp in this his first campaign.

The rain was falling as the column passed through the streets

of Allahabad, extending for nearly three miles between the fort and
the Grand Trunk Road leading to Cawnpore. As it marched, the
inhabitants, so lately in revolt, turned out to observe our first offensive
movement.* The Hindoos appeared indifferent or apprehensive;
but wherever a Mahomedan was seen there was a scowl on his brow
and a curse in his heart. Of such demonstrations our troops were
careless: they had started on a noble errand; they were animated
by the hope of being able to save, by the certainty at all events of
avenging, their countrymen at Cawnpore: like Cromwell's Ironsides,
there was a stern determination in their aspect, even in their very
tread, which showed the earnestness of purpose within. For the
first three days they marched at the ordinary rate of about thirteen
miles a day: the weather was hot, and there was more to be risked
in hurrying them on unnecessarily than was to be gained by forced
marches. Whatever might have been the prevailing impression
among the men, Havelock knew that Cawnpore had fallen. Major
Renaud, with his advanced party, seven hundred strong, was within
nineteen miles of Futtehpore. All his efforts were being exerted to
settle the country, and procure information from the front; and it
was to him that the General would look for the intelligence which
would quicken his movements. For the first three days, then, they
took the ordinary marches. The entire country was under water,
the rainy season having set in with great severity. Our troops,
however, marched cheerily on; the road presented one scene of
desolation, every one of the staging bungalows erected for the
accommodation of travellers had been pillaged and burnt down by
the insurgents; on the other hand, their blackened homesteads, and
the bodies of rebels hanging by half dozens from trees on the road-
side, and nick-named by our soldiers "acorns," afforded ample evidence that Renaud had not been slack in the work of retribution.

On the 11th the force arrived at Khagu, twenty-four miles from
Futtehpore. They had scarcely reached the ground when information was received from Renaud, himself then only five miles in
advance, that the enemy were advancing in considerable force on
Futtehpore, and that it was apparently their intention to hold that
place against us. Havelock could scarcely credit such good tidings:
no one indeed thought that they would be foolish enough to move
out of Cawnpore, and give us the opportunity of beating them in
detail. However, the authority was good, and the news positive.
Havelock therefore, sending orders to Renaud to be prepared to
join him with his detachment on the following morning, broke up
his camp at midnight.

After an hour and a half's marching, the two detachments met,
and went on together. The plan of the General was to halt about
six miles from Futtehpore, rest his troops for the day, reconnoitre
that place, and, if the enemy should be found in position there, to
move on him the following morning. In accordance with this idea,
on arriving at Belunda, within five miles of Futtehpore, the column

* Letter in a London Paper.

was halted, the men fell out to light their pipes and make a brew of tea, whilst a party of Volunteer Horse, under Colonel Tytler, went in advance to reconnoitre.

Whilst they are engaged in this important movement, it may be as well to return for a brief period to Cawnpore, and ascertain as far as possible the intentions and objects of the Nana Sahib.

Scarcely had that miscreant proclaimed himself Sovereign of the Mahrattas, when he experienced the cares and perils of his elevation. He found himself not the master, but the servant, of those mutinous Sepoys whom he had abetted in their treachery; many of them were anxious to proceed to their homes, and enjoy or secure their ill-gotten plunder. Others again, and in this line of policy the native officers of the 2nd Cavalry took the lead, pressed him to pursue his advantage, and exterminate the "Kafirs"* at Allahabad. The Nana himself was very much under the influence of these men; they had been the leaders of the revolt; they had influenced the Infantry regiments to turn and attack us; they had superintended the slaughter of our countrymen; they were relentless and violent in their hatred to us. The views of the Nana also coincided with theirs; he probably felt that he would never be safe at Cawnpore so long as a base for operations remained to us in the Fort of Allahabad; to be secure he must have more blood. He, therefore, was not indisposed to march against us.

The difficulty consisted in persuading the troops to leave their ease and plunder for a fresh campaign against the dreaded "Gora log." But he was well served with spies: all our movements were reported to him, and at this crisis he received information of the march of Renaud's column from Allahabad. This was just what he wanted. He communicated with the native officers of the 2nd Cavalry; then held a durbar, in which he pointed out the ease and facility with which Renaud's detachment might be cut off, and the treasure they had with them plundered.

Both these inducements and that belief in his own invincibility, which even the cowardly massacre of Cawnpore naturally produces in the mind of a native†, had the desired effect. An expedition was at once organised to crush Renaud.

It left Cawnpore on the morning of the 8th July, commanded by Sikka Singh, subadar of the 2nd Cavalry. At 8 o'clock on the morning of the 12th, as our troops were marching on to the encampment of Bolinda, the enemy's force, composed of 100 native artillerymen and twelve guns, 500 cavalry, 1400 mutinous Sepoys, and 1500 Mahrattas and armed insurgents, was passing through Futtehpore. They had advanced some little distance on our side of that place, their infantry, in column of route, marching along the high road, with three guns, a 6, a 9, and a 24-pound howitzer, a little in advance, and about half a mile in rear, the Mahrattas with two guns, an iron 18, and

---

* Europeans.

† A native classes every species of "Killing" with "courage." Even in his sports he is cruel; after having wounded a deer or a hare, he will prefer torturing it to putting it out of misery.

an iron 24-pounder, the cavalry on their flanks, when Colonel Tytler with his reconnoitring party rode up. He had scarcely halted his escort, and taken a position in advance to survey the enemy's position, when he was seen, and their entire cavalry dashed at him. There was nothing for it but to gallop back with the information to the General. That instant the assembly sounded, the troops fell in as cheery and hearty as possible, notwithstanding that a bright July sun was burning overhead, and they had just marched eighteen miles. The guns, eight in number, under Captain Maude of the Royal Artillery, moved to the front, and a cloud of skirmishers, armed with the Enfield rifle, aligned themselves with them, ready to concentrate their fire on the head of the enemy's column, which by this time was seen in the distance advancing. Behind the guns were the several detachments of infantry, forming a line of quarter-distance columns at deploying distance: the Volunteer Horse guarded the left flank. The bulk of the Irregular Cavalry was on the right.

These dispositions had not been completed, when the enemy's artillery, coming within distance, opened fire on our men, their infantry still remaining in quarter-distance columns; their cavalry, at the same time, wearing their cold-weather suit of French grey and mounted on stud horses, but armed in the native fashion, threatened our flanks. Their guns were permitted to fire two or three rounds before ours replied; but the moment our dispositions were completed, Captain Maude answered them, and in a few minutes it became a species of duello at 400 yards between our artillery and theirs, ours assisted by the skirmishing fire of the Enfield rifles. This appeared to paralyse them; its range took them quite by surprise, and, being quite unable to reply to it, they deserted their guns in a shorter space of time than it has taken to record it. Colonel Tytler, Captains Maude and Beatson, then raced up to have the honour of capturing the guns. They were all close together, and the honour may be equally divided, although Captain Beatson was first up. The infantry then deploying, advanced in pursuit, and although the enemy endeavoured to make a second stand by falling back on their 18 and 20-pounders, it was but momentary: they dreaded the Enfield rifle, but still more the bayonet, and they fled in confusion—Major Renaud, commanding the advance, pushing on their centre, composed of the main body of their infantry, and giving them no rest.

Meanwhile the enemy's cavalry were manoeuvring very steadily and with great precision on our flanks; they were anxious evidently to get round and take our infantry in rear; on our left they were checked by the steady attitude of our Volunteer Horse; but on the right we were nearly meeting with a disaster.

In that quarter was the remnant of the Irregular Cavalry that had remained faithful at Benares and Allahabad. They had hitherto acted with spirit against the insurgent villagers, but to fight their kinsmen was a different affair. They were advancing on the right of our line, when about eighteen or twenty horsemen (formerly of our own 2nd cavalry) advanced towards them at a trot, and called out to them in the most appealing terms to join them. Lieut. Palliser who commanded the Irregulars at once sounded the charge : he was followed most gallantly by Lieut. Simpson, the adjutant, but by only three or four of the men. Seeing this, the enemy's cavalry came down upon this handful, charged them, and somehow in the scrimmage, Palliser was unhorsed. It would then have gone hard with him, but that some of the men who had previously refused to follow him, rallied round him, and brought him off. At this place seven of the Irregulars were killed, and three or four wounded, while but one of the enemy's horsemen lay dead upon the field; three or four however were wounded.

While this was going on on the right our main body of infantry was passing through Futtehpore; the right column, consisting of two companies of the Madras Fusiliers and one of the 78th Highlanders, was making its way through the walled enclosures, gardens, and plantations that skirt the left of that town. At this moment they beheld the Irregular Cavalry coming towards them in full flight, pursued by the troopers of the 2nd (enemy's) cavalry. Captain Beatson, who was with the infantry, at once halted the column, and having succeeded by his coolness and commanding manner in halting the fugitives, directed a volley to be poured in upon the enemy : he never attempted to form our men into square, although they were expecting the order, but remaining in line, some even in skirmishing order, they succeeded not only in checking but driving off the enemy.

All this time the centre and left were pressing into and beyond Futtehpore. The town or village consists of but one narrow street, with lofty houses, high walls, and garden enclosures, on either side. This street was found to be choked up with the enemy's baggage, which had followed close upon his main column: so closely, indeed, were they packed that they presented the appearance of a defence run up by the enemy; but a few rounds of shrapnel and the action of the skirmishers on the flanks speedily dislodged the most hardy of their opponents, and caused them to abandon the whole of their stores. In the midst of the ruck were two new six pounders, with limbers and ammunition complete, besides large quantities of gun and musket ammunition; a little beyond, two tumbrils of treasure were found, one of which fell into the hands of the Sikhs and was no more seen.* Amongst the plunder which was taken on this occasion were ladies' dresses, worsted work, and other tokens of our lost countrywomen, the discovery of which served to make the men still wilder for vengeance.†

By the time the baggage had been cleared away from the town, the artillery had passed through, and a last parting shot had been sent at the enemy's infantry, it was past mid-day. The heat was intense; many of the men dropped down, struck by the sun, some never to rise again. These, indeed, formed the only casualties amongst the Europeans; their number amounted to twelve. The fury of the sun had effected more injury than the fire of the enemy.

* Correspondent, "Saturday Review." † Ibid.

In addition to their baggage, treasure, and camp-equipage, twelve pieces of ordnance fell into our hands; the enemy were too intent on flight to care to struggle for their guns.

It was nearly 1 o'clock before our wearied troops, who had marched four-and-twenty miles and fought a pitched battle on an empty stomach, reached their encamping ground; their tents were pitched, and it was on the hard ground and in the shade of the mango-trees that our exhausted countrymen sought for repose.

The action of Futtehpore, in the manner in which it was conducted, as well as in its result, was a type of many that were to follow. It showed that meeting the enemy face to face in the field, we must inevitably beat him; that he could not stand for an instant against our men: but it also evidenced that our deficiency in one arm, in cavalry, almost neutralised this vast superiority. We could beat the enemy, but we had no means of following him up; he was consequently able to take up a new position, often a stronger one, after each defeat.

If the Government had acceded to Captain Beatson's proposition already alluded to—if it had even adopted General Havelock's suggestion, of sending up the officers of disbanded corps to act as troopers—if it had called for volunteers from the infantry, and taking the horses from the native body guard, had sent them up by steamer, or by forced marches, in the middle of June, Havelock might have had at his disposal a body of 400 horse, splendidly mounted, and all drilled men. With these at Futtehpore, he could have destroyed many of the enemy; had they joined him even at Cawnpore, he could have annihilated him.

But of what avail was the iron firmness of our general, the unmatched bravery of our troops, placed under the control of red-tape officials? For want of cavalry, all their labours, all their exertions, all their privations were of comparatively little avail. The enemy, though invariably beaten, yet never followed up, aided too by that powerful sun under which they could move about with comfort, whilst its rays were fatal to our men, as constantly re-appeared, their leader rejoicing if, by the sacrifice of ten of his own followers, he could spill the blood of even one European.

On the 13th, the day after the action, Havelock halted his men, as well to give them rest as to bring in the captured guns and ammunition; much of the latter, which could not be brought on, was destroyed. It may here be mentioned that no sooner had the victory been gained, and our troops had entered Futtehpore, than the deputy-collector of that place, the man who had murdered Robert Tucker, Hikrimtoolah Khan, came out to meet us, little thinking that his crimes had been discovered. It is needless to add that he was at once seized, tried, and hanged.

On the 14th, the march was resumed. The road was strewed with evidences of the precipitancy of the enemy's flight, tents standing in their camp, chests of cartridges, and various articles of property. The morning was unmarked by any particular event, but one slight incident afforded an opportunity for disarming the Irregular Cavalry.

These men, after their disgraceful behaviour on the 12th, had been turned into baggage-guards. Whether they were unable to resist the temptation thus offered, or were actuated by a spirit of disaffection, is immaterial. On the morning of the 14th, as they were in rear with the baggage, the alarm was given that the enemy were in force in a village in front, whereupon the artillery was brought up, and a few rounds of shot and shell were fired into it. Hearing the firing in front, the sowars believed that a good opportunity offered to make free with the baggage. Fortunately, the alarm was a false one, and the plunderers were discovered in the very act. The Highlanders at once went after them; they were brought into camp, and at once disarmed and dismounted. Their horses were found useful for the public service.

It is an almost incredible, but well authenticated fact, that many of these men, disarmed on the 14th July, 1857, for base and treacherous behaviour, and for misconduct in the field on the 12th, were, on the 28th of August following, promoted to higher rank in their corps, one of them to the title of "Buhadoor" for "exemplary loyalty," and "conspicuous acts of devotion to the state," — their loyalty consisting in their refusal to face the mutineers on the 12th, their devotion in attempting to plunder the baggage of our army!*

On the evening of the 14th, intelligence was received that the enemy had entrenched themselves at Aoung, a small village some six miles distant. Our force then started on the 15th, in anticipation of a fight. Directly Havelock came within range, their guns opened upon him; our artillery, however, had been greatly strengthened by the guns captured at Futtehpore; they at once moved to the front, the skirmishers aligned with them, as on the previous occasion. The enemy also threw out skirmishers, and sent his cavalry to turn our right flank: the guns and the Enfield rifles succeeded, after a smart encounter, in driving them back, but only that they might make a wider detour, and fall on our rear. But a sergeant of the Highlanders, who had been left in charge of the baggage and sick, collected all the stragglers, and received the enemy with such a volley that they were glad to make off. Meanwhile, their guns in front had been silenced by ours, and our men, pressing onwards under Colonel Tytler, carried the village after some hard fighting. The enemy were not here, as at Futtehpore, taken by surprise; they expected us, and fought much better.

---

* Vide Government Gazette, 29th August, 1857.

The names of the men who were dismounted on the 14th July, and promoted on 28th August, were as follows:—

Repaldar Heera Singh, 13th Irregular Cavalry, received title of Buhadoor for exemplary loyalty to the state, — dismounted.

Naib Repaldar Maharaj Singh, promoted to Repaldar for conspicuous acts of devotion to the state, — dismounted.

Duffadar Ulta Hossen Beg, promoted to Jemadar for ditto, — deserted.

Kote Duffadar Delaur Hossein, promoted to Ressaidar for ditto, — dismounted.

Duffadar Khurrug Singh, promoted to Jemadar for ditto, — dismounted.

Duffadar Share Singh, ditto, ditto, for ditto, — dismounted.

As our men halted on the other side to rest after the engagement, which had lasted fully two hours, information was received that the insurgents had retired to a very strong entrenchment on the other side of the Pandoo Nuddy, and that they were then preparing to blow up the bridge. Forward again was the cry: the troops got up with alacrity, and recommenced their march. They had scarcely gone three miles, when the little nullah, swollen by the rains to the dimensions of a large river, the stone bridge intact, and the enemy's entrenchment on the other side, burst upon the view. The bridge was guarded by two long 24-pounders, and we had just become visible, when a puff of smoke was seen, and the shot came pounding amongst our advance. Our guns of smaller calibre never attempted to reply, but moved on steadily in face of a continuous fire till well within range, when unlimbering, they opened fire. The effect was instantaneous. The fire of the enemy ceased as if by magic. It subsequently transpired that the first discharge from our guns had smashed their sponge-staffs, and, having none in reserve, they could no longer load their pieces. Finding the firing suddenly cease, the general sent forward the Fusiliers under Major Renaud, whilst the guns turned on the cavalry. The Fusiliers, advancing in skirmishing order, and covering the rest of the force, quickly gained the bridge, dashed on to it with rare gallantry at a run, and drove the enemy before them. The victory was now gained, and the guns, limbering up and crossing the bridge, poured a last volley on the flying enemy. It was ascertained, after the engagement, that, had we not advanced that afternoon, the bridge would have been blown up, and we should have been left to cross as best we could. There were no boats available for the purpose, and the river was not fordable. Our loss must necessarily have been very severe. Of such importance is promptitude in war.

In these two actions, we lost about five-and-twenty men in killed and wounded. But the loss most sensibly felt was that of Major Renaud, of the Madras Fusiliers, a most able officer, who had hitherto always commanded the advance. He was wounded in the thigh by a musket ball, whilst cheering on his men to the bridge; he did not survive more than two days. His short career in Bengal had been most brilliant, and he died nobly doing his duty.

In these actions, too, the want of cavalry paralysed our successes. With four hundred men, the slaughter at the Pandoo Nuddy might not only have been avoided, but our men going on might have held the bridge, and the insurgents would have been in our power.

Let it be remembered that, as will be recorded in full detail presently, it was on that very evening that the Nana Sahib, enraged at the defeat and flight of his legions, murdered in the most savage, horrible, heart-rending manner, our countrywomen at Cawnpore. It is not only possible, but probable that, if we had had cavalry, this awful catastrophe might have been prevented. Not only might the rebels have been hemmed in, in the manner described in the preceding paragraph, but a detachment, pushing on that night before the news of the defeat of his troops could have reached the Nana, would, by their sudden arrival, have so terrified the Asiatic spirit, ready at all times to sink from excess of triumph to the lowest depth of depression, that he would have had neither time nor opportunity to execute his merciless intentions.

But we had no cavalry; and whilst the horses of the native body-guard were growing sleek in their stables near Calcutta, whilst hundreds of young officers were panting to flesh their maiden swords, and many infantry privates were available and anxious for the service, not a step was taken in the matter; no cavalry were embodied until it was "too late"* and for want of them our countrywomen were massacred.

Our tired soldiers bivouacked that night on the spot whence the last gun was fired at the retreating enemy. But to them there was little rest. That evening, Havelock received information that his most severe encounter would take place on the morrow, and that the Nana in person, at the head of 7000 men, would oppose his advance into Cawnpore, every defensible point of which had been strongly fortified.

This intelligence roused every one to fresh exertion. News had reached our camp the day before, that our unfortunate countrywomen were then alive, and our gallant troops were not without the hope that their exertions might not be altogether in vain — that they might yet arrive in time to save them. The very idea shook off all sense of fatigue. That night they moved on, proud in hope, and strong and stern in the thought of vengeance. Cawnpore was twenty-two miles distant: they marched that night and morning fourteen. Bivouacking then under the trees, and there cooking and eating their food, at 2 P.M. the signal for advance was given. They moved in the array of battle, the small body of volunteer cavalry in advance, the artillery behind, supported by the infantry. The heat was fearful: at every step some one fell out of the ranks, many never to return to them, and the calls for water were loud and continuous. After proceeding for about two miles, the force of the enemy became visible — every point guarded — the guns bearing on the road by which it was thought we must advance. But Havelock had determined to trust rather to generalship than to dash, or, to speak more correctly, to the combination of both. As soon then as he ascertained the position of the enemy's batteries, he still advanced his handful of cavalry to mask his movement, but made with the bulk of his force a detour to the right with the view of taking the enemy in flank. This masterly movement had all the effect he anticipated; the enemy's guns poured their showers of shot and shell in the direction of the cavalry, whilst the main body moved off unmolested. But our men had not proceeded half a mile before they were perceived, and the enemy at once changed the direction of their fire. Not a gun of ours replied. Havelock had resolved to reserve his fire, until it could take place with effect. Forward then, with sloped arms, our men advanced, trudging alternately through marshy and ploughed land, the fierce

* 23rd July.

sun beating down upon them, and the fire of the enemy taking effect around and amongst them. But one thought was in their hearts that day, a resolution to drive out the murderers of their comrades. Thus they progressed for about a quarter of an hour, till the turning-point of the flank march was gained. Then, wheeling up into one line with the artillery at intervals, they marched down upon the foe.

The enemy numbered about 5000 men: they had eight heavy guns in two separate batteries. Direct against these our troops advanced, the artillery coming forward and engaging the enemy's guns. So hot at this moment did their fire become, that our line was halted, and directed to lie down until our artillery should have silenced it.

But after a short interchange and pounding on both sides, it was found that the enemy's guns were so well protected that it would be impossible for our Artillery to silence them. There was nothing for it then but to try the bayonet. The Highlanders were lying down. Havelock came up to them, pointed to the enemy's battery, and told them to take it. The Highlanders rose, fired one rolling volley as they advanced, and then moved forward with sloped arms and measured tread like a wall—the rear rank locked up as if on parade —until within a hundred yards or so of the village, when the word was given to charge. Then they all burst forward, like an eager pack of hounds, racing to the kill, and in an instant they were over the mound and into the village. There was not a shot fired, or a shout uttered, for the men were very fierce, and the slaughter was proportionate.* Their general was with them. "Well done, 78th," said he. "You shall be my own regiment in future. Another charge like that will win the day." On they went then, through pools and mud, shouting and cheering, and the west battery was theirs.

Nor were the other regiments behindhand. Position after position fell to their unwavering line, the Sikhs vying with the Europeans. Devoid of cavalry, threatened on their flanks and rear, they were not diverted from the one great object of taking the batteries in front of them. The guns once in their possession, they felt sure that all other obstacles would vanish. Nevertheless their difficulties were all but insuperable. At one time they were entirely surrounded, and it appeared as though our soldiers would have to fight not for victory but for their lives. Still on they went. One officer, Lieut. Seton of the Fusiliers, having, with about forty men, got separated from his regiment, was dashed at by five hundred cavalry. Nothing daunted, Seton called his men round him, formed a rallying square, and with a rolling file firing from the Enfield rifles, &c., compelled them to retire.

The field was now almost gained; but there was one position which still kept up an unabated fire. A huge 24-pounder vomited forth continuous discharges; it was by one discharge from this gun that the 64th had lost six men in their first advance; they and the 84th were nearest it. Havelock went up to them and addressed a

---

* Correspondent, "Saturday Review."

few inspiriting words. "That gun must be taken by the bayonet; I must have it. No firing; and recollect that I am with you." There needed no more; the two regiments advanced, the grape from the battery crashing through them. They fired four times before they charged, but when they did charge their onset was irresistible. All opposition was now over, but the troops still advanced; as they came upon the ridge which immediately overlooks the grand parade, the artillery came to the front and chased the rebels into the town: here again the want of cavalry was keenly felt; with the aid of that arm the enemy might have been cut up almost to a man, his retreat on Bithoor intercepted, and the Nana himself captured. As it was, he effected his escape across the canal, and thence marched leisurely on his stronghold. Our army bivouacked for the night on the plain of Jubada.

Such was the battle of Cawnpore, in which 1000 British troops and 300 Sikhs, labouring under every disadvantage, a powerful sun over their heads, a merciless enemy in their front strongly entrenched, without cavalry, and with an artillery of inferior weight, defeated 5000 native troops, armed and trained by our own officers. Perhaps in no action that ever was fought was the superior power of arrangement, moral force, personal daring, and physical strength of the European over the Asiatic more apparent. The rebels fought well; many of them did not flinch from a hand to hand encounter with our troops; they stood well to their guns, served them with accuracy: but yet, in spite of this, of their strong position, of their disproportionate excess in number, they were beaten.

Napoleon has, in his memoirs, alluded to the immense effect which *morale* has on the physical efforts of soldiers. Never was the truth of this axiom exemplified to a greater extent than at Cawnpore. The enemy were traitors and rebels, who had gained possession of the station which they were now fighting for by the treacherous and cruel murder of their masters; they were men not only without honour, but devoid even of a conscience; they pretended to have revolted from us on account of their religion, and yet the Hindoo portion of them, at least, had committed or connived at enormities which, according to their own impure theology, would have caused the transmigration of their souls into the meanest species of animal; they had, in fact, been corrupted from their allegiance by appeals to their avarice, and they were now fighting in the sole hope of being able to retain the plunder which had accrued to them by treachery and murder. Assailed by the countrymen of those whom they had murdered and despoiled, with what heart could these men combat? Their negation of conscience was their only saving clause, for, with that guilty witness in their bosoms, their evil deeds must have choked them!

On the other hand our men, strong in the conviction not of the justice only, but of the holiness of their cause, seeing before them, not an enemy they could respect, but the vilest assassins, murderers of women and children, were animated by a zeal and fervour which nothing could repress or resist. Had you directed one of those men, on an ordinary day in cantonments, to walk ten miles under a July sun, fully armed and equipped, with sixty rounds of ammunition in his pouch, he would have considered it the most cruel order that could have been issued. But, animated by the holy feeling of revenging his murdered countrywomen, this was but a light undertaking. Neither the length of the road, the heat of the sun, the weight of his accoutrements, or the fire of the foe diminished his ardour: he was sensible when in action of none of these difficulties; he pressed on, conquering and to conquer, because he felt that his cause was a righteous cause, and that in no other quarrel could the strength, the intelligence, and the capacity with which he had been endowed by his Maker be more nobly or more worthily employed.

Thus inspired, no numbers were too disproportioned. Our troops bivouacked on the Cawnpore parade ground; no tents were pitched, but, after such a day's work, even the wet ground was a luxury; and though disturbed for a few minutes by a false alarm of an enemy, they slept, and slept soundly.

Our loss, in killed and wounded, was about a hundred. But chiefly was to be mourned the death of Stuart Beatson, the Assistant-Adjutant-General. Arriving from Persia in a weakly state of health, and actuated solely by devotion to his country, he had endured with fortitude and even pleasure, all the privations of the campaign. He had ever been foremost in the fight, and had never lost an opportunity of showing his capacity. Though suffering from the effects of fatigue, he shrank not from the anticipated dangers of the 16th of July. But the sun, more dreaded than the enemy, struck him down. Recovering from this shock, it was yet only to meet the more fatal onslaught of cholera, which carried him off on the following day. In him, Havelock lost one of his ablest followers, the most earnest, disinterested of soldiers. In addition to his military acquirements, Stuart Beatson possessed very considerable literary capabilities, which he was fond of exercising. His store of varied knowledge, his genial wit, and his kindliness of heart, made him a most delightful companion, one who will never be forgotten by the many friends who have been left to mourn his lot in India.

Our troops, I have said, slept on the night of the 16th. Let them sleep on, for the morrow will convey to them fearful tidings; while they rest, be it our task to notice the occurrences which had taken place in Cawnpore and its vicinity since we last parted from it. And first must be recorded the tragedy of Futtehgurh.

Futtehgurh is a small station on the right bank of the river Ganges, eighty-three miles above Cawnpore. It is the head of the agency for the manufacture of gun carriages, being, by its vicinity to the vast forests of the Serai, peculiarly adapted for the storing of wood. The agency yard itself is merely an enclosure surrounded by mud walls on three sides, abutting on the river on the fourth. Within these walls is a bungalow for the residence of the agent, and large go-downs for the reception of musket guns, carriages, ammunition, &c.

The rising in the Bareilly district (which will be treated of in another chapter), the revolt in Oudh, and the events at Cawnpore, had had their influence on the residents at Futtehgurh. They were thus cut off from all land communication with any of our military posts; the river alone was available. The troops at Futtehgurh consisted of a detail of Native Artillery, and the 10th Native Infantry. This latter was one of the regiments which had volunteered for and had proceeded to Burma, on the occasion of the late war with the King of Ava. It had there done good service. In addition to the officers of the 10th, there were at Futtehgurh the gun-carriage agent, Major Robertson, the judge, magistrate, and an assistant, Colonel Goldie, his wife, and his daughters, on leave, the chaplain, the Reverend Mr. Fisker, several indigo-planters, tent-makers, merchants, and others. Here, also, were the native Orphan Asylum, and a large native Christian community under the special care of the members of the American Presbyterian mission, a most devoted body of men. So great was the alarm amongst the non-military portion that, on the 3rd of June, they held a meeting, and resolved to leave Futtehgurh by boat on the following day, it having been currently reported that the 10th had resolved to mutiny on the 5th. The party, consisting of about 166, including women and children, started accordingly at one o'clock on the morning of the 4th, and got on very well as far as they went. The next morning they were joined by three officers of the 10th, with the information that that regiment had mutinied.

This intelligence was untrue. The fact was, that there was an attempt to break out of the jail; some of the convicts actually did get out, and, firing a portion of the station, advanced towards the cantonment. It was this that the three officers mistook for the mutiny of the regiment, and to avoid its effects they went off to join the boats; had they remained, they would have seen their own men turning out willingly and beating back and securing the jail-birds.

The boats meanwhile went on, but were fired upon by the villagers; information also reached the fugitives that the Oudh troops had assembled a little below to obstruct their further passage. Whilst they were debating on their plans, Hurdeobukhsh, an Oudh landholder, and owner of the petty fort or "gurhee" of Dhurrumpore, offered them protection, if they would remain with him. The counsels were divided. Forty, however, including two of the officers, the collector, Mr. Probyn and his wife, and Mr. Edwards, accepted the offer. The boats, then carrying only 126 passengers, went on downwards towards Cawnpore; they could have met with little obstruction, as it is known they reached that station on the 12th. But tidings of their arrival had preceded them; they were intercepted and taken on shore, and massacred by Nana Sahib in the manner recorded in the seventh chapter. Meanwhile the majority of the party, which had taken refuge at Dhurrumpore, hearing that the troops at Futtehgurh had not mutinied, resolved to return thither. This they did. Mr. Probyn, his wife and family, and Mr. Edwards, alone remaining.

At Futtehgurh all had been quiet: the military had been engaged in as far as possible providing against an outbreak. Still the behaviour of the 10th had been on the whole satisfactory. A few of the young Sepoys had indeed on one occasion shown a refractory spirit, but the firmness and promptitude of the colonel — Colonel Smith, a capital officer — had put it down most effectually. Had they been left to themselves, all would still have gone well; but they were about to be exposed to new dangers and temptations.

On the 15th June, the revolted 41st Native Infantry, fresh from the slaughters of Seetapore and Mohammerah*, arrived on the left bank of the Ganges opposite Futtehgurh. They at once sent over to the 10th an invitation to join them in murdering their officers and seizing the treasure. But the men of the 10th, even if they would have accepted the former proposal, saw no advantage in sharing treasure which was already *de facto* theirs. They accordingly replied to the 41st that they would have nothing to do with rebels and traitors, and were resolved to remain true to their salt. At the same time, by order of their commanding officer, they zealously set to work in breaking up the bridge of boats which connected the right bank of the river with the left, and in sinking all the other boats they could lay hands on.

On the evening of the 17th June, however, the 41st, having ascended the river, found the means of crossing, — the same having been furnished, it is supposed, by the Nawab †,— and that night marched down towards Futtehgurh. On hearing of their approach, there was a great commotion in the lines of the 10th; many wished to remain faithful; others were as resolved to take possession of the treasure. A bold movement decided them; the Grenadier Company seized the bullocks, yoked them to the treasure cart, and marching to the Nawab, saluted him as ruler of the district; the treasure, however, they kept to themselves. They then, joining the 41st, marched to attack the Sepoys who remained faithful to us; many of these, seeing the course of events, joined them, but a few, conspicuous amongst whom was the havildar major, still held out, even to blows; but they were beaten and dispersed, and the havildar major hanged as an example to the rest.

Meanwhile our countrymen and women, one hundred and ten in number, of whom thirty-three only were able-bodied men, had retired into the Agency Compound, which served them as a fort. They had about three hundred muskets, seven guns, viz. three, six, and nine-pounders, and twelve, eighteen, and twenty-four pound howitzers, and a small brass mortar. But there was a very limited supply of ammunition, — even of gunpowder, — and they lay therefore under the necessity of husbanding their resources as much as possible.

On the 27th June the attack on their position began. It is needless to follow them through the daily round of their defence, varied

---

* To be recorded subsequently.

† The Nawab of Futtehgurh, a Mahomedan and a man of great influence, has since assumed the government of the district.

as it was by few uncommon incidents. Suffice it to say that after defending themselves with great spirit up to the 4th July, with two practicable breaches in the walls, with a mine underneath them almost ready to be sprung, wearied with fatigue, two of their number killed, others disabled, they resolved on evacuating their position, and trusting to the Ganges. On the 4th July, accordingly, they embarked in three boats, and started. As they passed the fort, the Sepoys saw them, and calling out, "The Feringhees are running away," pursued them with a hot fire for about a mile along the banks, but happily without effect.

They had not proceeded far before one of the boats became unmanageable, and they shifted into two. In these they proceeded in safety as far as a place called Singheerampore. Here, unfortunately, one of the boats grounded. Guns were immediately opened upon her from the bank, and although our countrymen, wading in the water, made many efforts to shove her off, they were all fruitless. They had been in this position half an hour, when two boats, apparently empty, were seen coming down the stream; on approaching them, they were found to be filled with Sepoys, who immediately opened a strong fire of musketry on our party. Not content with this, they came close and commenced boarding the boat. On seeing this, and finding resistance ineffectual, our countrymen resolved rather to fall into the hand of God than of man, and to trust rather to the Ganges than to the mercy of the Sepoys. In carrying out this resolve, many of course were drowned, — all the ladies and children. But Major Robertson, and Mr. Churcher, junior, succeeded in reaching the shore, and were cared for by friendly natives. Mr. Fisher too, and Mr. Jones*, swam on and were taken up by the sole remaining boat.

But on board of this everything was in confusion; attracted, however, by voices from the shore, they put in for the night, and were kindly received by the villagers. Here Mr. Jones, suffering intensely from a wound, remained, careless of the fate that might be in store for him, and to this circumstance he owed his life. The remainder of the fugitives started on the following morning, and proceeded safely as far as a village just above Bithoor, of which † a man named Jussa Singh was the Zumindar. As they were passing this, the people on the bank called out that their Rajah was friendly to the British. Allured by this statement they took the boat into the bank, but they had no sooner landed than they were made prisoners by the Zumindar. Information of their seizure was forthwith sent to Nana Sahib, who immediately despatched carriages and other conveyances for the ladies and children, twenty-three in number, whilst the men, of whom there were twelve, walked. They were, with the exceptions already noted, the sole survivors of the Futtehgurh party. On arriving at Cawnpore, on the evening of the 11th July, they were thrust into the little house in which our country-

---

* From whose narrative these particulars are chiefly taken.
† Statement of Lall Khan.

women, the survivors of the tragedies of the 27th and 28th of June, were congregated.

Here they were, in a small, confined building, lying in filth, without comfort of any sort, their food, bread, water, and salt, their bedding, the hard floor. Surrounded by savages who insulted them, who took a delight in their miseries, their children pining, even dying before their eyes, themselves powerless to help them — what must have been their feelings? They must at least have felt satisfied that, in the event of their murder, they would be terribly avenged. Hoping, perhaps, that they might be relieved, they must at times have anticipated their fate. Themselves Englishwomen, accustomed all their lives to exact courtesy from others, they must, even at the last hour, have been animated by a proud consciousness that England's hand would yet reach the fiends that were tormenting them. The inscriptions on the wall prove this; these show that our murdered ladies were animated by a full conviction that we should advance, and that speedily, to the rescue, though not in time to save, yet certainly to avenge them.

And it must be acknowledged that of those who have been engaged in the terrible work of retribution, all parties but one have done their duty nobly. Our generals, our officers, our soldiers, have lost no opportunity of dealing out a vengeance as prompt as it has been severe. The Government of India alone has held back; the Government of India alone, by its representatives in Government House, has openly proclaimed its sympathy with our "poor Sepoys." Not a word for our suffering soldiers, not a syllable of commiseration for our murdered countrywomen: but even after the event I am now about to record had been published, for whomsoever sympathy might have been felt, it was expressed at the parties in Government House only for the Sepoys who had been disarmed because they had conspired!

It will presently be shown that these were not mere words: that all the acts of the Government of India have tended to show, that they considered these mutinous, murdering Sepoys in the light of pet children, who should be coaxed back to their duty, and in no case punished for their bloody deeds.

People have talked, and may still talk, of strengthening the hands of this Government? Of what use is it to strengthen the hands when the head is weak, the heart tainted, the blood cold — the whole system rotten. To strengthen the hands of such a one, is to infuse fresh poisonous virus into the body, to give greater capabilities for mischief.

To return to the sad story of our countrywomen. There were upwards of one hundred and eighty of them in that little two-roomed house that has been so often described. On the morning of the 15th, the Nana's best troops had gone out to stay our progress at Pondoo Nuddy; in the evening they came back baffled, beaten, savage. Defeated by our men they resolved to work vengeance on our unarmed women. The Nana was nothing loth. He forthwith gave the order for an unreserved massacre. It was a congenial task for the fiends by whom he was surrounded. With every kind of weapon, from the bayonet to the butcher's knife, from the battle-axe to the club, they assaulted these English ladies; they cut off their breasts, they lopped off limbs, they beat them down with clubs, they trampled on them with their feet: their children they tossed upon bayonets: blood flowed like water, but they were not glutted, nor did they quit that building, till they were satisfied that not a living soul remained behind them. The bodies yet warm, in some life not yet extinct, were dragged into a well hard by, limb separated from limb, — all were thrown in in one commingled mass: the blood was left to soak into the floor, to remain a lasting memento of insatiable vengeance.

It was this sight which met our victorious soldiers on the 17th July, as they entered the re-conquered station. The 84th in advance marched across the canal, and scoured the town, but scarcely one rebel soldier was to be seen; they had all left on the previous evening for Bithoor, after blowing up the magazine in their retreat. As our troops moved on, a dark looking man, apparently almost mad with terror, rushed towards them, and announced himself to be the sole survivor of the Cawnpore massacre. This was Mr. Shepherd, a commissariat clerk; he had left the entrenchment in June, two days before the surrender, in the disguise of a cook. Being almost at once apprehended, he had been taken before the Nana, and sentenced to hard labour on the roads. During the panic of our advance on the 16th, he had been apparently forgotten, for he found no obstruction in the way of his escape. He has since written a lucid narrative of the events of the siege, which must form the basis of any authentic history of that fearful period. The troops then encamped, and the officers proceeded in their search for survivors. Too soon the dismal truth broke upon them; there were not wanting men to point out to them the charnel-house. It was a flat-roofed building, containing two rooms, with a court-yard between, in the manner of native houses. The floor of the inner room was found two inches deep in blood, — it came over the men's shoes as they stepped. Ladies' hair, back combs, parts of religious books, children's shoes, hats, bonnets, lay scattered about the room; there were marks of sword-cuts on the walls low down, as if the women had been struck at as they crouched. From the well at the back of the house the naked bodies, limb separated from limb, protruded out. It was a sight sickening, heart-rending, maddening. It had a terrible effect on our soldiers. Those who had glanced upon death in every form, could not look down that well a second time. Christian men who had hitherto spared a flying foe, came out bearing a portion of a dress or some such relic in their hands, and declaring that, whenever they might feel disposed for mercy, they would look upon that, and steel their hearts.

Meanwhile, Havelock had sent on the 15th a pressing message to Neill at Allahabad for reinforcements. This officer, who, possibly to compensate for his supersession, possibly to ensure him against the recurrence of such a calamity, had been created a Brigadier-General, sent off two hundred and twenty-seven men that same afternoon, and started himself on the 16th. He arrived on the 20th. On the previous day Havelock had marched with a strong detachment of his force towards Bithoor, over a very difficult country, in which the enemy was reported to be strongly entrenched. But Havelock met with no opposition, the Nana despairing of success had crossed with the main body of his troops into Oudh, leaving behind him fifteen guns, several horses, and cattle of every description. His palace was fired, and his magazine blown up; our troops then returned to Cawnpore with their spoil, to prepare for fresh toils, and renewed exertions.

Before following them in this undertaking, it will be necessary to review the position of our troops in Lucknow.

We left them there on the 2nd of June, holding the Residency, Muchee Bawun, and the cantonments. But in the interval between the 2nd and the 30th, the whole of Oudh had risen, and although our troops were not very closely invested, still they were surrounded, and in no little danger. The native troops, those belonging to the 13th Native Infantry especially, six or seven hundred in number, had for some time remained staunch, and by their means they were enabled to maintain an imposing front, and to overawe the rebels from attacking them. Their communication by means of cossids or native messengers was still open, and it was through Sir Henry Lawrence, that the disastrous events at Cawnpore were first made known to the Government. On the 14th of June Sir Henry received a message from General Wheeler, asking for aid: it pained his noble heart to be compelled to refuse, but he could not spare one company without endangering the lives of those for whom he was responsible; but he sent off a message at once to Calcutta, pointing out in the strongest terms the perilous hazard to which Wheeler was exposed.

His own position was full of danger. Although able himself to despatch messages, none were received by him. On the 24th June, he wrote to Colonel Neill, then commanding at Allahabad, that he had received no intelligence from any quarter for twenty days, and that from every side the mutineers were threatening him. Nearer and nearer did they advance; the provisions of our garrison were gradually failing them. Still Sir Henry Lawrence and most of the officers were of opinion that it would be the wiser plan to endeavour to hold their own position, and to procure provisions by sorties, than to risk the safety of the entire force by an attack upon the enemy's positions. But one or two so very strongly held an opposite view, believing that our inaction would only increase the number of our enemies, and that we had only to appear to be victorious, that Sir Henry gave in, and towards the end of June, resolved to take the first favourable opportunity of making a dash at the enemy.

On the 29th June, information was received, that a large body of the enemy, some 6000 in number, preceded by an advanced guard of about 1,000 men was advancing steadily from Fyzabad, in the direction of the canal, and that the smaller party would arrive the following morning. It was at once determined to take hold of this opportunity and to destroy that advanced body. Accordingly at daybreak on the 30th, a party consisting of three companies of H.M. 32nd, thirty volunteer cavalry, eleven guns, including an 8-inch howitzer, manned by native artillerymen, and 120 sowars, went forth from the cantonment; they marched about six miles to a place called Chinbut, when, instead of only 1000 men, they found the entire insurgent army in position behind a village, in which they had fixed a battery of heavy guns. From these, on the approach of our men, they opened a very heavy fire. Our artillery, however, reserving its fire till well within range, replied with such effect, that that of the enemy was silenced, and their centre was forced back. The victory was ours, when at this critical moment our artillerymen of the Oudh battery overturned the guns into the ditches and abandoned them, thus totally exposing our flanks. On these the enemy's horse at once made a dash, and it required all the coolness and intrepidity of our men to effect their retreat to the Residency. Our loss was very great: of the three companies of the 32nd, and the European artillery, 130 were left on the field; we lost besides three light guns and one 8-inch howitzer; we forfeited our prestige, and, what was of even greater importance, Sir Henry Lawrence received a severe wound.

The rebels followed up their success with extraordinary pertinacity. Before 12 o'clock that day, round shot and shell were flying into the Residency, and Sir Henry Lawrence felt that his position was ten times as bad as before the attack. He wrote to General Neill that day, that unless relieved within fifteen or twenty days, he would scarcely be able to hold his ground.

It became also necessary, in consequence of the defection of the natives, and of our loss in Europeans, to contract the position. The cantonments were abandoned on the 1st, and on the 2nd, as much ammunition and supplies as could be taken away having been moved out of it, the Muchee Bawun was blown up, and the besieged were all concentrated in the Residency. On the 2nd and 3rd, by these movements, by the accumulation of one month's supplies, and by the proved ability to repulse all the attacks of the enemy, the spirit of our men revived, and they were reported as being hearty and confident.

On the following day (the 4th), Sir Henry Lawrence was killed by the bursting of a shell in the room in which he lay wounded.*

In him India lost one of the worthiest of her adopted sons. An honest and able administrator, an artillery officer of marked ability in his profession, a good Christian in whatever situation he had been placed, he had been able to advance at the same time the interests of his country and of his God. Unlike the Government of which he was the agent, in his eyes those duties were not antagonistic. The consequence was, that he, sooner than any man, gained the respect and admiration of those amongst whom he was placed, and he was thereby rendered able to perform actions, which in men inferior in capacity, and less reliant on their conviction of right, would have been deemed hazardous and imprudent. But not to great things alone had his attention been turned: his was a mind active to ferret out suffering, in order that he might relieve it. Impressed, after the Sutlej campaign, with the unhappy condition of the children and orphans of the soldiers who had been struggling for their country, he established, in 1846, the Lawrence

* He was struck on the 2nd, and died on the 4th.

Asylum, a noble institution, in which a Christian education, and, if possible, employment, is provided for the wards. But in every department of life his active benevolence was conspicuous. He was in fact a man, great in the world's estimate of greatness and good, if sincerity of belief, abnegation of self, and untiring devotion to duty, constitute goodness.

Almost immediately before the Chief Commissionership of Oudh had been offered to him, his medical adviser had recommended his return to England, assuring him that his life would not be worth two years' purchase if he remained in India. But the terms in which the virtual government of Lucknow were offered forbad him to think of life. He was a man selected in a crisis: what was life to him, except as his existence might benefit others? He at once accepted the position, and by so doing saved the lives of our countrymen at Lucknow, by at least deferring the catastrophe.

He died on the 4th July: not till the 21st September did the Government of India notice his demise, and then only because the merchants and public of Calcutta threatened to hold a public meeting to do honour to his memory. The press, gagged as it was, had spoken out on his behalf, but,—he was a military man—his measures, so far as he could regulate them, had been eminently successful—his administration had formed a marked contrast to the administration of India and the north-west provinces. The Government could afford to praise Mr. Colvin: no amount of encomium from Lord Canning could elevate Sir Henry Lawrence in the public estimation!

Hence, probably, the more than ten weeks' silence!

On Sir Henry's decease, the direction of affairs was assumed by Major Banks, an officer of very great ability. From the 4th to the 20th July, the siege assumed as it were a chronic form: the enemy daily firing, but doing little damage, our garrison remaining closely packed within the walls, officers and men alike working at the defences with untiring industry. These were of the meanest description; but such was the innate dread of the European face to face, that the enemy seldom ventured on a real attack.

But on the 20th July they were more bold. They had probably heard of the state of affairs at Cawnpore, and were resolved at one effort to exterminate the Lucknow garrison also. They came on in swarms, pounding with their heavy guns; their fire of musketry was incessant; their numbers were actually countless. They had every advantage; yet, in spite of their numbers, their perseverance, their showers of shot and shell, our countrymen never yielded an inch, but compelled their assailants, before the shades of evening had fallen, to desist from the attack.

This happened on the 20th July. On that date Havelock was crossing the Ganges to relieve them: it is time we should return to him.

Having demolished Bithoor, and having been joined by all the reinforcements he could expect, Havelock made preparations for crossing his little army into Oudh. Fortunately the means were at hand. The little steamer "Burhampooter," which left Allahabad on the 30th

July, having on board Lieutenant Spurgin, and a hundred Fusiliers, armed with Enfield rifles, and two guns, had arrived, after effecting capital service on the way. At one spot a little above Allahabad, guns had opened out on her from the bank. Lieutenant Spurgin at once went on shore with a detachment, charged the gun, put the enemy to flight, and captured it. The range of the Enfield rifles had effectually cleared both banks of the many small parties who were lying in wait there in hopes of a repetition of the tragedy of Cawnpore or Futtehgurh. The steamer managed to reach Cawnpore about the same time as Havelock's column, her instructions having been to co-operate with it as far as possible, and on no account to steam on in advance.

On the 21st July Havelock commenced crossing his artillery, the infantry following on the succeeding days. On the 25th, the whole force, amounting to about 1500 men, were united on the left bank, holding the only road to Lucknow, thence fifty miles distant. All the sick and wounded were left at Cawnpore, under General Neill, who, with three hundred men at his disposal, had received directions to maintain that station, and to restore order in the district. How well he executed both these commissions will be recorded a little further on.

Havelock crossed over on the 25th, and advanced that day to Nungurwar, a little village five miles on the Lucknow road. Here he halted, in order to complete his arrangements for the carriage of his ammunition and supplies. The men were without tents; the entire country was under water, and along the hard road alone could any advance be made with rapidity. This was a very great disadvantage to an attacking force, as the villages were all built upon the road, which, being straight without any windings, could be entirely commanded by the guns placed in them. The state of the country, therefore, compelled every attack to be made in the face of a heavy fire, without any possibility of avoiding it by a flank movement.

On the 29th July, every arrangement having been completed, Havelock set out at five o'clock in the morning. He had not proceeded five miles before the advanced pickets of the enemy warned him that he was approaching their strong position. He at one deployed his infantry, halted them in a clump of trees, and ordered them to lie down. The Fusiliers and Highlanders in skirmishing order, with two guns aligned with them, he moved to the front. He found the enemy occupying a very strong position in the village or town of Oonao, stretching for about a mile along his front, and terminating on either side in an impassable swamp. In advance of it was a succession of small gardens and walled enclosures, filled with the enemy's skirmishers; the town itself was intersected by a road, at a distance of about a quarter of a mile from its extreme right. This road was commanded by the loopholed houses on either side of it, whilst batteries were so placed as to be able to pour a concentrated fire on any troops advancing against the town. In addition to this, our preparations had scarcely been completed, when another body, the remnants of the cavalry of Nana Sahib, were observed advancing on our left rear, thus threatening our communications. They were commanded by Jussa Singh, the villain who had entrapped the fugitives from Futtehgurh.

Nothing daunted by the strength of the enemy's position, Havelock, after a brief reconnaissance, gave the order to advance. It was obeyed with alacrity, the artillery, as usual, reserving its fire till well within range: they then opened, and made such good practice that that of the enemy was speedily silenced. Still, however, they kept up a very galling musketry fire from the walled enclosures and loopholed houses guarding the approaches to the road. Havelock therefore ordered the 64th to drive them out of these outworks. They rushed forward at once; but one of their number, whose name deserves to be recorded, Private Cavenagh, a man of great personal strength, dashed in front of the line, cleared the wall with a bound, and found himself face to face with at least a dozen sword armed Mahomedans. He killed one or two of them; but before his comrades could join him, he had been overpowered, and literally hacked to pieces. His death was speedily avenged; the 64th on one side, the Madras Fusiliers and Highlanders on the other, were quickly amongst them. Lieutenant Bogle of the latter corps attacked a house filled with armed fanatics; and though wounded severely in the attempt to penetrate it, his object was attained. The rebels were either bayoneted, or driven helter-skelter through the town, and their strong position was gained.

But though the town was gained, the enemy had not yet given up all hope of victory. As our troops debouched from the narrow road on to the plain beyond, the rebel cavalry, which were in swarms, made as if they would attack them; but they wanted the pluck to charge the thin red line that at once formed up to receive them. Their infantry, however, had taken up a new position in the open, and were still threatening us. Thereupon Havelock, collecting his men, advanced upon them at once in echellon of batteries and detachments from the right. They scarcely waited the attack, but at the first charge made off, leaving all their guns in our possession. Our loss in this engagement was eighty-eight in killed and wounded: theirs was necessarily more severe.

It was now half-past eleven o'clock, and there was a burning sun overhead. The general, therefore, halted to allow the men to take their breakfast and a little rest. At two, P.M., the advance was again sounded, and our men, refreshed, but suffering fearfully from the intense heat and the burning sun, moved on: they passed at about two miles the little river Lôn without opposition. Four miles beyond they came to a large gheet, or pond, the water of which, owing to the general inundation, was running like a river: on the opposite side of this, in the town of Bessaruthgung, the enemy, strongly entrenched, were awaiting our arrival. Bessaruthgung is a walled town, situated in an open country; not a tree was there anywhere to afford shelter for our skirmishers: it is surrounded by a wet ditch, and in front of it the gheel referred to; in rear of it is a still larger piece of water, having all the appearance of a lake at this season, crossed by a narrow causeway and bridge. It is flanked on either side by a swamp. The road approaching to it was commanded by four pieces of cannon, mounted on a round tower, by which the gateway was supported. Havelock having reconnoitred, thought that it would be possible to cut off the enemy from the causeway in rear, whilst he attacked them in front. The 64th he detached on this duty: whilst they waded up to their hips in the swamp on the right of the town, he advanced with the main body, the guns in front, interlined with skirmishers, direct against the town. The enemy's fire was heavy, but their guns had too high an elevation, and did little damage: ours, on the contrary, played with great effect on the gateway. Under their cover the Fusiliers and Highlanders steadily gained ground. When within charging distance they rushed forward with the bayonet. There was a sharp but short struggle at the earth-works, the enemy fighting with great determination; but no sooner were these gained — Lieutenant Dangerfield, of the Fusiliers, showing his men the way over — than the town was in our possession, the enemy retreating by the causeway to the village on the other side of the lake, from which they kept up an unintermitting fire all night.

It was six o'clock before even the town was gained, and our troops were completely knocked up. All had behaved nobly: Colonel Tytler, scarcely able to sit his horse from sickness, had given to the General "glorious support." Officers and privates had vied together in the terrible struggle. But if they had done well they had also suffered severely. Numbers of them had been struck down by the terrible sun; others, from the damp, the exposure, the want of dry clothes, had fallen victims to cholera and dysentery: in two days, from these causes and the fire of the enemy, the effective strength of the force had been reduced to 1200 men. The General found, indeed, that from these combined influences he was losing at the rate of fifty men per diem. He could leave no men behind to keep open communication with Cawnpore; all the wounded must accompany him. There were still thirty-six miles between him and Lucknow. As the enemy fell back they approached their resources, as we advanced ours became fewer and less available.

These considerations probably induced General Havelock to retire for the present to Cawnpore, with the intention, not of abandoning our garrison at Lucknow, but of making a new advance after having deposited his sick and wounded in a place of safety.

On the following morning the troops were allowed to rest. At noon all of them were moved into the town of Bessaruthgung, and orders were issued to prepare for a move at two o'clock, P.M. Great was the surprise of the men when they ascertained that this move was to be in retreat; that they were to abandon the ground they had gained after so much hard fighting: it dispirited them. But as they came to reason on the subject, they admitted the prudence of their General. The force retired that night to Oonao, and on the following morning (31st July) to Mungurwa. From this point Havelock detached his sick and wounded into Cawnpore (five miles distant), detailed to General Neill the cause of his retirement, and begged that officer to send on all the reinforcements that he could spare.

Meanwhile Neill had been engaged in the work of restoring order at Cawnpore. His first object was to render his own position secure. To this end he selected a high piece of ground, on the river bank, commanding every approach to it, and made an entrenched camp. He then authorised a levy of sweeper police *, and issued a proclamation, that if within seven days from that time goods, proved to have been the property of our murdered countrymen, were found in the possession of any native, he would be liable to be hanged; at the same time a rigid search was instituted throughout the city, the bazaar, and the neighbouring villages, and an immense quantity of plunder was recovered. Every day, too, rebel Sepoys and others were brought in; were it proved that they had taken a part against our countrymen, they were taken to the charnel house, and compelled with their own hands to wipe up a portion of the blood of our murdered ladies. This operation was in itself sufficient to deprive them of their caste, and they went to the performance of it with more abhorrence than to the gallows. It may appear incredible, but it is a fact, that the high civilians, amongst them a secretary to Government, in Calcutta, disapproved of this proceeding, pronouncing it unchristian, inasmuch as it deprived the victims, in their last hour, of all hope of heaven; as if those blood-stained scoundrels, who had lived all their lives without honour and without a conscience, whose theory of an after-death state consisted in a belief in transmigration of souls, possessed any real sense of religion! If they had had any, the contemplation of their own deeds would have been more harrowing than the performance of an act, the degradation of which, in their eyes, consisted in their being seen to perform it; but as they had none, it were surely far better that their punishment should be aggravated, and that they should leave this world with the conviction that their vile souls were about to migrate into the bodies of cats and monkeys!

So at least thought Neill. He was not to be disturbed by the scruples of men† who were ever the most violent antagonists of their own religion, and, in spite of their remonstrances, the wiping up the blood and the hanging went on without interruption. Amongst those who underwent this disgrace and this penalty was an old subadar of the 1st Native Infantry, who had been most fierce in his animosity against our countrywomen. Had he known that in his last moments he possessed the sympathy of our Members of Council and Secretaries, his end might have been more dignified than it was!

By these and similar energetic measures order was soon restored in Cawnpore; the defences also progressed rapidly, and confidence in the stability of our rule began once more to prevail amongst the well-inclined natives.

Neill received Havelock's message on the 1st August; he at once took charge of the sick and wounded, and sent on to him every available man he had, trusting to his own *prestige* and the convales-

---

* Men of the lowest caste.
† The members of the Government of India who oppose Christian education and support Juggernath!

cents in hospital to keep his entrenchment. In this he acted a noble part,—a nobler never was performed. Havelock had superseded him, but he risked his own safety to ensure the success of Havelock's onward movement.

This latter General, having got rid of his non-effective men, and having received a small reinforcement, which brought up his force to about fourteen hundred men, again prepared for offensive operations.

On the 4th of August, having completed his arrangements, he sent his cavalry to reconnoitre. Oonao was found evacuated, but as they neared Bessaruthgung it became evident that it was there that the enemy had resolved to make a stand. They had apparently taken up a very strong position in rear of the town, in a row of smaller hamlets abutting on the lake beyond it. Being fired upon on their approach, our men retired to Oonao, and bivouacked for the night; they were there joined by the main column. Next morning (the 5th), at dawn of day, our troops marched. There were but six miles between them and the enemy, and the ground had been trodden over before. As they came near, Havelock went forward with the cavalry to reconnoitre their position. It was very strong, and Havelock, notwithstanding the difficulties of the ground, resolved to attempt to turn it. With this view, sending up the cavalry to the front, to within about seven hundred yards of their position, to occupy their attention, he ordered the light guns and a portion of the infantry to make a flank movement to the right. This manœuvre succeeded; the enemy were completely taken by surprise, and after a brisk cannonading, in which our shells did fearful execution amongst them, they evacuated their first position, and fell back upon a second on the other side of the lake.

Here it was impossible to turn them : the only practicable road was a kind of causeway and bridge across the lake. Our men, pushing over this, found the enemy in great force, occupying a second line of villages. From these a heavy fire at once opened upon our advance, but their guns being badly laid, the shot went prinicpally over the heads of our men : these dashed on unhesitatingly, and drove the enemy from village to village, until they fled into the plain beyond. Here they could no longer be followed up: their horse artillery, and their swarms of cavalry, effectively protected their retreat; our men too were knocked up, and it was necessary to spare them as much as possible.

That evening cholera again made its appearance amongst our men : this circumstance, our losses, and the strong position taken up by the enemy, again induced Havelock to retreat. The next morning, accordingly, he once more retired upon Mungurwa.

Here he lay recruiting his men for four or five days; but resolving not yet to give up Lucknow, he again, on the morning of the 11th, moved them in that direction. His intentions he had kept to himself, and no one in the force knew whither they were going, or how long they were to be absent. The force was by this time reduced to about a thousand men, but the same daring spirit still animated all, and they were relieved rather than dispirited, when the order to advance was given. They moved out that morning in the old order, the volunteer cavalry in advance, the artillery in the centre, the main body of the infantry supporting it. On approaching Oonao, they came across the enemy's advanced picket. About three miles beyond, their new position came in view, stretching about five miles, with strong batteries of guns at intervals; and their centre so well masked by walls, gardens, and entrenchments, as to be almost invisible. In front was their cavalry in skirmishing order. It was not the object of the General to provoke an engagement that day; he accordingly gave orders to retire slowly on Oonao. This operation was performed in perfect order, without any molestation from the enemy. It was dusk when our force reached that place; no supplies were ready for them, and they went dinnerless to bed on the wet ground. In the middle of the night a heavy shower came on, which did not tend to their comfort. Nevertheless at dawn of day they rose uncomplaining, rendered perhaps even more eager, from their hunger, to have a dash at the enemy. In anticipation of meeting him at the same spot where they had seen him on the previous evening, they marched at sunrise. Soon they came upon him; his line drawn up in the manner previously described, his guns well sheltered, his cavalry on the flanks: in front of him a broad open plain, across which our infantry must advance unsheltered, and with but a handful of cavalry to protect their flanks. Their line, as I have said, stretched out for about five miles; ours, on deploying, did not extend half a mile: there could not have been less than 20,000 of them in the field. Havelock must then have felt, if he had not been sensible before, that, although he might beat these men, he could never, with his present force, hope to reach Lucknow. In their relative positions, and with their relative forces, there was but one mode of proceeding: manœuvring was out of the question; he must beat them by the exhibition of sheer British pluck, or not at all. No one knew this better than the General: his position, indeed, was something similar to that of Sir Charles Napier at Meeanee, and he adopted similar tactics.

Covered by artillery and skirmishers, our troops advanced in echellon of battalions from the right. As they came within range the enemy unmasked his batteries and poured in a deadly fire; round shot, shell, canister, grape, and shrapnel flew around, about, and amongst our men; fortunately their guns were levelled too high, and the round shot principally went over the heads of our advancing array: still the fire was fearful; it did not, however, for an instant check our men; on they went covered by the guns, till at length these latter had obtained a sufficiently advanced position to get a flanking fire on the enemy's line: this appeared to paralyse them, and at the same moment the Highlanders, who were on the extreme right, making a dashing charge, carried the enemy's left battery of two guns. This completed their panic, they at once turned and fled, and our guns and their own captured batteries turning on them completed their confusion. On the left we had been equally successful. There the enemy's cavalry had attempted to turn our flank; but the

Madras Fusiliers nobly repulsed them: they fled with the remainder of the line.

The victory was gained; but it was one of those victories which must have called to the General's mind the despairing exclamation of Pyrrhus. He had lost one hundred and forty men out of a thousand, and had not advanced ten miles on his road to Lucknow. There was but one course to pursue,—to abandon all thought of reaching that place for the present, and to fall back upon Cawnpore. If there had been wanting any further argument to persuade him to this measure, he had it in the intelligence which reached him about this time, that the Nana Sahib had crossed in great force, and was threatening that station.

His mind was made up. But he held possession of the field of battle; rested on it for two hours, then taking with him the two guns, trophies of the victory, slowly retired on Mungurwa. The following morning, the 13th August, he recrossed the Ganges, and rejoined General Neill at Cawnpore.

He found this officer threatened on all sides: on his right, the Nana Sahib had re-occupied Bithoor in great strength, pushing out his advanced pickets towards the station; on his left, and occupying the plain of Subada, was another detachment of rebels threatening the station. Until the arrival of Havelock, Neill had been unable to leave his entrenched position to attack one party, without leaving that position exposed to the other. However, he was now able to act otherwise.

Havelock arrived on the evening of the 13th of August. The 14th was devoted to rest; on the 15th Neill moved out and attacked the enemy posted near the ground on which the battle of Cawnpore was fought, about six miles from his camp. They could not stand before him; they did not even attempt more than a nominal resistance, and fled almost at the first discharge. The mere fact of Neill going to attack him had the most beneficial effect, and it enabled Havelock to concentrate all his forces for a final attack upon Bithoor the day following. This was the more necessary, as the cavalry pickets of the enemy had shown of late more than usual boldness, and had advanced even into the suburbs of Cawnpore itself.

On the succeeding day (the 16th) Havelock accordingly resolved to beat up the enemy's quarters at Bithoor. Leaving a small detachment in the entrenched camp, he marched at daybreak with the remainder, about sixteen hundred in number. About mid-day they came upon the enemy, drawn up in three lines. The first line consisted of an entrenched and all but completely masked battery in the heart of a dense field of sugar-cane,—the cane rising high above the heads of the men, — defended with very thick mud ramparts, and flanked on both sides by entrenched quadrangles filled with Sepoys, and sheltered likewise by plantations of sugar-cane. The two villages formed as it were the supports of this formidable position, being situated at some distance to the rear, one on either flank. The rebel army was arrayed in front of the entrenchments, ready to give us battle; they consisted principally of Sepoys from the 34th (whose disbandment at Barrackpore in May 1857 was thought by the Government to have suppressed the spirit of mutiny), the 42nd, and 28th Regiments, who up to this time had not met us on the field; they were perhaps on that account the more confident.

On observing the enemy's position, and their infantry drawn up in front of it, Havelock brought his guns to the front, and opened upon them; but it soon appeared that this was only a part of their plan to draw us on, for no sooner had our guns opened, than the enemy retreated into their defences, and their guns at the same moment poured in a tremendous shower of shot and shell on our advancing line. During the twenty minutes that this was kept up our men lay down, replying with their rifles, our artillery also blazing at them. But at the end of that time, finding that our guns made little impression, and did not even silence their fire, although within six hundred yards of their position, Havelock resolved to have resort to the bayonet. A simultaneous advance was made in skirmishing order on the entrenched quadrangles before alluded to. These were quickly cleared, the Sepoys retreating to the two villages in rear: whilst the Madras Fusiliers went in pursuit of these, the 78th Highlanders advanced on the battery, alternately lying down and moving on, as it vomited forth its fierce discharges of grape and canister. The rebels, confident in their position, awaited the approach of our men; but no sooner had the foremost of them cleared the parapet, than the Sepoys' hearts failed them, and they fled in confusion. Their position was so strong, and our men were so exhausted by the heat of the sun and by their own exertions, that a determined stand here might have changed the fortunes of the day. No fact, however, has been more clearly established in the course of this insurrection, than that Asiatics, whatever may be their strength, cannot resist the charge of the smallest number of Englishmen: there is something in the sight of Europeans advancing at a run, with stern visage, bayonets fixed, determination marked in every movement of the body, which appals them; they cannot stand it, they never have stood it yet.

Meanwhile the Fusiliers, pursuing the enemy out of the entrenched quadrangles, came down upon the loopholed villages in the rear. Not an instant did they pause, but, rushing into them, gained them with scarce a struggle,—the enemy being quite unable to make head against their impetuosity. In rear of these villages was a little bridge leading to the town: across this the Fusiliers, now joined by the whole force, drove them, a few only endeavouring to make a fruitless stand; these were bayoneted; the remainder fled, followed by our men right through the town. Further it was impossible to pursue them: our troops, exposed to a hot sun and undergoing fearful exertions, were completely knocked up: they bivouacked on the ground they had won, and the next morning returned to Cawnpore, to take up a commanding position on the plain of Subada, close to the spot on which our heroic garrison had so long defended themselves.

With this action terminated Havelock's first grand campaign for the relief of Lucknow. Strictly speaking, perhaps, it was concluded on the day on which he recrossed the Ganges. In this great effort he had fought five pitched battles against an enemy vastly superior in numbers; he had been compelled to leave open his communications—

to carry with him sick and wounded—to dare the rays of a scorching, often a deadly sun—to march without tents—to carry with him every article of supply. With these difficulties to encounter, he had advanced three times, and three times had struck so great a terror into the enemy that his retreat had been invariably unmolested. He found, indeed, that he could gain victories, but that for want of cavalry he could not follow them up; that the enormous numbers of the enemy enabled them to recruit, and more than recruit, their losses as he advanced; that another large body, under the Nana Sahib and Jussa Singh, was always ready to interpose between him and the Ganges. He fought, in fact, more conscious that victory would secure his retreat, than facilitate an advance, which, with his numbers, was impossible.

His countrymen in England have paid homage to his deeds—feeling a national pride in one who fought so nobly, so earnestly, with such an end in view; but the Government of India—his masters—what did they do? Testing everything, as was their wont, by the result, they only saw that Havelock had failed to relieve Lucknow. Careless of the sun, more deadly than the foe,—of the small numbers,—of the want of cavalry,—they superseded him. And the noble-hearted Havelock had scarcely recrossed the Ganges, conscious that he had deserved the gratitude of his countrymen, when he learned that reinforcements were on their way up, but that they were under the command of Major-General Sir James Outram, his superior officer.

It is nothing to the purpose to state that Sir James did not subsequently assume the command: it was the intention of the Government that he should take it; they did not count on his abnegation of his own rights.

CHAPTER VIII.

CALCUTTA TO 5TH AUGUST.—DINAPORE, PATNA, ARRAH, GYA.—THE CLEMENCY ACT.— MR. J. P. GRANT.

REPORTS of the terrible fate of our soldiers and countrywomen at Cawnpore had reached Calcutta early in July, but it was not until the 17th of that month, when Havelock telegraphed down the account alike of his victory and of their murder, that all hope of their surviving disappeared. Then, indeed, the agony of suspense was succeeded by the deadening height of despair. But as that feeling gradually wore off, there sprang up in its place a desire for retaliation, an unrepressed eagerness for vengeance on those who, to the crimes of revolt and treachery, had added those of murder and torture. Such was the effect, alike on those whose relatives had been massacred, and on the great body of the European public. Every heart panted for news from Havelock, sympathising most deeply with his noble efforts. General Neill became even a greater favourite. His stern measures for the restoration of order at Cawnpore, his contempt for the instructions he received to be merciful to these villains, stamped him at once as the man for the occasion. His praise was in every one's mouth, whilst in all ranks of society the measures of the Government earned only contempt.

And truly did the Government of India deserve it: all their measures had been too late! They had been over-confident and vainglorious when the horizon appeared likely to clear, depressed and suppliant when the clouds seemed to gather around them. So it was, as we have seen, in the matter of the Calcutta Volunteers, and with reference to the raising of a corps of Yeomanry Cavalry; so it was, to an extent far greater and infinitely more culpable, as we shall now see exemplified, in their dealings with the Court of Katinandoo. That city is the capital of the vast district of Nepâl, a mountainous country lying due north of Bengal Proper. Its people are bold, hardy, and resolute; possessing, like all mountaineers, a supreme hatred and contempt for the inhabitants of the plains, over whom they had often asserted their superiority. The entire power of the government of Nepâl was in the hands of Jung Buhadoor, a man the very type of the better class of his countrymen, and endowed in a supreme degree with vigour, energy, and power of will. His visit to Europe, some eight years ago, had impressed upon his mind a deep conviction of the power and resources of England, and had made him sensible that it were better policy for him to retain the friendship and alliance of her people. In the intrigues which brought about the revolt of the native army he had no share. Under no circumstances could that revolt advance his interest or the interests of Nepâl, and he never, from the moment of the outbreak, gave the smallest encouragement to its abettors.

In the month of May, as we have seen, the Government of India felt very confident of the speedy repression of the insurrection. Even in the beginning of June that confidence was unabated; they were expecting by every post to hear of the fall of Delhi; and the fall of Delhi, they felt sure, would tranquillise the country. But there was one man, an Asiatic, who knew differently, who was aware that our troubles were only commencing, and that unless the insurgents should commit the grossest errors (which happily for us they did commit), there would be an end temporarily to our rule in India. Certain of the accuracy of his information, and well aware that nothing but promptitude could save us, he communicated his opinion, and made offers of assistance in men to Major Ramsay, our political agent at the Court of Katinandoo. This officer, like all the Ramsays, a very able man, entered at once into the views of Jung Buhadoor and the Nepâl Durbar, and without any delay transmitted an abstract of the Prime Minister's opinions, together with his offers of assistance, to the Supreme Government in Calcutta.

Unfortunately, the letter containing this offer arrived at a time when the political barometer pointed to "fair." Not only, therefore, was the proposal refused, but refused in terms which, so far as our political agent was concerned, were most uncourteous.

But the ink with which this "wigging" had been penned was scarcely dry, when tidings from Oudh, Azimgurh, Benares, Allahabad, Cawnpore, Jhansie, Rohilcund, came pouring in, each brimful of disaster. The Government at once perceived that Jung Buhadoor had not been so ill-judging, nor Major Ramsay so hasty, as they had supposed ; they, therefore, after an interval of ten days, signified their willingness to accept the six Nepâl regiments, which Jung Buhadoor had placed at their disposal.*

Jung Buhadoor, still anxious to show his devotion to the British cause, at once sent a favourable reply, and ordered his six regiments to move to Goruckpore, thence to proceed to Lucknow. Had this move been made even at that time, such a diversion would have been created that the relief of Lucknow would have been an easy, or, at all events, a feasible matter; but we were fated to have one more instance of the hap-hazard and hand-to-mouth system on which the Government of India is conducted. By the time that the Goorkhas were well on their way to Goruckpore, another change in the barometer had taken place. Benares, Allahabad, Azimgurh had been quieted, Cawnpore had been re-occupied, and Havelock was preparing to advance upon Lucknow. His success was looked upon as certain. Where then was the necessity for employing the Goorkhas? The order was transmitted to them on no account to advance beyond Goruckpore. Again, however, our necessities compelled us to apply for them: they were sent on, and have since performed excellent service, showing how they might have assisted us in the earlier stages of the revolt. They now, supported by a handful of Europeans, form our only column of defence for the Benares district, against a force of 15,000 rebels who are threatening it.

The foregoing is a sample of the foreign policy of Lord Canning ; his domestic measures were scarcely more happy.

Patna, the chief city in the province of Behar, contains upwards of 300,000 inhabitants, a large proportion of whom are Mahomedans. It is situate on the right bank of the river Ganges, 380 miles northwest of Calcutta, and ten miles east of the military station of Dinapore.

The small civil stations of Gya, fifty miles to the south, Dinprah, forty miles to the north, and Arrah, thirty-five miles to the west of Patna, are entirely under the control of the Commissioner of that place.

At the time of which I am treating, the Commissioner was Mr. William Tayler, a civilian, very proud of his "order," and a great upholder of their rights and dignities. He was at the same time a gentleman and a scholar, possessing good abilities, an elegant mind,

* It would be by no means an unprofitable occupation to trace the connection of the acceptance of this offer with the Gagging Act. The "Friend of India" was warned for treating of the probability of India becoming Christianised on the 25th June: on the 25th a favourable answer to the application of Government had been received from Jung Buhadoor.

and a large fund of common sense. Thus it happened, that although starting as Commissioner wedded to the time-honoured principle of "India for the Civil Service," he had sense enough to perceive that an adherence to it would swamp the vessel he was piloting—and he threw it over. By so doing, he saved Patna and lost his appointment.

It may be easily imagined that with a rebellion incited, fostered, and kept up by Mahomedans, a city, in which men of that religion formed a preponderating class, must be an object of no ordinary anxiety. From the days of Meer Kassim Ally, Patna had always been a rebellious city. Even so lately as 1846, its Mahomedan nobility had endeavoured to take advantage of our balanced fortunes on the banks of the Sutlej. They had then succeeded in corrupting some of the native officers and Sepoys stationed at Dinapore. What might not be expected now, when our own native troops had spontaneously, apparently, revolted, and when our European troops lay scattered and beleaguered all over the country? And in fact the question which, not private individuals only, but secretaries to Government also, asked themselves, when news of the revolt of the half of India reached them, was this, "Why has not Patna risen?" For weeks and weeks the intelligence was expected. Every letter described the city as being "shaky." The wonder at its long state of quiescence was increased by the contemplation of the military means at the disposal of the Government to coerce it. To ascertain what those means were, we must transport the reader for a moment to Dinapore.

Dinapore lies, as has been stated, ten miles westward of Patna. This station was garrisoned by H. M. 10th Foot, three regiments of Native Infantry, the 7th, 8th, and 40th, one company of European and one of Native Artillery. These regiments had hitherto been "staunch;" that is to say, they had not mutinied; but two of them at least had given intimations which ought to have been sufficient, that the opportunity alone was wanting.

The regiment supposed by their own officers and by the Government to be actually loyal, was the 40th, one of the corps lately returned from Burma: its officers were good officers, and if they believed in their men, it merely proves the falsity of the charge which Mr. Mangles and others have levelled against the officers of the Bengal Army.

The station and the military division of Dinapore were commanded by Major-General Lloyd, an officer who in his day had done excellent service. Only in 1854 he had been selected by the Government of Lord Dalhousie to suppress the Southâl insurrection, and right well had he done it. He was an old man, but he had grown old in the service of his country, and that service had been passed chiefly amongst Sepoys. Take the world at large, and see how few men verging upon seventy would have been fit to control a crisis of this sort—a crisis the more trying to General Lloyd, as he was called upon to forego the experience of forty years, and to doubt those very men who under himself had, in numerous instances, given proofs of their devotion to the Company.

He had indeed no ordinary task. He was in constant communication with the Commissioner of Patna to preserve the order of the district; he had only European troops sufficient to look after the native regiments.

The district which the troops at Dinapore are supposed to command is indeed an enormous one. It extends on the north side to the very foot of the Nepâl Hills, on the east to Berhampore, on the west to Benares, on the south to Hazariebagh and Rampore; on the north alone, at the station of Segowlie, distant about a hundred miles, was a corps of irregular cavalry, a detachment from which had been located at Patna: to that place also, as a measure of security, Captain Rattray's new Sikh levies had been ordered.

It will thus be seen that to maintain the security of the Patna district, the Commissioner had very little effective military aid upon which he could rely: he had to depend entirely upon his own energy and foresight, and the influence which he could bring to bear upon others.

He had been trained, as has been stated, in the school of "India for the Civil Service;" as an adept in the practice of that school, he had earned the applause of Mr. Halliday, on the occasion of the vice-regal visit of the latter to Patna, two years before, and he had been looked upon as a most promising pupil.

He was so indeed, as are many civilians, most excellent men naturally, so long as their eyes are blinded by prejudice, routine, prescription. But this terrible insurrection had scarcely raised her Hydra-like head, before the scales fell from Mr. Tayler's eyes; he felt that the gods he had worshipped were no gods: — he acted at once the part of a true Englishman; he threw away his theories to the winds, and exerted all his endeavours — not to gain applause from Mr. Halliday, but to save Patna!

In this attempt he was ably seconded by Major Holmes, the officer who commanded the Irregular Cavalry Regiment (the 12th), already noted, at Segowlie. Constant intercourse passed between the two, and they had both come to the conclusion that Repression, not Conciliation, was the policy to be pursued in the crisis.

This, unfortunately for Mr. Tayler, was antagonistic to the principle which had been adopted by the leaders of the Civil Service, of whom Mr. Halliday, Lieutenant-Governor of Bengal, Mr. Grant, a Member of Council, and Mr. Beadon, Home Secretary, were the chiefs. They had laid it down as a maxim, that no corps ever mutinied which was properly commanded, and that a civil district had no business to revolt, inasmuch as this was a mere military mutiny. But Mr. Tayler, although he was aware of the existence of this principle, refused to be a *doctrinaire* of this stamp. All Patna wanted but the opportunity to rise: he was face to face with incipient mutiny: like a bold, fearless man, he determined to take the initiative, to arrest the ringleaders, and, by paralysing their plans, to check the revolt in the bud.

The opportunity was not long wanting.

The fact of a conspiracy being on foot had been made clear by the perusal of intercepted letters. At the head of it was the Moulvie Ally Kurem, a man of great wealth, large estates, and corresponding influence. He was indeed the soul of the plot. Mr. Tayler resolved to lose no time,—to arrest him and the other ringleaders at once, and bring them to prompt trial. A party accordingly was sent to seize him, but the Moulvie was well served. Unknown to us he had stationed horses along the road in anticipation of some such catastrophe as that which was impending. He had scouts upon the look-out. No sooner did they inform him that a party, with Mr. Lowis, one of the civil subordinates, at its head, was on its way to his house, than he mounted his elephant, and started in the direction he had previously resolved upon. He was seen and pursued, but no sooner did our men buoy themselves with the hope that they were gaining upon him, than they observed him descend from his elephant, mount a very powerful horse, and gallop off.

He has not since been re-captured.

But although the principal conspirator escaped, the subalterns were not so fortunate. But before referring to their capture, it is necessary to allude to the ebullition on their part which preceded it.

On the evening of the 3rd July, sixty or seventy fanatics, raising the cry of religion, beating drums, unfurling the green flag, and calling out "Ya Allah," rushed to attack the Roman Catholic cathedral, situate in the very heart of the city. No sooner had intelligence of this reached our authorities, than Rattray's Sikhs were ordered down to the spot. Dr. Lyell, the opium assistant, thinking that his presence would overawe the rioters, and being well mounted, rode on in advance. As he approached them, several shots were fired at him, one of which took effect. He fell never to rise again.

The moment was critical. Had it been attempted now to carry out the policy of conciliation, it had been all over with Patna. The sight of blood had roused the evil spirits of the populace; their number was increasing, when at this moment arrived the armed and disciplined Sikhs. The feeling with which the Sikhs regard the Mahomedans is one of intense and bitter hatred; when, therefore, they came upon this crowd of fanatics, howling out pæans in honour of a religion which they detested, their fury was ungovernable; they rushed with a will upon the undisciplined mass, and dispersed them in a moment.

The next morning the city underwent a complete search. Thirty-one ringleaders were apprehended. Amongst these were Pera Ally, an emissary from Lucknow, Shekh Ghuseeta, the Jemadar of Lootf Ally Khan, the richest banker in the town, and Lootf Ally Khan himself.

The three men named above were unfortunately[*] reprieved, with the view of eliciting more information from them. Of the thirty-one who were seized, fourteen were hanged that same afternoon, in company with a man named Waris Ally — the Jemadar of the

---

[*] I say unfortunately, because Mr. Samuells, the successor of Mr. Tayler, released them.

Moulvie Ally Kureem. When taken to the gallows this worthy exclaimed in a loud voice, " If there is any one here who professes to be a friend of the King of Delhi, aid me."

These vigorous measures saved Patna for the moment, but not an hour passed by without a risk of an insurrection, and Mr. Tayler's unceasing vigilance alone enabled him to discover the plotters. By means of a native Christian at Moughyr, a correspondence was brought to light which proved that the flight of the Moulvie Ally Kureem had by no means quelled the spirit of revolt, that the train was laid, and that the conspirators were only waiting for the opportunity to fire it.

By dint, however, of constant arrests, and an unceasing use of hemp, the city was kept quiet: the inhabitants were over-awed. Major Holmes, on the Segowlie frontier, pursued the same policy: the greatest cordiality existed between the Commissioner and himself: they were one on the subject of the only course to be pursued: they followed it, and maintained order in the district as well as in the city.

But these constant arrests, these continual hangings, the credit which they brought to Mr. Tayler from the planters and mercantile community,—even from the fettered press of India,—were all galling to Mr. Halliday. They falsified his maxim that this was a mere revolt of the soldiery. They rendered patent to the world that the largest civil district under his control was surging with revolt. They endangered the stability of the exclusive Civil Service. Mr. Tayler, too, had committed another act of "imprudence," which was not likely to further his interests with his superiors. He had suspended one of his subordinates, Mr. Lowis. Now Mr. Lowis was a son-in-law of Mr. Mangles. Mr. Mangles was Chairman of the Court of Directors, and prime patron of the Government of Bengal. The inference is easy.

Before, however, that Government could recall a man whose energy was at the same time saving Patna and spoiling their crude theories, it was necessary to provide a pretext for so strong a measure. This was not long wanting; it will appear in its proper place in this history.

The disaffection prevailing in Patna, and the threatening attitude of the three native regiments stationed at Dinapore, had not been viewed without alarm by the mercantile community of Calcutta. Their interests were in a great measure bound up in the district of Tirhoot, of which Patna and Dinapore were the two most important stations. As the great indigo-producing portion of Bengal, they were more than any class interested in the maintenance in it of peace and order. Any revolt at this period, before the plant had been cut, and even subsequently during the process of manufacture, would have been fraught with ruin to many of them. The measures of Mr. Tayler therefore met their warmest approval; they saw in him just the man for the occasion. At the same time they were sensible that all his arrangements, his vigilance, and his energy were liable to be rendered nugatory by any *émeute* or disturbance amongst the troops at Dinapore. They had indulged the hope that those regiments, like their brethren at Barrackpore, would have been disarmed — such a step would have put to flight all their fears, and have inspired them with a confidence in the Government which had hitherto been wanting. It was easy of accomplishment. Her Majesty's 10th Regiment was on the spot; one wing of the 37th Foot was on its way up, and the 5th Fusiliers, 800 strong, arrived from the Mauritius on the 5th July.

The subject was early in that month debated in Council: the minutes of that discussion have not yet been published; its result is before the world. That result added another proof to the many that had preceded it, that the Government of Lord Canning was not above half-measures; that it was ready, in order to have a scape-goat, to shift responsibility from its own shoulders. The Supreme Council decided in this important matter, that it would not take upon itself the responsibility of ordering the native regiments at Dinapore to be disarmed; neither would it assume the responsibility of directing that those corps should retain their arms; but, casting the entire responsibility on Major-General Lloyd, it left it optional to him to disarm them or not, as he might think fit.

To cast the sole responsibility of an important measure upon an agent, is to say to him, we have confidence in you; we are ready to abide by what you do; we are ready to support you; we are perplexed and divided; act as you think best. A Government has no right to turn round to the public, after committing their power to their own agent, and that agent has acted, and acted unfortunately, and to say, "This is not our act, it is the act of our agent; we atone for it by turning him out." A Government by throwing all responsibility on an agent, becomes itself responsible for his acts, and must share with him the blame or praise. It is the more necessary that this rule should be applied in the present instance, because the Government was aware of General Lloyd's partiality for the Sepoys, that he could not bring himself to believe that they would mutiny, and that he had already on a previous occasion avoided disarming them when the opportunity presented itself.

This decision of the Government was not published, but it was privately communicated to the members of the mercantile community. It failed to satisfy them: they too, knew the disposition of General Lloyd; they felt satisfied that he had no heart for disarming the Sepoys; they saw their interests, and, with theirs, the interests of the European settlers in India, — a class of men whom the leaders of the Civil Service discouraged in every possible manner,—abandoned, by the cowardice of the Government, to the prejudices of a feeble old man.

There was one course still open to them — to appeal in a body to the Government, and to endeavour, in a personal interview with Lord Canning, to point out to him the course which they humbly deemed both feasible and advisable. They came to this resolution on the 17th of July.

But Lord Canning was a great man in petty things. This

uncalled for opinion of men, who were in no way connected with the Government, appeared to him very like trenching upon his prerogative. He resolved to show them that the will of the Governor-General of India was perfectly independent of the feelings of those who possessed the only real stake in the country.

When therefore, on the 20th July, the deputation reached him, pointed out how their interests were involved in the maintenance of peace and order; how both were threatened by the attitude of the regiments at Dinapore; how disarming them would quiet the public mind and possibly restore confidence; how that the most favourable opportunity now presented itself for carrying out that measure, as the 5th Fusiliers had left by steamer on the 12th and would be off Dinapore on or about the 22nd; how that disembarking from the steamer, disarming in conjunction with the 10th Foot the mutinous regiments, and then re-embarking, would be the work of less than three hours,—Lord Canning replied, "They shall not stop for one hour." He said more, but that was the main point of his speech. He was very curt, and very ceremonious.

This was on the 20th July: if a message had been sent to Dinapore on that day or the following, to comply with the request of the merchants, the calamities which subsequently followed would have been avoided. As it was, and because Lord Canning would not allow the 5th Fusiliers to stop one hour, they were detained three weeks at one of the most critical periods of the revolt. Before tracing out the result of his obstinacy, it may be convenient to notice another characteristic act of the Government of India.

The bearing of the natives of Calcutta, the Mahomedan portion especially, had given no little cause for anxiety: they outnumbered the European population by about twenty to one, and it appeared quite possible that fanaticism, combined with the hope of plunder, might induce them to rise at any moment. It was known, too, that the suburbs were crowded with disbanded and disarmed Sepoys, and some of them had been heard to express their conviction that the rule of the Company was about to close. The means of providing them with weapons were at hand: the bazaars and streets in the outskirts were crowded with armourers and venders of swords and muskets, and it was remarked that they were driving a rattling trade. This circumstance, combined with the insolent demeanour of the Mahomedans, the experiences of Cawnpore and other stations, and the near approach of a Mussulman festival, the celebration of which invariably caused great excitement amongst the votaries of that religion, conjoined to impress upon the European inhabitants the policy of adopting some precautionary measure. The grand jury had, on the occasion of their being sworn in, forwarded an address to Lord Canning, urging the disarming of all natives in Calcutta, and the mercantile community had adopted with alacrity this suggestion, and had petitioned the Governor-General on the subject. But Lord Canning, impressed with the dogma of "imperial legislation," that is, with the necessity of treating the loyal and the rebellious on the same terms, after many delays, caused a project of law to be introduced into the Legislative Council, by which Europeans and natives were to be alike disarmed; thereby rendering it penal for the former to possess without a license (which a native magistrate might refuse) a weapon wherewith to defend himself against the murderous assaults of the latter. This was imperial legislation with a vengeance.

On the 31st July, a few days after the Dinapore mutiny had been known, just one fortnight after the details of the horrible massacre of our countrywomen at Cawnpore had been published, when every post brought accounts of some fresh deed of atrocity, some new instance of the blackest treachery on the part of our Sepoys, occasion was taken to publish a manifesto*, in which the members of the Civil Service, with Lord Canning as their accomplice, laid down their patent scheme for the suppression of mutiny and insurrection.

In this document a free pardon was offered to all mutineers against whom it could not be proved that they had been guilty of any heinous crime against person or property, or that they had aided and abetted in the commission of such crime.

Sepoys who had mutinied without murdering their officers were to be treated with all reasonable leniency.

No deserters from disarmed regiments were to be apprehended, unless with arms in their possession.

Other mutineers against whom it could not be proved that they had murdered their officers, were to be sent for trial to Allahabad.

These were the principal provisions of this celebrated order, which the *Times* has well designated "The clemency of Canning"—an order which will remain a lasting stamp of the manner in which civilians meet mutiny and revolt. To secure its being efficiently worked, a member of the council that framed it, Mr. John Peter Grant, was sent up to Benares, copies of it were transmitted to the Lieutenant-Governor of the North-West Provinces, and to all the Commissioners in the Province of Bengal. At the same time Mr. Tayler, the commissioner of Patna was removed from his appointment, and replaced by a gentleman pledged to maintain the cause of his own exclusive service.

The effect of the document above alluded to, published as it was at a time when Havelock was being driven back by the men to whom it specially bore reference, was to impress them with an idea of our weakness which nothing could eradicate. They saw us, at a time when they were beleaguering our countrymen at Lucknow, suddenly offer them, under very easy conditions, a free pardon. It had all the effect upon them of an offer to sue for peace, it emboldened them to renew their efforts, to push us hard whilst we were in distress, to exert themselves more than ever against us.

It is almost needless to add that when this resolution of the Supreme Government was sent up to the gallant Neill, with an order that it should be enforced at once, he declined paying any attention to it. The district of Cawnpore, he replied, was under martial law, and according to the provisions of that law, and of no other, would

* Resolution of Government of India, No. 1359, 31st July, 1857.

he act. It is currently reported that for this act of disobedience he would, had he survived, have been brought to a court-martial. The government would have found it difficult to assemble fifteen officers who would have convicted him.

Meanwhile, the governmental policy had been yielding its natural fruit at Dinapore. General Lloyd had received the instructions by which the sole responsibility of disarming the Sepoys devolved upon him; but he too bethought him of a half measure: he was permitted to take away the muskets to prevent the Sepoys from rising; the same end, he imagined, might be attained by depriving them of their percussion caps. Accordingly, on the morning of the 25th July, he gave orders for carrying this measure into effect. It may be necessary, before describing the manner in which this was performed, to give a slight sketch of the station.

Dinapore lies, as before stated, ten miles west of Patna, on the right bank of the Ganges. The European troops are cantoned in a large square immediately to the west of the native town; beyond this, and still immediately on the bank of the river, is a smaller square; outside this are a few houses, and further on the native lines; on the other side of the lines was the magazine in which the caps were kept. It will be seen, then, that to bring away the caps from the magazine into the European part of the cantonment, it was necessary to convey them along the front of the lines of the Sepoys. This measure, therefore, like all half measures, was more dangerous than disarming.

However it was tried. On the morning of the 25th the 10th Foot and the Artillery were drawn up in the large square already alluded to, whilst two bullock-carts were sent down to bring away the caps under the charge of an officer; the caps were taken from the magazine, and stowed in the carts, which then set out on their return. As they passed the lines of the 7th Regiment, a great commotion was visible; the Sepoys were parading for guard, but they broke their ranks, and rushed forward, shouting, one of them calling out in a loud voice, "Kill the sahibs! don't let the caps be taken away." But their officers went amongst them, and even forced them to abstain from any further demonstration; the men returned sullenly to their posts, and the carts went on. All was now supposed to be over, the Europeans were dismissed to their lines, and the General, congratulating himself on the success of his manœuvre, went on board one of the steamers, which had that morning arrived, to lunch. It had been previously arranged, that in the event of any disturbance two musket shots in quick succession should be fired by the European guard at the hospital — a large building between the smaller square and the native lines, and commanding a good view of the latter. At half past one, the sound of these shots was heard; instantly the 10th Foot, two companies of the 37th Foot which had arrived the day before, and the Artillery, turned out. It appeared that, previous to going on board the steamer, the General had issued an order that the caps actually in the possession of the Sepoys should be given up. But these latter, when called upon to obey, had fired upon their officers. When the Europeans came within sight of their lines, all was uproar and confusion, but a few shots from the Enfield Rifles of the 30th who were in advance, and a sharp fire opened upon the Sepoys from the roof of the hospital, soon cleared the scene. The Sepoys made off with precipitation, leaving behind them the greater part of their property. The Europeans followed them up to the limits of the cantonments, burning their lines as they advanced. They were then halted ; there was no one to give orders, no general, and no one would take the responsibility. It was a bad business as it was; and, serving under a Government which judged only by the result, no one would run the risk of making it worse.

A few of the Sepoys endeavoured to cross the Ganges in boats, but the steamer at the Ghat opened fire upon them with considerable effect; the main body therefore took their way towards the Soane river in the direction of Arrah. Information was instantly transmitted to the residents of that little station in order that they might be prepared to avoid, or to give a warm reception to their unwelcome visitors.

Arrah is only five and twenty miles west of Dinapore, but it is separated from it by the Soane; and it was hoped that this river, swollen by the rains, would oppose an effectual bar to the passage of the mutineers. But for three days they were left unpursued ; leisure was allowed them to procure boats, and even to cross by the ferry, and they experienced no difficulty in passing over a river which might have been made an insurmountable obstacle. They received assistance too from a quarter on which we had even reckoned for opposition to their movements.

No sooner was it known in the district that the troops had risen at Dinapore than Koour Singh, a large landowner, possessing estates in the neighbourhood of Arrah and all along the banks of the Soane, declared in their favour. He was a known bad character, and was supposed to be in communication with Nana Sahib : at the same time he was permitted unmolested to carry out his schemes. He it was who procured boats for the passage of the mutineers across the Soane, and it was he who advised them to march without delay on Arrah, plunder the treasury, murder the residents, and then, crossing the Ganges at Busat, to make at once for Ghazeepore and Oudh. It was a bold plan, and was very nearly succeeding. The Sepoys mutinied on the 25th, on the 26th they crossed the Soane and were joined by Koour Singh ; on the 27th they arrived at Arrah, let loose the jail-birds, plundered the treasury, and attacked the residents.

But these latter had not been idle in anticipation of the visit which they were now awaiting : they had, under the direction of Mr. Boyle, a civil engineer, fortified a small detached two-storied house, fifty feet square, with a flat roof. In this they had stored supplies of meal, wine, beer, water, biscuit, and sheep. Their only garrison consisted of fifty Sikhs : these, however, were true to the very core. The Europeans numbered only sixteen, but they were well armed, and besides possessed the prestige attaching to their country. They might, had they chose, have abandoned the station to the mutineers ; but they were Englishmen, and resolved rather to defend one corner of it than to submit to so humiliating an alternative.

On the morning of the 27th, the Sepoys, having gutted the station, came down to attack them. They advanced boldly at first in unbroken order ; but being met by a steady, well-directed fire, they changed their tactics, and occupying Mr. Boyle's own house — only sixty yards distant — commenced, from it and from the trees which stood around it, an unintermitting fire. At the same time they offered every possible inducement by bribes and threats to the Sikhs to join them. Their own countrymen, serving in the ranks of the mutineers, were employed as mediators, but without effect. The Sikhs remained staunch: their courage and their fidelity were alike proof, and they showed throughout the siege an unwavering attachment to our interests. On the 28th the rebels brought two small guns to bear upon the besieged: these they fired as fast as they could manufacture some species of projectile: the house in which our countrymen were shut up, was riddled, but they themselves were unhurt. Every evening a Sepoy standing behind a pillar of the house occupied by the enemy, was in the habit of offering terms — in the name, not of Koour Singh, but of the commander of the allied forces, a subadar of the 8th Native Infantry. It is needless to say his "terms" were rejected, and it is satisfactory to know that the worthy at whose instigation they were made — the subadar of the 8th — was subsequently killed. He did not happily fall into the hands of Mr. Grant.

Meanwhile intelligence of the beleaguered state of the Arrah residents had reached Dinapore, and it was resolved to equip forthwith an expedition to relieve them. Accordingly, on the evening of the 26th, 193 men of the 37th Foot started to steam up the Soane, with the intention of landing at the spot where the road to Arrah joins that river. Unfortunately the steamer, running on after the moon had gone down, stuck on a sand-bank. Here she remained for six and thirty hours. Information of the catastrophe having in the meanwhile reached Dinapore, it was resolved to despatch another steamer with a detachment of the 10th Foot, to take on the troop-boat attached to the first steamer, and to carry out the original resolution. This they did. Starting with 150 of the 10th Foot, and seventy Sikhs, she came up to where the first steamer was lying, detached her troop-boat with the 37th on board, and then steamed up to the appointed spot. Here she arrived at 4 P. M. on the afternoon of the 29th, and disembarked her force. This amounted to 410 men, under the command of Captain Dunbar of Her Majesty's 10th Foot.

The point at which they disembarked was but twelve miles from Arrah, and about four miles from it was an unfordable nullah, traversable only by boats. The detachment commenced its march immediately after landing, led by a native guide, who informed them that Arrah had been evacuated by the rebels. On arriving at the nullah, Captain Dunbar was strongly advised to bivouack for the night ; but finding boats on the right bank ready for crossing, and being strongly urged by the guide, he persisted in pushing on. He accordingly crossed, and marched in military order, an advanced guard in front feeling the way. At last the guide announced that Arrah was gained:

there was no sign of life anywhere: all was still. Captain Dunbar thereupon called in the advanced guard, and moved on in column of march. He had scarcely proceeded ten paces before a volley was fired into the party from a clump of trees close in their front, whilst from both flanks almost simultaneously there commenced a leaden shower. Captain Dunbar and several of the officers were shot dead at the first discharge; the enemy was invisible: our men appeared to be surrounded; their commanding officer had been shot. Great confusion ensued; the men got separated from one another, and feared to fire on their comrades. After an interval of about a quarter of an hour, order to a certain extent was restored, and the men retired to a small enclosure which afforded them some cover, and enabled them to keep together. The enemy, however, fired upon them all night. As morning dawned, they found themselves much reduced in numbers, the men dispirited, and altogether unable to resume the offensive. They therefore turned their faces towards the Soane. They had, however, scarcely moved out of their cover before they were followed by the enemy, who, advancing in skirmishing order to the number of three thousand, and keeping at a very respectful distance, poured in an unceasing fire. In vain did our men endeavour to keep them off with musketry: in vain did they attempt to drive them back by a successful charge: as they advanced the enemy fled: as they retired, again the foe returned to the pursuit. To be wounded was a worse fate than death; for it was impossible to carry away those in that condition, and a man with a broken limb was reserved for that most dreaded of all fates—the tender mercies of the Sepoys. At last the nullah was reached, and to the delight of the survivors the boats were all on the left bank. Two of them were filled and shoved off; but the nullah had gone down a little in the night, and all the other boats had become fixed in the mud. Meanwhile the enemy were advancing: from the front and on both flanks they poured in their fire. The number of our men was few: any fate was better than falling into the hands of the Sepoys: there was no longer any hesitation: as if by mutual consent, they stripped off their clothes, and plunged into the stream, and swam for dear life.

Many were drowned, many were shot, but more reached the right bank: their difficulties were then over: the steamer was gained in safety, and with heavy hearts they paddled back to Dinapore. Such was the issue of the first attempt to relieve Arrah. Out of the party fifty only were untouched: out of fifteen officers, three only unwounded. The truth is, the fault lay with the commanding officer: our men fell into an ambuscade. Captain Dunbar's first fault was in not halting on the right bank of the nullah till daylight; his second, in trusting to the assurances of a native guide, in a case in which natives were concerned; his third, in not marching in military order. Any one of these mistakes would have been sufficient to cause a check; the three combined occasioned a disaster.

The attempt to relieve our countrymen at Arrah from Dinapore only increased their perils, for its ill-success flushed the Sepoys, and encouraged them to push their efforts against them with more determination than ever. The situation of the garrison would have been hopeless but for the occurrence of a series of seemingly fortuitous events, which can be regarded in no other light but providential intervention.

Major Vincent Eyre, an artillery officer of great ability, had left Dinapore in a steamer *en route* for Allahabad with half a company of European Artillery, and two 9-pounder guns and a 24-pounder howitzer. He arrived at Ghazeepore, half way between Dinapore and Allahabad, on the 28th. Here for the first time he received intelligence that our countrymen were beleaguered in Arrah. His chivalrous spirit could not endure the idea of their being allowed to remain in that position without an attempt being made to relieve them : he accordingly went to the authorities, and pointed out to them the ease with which an attack might be made from Busar by a party under his orders, which could also co-operate with any demonstration from Dinapore. The news of the Arrah disaster had not reached any of them, and willing to afford some assistance, the Ghazeepore authorities offered Major Eyre five-and-twenty Highlanders. This would increase his entire force to but sixty men, but Eyre at once accepted the offer, and embarking the Highlanders, turned the head of the vessel, and steamed back for Busar. Fortunately, on arriving there on the 30th July, he found a steamer and flat with 150 of the 5th Fusiliers on board. He gladly availed himself of their services, and sending back the Highlanders to Ghazeepore, with a force now increased by the Fusiliers, and volunteers from the Stud and Railway Departments, to about 200 men, he on the evening of the 1st August pushed on. That night, or rather the next morning, they reached the Shahpore, a village twenty-eight miles distant, and here they received the first intelligence of the Arrah disaster. This only made them the more desirous to hasten on to the rescue. At 2 P.M. on the 2nd Eyre renewed his march, having to halt occasionally to repair the bridges which had been broken down or cut through. It was about sunset when they arrived at Goojeerajgung, about nine miles from Arrah. Here it was known that there was a very strong bridge over a nullah, and Eyre fully expected to find it broken down : to his surprise it was in capital order. Some were of opinion that he should take advantage of the neglect of the rebels and push on at once. But Eyre was too prudent : he did not fancy a night march into an enemy's country, and he resolved to halt where he was, the only approach to his camp being covered by the bridge. It was fortunate that he did come to this resolution : the bridge had not been broken down, solely that he might be tempted to cross it; preparations had been made to receive him a little distance on the other side, and, had he moved on, there can be no doubt but that he would have shared the fate of the Dinapore party. But he was happily proof against the temptation : it was no light one, for it seemed to them all possible that the delay might make all the difference in the fate of the garrison of Arrah.

At break of day next morning Eyre resumed his march, but had not proceeded above a mile before he discovered that the copses in his front and on his flanks were filled with Sepoys. The road beyond them was bounded by inundated rice-fields on both sides. Observing that the enemy were more intent upon taking him in flank than in guarding their own front, he resolved to push on, under the cover of his skirmishers, armed as they were with the Enfield rifle. The enemy fell back before him, abandoned the copses, and hastened to take up a new position.

Beyond the copses was a large marshy plain, unprotected by cover of any kind; beyond this again were some thick clumps of trees, the approach to them defended by a small river, spanned by a bridge; behind the trees were the houses which formed the village of Beebeegunj. The Sepoys had made this their main position, and had strengthened it in every possible way; the bridge had been broken down, earthen breastworks thrown up on the opposite side of the river, and every house in the village occupied in force. Their numbers were estimated at from 2000 to 2500. Eyre having reconnoitred, concluded that with his force their position was unassailable in front: he resolved therefore to turn it. Masking this movement by the fire of his guns, he diverged to the right, taking a course parallel to the river, in the direction of the railway embankment by which it is crossed. His intention had no sooner become evident to the rebels than they left their entrenchment, and proceeded in the same direction on their side of the river, keeping upon our men a hot fire. It seemed as though the victory ought to lie with the party which first reached the railway embankment, for close to it was a large clump of trees which commanded the angle of the only approach. In this the Sepoys had a great advantage over us; our men were moving across partly swampy, partly rugged and broken ground—they had a hard soil to traverse; we were encumbered with guns—they had none. However, our men pushed on with a will, and with every hope of being beforehand with them, until within 300 yards of the railway line.

Here the ground was broken and rugged; the guns were moved with difficulty, and it was found impossible to get them on to the line. The Sepoys saw their advantage: they had reached the woods already alluded to, which quite commanded the road by which our men must pass. Under cover of these they poured a very brisk fire on Eyre's party, but these latter were not entirely unsheltered by trees, and Eyre at this moment getting the guns into position, opened upon them a heavy fire of shot and shell. But the Sepoys were bent on mischief. Led by their subadars, they made several very gallant and very desperate efforts to gain possession of our guns, and their numbers were so great that these were in very great peril. All this time the Fusiliers, moving in advance in extended order, were interchanging volleys of musketry with the enemy, whose numbers, however, were so great that they were able at the same time to occupy our infantry, and attempt to carry our guns. It became evident by this time that a much longer continuance of these tactics must end in our discomfiture, more especially as our gun-ammunition was almost exhausted, and of the sixty rounds carried by the men more than half had been fired away. The rebels, too, were becoming bolder, from observing our stationary tactics. Seeing this, Eyre resolved to have recourse to the bayonet — that glorious weapon which has never yet failed in the hands of England's sons. Accordingly the word was given, and with hands well down and hearts in their right place, this band of less than 150 men, extending over 300 yards and led by their gallant commandant Captain L'Estrange, bore down to the charge. Conspicuous on either flank, as the best mounted officers present, were Captain Hastings of the Stud Department, and Mr. Kelley of the Railway — both big men on big horses, charging with, and cheering on the infantry. On they came to that wood from which so many volleys had been poured forth on our devoted band. But the Sepoys would not wait for them. Sheltered behind trees they would have fought for hours; but here, as in Oudh, the sight of the cold steel was sufficient to scare them ; they broke and fled. The victory was now gained ; the enemy gave up the contest and fled in confusion. Our troops followed them up to within four miles of Arrah, when their further progress was stopped by an impassable river. They therefore halted whilst the engineers prepared a temporary bridge.

The reader, judging from the account I have given of this action, may imagine that the infantry charge ought to have been made sooner in the day. Such a judgment would, at least, be hasty. If there were any quality exhibited throughout the action, which called forth more than any other the admiration of all, it was the coolness and complete self-command displayed by Major Eyre. This officer showed that he possessed all the abilities which, fifteen years before, had brought him prominently to the notice of Lord Ellenborough. On this occasion, he had guns and few infantry: the enemy had no guns and swarms of foot-men. It would have shown the most culpable rashness on Eyre's part, if he had dashed at them with his handful of men, without endeavouring to make them sensible of the power of his guns. The moment he saw that they were too strongly posted for his artillery to dislodge them, he let go the infantry, and drove them out. If they had had the heart to resist, then our position would have been very critical. It was, in fact, a last resort. Like a good general, he husbanded it till the proper moment arrived, and then, by using it effectually, assured himself of victory. The gallantry of officers and men, as well as of the volunteers, was most conspicuous. Lieut. Wild, an officer of the 40th—the men of which corps were fighting against him—was observed to be everywhere, distinguished from all his comrades by wearing his red-jacket. But all were animated by the same noble spirit, and it is gratifying that all were spared to reap the fruits of their success. Our losses were little more than nominal.

Meanwhile, the party in the little house at Arrah were still holding out bravely against the foe; their hope never wavered, their hearts never sank. Every assault of the enemy was repulsed with loss; all his offers of terms repelled with indignation. On the third day, water began to run short; a well was dug within the house in less than twelve hours. Did the enemy raise a barricade, ours grew in proportion; did a shot strike a weak place in the defence, it was made twice as strong as before. But, perhaps, their greatest danger consisted in the possibility of their being undermined. This also was attempted. The mine was dug, the powder was stored, the train was laid; why it was not fired yet remains a mystery. But the probability is, that the party on watch over the house were awaiting the return of their victorious comrades from Beebeegunj. Return they did, but how? Broken in spirit, tumbling down, after the manner of Asiatics, from the fever heat of exultation to the zero of depression, seeing an enemy in every shadow; they came but to warn their associates to fly with them. And fly they did, leaving in their haste the train which was ready for the spark unfired. The next morning Eyre arrived. Great were the congratulations on all sides. The little house in which our countrymen had held out so long was quite a picture; not a single brick unmarked by shot or bullet. Yet in it, for seven days, a few Englishmen had resisted the attacks of three thousand men. Honour to them! They all deserve the admiration of their countrymen. But, by common consent, foremost amongst them stands the civil engineer, Mr. Boyle. He it was who planned the defence; he it was who laid in stores and supplies; he it was whose engineering skill enabled the garrison to render nugatory all the efforts of the foe. The mine to which I have cursorily alluded had, under his instructions, been countermined, and another blow of the pick would have broken into it. The heroic exertions of Messrs. Wake and Colvin are also deserving of the highest praise; it was to the acuteness of the former that the garrison discovered that a mine was being attempted; whilst the untiring exertions of the latter were remarked by all.

But not the least amount of praise must be awarded to the Sikhs. Fighting for aliens against their own countrymen, for there were many of these latter in the ranks of the rebels, they displayed throughout a fidelity and a staunchness which was the more to be admired as it had become so rare; they knew that in case of our defeat they would receive no mercy from the Sepoys,—that an act of treachery, on the other hand, would ensure them the warmest welcome. But such an idea was never entertained for an instant; they had at the outset announced their intention of casting in their lot with us, and from that resolve they never swerved.

Eyre's first act after arriving at Arrah was to send in to Dinapore a report of his proceedings, together with a request that ammunition might be sent out for his detachment. His requisition was acceded to; and it having been ascertained that the Sepoys had rallied at Jugdeespore, between twenty and thirty miles south-west of Arrah, and that Eyre had proposed following them up, a detachment of two hundred men of the 10th, under Captain Patterson, burning to revenge their comrades, were sent to join him. On coming within sight of the enemy, it was found impossible to restrain the impetuosity of these men; Eyre accordingly let them go. They charged with a shout of fury, and taking three guns as they rushed on, at length came to a hand-to-hand *mêlée* with the enemy. Then did they execute terrible vengeance — a vengeance which was sufficient to wring tears of blood from the heart of Mr. Grant and his co-sympathisers with the mutineers. Happily Eyre was not a *doctrinaire;* he had witnessed the mangled remains of our countrymen at Arrah, and he did not check the furious onslaught of our avenging soldiers. The charge of the 10th was decisive; it struck a terror into the hearts of the rebels; they were now utterly broken and fled in dismay. The district of Shahabad was at once cleared of their presence, and those that were not killed hastened under the guidance of Koour Singh to find refuge in a more congenial part of the country. By their departure Eyre's further detention in Behar became unnecessary, and he returned to gain fresh reputation on his road to Cawnpore and Lucknow.

We must now return to Patna.

Scarcely had Mr. Taylor, the Commissioner, received intelligence of the mutiny at Dinapore, followed by the disaster at Arrah to the west, than news reached him that two companies of the 8th had revolted at Hagareebagh to the south, and that the 12th, the most trusted regiment of Irregular Cavalry, had risen in insurrection at Legowlie to the north, and had murdered their commanding officer, his own most valued coadjutor, Major Holmes. It was too true. The regiment had been doing splendid service up to the 25th of July. Major Holmes had reported most favourably of them, and this officer had been quoted as an example of the truth of Lord Canning's axiom, that no regiment which was properly commanded would mutiny. But on the evening of the 26th, as he was driving out in his buggy with his wife, a daughter of the heroic Sale, four sowars rode up to him with their swords drawn, and almost before he knew what they wanted they had beheaded both himself and Mrs. Holmes. The regiment then rose, murdered the doctor, his wife and children, plundered the treasury, and let themselves loose on the country. The fears of the mercantile community, expressed on the occasion of their interview with Lord Canning, were thus so far realised. The native troops had not been disarmed; they had mutinied; the entire district was at their mercy. It appeared to the Commissioner of Patna that the natural course of the mutineers would lead them to those small civil stations — the arteries of Patna — in which the local treasuries were deposited; he accordingly issued a circular to the magistrates of those stations which lay most prominently in the route of the mutineers, directing them to retire, with their treasure, if possible, on Patna, leaving, for the present, the district unprotected. It was this order which was made the pretext for his recall.

At the little civil station of Gyah, to which, amongst others, this order was transmitted, Mr. Alonzo Money was the magistrate. The troops there consisted of forty Europeans of the 84th, and 116 Sikhs. Eighty men of the 64th Foot had left two days before for Patna. Mr. Money, on receiving the circular, called a meeting of the residents, read out the Commissioner's orders, and announced his intention of abiding by them. The roads being considered impracticable for wheeled carriages, it was resolved to abandon the treasure, 70,000*l*. It must be premised that the station of Gya lay on the direct route from Hagareebagh to the north-west, and the residents were daily expecting a visit from the mutineers.

On the morning of the 31st of July, the party started, every European in Gya abandoning that station, their houses, property, the Government stores and money. They had not ridden far before the idea came into the head of Mr. Hollings, an uncovenanted servant of Government—that is an "adventurer" in Governmental employ—that this was a very shameful abandonment. The more he brooded over the idea, the more satisfied did he become of its being well founded. He accordingly rode up to Mr. Money, and mentioned his convictions on the subject. Mr. Money, who had felt uneasy himself on the very point, cordially sympathised with him, and adopted on the spur of the moment the resolution of returning. He halted the party, announced his individual intention, asked none of them to join him, and in company with Mr. Hollings alone rode back. He found the station in the same order as when he had left it; nothing was disturbed, the native police were doing duty over the jail and over the treasury as when he had set out. His first measure was to send a despatch for the return of the company of the 64th Foot which had left two days before; his second to endeavour to re-assure the minds of the native population, an attempt in which he was but little successful.

On the 2nd of August, the company of the 64th returned, and Mr. Money busied himself in procuring wheeled carriages for the treasury. Still everything was apparently secure; but on the 13th, as Mr. Money was going out of his house, he heard a fearful yell, and perceived the convicts from the jail accompanied by the jail-guard rushing toward his house. Fortunately, a horse ready saddled was awaiting him at the stable close at hand. He instantly mounted, galloped to the treasury, turned out the Europeans, yoked the bullocks, and set out in the direction of Shergotty, in the hope of soon getting on to the Grand Trunk Road. He had not proceeded five miles before the crowd of savages, filling the air with discordant cries, was seen approaching. They had not perhaps counted on the warm reception which they met with, and which had the effect of completely dispersing them. Mr. Money then, unmolested, pursued his journey to Calcutta, whither we must precede him.

The account of Mr. Tayler's circular, of Mr. Alonzo Money's successful disobedience of its provision, had no sooner reached Calcutta than Mr. Tayler was suspended. This was not the real cause—that has been previously pointed out; but the Bengal Government was glad to pounce upon Mr. Tayler's first indiscretion, to replace him by a man after their own heart.

Whether Mr. Tayler's order to abandon the small stations of the Patna division were an indiscretion or a crime, or whether it were a wise forethought, is a point upon which public opinion in India is still divided. That gentleman has set forth in a pamphlet lately published, that he intended the order to be discretionary, and that in no case did he contemplate the abandonment of the treasure. If this be the case, and in the absence of the circular itself it may be accepted as a correct account, Mr. Tayler's order possesses the character of a wise and prudent measure. The entire country was swarming with revolters; the small stations were weakly garrisoned and isolated,

It were surely then wise to accord to the chief person in authority at those stations liberty to retire, if needs be, with the treasure to the chief town of the district, there to mass the available forces. If this was all that Mr. Tayler did, he is scarcely deserving of blame.

And in that view the conduct of Mr. Money loses much of its chivalrous aspect. In any case he was wrong to leave the station, unless he conceived he were threatened by an overwhelming force; and when once he resolved on returning, it was very courageous, but not very wise, not to order back the escort and residents also. Fortune favoured him, as it so often favours those who are brave and self-reliant; but it is unfortunate that the firmness which he displayed after his conversation with Mr. Hollings had not been exerted prior to his desertion of Gya. By that means the whole scandal would have been avoided.

These gentlemen received their reward. Mr. Money, the civilian, was promised almost immediate promotion from a grade in which he received 100*l.* per mensem to another wherein that salary would be doubled. The allowances of Mr. Hollings, the "uncovenanted," received an addition of 20*l.* per mensem.

A new era was now about to be inaugurated. On the 30th July, the circular known as "Canning's Clemency" was issued; on the 4th August, Mr. J. P. Grant was sent up country to carry out its provisions; on the 5th, Mr. Samuells was appointed Commissioner of Patna, on the principle of conciliation, and Ameer Ally, a Mohammedan pleader, directed to proceed with him as his assistant; and finally, General Outram, who had arrived in Calcutta on the 1st, was on the 5th appointed to the joint commands of Dinapore and Cawnpore, thus superseding the incapable Lloyd and the noble-hearted, indefatigable Havelock!

All India stood aghast at these changes, all in the wrong direction. But the public voice was dumb, for the Press was gagged, and letters to England formed the only outlet for public opinion. On that account perhaps the thraldom was the more keenly felt; for, from the drawing room to the barrack, the tone of society was very bitter against Lord Canning and his advisers.

CHAPTER IX.

GWALIOR. — CENTRAL INDIA. — AGRA. — ROHILCUND.

THE state of Agra and the surrounding districts, up to the beginning of June, has been already related. From that date its fate, and the fate of India, it may be said, was entirely dependent upon the movements of that large body of men who form the Gwalior Contingent. It will be convenient, then, primarily to notice the influences under which those men, most of them natives of Oudh, first rose against their officers, and were subsequently persuaded to abstain from adding their weight, at that critical period, to the burden which was then almost bowing us to the earth.

When, in 1843, Gwalior lay at the feet of Lord Ellenborough, its army discomfited, their leaders disheartened, and its king a minor, that far-seeing nobleman conceived the idea of so binding it to our interests, that without any violation of faith, without any infringement of, the rights of the native ruler, it might be hereafter a source of strength to our empire; and the means by which he proposed to accomplish this result were these. To the lawful ruler, of whose infancy his counsellors had taken such unwise advantage, Lord Ellenborough returned the whole of his patrimony. But his army he disbanded. In lieu of it, he raised another army, officered and paid by British officers — the money for the purpose being furnished by the Maharaja. He placed near the person of that prince a resident, armed with plenary powers, whose duty it should be to guide, instruct, and educate the youthful monarch; to make his policy, though he remained Maharaja, and in name the despotic master of Gwalior, entirely dependent on the views and instructions of the British Government.

By these means, no shock was offered to the feelings of the native princes: these were not suddenly and rudely, even treacherously, as in the case of Oudh and Nagpore, made to feel that their existence depended on the pleasure of one man. On the contrary, the generous policy of Lord Ellenborough drew from them all the expression of satisfaction, with a devotion to our rule. Nor was it in any other respect a less wise policy. Instead of weakening our empire, as was done in the two instances referred to, by transferring to our rule, and to a more dreaded ordeal — to our civil courts, a wild, rude, untamed people, untaught in the technicalities and trickeries of law, he strengthened it by retaining them under their native laws, and by imparting thereby a sense of security to all who had inherited or purchased property under the ancient *régime*. It was hoped too that the Maharaja, as he grew up to manhood, perceiving the stability of the tenure by which he held his possessions, secure alike from all fear of his protectors, the British, and from the danger of combination among his own officers, would recognise and appreciate the tie which bound him to our rule, and would use all his efforts to strengthen rather than to break it.

Of all the schemes which the penetration of statesmen has shadowed out, there is not one which has been more justified by the result than that embodied in the policy adopted by Lord Ellenborough towards Gwalior in 1843.

Whilst other provinces under the systems of those who had preceded and who came after him — whilst Affghanistan under Lord Auckland, the Punjab*, under Lord Hardinge, Oudh under Lord

---

* It is readily admitted that the Punjab, since its annexation in 1848, has shown splendid results; but it is equally a fact, that the system under which she has been so ably administered was borrowed by Lord Dalhousie from Sir Charles Napier's administration of Sinde.

The plan, too, first adopted to any great extent by Sir Charles Napier, of em-

Dalhousie, have proved thorns in our sides, Gwalior has been a tower of strength. She has been an outwork, as it were, of Agra, and at the same time has overawed and kept in subjection to us, the chiefs of Rajpootana, Dodypore, and the petty rajas of Central India. Before the battle of Maharajpore she had been the source of unceasing anxiety to our Government.

The Maharaja, now a grown man, has perceived that Gwalior had had her crisis: that the administration of her affairs had, been committed to him on the sole condition of dealing out impartial justice to his subjects: he has seen that he possessed great social power, a princely revenue, a high status amongst native princes, an army officered by Europeans. He had therefore no want; there was nothing to tempt him to offer any opposition to British rule: he had no sympathy in common with the Mahomedan sovereigns of Delhi and Oudh: his interests and ours had become identical.

Such was the result of Lord Ellenborough's statesmanlike policy in 1843. It was destined, as I shall now proceed to show, to save our empire in 1857.

On the revolt of Delhi becoming known at Gwalior, the Maharaja at once resolved to cast in his lot with the British: he sent his bodyguard, men of his own Mahratta clan, to Agra, where they were most successfully employed, and placed at the disposal of Mr. Colvin the entire Contingent. But it soon became evident that the causes which had induced our own native army to mutiny had infected the Sepoys of the Gwalior Contingent with the virus of revolt. The first symptom of it appeared at Hattrass on the 28th May *, when a portion of one of the cavalry regiments under the command of Lieutenant Cockburn revolted and went to Delhi; again, in the beginning of June, one of the regiments of the Contingent stationed at Neemuch mutinied; those at Augur and Sullutpore followed these examples; and finally, on the 14th June, those remaining at Gwalior rose in the night and massacred their officers.

The Maharaja was in no way to blame for these calamities: the troops which had mutinied were not Gwalior men; they came from Oudh, and had been enlisted by us. Like the rest of our native troops, they had been seduced by the emissaries of the former sovereign of their country — the king of Oudh — to rise against us; they received their orders from another power than that at Gwalior, and obeyed them.

Nevertheless, no sooner had they murdered their officers, than they placed their services at the disposal of the Maharaja, and begged him to lead them against Agra. At this time not only did the insurgents occupy Delhi, but the entire country north-west of Agra had risen in

ploying hardworking subalterns on moderate salaries to do the work of highly paid civilians, has been tried in the Punjab with the best effect.

It is not necessary to enter into the reason now why a different policy was put in force with respect to Gwalior and Sinde. It was absolutely necessary that it should be so; any measure short of the annexation of Sinde would have been destruction to us. One remedy will not cure every constitution.

* Vide Chapter I.

revolt; our garrisons were beleaguered at Cawnpore and Lucknow; and the aspect of our affairs was in the highest degree unpropitious. If, therefore, the policy adopted in 1843 had been a vicious policy like that pursued towards Affghanistan in 1838-39, if it had been a selfish and grasping policy like that carried out towards Oudh in 1856, now would have been the Maharaja's opportunity — most favourable the moment for recovering his lost authority: it was merely necessary to accede to the proposal of the mutinous Contingent to revenge himself on the British. Had he so acceded, had he put himself at their head, and, accompanied likewise by his trusty Mahrattas, proceeded to the scene of action, the consequences would have been most disastrous to ourselves. He would have brought at least twenty thousand troops, one half of them drilled and disciplined by European officers, on our weak points. Agra and Lucknow would have at once fallen. Havelock would have been shut up in Allahabad; and either that fortress would have been besieged, or the rebels, giving it a wide berth, would have marched through Benares on to Calcutta. There were no troops, there was no fortification to stop them. But, happily for us, the policy inaugurated by Lord Ellenborough, unlike many other excellent measures introduced by that nobleman, had not been repealed; and the Maharaja felt that a Mahomedan power raised upon the ruins of the British would be of all things most unfavourable to his interests, that, in fact, his prosperity depended upon our supremacy. He was, however, to a great extent in the power of the Contingent troops: he could not coerce them: he was compelled therefore to temporise.

It was a difficult matter. It was not the Maharaja's object, acting for our advantage, simply to decline going with the troops himself: he saw that, to whatever part of our territories they might proceed, they would inflict terrible damage on our interests, and that his refusal to go with them would be useless unless he managed to detain them altogether, or until such time as our resources should be better able to ward off their attack.

But, in spite of the difficulty of the case, he managed it. By liberal donations of pay, by pretended difficulties in the way of procuring carriage, by all the arts to which an Asiatic mind can have recourse, he did manage to detain them. Nay, more, when the Mhow mutineers and the rebel troops of Holkar, 3000 strong, passed through his territory, he actually so temporised with the Gwalior troops as to prevent their accompanying the former in their expedition against Agra. He could not keep them back much longer, but he detained them up to the proper time; they finally rose against him, left Gwalior on the 16th October, and, after many marches and counter-marches, arrived at Cawnpore in time to fall into the hands of Sir Colin Campbell, on the 7th December.

Meanwhile the 3000 men above alluded to moved on to Agra; but, before referring to their doings at that station, it will be necessary to give a sketch of the risings in the principal districts in Central India.

The revolt at Neemuch, long previously threatened, took place on the 3rd June. The regiments at that station consisted of the 72nd Native Infantry, the 7th Regiment of the Gwalior Contingent, and a wing of the 1st Bengal Cavalry. Their mutiny was characterised by the usual occurrences. Loud protestations of fidelity on the part of the men until their arrangements had been completed; then a sudden rise, and an attempt, more or less successful, to massacre their officers. At Neemuch, fortunately, there was a fortified square, in which our countrymen and women were able to find shelter at the commencement of the outbreak: and before this was threatened, they had time to make some preparation for escape. The rebels, thus masters of the station, plundered the treasury, and made for Delhi. Their operations there on the rear of our force, and their sudden assault on Agra, will be detailed in due course.

At Nusseerabad, about one hundred and fifty miles nearer to Delhi, the revolt had commenced even earlier: the troops here were the 15th and 30th Native Infantry, a battery of Native Artillery, and the 1st Bombay Lancers.

The mutiny commenced at 3 P.M. by the men of the 15th and the Artillery taking possession of the guns, and bidding defiance to the officers; the 30th appeared to hesitate at first, but it was not long before they also joined. The officers were fired at on all sides, and many of them escaped very narrowly. In this situation, the Bombay Lancers were brought up. As they approached, the guns opened fire upon them. In vain they tried to charge: every attack was repulsed; and their officers, leading them on with great gallantry, suffered out of all proportion. Finding it fruitless to persevere, the Lancers desisted, and contented themselves with covering the retirement of the women and children to a place of safety. The mutineers then made their way to Delhi, and managed to reach it in time to take an efficient part in the defence.

The regiments at Mhow consisted of the 23rd Native Infantry, a wing of the 1st Cavalry, and a company of European Artillery. The mutiny first commenced at Indore, some thirty miles distant, the residence of the Maharaja Holkar, and of the Governor-General's agent. The Maharaja himself was quite innocent of any share in the catastrophe: his troops had caught the infection, and turned against us in spite of him. But a sufficient number of the Bhopal Contingent, who were fortunately on duty there, remained faithful long enough to enable Major Durand and the residents to retreat uninjured.

That same day an account of the occurrence reached Mhow. That very morning two guns had been sent out on the Bombay road to join General Woodburn's advancing column; but on the news of the revolt at Indore orders were transmitted to recall them. The men who were ordered to bring them back showed little alacrity in turning out, and on arriving up to the guns seemed unwilling to coerce the gunners. However, the remonstrances and example of their officers prevailed, and the guns were brought back. The bearing of the men, however, was sulky and unsoldierlike.

These circumstances being reported to the commanding officer, the European Artillery was ordered into the fort. Thither also the ladies repaired. That very night, as their officers were sitting at dinner close to their lines, the men rose, fired upon them, killed two or three, plundered the station, and then made the best of their way to Gwalior. The great body of the officers found refuge in the fort. Here we must leave them for the present, whilst we follow the fortunes of our countrymen at Agra.

Towards the end of June the country all around Agra had assumed so threatening an aspect, that the residents had all been ordered into the fort, and the Kotah Contingent, then supposed by Mr. Colvin to be trustworthy, was moved up to the assistance of the garrison. It had certainly performed good service up to the time of its reaching Agra, collecting revenue, hanging mutineers, and burning villages; but it had scarcely arrived at the seat of the Lieutenant-Governorship before the men mutinied, firing upon their officers. Next day the Neemuch mutineers arrived within four miles. The authorities had been expecting them, but had forborne to mention their fears: the consequence was that much property belonging to those who could least afford to lose it was destroyed. However, hearing of the approach of the rebels, it was resolved to meet them. They numbered about four thousand men, of whom one-half perhaps had been disciplined by us. Our force consisted of seven companies of the 8th Europeans, one company of European Artillery, and a few volunteer cavalry. The enemy had eight guns, which they had strongly posted in the little village of Sussia, on the road to Futtehpore Sikri, being themselves encamped on the plain beyond. Our force advanced against them in line, the artillery being on the flanks, the cavalry on the rear. When about six hundred yards from the village, their artillery opened upon our line: it was immediately replied to by D'Oyley's battery with so great effect that they were temporarily silenced. A charge of infantry at this time, such as Havelock ordered at Cawnpore, and Eyre directed at Beebeegunj, would have gained us the day; but no one of those possessing authority could appreciate the crisis, and, instead of a charge, a cautious advance was directed. But the enemy had gained courage from our inactivity. The gunners returned to their guns, and opened a fire on our line with great effect; at the same time their cavalry threatened our flanks and rear, and their infantry, advancing in skirmishing order, gave us great annoyance. It was at this time, as we were advancing too slowly for heroic souls, that Captain D'Oyley, seated on one of the gun-carriages, was mortally wounded. His horse had been previously shot under him. When struck, he called out in a loud voice, "Follow them up, follow them up," and still continued, for a short time, to direct the advance of the battery. He knew that his wound was mortal, but still he gave his orders. When at last he was overcome with pain, he turned to the man nearest him, and said, "They have done for me now; put a stone over my grave, and say that I died fighting for my guns." He did not survive long.

Meanwhile our slow advance had had some effect, for the enemy had abandoned the village to a charge of two companies of the Europeans, and the day seemed our own, when it was discovered that all our ammunition was exhausted. There was nothing for it then but a retreat, as our creeping movements had permitted the enemy to carry away his guns. Retreat then we did, threatened by the cavalry, even surrounded. Had they had any pluck, they might have cut up every man of our party. But they still feared the red-coated European; and our force, scarcely beaten, but certainly baffled and humiliated, at last found shelter under the walls of the fort. Our loss on this day was one hundred and forty, out of five hundred engaged; that of the enemy was not known. Strange to say, he did not think of following up his advantage, but took the road to Muttra and Delhi the next day, contenting himself with letting out from the jail four thousand of the most determined villains in India. Our countrymen were thenceforth confined to the fort, whence they were subsequently released by the arrival of Colonel Greathed's column, of which an account will be given hereafter.

Before proceeding to the north-west, and detailing the circumstances connected with the siege and recapture of Delhi, it will be necessary very briefly to refer to the events which had been passing in the districts surrounding that city, as well as in the rich province of Rohilcund.

In the end of May, the men of the Hurrianah Light Infantry, a local battalion stationed at Hausi Hissar and Sirsa, and part of the 4th Irregular Cavalry, rose upon their officers and the European residents, massacred many of them, and, after plundering the entire district, made for Delhi. Every village in that part of the country is a castle on a small scale: the inhabitants, sympathising with the mutineers, rose almost simultaneously with them, and declared for the cause of the King of Delhi. They did more: every unfortunate straggler who fell into their hands was ruthlessly butchered. And yet, many of the villages in which these deeds were perpetrated have been spared. It is a fact, to which there are hundreds of witnesses, that when, after the capture of Delhi, Colonel Greathed's column reached one of the largest of these rebellious towns, notorious for the cruelties which had been perpetrated within its walls—in which too the decapitated skeleton of an European woman was still exposed, bearing besides marks of the infliction of torture—that village was, at the earnest prayer of the civilian who accompanied the force as "political adviser," it is supposed, actually spared. Does the reader ask why? Because it supplied a large revenue to the Government of the North-West Provinces. These are some of the sordid considerations which the agents of the East India Company allow to interpose between our soldiers and retributive justice. But this is but an ordinary instance; others remain to be told which proclaim even more clearly the cold-blooded nature of our rulers, their want of sympathy with humanity, if that humanity be allied to their own.

The important province of Rohilcund, lying east of Oudh and north-west of Delhi, is inhabited by a race of Mahomedan warriors, the descendants of the victorious Affghans who settled in that country nearly a century and a half ago. Notwithstanding that lapse of time, they had retained, in all its perfection, their national character: they were brave, treacherous, revengeful, very idle, careless of any occupation save that of a soldier. Hence this race supplied many recruits to our Irregular Cavalry. Its daring, dashing service was peculiarly suited to men of their disposition, and there were always numerous applicants for the vacancies which occurred.

We had three military stations in Rohilcund,—the principal and most important at Bareilly, the chief town of the province. Here, when the Delhi outbreak occurred, were the 8th Irregular Cavalry, the 18th and 68th Native Infantry, and a battery of Native Artillery, — not a single European besides the officers and residents.

From the very day that the news arrived the infantry regiments had shown their sympathy with the mutineers. But the 8th Irregular Cavalry, one of the best corps in the army, and commanded by a very gallant officer, Captain Mackenzie, evinced every disposition to continue loyal. So well had the men behaved, and to such an extent were they trusted by all, that Captain Mackenzie was empowered to raise several additional troops for permanent service, and the lines of the Irregular Cavalry were appointed as the place of rendezvous in the event of an outbreak. That these men were at the time faithful, cannot be doubted: many of them evinced their fidelity shortly afterwards by leaving house and home, wife and children, to the mercy of the insurgents, whilst they followed the fortunes of their officers to the bleak hills of Nynee Tal. But the great bulk of the men were unable to resist the combined influences of religion and example, and the golden prospects held out to them by the tempters. Foremost amongst these was Khan Bahadoor Khan, a pensioner of Government, and the nearest descendant of the famous Rohilla chief, Hafiz Rahmut. This man, in fact, received a double pension,—one as the heir of Hafiz Rahmut, the other in his capacity of retired Principal Sudder Ameen.* He enjoyed the entire confidence of the authorities at Bareilly: he was closeted daily with the commissioner and the magistrate, who concerted plans with him for the preservation of order. He was an old, venerable-looking man, with a soft, insinuating answer: his interests were supposed to be bound up with ours. Little did the magistrate imagine, when he announced his conviction that Delhi must fall in a week, that the hearts of the people were with us, and that the cavalry would remain staunch, that the old man listening apparently so respectfully was laughing in his sleeve, that he himself was the soul of the conspiracy, that the entire district, and the infantry regiments, were ready to rise at a signal from him, and that he was busily engaged in seducing the Irregulars by means of Mahomed Sheffie, a resaldar whom he had gained over to his interests.

But so it was: the hoary traitor had, under the mask of servility, wound himself into our confidence, and he employed the hold which he had thus gained on our authorities to bring about their destruction.

* Native judge.

All was ready by the end of May. In the morning of the 31st a servant, who had been sent with letters to the post, reported that he had found the office surrounded by armed Sepoys, who had tore up the letters: information came from another quarter to the effect that the Sepoys had resolved on rising at eleven o'clock, and that they had told off parties to each bungalow to murder all their officers. The cavalry were at once ordered to turn out, but before they could be got ready the revolt had commenced. As the clock sounded eleven, the Sepoys of the 68th rushed furiously out of their lines, seized the guns, and turned them upon the mess-house, firing grape into it. The officers immediately mounted their horses, and, finding it worse than useless to attempt to restore order, rode across the parade ground to the Irregular Cavalry lines, exposed all the time to a galling fire. At the same time both the 18th and 68th Sepoys went off in parties to execute their murderous commissions. One of these came across Brigadier Sibbald, a fine old soldier, riding towards the Irregulars: they saluted him with a volley which produced instant death. Most of the other officers reached the cavalry lines in safety.

There, indeed, had assembled by this time almost all the residents of the station, civilians, military men, merchants, and others. They found Captain Mackenzie and his adjutant, Lieutenant Beecher, haranguing their men and endeavouring to keep them together; but some were already sneaking off, and the disposition of others seemed doubtful. Colonel Troup, who commanded on the death of the Brigadier, saw at once that they too were gone, and gave the order to retire on Nynee Tal, a hill-station a hundred miles distant. Captain Mackenzie, however, was anxious to give his men the opportunity of proving themselves faithful. But he had scarcely returned from taking Colonel Troup's orders than the left wing went bodily off and joined the mutineers. They halted at the magazine, raised the green flag of Mahomed, and called on the others to join them. In spite of every solicitation of their officers, they obeyed: out of the entire regiment assembled that day at Bareilly, nineteen only remained faithful, and these escorted their officers and the refugees to Nynee Tal, leaving, as I said before, their property and families behind them. The residents whom choice or accident caused to remain were brutally murdered. Khan Bahadoor Khan himself taking a leading part in the atrocities.

At Moradabad and Shahjihanpore, the two other military stations in Rohilcund, the troops rose almost immediately after. At the former place, indeed, the 29th Native Infantry only joined their comrades when coerced by the arrival of the mutineers from Bareilly; but at Shahjihanpore the 28th revolted with a will, surrounded the Christian residents as they were at church, and murdered almost all of them. A few who escaped managed, after incredible difficulties, to reach the little fort of Mohammerah in Oudh; but, compelled to leave this place of refuge, they endeavoured, under an escort of men believed to be faithful, to make their way towards Lucknow. On the road they were met by the 41st Native Infantry, red with the blood of the Europeans stationed at Seetapore : by these they were one and all brutally murdered ; some of the servants alone escaped to tell the tale.

Meanwhile the mutineers from these three stations having plundered all the treasuries and accumulated enormous quantities of spoil, prepared to take it with them into Delhi. They were about 5000 strong, and had with them 400,000*l.* in silver, laden on country carts. They crossed the Ganges within thirty miles of Meerut. We had in that station a thousand Europeans doing nothing beyond guarding an entrenchment; and yet the general commanding did not attempt in the slightest degree to interfere with their passage. They even lay at Gurmuckteser for some days, whilst they sent over their baggage, and, to keep our men off, sent the General taunting messages that they were about to attack him, a threat which sufficed to make him keep his Europeans within the entrenchment. How the spirits of the gallant young officers, panting to revenge their countrymen, chafed at this inaction, may be imagined. More than one implored the General to permit them to go with even 500 men to attack the rebels as they were crossing : but he would not hear of it. Meerut, he said, was too important a station to be left undefended. Most true! But there are some cases in which a bold attack is the best defence, and this was one of them. The defeat of the Rohilcund rebels at Gurmuckteser Ghât would have struck terror into the surrounding district, and would have had even a material effect on the siege of Delhi.

But it was not to be : this force, laden with the plunder of Rohilcund, marched within thirty miles of a thousand Europeans, crossed the broadest river in India in boats, traversed the country, exposing their left flank to our inactive forces, and finally reached Delhi on the 1st of July,— a very critical period for the garrison of that city,— without a shot having been fired at them in anger.* Let us turn from the contemplation of one of the most disgraceful passages in the whole course of the rebellion to recount the progress and result of the siege of Delhi.

CHAPTER X.

DELHI.

THE easy conquest of a place, the most important in India, because traditionally the seat of Indian sovereignty, had the most pernicious effect on the minds of every class of native. It convinced the wavering, unnerved the staunch, and furnished the last inducement for the yet dissimulating to throw off the veil and openly proclaim themselves rebels and traitors. Once, therefore, in the hands of the

---

* I have not given the name of the general officer who commanded at Meerut at the end of June, because it is possible that General Hewitt may have previously left. Whoever he may have been, he deserves to stand in a literary pillory.

insurgents, Delhi became the rallying point for all the mutinous and disaffected in the Doab. Muttra, Kurnaul, Bareilly, and all the surrounding stations contributed their quota of rebels to garrison the captured city. With vast supplies of warlike stores in their possession, and ample time afforded them to concentrate without interruption, no wonder that, before a single besieger appeared before its walls, Delhi was a stronger place than any that had ever offered resistance to a European force in the East. The news of its capture reached General Anson, the Commander-in-Chief, while on a shooting excursion in the hills, on the 12th May. He at once issued the necessary orders for the formation of a force at Umballah, whither he himself proceeded in all haste, arriving there on the 22nd. There were at Umballah at this time the following troops, commanded by Major-General Sir H. W. Barnard: — Her Majesty's 9th Lancers, two troops European Horse Artillery, 4th Light Cavalry (native), and the 5th and 60th Regiments Native Infantry, with a detachment 9th Irregular Cavalry. At the hill stations of Kussowlie, Dugshai, and Subatho, all within sixty miles of Umballah, were Her Majesty's 75th, and the 1st and 2nd Fusiliers respectively; these regiments were immediately ordered down, marched on the 14th, and reached Umballah on the 17th May. That night a force, consisting of four companies of 1st Europeans, one squadron 9th Lancers, and two guns Horse Artillery, were despatched to Kurnaul, to quell disturbances taking place there. General Anson followed on the 23rd, with the following troops: — four guns, two troops 1st brigade Horse Artillery, 2nd troop 3rd brigade and 3rd troop 3rd battery Horse Artillery, and 4th company 6th battery Artillery; Her Majesty's 9th Lancers, one squadron 4th Lancers, 75th Foot, six companies 1st E. B. Fusiliers, Head Quarters and six companies 2nd E. B. Fusiliers, 60th and 5th Regiments Native Infantry. He reached Kurnaul on the 25th, and died on the 27th May.

Major-General Barnard then assumed the command, and, pushing on, arrived at Alleepoor, ten miles from Delhi, on the 8th June, having been joined by the siege train from Phillour on the 6th, and by the force under General Wilson on the 7th. On the 23d May, the Commander-in-Chief had despatched to General Hewitt at Meerut the following lucid and definite instructions :—

(INCLOSURE 18.)

" *The Commander-in-Chief to Major-General Hewitt.*

" My dear General,   " *Umballah, May* 23, 1857.

" I wish to place you in possession of what has been done and is doing here, and of my ideas with respect to the future movements of the force from Meerut, which will be required to join this column in its advance towards Delhi.

" The force from Umballah consists of the 9th Lancers, one squadron 4th Lancers, Her Majesty's 75th foot, 1st European Regiment, 2nd European Regiment, 60th Native Infantry, two troops of Horse Artillery.

" They are formed into two small brigades. Brigadier Halifax commands the 1st, composed of two squadrons Lancers, Her Majesty's 75th Foot, 1st Europeans, 3rd troop 3rd brigade Horse Artillery of six guns.

"Brigadier Jones will command the 2nd Brigade — 2nd Europeans, 60th Native Infantry, two squadrons 9th Lancers, one squadron 4th Lancers, 2nd troop 3rd brigade Horse Artillery, six guns.

"Four companies 1st Fusiliers, one squadron of 9th Lancers, two guns Horse Artillery, were moved to Kurnaul on the 17th, and arrived on the 20th.

"Six companies of 1st Fusiliers followed on the 21st.

"Her Majesty's 75th Foot and 60th Regiment Native Infantry march on the 22nd.

"One squadron 9th Lancers and four guns will march on the 24th or 25th.

"The above will all be at Kurnaul on the 28th.

"The 2nd Europeans, 3rd troop 3rd brigade Horse Artillery, will probably follow on the 26th. The whole will be at Kurnaul on the 30th.

"I propose then to advance with the column towards Delhi on the 1st, and be opposite to Bhagput on the 5th. At this last place I should wish to be joined by the force from Meerut. To reach it four days may be calculated on.

"This would require your movement on the 1st or 2nd, according to circumstances. By that time it is hoped you will have made every preparation.

"Irregular detachments have been sent on the road to beyond Paneeput to stop plundering, and to protect the well disposed.

"The road has also been opened to Meerut. Captain Sanford arrived here with your despatches early on the morning of the 23rd, and found no obstruction.

"A detachment of 150 sowars of the 4th Irregular Cavalry will leave Kurnaul to-morrow; 25 will be posted at Shamlee, 50 will proceed to Mozuffurnugger, to restore confidence in that district, and to punish any villagers and marauders that may have been concerned in the plundering of that place.

"I have directed 75 to proceed direct to Meerut and to place themselves at your disposal; they will be under the command of an European officer. You will then be enabled to secure carriage for your troops, if you still require it. You must ascertain whether there are any difficulties on the road from Meerut to Bhagput, and the best mode of overcoming them.

"It would be very desirable to push forward some reconnaissance to as near Delhi as possible. It is reported here that a detachment of the mutineers, with two guns, are posted on the Meerut side of the river. They should be captured, and no mercy must be shown to the mutineers.

"On the 20th, I sent a detachment of 2nd company of the 5th Native Infantry and a squadron of the 4th Lancers towards Saharunpoor. I have the satisfaction of having heard that they arrived just in time to save that place from pillage, and that confidence is restored there. I hope that the occupation of Mozuffurnugger will tend to tranquillise that district.

"Many of the 5th Native Infantry have deserted, but it is gratifying to find they have done their duty when detached.

"Two companies have been sent to Roopur on duty. The remainder, with light companies of the 2nd European Regiment, will be left to guard these cantonments.

"If any families at Meerut would consider themselves more secure in the hills, they might go there with safety.

"A small siege-train has left Loodiana and is expected here on the 26th. It will require eleven days to get it to Delhi. It may join us at Bhagput on or about the 6th, the day after that I have named for the junction of your force.

"I depend upon your supplying at least 120 artillerymen to work it.

"You will bring besides, according to statement received, 2 squadrons of Carbineers, a wing of the 60th Rifles, 1 light Field Battery, 1 troop of Horse Artillery, and any Sappers you can depend upon, and of course the non-commissioned European officers belonging to them. I wish to know whether you have any information respecting troops or guns coming from Agra, or the co-operation of any native States.

"I beg you will communicate this to the Lieutenant-Governor at Agra, and to the Secretary to Government at Calcutta — telegraph and letter.

"Any change in the above shall be communicated to you instantly.

"I remain, &c.,
"GEORGE ANSON.'

Acting upon these, Brigadier-General Wilson left Meerut on the 27th May with the force in the margin, and arrived at Guzeeoodeen Nugger on the 30th. At this place the little river Hindun is crossed by an iron bridge, which, as it formed part of the high-road to Delhi from Meerut, it was of the utmost importance to guard. The rebels had sent out a large force with siege-guns to take possession of this bridge; and accordingly, at four o'clock, P. M. of the day of his arrival, General Wilson found himself attacked by the enemy, who had taken up a very advantageous position on some rising ground about a mile from the British camp on the other side of the river, whilst a company of 60th Rifles was detached to hold the bridge. The two 18-pounders replied to the heavy guns, and four guns of Major Tomb's troop Horse Artillery, supported by a squadron of Carbineers, moved along the bank of the river to outflank the enemy's position. They were supported by two companies of the 60th Rifles, four guns of Major Scott's battery, the Sappers, and a troop of Carbineers. The movement completely succeeded: the raking fire from the 6-pounders disconcerted the enemy, whose fire slackened, and shortly ceased. The Rifles were then ordered to advance, which they did in the most dashing style, capturing all the guns, ammunition, and stores of the enemy, who took to flight, pursued by the Carbineers under Lieutenant-Colonel Custance. In this battle, the first in which they had met us in the open field, the mutineers fought most determinedly. "They actually," writes one engaged in the action, "crossed bayonets with us, and met their death like Trojans," and did not relinquish their guns before they had attached slow matches to the ammunition waggons, one of which exploding caused the death of Captain Andrews and four men of the Rifles. The next day about one o'clock the insurgents appeared in force almost on the same ground from which they had previously been driven. After movements on our part similar to those of the day before, a general advance was ordered and the rebels were driven from their position, and the ridge was crowned. The British force, however, was so knocked up by the sun, that the enemy was not pursued, and succeeded in carrying off all their guns.

400 rank and file 6th Rifles.
200 6th Carbineers.
1 Horse Field Battery,
Half troop Horse Artillery.
Head-quarters of Sappers and Miners, about 100 men of all arms.
2 18-pounder guns.

On the 3rd June, General Wilson was reinforced by the Sirmoor battalion (Goorkhas) 600 strong. On the same day he marched towards Alleepoor, where on the 7th he joined the Commander-in-Chief, whose force had been somewhat augmented in the meantime by troops from the contingents of the Putteala and Jhund Rajahs. Sir H. Barnard broke up his camp on the 8th at one A. M., and after marching ten miles found the enemy fully prepared to dispute his advance, in a strong intrenched position with a canal in his rear, at a place called "Badul ka Serai." The British force, divided into three brigades, was disposed as follows: — The 1st brigade, under Brigadier-General Showers, was to act on the right of the main trunk road, along which the column was to advance; the 2nd brigade, under Brigadier-General Graves, was to take the left; and the 3rd brigade, under Brigadier-General Grant was to gain the opposite side of the canal, and recross it below and in rear of the enemy's position as soon as the action commenced, so as to take the enemy in flank: the heavy guns were to remain in position on the road, the rest of the artillery to act on either side. As soon as the advanced picket met the enemy, these brigades deployed, leaving the main road clear. The enemy's guns, served with the greatest precision, now opened upon the advancing troops, causing considerable loss, the second shot killing Colonel Chester, the Adjutant-General. The light field-pieces which replied to them failing to silence guns of such heavy calibre, the 75th were ordered to advance and take the battery. This was done, as General Barnard says, "with heroic gallantry,"— the 1st Europeans supporting the attack. The 2nd brigade now coming up and threatening their right, and the 3rd brigade their left, the enemy abandoned the position entirely leaving their guns on the ground. Knowing from the natives of the country, that if he halted a similar opposition might be offered him the following morning, General Barnard determined to push on, and his victorious though exhausted army was nothing loth. Arriving at a point where the road branched off to the left through the Delhi cantonments, it became advisable to divide the army into two columns, one of which should take the branch, and the other the main road. To General Wilson was given the command of the former column, which had to fight its way through lanes and gardens enclosed by high walls and other obstacles, affording cover to an enemy as far as Hindoo Rao's house on the ridge to the extreme right of the cantonments. General Barnard, commanding in person the column proceeding to the left, soon came in sight of the enemy strongly posted on the elevated ridge which separates Delhi from its cantonments. Making a rapid flank movement under cover of the cantonment itself, General Barnard succeeded in gaining the ridge ere the enemy could get their guns into a new position to oppose him. Taken in flank and rear, the out-manœuvred rebels hastily fled, abandoning their guns, twenty-six in number, ammunition, camp equipage, and even wounded men. The whole ridge was at once in our possession, and the army was placed in position upon it. General Barnard meeting General Wilson at Hindoo

Rao's house, which became Army Head-quarters. The goal was now reached. Delhi, the city of horrors, the loathsome refuge of thousands of murderers and traitors, lay beneath our army, and distant but a mile. Welcome as the sight was to our brave little band of soldiers, few could gaze at the immense extent of the city and its formidable defences, without feeling that to attempt a "coup-de-main" with such a force, would be to risk our all upon a rash and perhaps profitless enterprise. It was determined, therefore, to retain the position on the ridge until adequate reinforcements should arrive, and in the meantime to throw up batteries at a distance of 1500 yards from which to shell the city. The extreme right of our position, or the house of Hindoo Rao before mentioned, was the nearest to the walls of Delhi, and faced in a south-easterly direction the Moree Bastion and Gate, the most salient point opposed to us. Here then were placed our batteries. A little on the left, on the ridge which from this point took a north-easterly direction till it joined the river Jumna, was a strong picket in an old mosque, and to the left of that a building called the Flag-staff Tower. Immediately behind this tower lay the cantonments, where the bulk of our force was encamped, protected from the fire of the enemy by the ridge itself, on whose slope descending towards the camp were still the ruined huts of the mutinous regiments and the houses of the unfortunate officers. Behind the camp flowed a small river, taking a northerly course through the plain, and joining the Jumna a few miles above Delhi. This river was crossed by several bridges which however were commanded by some of our heavy guns. The right of the camp was defended by a field-battery, placed upon a convenient elevation, and called the "Mound Battery." To the right of this battery, and almost in rear of Hindoo Rao's house, was a suburb of Delhi called the "Subzee Mundee." It consisted of old houses, gardens with high walls, narrow streets and lanes, affording the very cover behind which only the Sepoy is brave, and in which, as the sequel will show, some most desperate hand-to-hand fights occurred. Similar suburbs intervene between the actual defences of Delhi and the whole front of our position. The defences of Delhi enclose an area of about three square miles; they consist of a series of bastions connected by long curtains, with occasional martello towers to aid the flanking fire: these bastions rise about sixteen feet above the general level of the ground, and are built of masonry twelve feet thick; the curtains are also of masonry and about the same thickness and height. Each bastion mounts eleven guns, one at the salient, three on each face, and two on each flank. Running round the base of these bastions and curtains, is a berm or terrace varying in width from fifteen to thirty feet, and having on its exterior edge a wall eight feet high loopholed for musketry. This wall is a continuation of the escarp wall of the ditch, which descends to a depth of twenty feet, and is twenty-five feet wide. The counterscarp is not of masonry, but is a mere earthen slope of easy incline, the glacis is about sixty yards wide, and covers scarcely half of the walls. On the eastern side of the city runs the river Jumna, on whose banks stand the palace of the king, and the old fort of Selimgurh, fronting which is the bridge of boats leading to Meerut. At the north side of the king's palace is the Calcutta Gate, and, following the defences in a north-westerly direction, is the Magazine, St. James's Church and the main guard. This was the extreme point of the face which our position fronted, and is the northernmost point of the city walls. Going still round to the left in a northerly direction, we come to the Cashmere Gate, and then to the Moree Gate and Bastion, on which our first fire was directed. This forms the left point of the face opposed to us. To the left of this again, the walls circling towards the river in an arc of which the Calcutta Gate would be about the centre, were the Cabul, Lahore, Furaskkhana, Ajmeer, Toorkaman, and Delhi Gates. Outside the Ajmeer Gate was a crown work for the defence of the tomb of Ghazee Khan. During the rainy season the river Jumna almost washes the walls of the eastern face of the city, rendering it unassailable. With the exception therefore of the three-quarters of a mile faced by our army, the enemy had free ingress and egress through the walls of the city, into which reinforcements from almost all quarters daily poured. The numerical strength of the Sepoys within the walls, on the 8th June, was estimated at 7000. On the 9th General Barnard was joined by the Guides (horse and foot), from the Punjaub, who had marched 600 miles in the extraordinary short period of twenty-two days. They were engaged on the afternoon of the day of their arrival in repelling the first of a series of assaults on our position, that occurred almost daily up to the actual storming of the place, and it was in this action that they lost their gallant young second-in-command, Quintyn Battye, a soldier of extraordinary promise. The enemy invariably endeavoured to turn our position, and was on every occasion repulsed with great loss. It would be mere repetition to describe each separate assault, and I shall therefore select only one or two of the most desperate:— The 23rd June, the 100th anniversary of the battle of Plassey, was the day predicted by the Hindoo seers for our downfall. It was the one specially selected for the General Massacre of Europeans throughout Bengal (if not India), and was by a coincidence favourably ominous both to the Festival of the Ruth Juttra of the Hindoos and the first day of the new moon sacred to the Mussulmans. The attack begun on our right from the suburb of the Subzee Mundee. The object of their attack was to get possession of our battery on the hill, but finding that they could not succeed, they confined themselves to the gardens and houses of the suburb, where a most desperate hand-to-hand fight continued for many hours. Fortunately the bridges in our rear had been blown up the day previously; yet notwithstanding that this relieved the army of all anxiety for its rear, and left a larger disposable moveable force, such was the determination with which the rebels fought that it was necessary to order out Rothney's Sikhs, who had only arrived that morning after a night march of twenty-four miles. It was not until after sunset that all resistance was overcome, and the enemy retired into the city through the Lahore Gate exposed to a fire of three eighteen pounders, which committed immense havoc amongst them. The enemy's loss was estimated at 1000 men. In one inclosure 150 were bayoneted, so desperately did they cling to cover. The casualties on our side were 180 killed and wounded, of whom 45 were Europeans of the 1st and 2nd Fusiliers and 60 Rifles, who bore the brunt of the battle. On the next day Colonel Chamberlain arrived to fill the post of Adjutant-General of the army. On the 26th appeared the first symptoms of disunion amongst the rebels in the desertion from the town of the 9th Native Infantry: they fled in great confusion, and were fired upon from the walls; after wandering about for a week or so, they surrendered themselves and claimed pardon under Mr. Colvin's proclamation. On the 28th our army was reinforced by 1000 men from the Punjaub; and on the 1st July the head-quarters, and a wing of Her Majesty's 61st from Ferozpore, arrived in camp. On that day was seen from our batteries on the ridge a large encampment on the other side of the Jumna; it was the whole body of the Rohilcund mutineers from the three stations of Bareilly, Moradabad, and Shahjehanpore, four regiments of infantry, one of irregular cavalry, and a battery of artillery. For a time it had been hoped that they would find the Ganges impassable, but the anticipated rise of the river did not take place; it was crossed at Gurmuktesur, the usual place of passage, the Doab was traversed, and Delhi was attained. For two whole days our troops had the mortification of watching the long train of men, guns, horses, and beasts of burden of all kinds, streaming across the bridge of boats into the city, without the possibility of preventing or in any way annoying them. An immediate attack on the part of the reinforcements was anticipated from the known practice of the insurgents with regard to new comers. Accordingly on the afternoon of the 3rd, they came out in force, and threatened the right rear of the English position. But, finding our men well prepared, they drew off and marched away several miles to our rear along the Kurnaul road as far as Aliepoor, the place where our army bivouacked the night before the advance upon Delhi and the first brush with the enemy.* Finding no enemy to oppose them, they returned, and though twelve guns and 1000 infantry, and two squadrons of cavalry had been sent out by General Barnard to intercept them, the rebels, after a short artillery fight, continued to effect their retreat with the loss only of a little baggage. On the 3rd, the force was joined by "Coke's Corps" of Punjaub Irregulars. On the 5th General Barnard died, the last of the officers that formed the council of war at Umballah. General Reed, an old officer in bad health, in virtue of his seniority, succeeded to the command in chief. On the 9th the enemy added a first attempt at stratagem to his usual mode of attack. He detailed to our rear a body of cavalry, who, advancing slowly, were mistaken for our 9th Irregulars. It was not until they came upon our advancing picket, consisting of two light guns and about 80 of the 6th Carbineers, that they were dis-

* Letter from an officer present.

covered. The artillery officer in command of the guns (Lieut. Hills) was about a hundred yards in front of his guns with the party of Carbineers, who, from some unexplained reason, immediately on catching sight of the enemy's cavalry, turned and fled. The guns being limbered up, Hills could do nothing; but rather than fly he charged by himself.* He fired four barrels of his revolver and killed two men, throwing the empty pistol in the face of another, and knocking him off his horse. Two horsemen then charged him, and rolled him and his horse over. He got up with no weapons, and seeing a man on foot coming at him to cut him down, rushed at him, got inside his sword, and hit him full in the face with his fist. At that moment he was cut down from behind, and a second blow would have done for him, had not Tombs, his captain, the finest fellow in the service (who had been in his tent when the row began) arrived at the critical moment, and shot his assailant. Hills was able to walk home, though his wound was severe, and on the road Tombs saved his life once more by sticking another man who attacked him. The enemy's horsemen charged right through the camp, firing into the tents. They halted, however, in our rear, on the banks of the canal, and there made a stand. They were taken in flank by some guns under Major Tombs, and ridden down, almost to a man, by some of the 6th Carbineers, and mounted guards from the Subzee Mundee road. Meantime a general attack upon all our pickets was made by about 6000 of the enemy in front; it was repulsed, after some severe fighting, with immense slaughter, and the enemy was driven as usual into the gardens and inclosures of the suburbs, from which they were dislodged at the point of the bayonet, our guns making lanes in their ranks as they retreated into the city. Similar actions were of almost daily occurrence, so that up to the 31st July no less than 23 battles had been fought, in which 22 officers and 296 men had been killed; and 72 officers and 990 men wounded. Our force at this date consisted of 6200 effective men, and 1060 sick and wounded. General Reed had been compelled, by ill health, to go to the hills; and General Wilson of the Artillery had taken the command, Colonel Baird Smith being Chief Engineer: two abler officers it would have been difficult to find in India or elsewhere. The General had now determined to act entirely on the defensive until the arrival of Nicholson's column with another siege train, should sufficiently strengthen his hands to attempt the final assault. On the 7th, our engineers made an ineffectual attempt to blow up the bridge of boats by floating down infernal machines, so arranged that they should explode when they came in contact with anything. An officer writing from the camp, about this time, gives the following description of it: — "What a sight our camp would be even to those who visited Sebastopol! The long lines of tents, the thatched hovels of the native servants, the rows of horses, the parks of artillery, the English soldier, in his gray linen coat and trowsers (he has fought as

* Letter to the "Times."

bravely as ever without pipeclay) the Sikhs with their red and blue turbans, the Affghans with their red and blue turbans, their wild air, and their gay head-dresses and coloured saddle cloths, and the little Goorkhas, dressed up to the ugliness of demons in black worsted Kilmarnock hats and woollen coats, the truest, bravest soldiers in our pay. There are scarcely any Porbeas (Hindoos) left in our ranks, but of native servants many a score. In the rear are the booths of the native bazaars, and further out on the plain the thousands of camels, bullocks, and horses that carry our baggage. The soldiers are loitering through the lines or in the bazaars. Suddenly the alarm is sounded, every one rushes to his tent. The infantry soldier seizes his musket and slings on his pouch, the artilleryman gets his guns harnessed, the Affghan rides out to explore, in a few minutes every one is in his place. If we go to the summit of the ridge of hill which separates us from the city, we see the river winding along to the left, the bridge of boats, the towers of the palace, and the high roofs and minarets of the great mosque, the roofs and gardens of the doomed city, and the elegant looking walls with batteries here and there, the white smoke of which rises slowly up among the green foliage that clusters round the ramparts." Yet it must not be supposed from this *couleur-de-rose* sketch that our troops were enjoying much rest; they were harassed by almost daily attacks, to repel which required almost every available soldier in camp. The season was most inclement, the rains being at their height, and the men were frequently under arms for hours without any shelter whatever. There was hot work in store for them. Nicholson, the Bayard of the Punjaub, had pushed on in advance of his column, and arrived in camp on the 8th of August. This gallant and comparatively young officer was a brevet Lieutenant-Colonel and regimental Captain in the 27th Native Infantry, and at the time of the breaking out of the mutiny was a 1st class Deputy-Commissioner in the Punjaub. On General Chamberlain being sent to Delhi, Colonel Nicholson, with the rank of Brigadier, was ordered to succeed him in command of the moveable column which had been organised at Wuzeerabad. This column consisted, on the 22nd of June, when Nicholson joined it, of the following troops:—

> Dawe's troop, Horse Artillery.
> Two guns, Smyth's troop (Natives).
> Bourchier's Light Infantry Battery.
> Her Majesty's 52nd Light Infantry.
> 2nd Punjaub Light Infantry Sikhs.
> 35th Bengal Native Infantry.
> Wing 9th Bengal Cavalry.
> Mooltanee Horse.

This force was, however, speedily reduced, for on the mutinying of the troops at Sealkote, on the 9th July, it was considered necessary to disarm the 35th Native Infantry, the cavalry and the native gunners of Smyth's troop. This was done at Umritsir, and immediately afterwards Brigadier Nicholson started with Her Majesty's 52nd and artillery to cut off the Sealkote mutineers, who would, it was thought, endeavour to join the Irregular Cavalry stationed at Goordaspoor; starting at 8 P. M., they reached that station, distant forty-four miles, the artillery in sixteen hours, the infantry (in carts) in nineteen. On the next day, spies brought word that the enemy were crossing the Ravee, and then might Brigadier Nicholson have closed his glass and said, " The day is ours." Marching out at 10 o'clock in the morning, in a couple of hours they came in sight of the enemy drawn up in battle array. Our guns opened immediately they got within range, and Pandy made a feeble attempt at a charge. His small body of cavalry actually rode into the Horse Artillery, but were cut down to a man. Then came the *sauve qui peut*, and they were unmolested in their flight, for there was no cavalry to pursue them. They took up a position upon an island in the river, where they threw up a parapet for their single gun, a 12-pounder. On the 14th General Nicholson crossed the 52nd, a point below the enemy's position, unobserved, and sweeping the entire island, killed or drove into the river every soul opposed to him. On the 25th of July Nicholson crossed the Beas, and commenced his march towards Delhi, which was reached by himself on the 8th, and by his troops on the 14th of August. How welcome was such a reinforcement need not be told. While it revived the ardour of the worn-out besiegers, it depressed in a far greater degree the spirits of the besieged. From the 14th of August to the 14th of September, the latter hazarded but one attack. On the 28th of August General Nicholson's brigade, of the strength in the margin, was ordered out to intercept a force of the enemy reported to have left Delhi with the intention of cutting off our expected siege-train. He marched at daybreak, and after crossing two difficult swamps arrived at a village called Naugloo, about nine miles to the north of our position, where he obtained intelligence of the enemy being expected at Nujuffgurh, a place about five miles further on. He arrived there about 4 P. M., and found that the enemy, 7000 strong, had taken up a strong position in front of the town of Nujuffghur, with their left centre resting on an old serai, in which they had four guns. Between this point and a bridge crossing the Nujuffgurh Canal, they had nine more guns. After a hasty reconnoisance, General Nicholson determined upon attacking their left centre, which seemed the key of the position, and then changing his front to take their line of guns in flank, and drive the enemy towards the bridge. Reserving 100 men of each of the corps, he sent Her Majesty's 61st and 1st Fusiliers, and 2nd Punjaub Infantry, with four guns on the left flank, and ten on the right, to carry the position. This was done in the most brilliant manner, with scarcely any loss, and following out his previously arranged movement with perfect success, the enemy were soon in full flight over the bridge, leaving the whole of their guns in our hands. The column bivouacked that

1 squad. 9th Lancers,
16 guns Horse Artillery,
120 Guide Cavalry,
200 Mooltanee Horse,
Wing of H.M. 61st,
1st European Battl. Foot,
1st and 2nd Punjaub Irr.
30 Sappers and Miners.

night at the bridge without food or shelter of any kind, and after blowing up the bridge the next day, marched back to camp, which it reached in the evening. On the 4th of September, the siege-train from Ferozpore, consisting of 32 pieces, 24-pounders and 10-inch mortars and howitzers, came in. Up to this time we may be looked upon as having been rather the besieged than the besiegers, for the guns at our disposal were quite inadequate to compete with the heavier metal with which the enemy returned our fire; now, however, with fifty-four heavy guns, the siege might begin in earnest, and our general and his engineers lost no time in setting to work. Ground may be said to have been first broken before Delhi on the 7th September. This usually laborious process was materially assisted by the nature of the ground, which was scored by a series of nullahs, running almost parallel to our position in the direction of the Jumna. These nullahs, which served only to drain the eastern slope of the ridge, were dry at this season of the year, and afforded capital cover for our troops. On the night of the 7th, No. 1 siege battery was commenced; it consisted of four 24-pounders, destined to demolish the Cashmere Bastion, distant 850 yards; and five 18-pounders and one 8-inch howitzer, to silence the fire of the Shah Bastion, distant 700 yards.

During the day and night of the 8th, the whole of these guns were got into position, and commenced a most destructive fire upon the enemy's works. On the night of the 10th, No. 2 battery was constructed, and opened fire at half-past 5 o'clock, A M. of the 11th; it was armed with nine 24-pounders, intended to breach the curtain adjoining the right flank of the Cashmere Bastion, distant 500 yards, and seven 8-inch howitzers, and two 18-pounders, to batter the bastion itself, destroy its masonry parapet, a small tower in the curtain, and the musketry parapet on its left face. No. 3 was armed on the night of the 11th with six 18-pounders, at a distance of 160 yards, to demolish the Water Bastion, and twelve $5\frac{1}{2}$-inch mortars to shell the interior of the bastion. This battery opened at 1 P.M. on the 12th. No. 4 mortar battery was ready on the evening of the 9th. It was, however, ordered not to open fire until the morning of the 11th, on which date it saluted with a storm of shell, from four 10-inch and six 8-inch mortars, the Cashmere and Water Gates and bastions, the church, and Skinner's House. "At different times," says Colonel Baird Smith, in his despatch, "between the 7th and 11th, these batteries opened fire with an efficiency and vigour which excited the unqualified admiration of all who had the good fortune to witness it. Every object contemplated in the attack was accomplished with a success even beyond my expectations, and I trust I may be permitted to say, that while there are many noble passages in the history of the Bengal Artillery, none will be nobler than that which will tell of its work on this occasion." On the night of the 13th the breaches were pronounced practicable, and instant orders were issued for the assault to take place next morning. The assaulting force was divided into four columns as follows:—

		Men.
1st, Brigadier Nicholson commanding	Her Majesty's 75th	300
	1st European Battalion, foot	200
	2nd Punjaub Irregulars	450
2nd, Brigadier Jones, Her Majesty's 61st, commanding	Her Majesty's 8th	250
	2nd European Battalion, foot	250
	4th Regiment Sikhs	250
3nd, Colonel Campbell, Her Majesty's 52nd, commanding	Her Majesty's 52nd	200
	Kemaon Battalion	250
	1st Punjaub Irregulars	500
4th, or Reserve, Brigadier Longfield, Her Majesty's 8th, commanding	Her Majesty's 61st	250
	4th Sikh Rifles	450
	Belooch Battalion	300
	Jheend Rajah's troops	300
	Her Majesty's 60th Rifles	200

The first column was destined to assault the main breach, the second the breach in the Water Bastion; the advance of both was covered by a battalion of Her Majesty's 60th Rifles. The third column was directed against the Cashmere Gateway; it was preceded by an explosion party covered by the 60th Rifles. The fourth column was kept in reserve. The 1st Bengal Fusiliers, headed by Brigadier Nicholson in person, escaladed the left face of the Cashmere Bastion, while the 75th and 2nd Punjaub Infantry carried the breach on the left of the Cashmere Gate. The bastion carried, the column reformed and, moving rapidly to the right, carried the various bastions up to the Caubul Gate; on reaching the head of the street at the Caubul Gate, the enemy made a resolute stand but were soon driven forward. Pushing on along the rampart road, the column was checked by a heavy fire from two guns commanding the road, which at this point was so narrow as scarcely to admit of four men abreast. After endeavouring for two hours to effect a passage, the column was withdrawn to the Caubul Gate, where it was met by Brigadier Jones's column. It was whilst rallying the men to a last charge down that fatal passage that the brave Nicholson received his mortal wound. The 2nd column carried the breach in the Water Bastion, and, turning to the right, followed almost in the footsteps of the 1st column, joining them as before stated at the Caubul Gate.

It was the duty of the explosion party to blow in the Cashmere Gate, and the way in which this desperate service was performed cannot be better told than in the words of Colonel Baird Smith. " The party was composed, in addition to the two officers named, of the following:

Serjeant John Smith,
„ A. B. Carmichael, and
Corporal F. Burgees, alias
Joshua Burgees Grierson, } of the Sappers and Miners.

Bugler Hawthorne, Her Majesty's 52nd.
14 Native Sappers and Miners.
10 „ Punjaub Sappers and Miners.

Covered by the fire of Her Majesty's 60th Rifles, this party advanced at the double towards the Cashmere Gate,—Lieutenant Home, with Serjeants J. Smith and Carmichael, and Havildar Madhoo, all of the Sappers, leading and carrying the powder bags, followed by Lieutenant Salkeld, Corporal Burgees, and a section of the remainder of the party. The advanced party reached the gateway unhurt, and found that part of the drawbridge had been destroyed; but passing across the precarious footing supplied by the remaining beams, they proceeded to lodge their powder against the gate. The wicket was open, and through it the enemy kept up a heavy fire upon them. Serjeant Carmichael was killed while laying the powder, Havildar Madhoo being at the same time wounded. The powder being laid, the advanced party slipped down into the ditch, to allow the firing party under Lieutenant Salkeld to perform its duty. While endeavouring to fire the charge, Lieutenant Salkeld was shot through the leg and arm, and handed over the slow match to Corporal Burgees, who fell mortally wounded, just as he had successfully performed his duty. Havildar Tiluk Singh, of the Sappers and Miners, was wounded, and Ram Hetch, Sepoy of the same corps, was killed, during this part of the operation. The demolition having been most successful, Lieutenant Home, happily unwounded, caused the bugle to sound the regimental call of the 52nd Regiment as the signal for the advance of the column. Fearing that amid the noise of the assault the sound might not be heard, he had the call repeated three times, when the troops advanced and carried the gateway with entire success." The gateway was stormed with a cheer, and the entire column entered the main guard. Re-forming, it then advanced with the intention of occupying the Kotwallee (Police Court), and, if possible, the Jumma Musjid. Clearing the Water Bastion, the church, and the "Gazette Press" Compound, the column proceeded through the Cashmere Gate Bazaar, arrived within about 100 yards of the Jumma Musjid, when it was found that the arches and gates of that building had been bricked up, and could not be forced without powder-bags or artillery. After remaining for half an hour under a galling fire of musketry from the houses, in the expectation of hearing of the successful advance of the other columns, Colonel Campbell deemed it prudent to retire upon the Begum's Bagh, or garden, a large enclosure, which he held for one hour and a half under a fire of grape and musketry. The Kumaon battalion, which, having diverged to the right, had for some time held the Kotwallee, here rejoined the column, which now fell back upon the church. Meantime, the Sirmoor battalion and the Guides made an attack upon the enemy's position in the suburbs of Kissengunge and Pahareepore, with a view of driving in the rebels and supporting the main attack by effecting an entrance at the Cabul Gate after it should be taken. This attack was supported by the cavalry under Brigadier Hope Grant, 9th Lancers, and Horse Artillery under Major Tombs. Though conducted with the utmost gallantry, this attack failed in its object: the enemy, however, abandoned their position the next day, leaving their guns in our hands.

At the close of the day, the whole of the defences, from St. James's Church to the Caubul Gate inclusive, then remained in our hands. Our loss in killed and wounded was severe, viz. 1160,—283 under the former head, including 7 officers; 877 under the latter, including 57 officers. On the walls were captured 37 pieces of ordnance. On the 15th, the magazine was breached, and carried by assault on the 16th. It was found to contain no less than 171 guns and howitzers, most of them of the largest calibre. The resistance of the enemy now became less determined, large bodies deserted, and the townspeople crowded out of the city. Every available mortar was now turned upon the palace, the old fort of Selimgurh, and the southern part of the city. On the 17th and 18th, advance posts were taken up in the face of considerable opposition, and on the 19th, the Buree Bastion was surprised and captured. On the 20th the troops pushed on, occupied the Lahore Gate and the other bastions and gateways, until the whole of the defences were in our hands. On the same day the gates of the palace were blown up, and the head quarters established there.

In the history of sieges, that of Delhi will ever take a prominent place. Its strength, resources, and the prestige attached to it in the native mind, combined to render formidable this citadel of Hindostan. Reasonably might the "Northern Bee," or the "Invalide Russe," question our ability to suppress this rebellion, if they drew their conclusions from the numerical strength of the little band that first sat down before Delhi. But the spirit that animated that handful of soldiers was not simply the emulative bravery of the military proletarian. The cries of helpless women and children, ruthlessly butchered, had gone home to the heart of every individual soldier and made this cause his own. There was not an Englishman in those ranks, from first to last, that would have consented to turn his back on Delhi without having assisted in meting out to those bloody rebels the retributive justice awarded them by his own conscience, his country, and his God. It was this spirit that buoyed them up through all the hardships of the siege, that enabled them for four long months of dreary rain and deadly heat, to face disease, privation, and death, without a murmur.

It was for the "crowning mercy" of that day of assault that every heart throbbed with intense longing; it was in the fixed determination to do or die, that, silent with pent-up hate, every soldier dealt his death-thrust on his brutal foe. Quarter was neither asked nor given, and when at the Cashmere Gate, the charred remains of a British soldier were found about a stake, to which he had been tied, it is not to be wondered at that even the wounded, abandoned by the enemy, met the fate they had failed to find in the field. For two days the city was given up to the soldiery, and who shall tell in how many obscure corners the injured husband, son, or brother, took his blood for blood. How the King was taken prisoner, and two of his sons shot, and how the reign of red tape supervened on General Wilson's departure to the hills for his health, I shall tell in a future chapter; but I shall not delay till then to tell the people of England, that, at the time I am writing, the King is still royally treated; that a surviving prince rides in state, with two British officers attending upon him; and that the cherished mosques and temples of Mussulman fanatics and Hindoo idolaters are still preserved intact in this modern Sodom.

THE END.

Printed and bound by Antony Rowe Ltd, Eastbourne

COMPLETE NARRATIVE

OF

THE MUTINY IN INDIA,

FROM ITS

COMMENCEMENT TO THE PRESENT TIME,

COMPILED FROM THE MOST AUTHENTIC SOURCES;

INCLUDING

MANY VERY INTERESTING LETTERS FROM OFFICERS AND OTHERS ON THE SPOT.

WITH

Eight Illustrations, drawn on Stone, of the most important Events.

EDITED BY

THOMAS FROST, Esq.

SECOND EDITION.

LONDON:
PUBLISHED BY READ AND CO., 10, JOHNSON'S COURT,
FLEET STREET.

LONDON:
WILLIAM STEVENS, PRINTER, 37, BELL YARD,
TEMPLE BAR.

NARRATIVE

OF THE

MUTINY IN INDIA.

SELDOM has news of more absorbing interest flashed along the wires of the electric telegraph than the intelligence which was received by its agency on the 26th of June, of the mutiny of the Bengal army, the massacre of Europeans, and the proclamation of a descendant of the great Mogul as King of Delhi. Only three days had elapsed since a meeting had been held in the metropolis to celebrate the centenary of the battle of Plassy, whereat the first steps were taken towards carrying out a proposal to erect a monument to the hero of the day—Robert Lord Clive—by whose military genius and daring the empire of Britain in the East was founded. The lapse of a hundred years seemed but to have consolidated our power, and if ever a thought of the possibility of its diminution crossed the mind of rulers or people, it was from an European foe that the peril was apprehended. The aim of Napoleon, which was the prime motive for the invasion of Egypt, was patent to Europe; and the ambitious designs of Russia, which have prompted all the intrigues of that power in Persia and Bokhara, have frequently aroused the fears of far-seeing politicians. But the possibility of any danger to the stability of our Indian empire from an internal source was never dreamed of. Every successive war with the native princes served only to extend the limits of our rule, and to increase the prestige of our power. There had been Sepoy mutinies, it is true, as at Vellore in 1806, and at Barrackpore in more recent times, but they arose out of very superficial causes of discontent, unshared by the native population generally, and were promptly and effectually suppressed. Hence, the evidences of disaffection among the troops of the Bengal Presidency, which preceded the outbreaks at Meerut and Delhi, elicited little attention in this country, where, indeed, Indian affairs have hitherto awakened a comparatively small share of public interest.

At this distance from the scene of the events, it is difficult to form an opinion as to the causes of the outbreak; but it is undeniable that discontent has been smouldering among the native population generally, as well as among the troops, for a considerable period. It is true that many of the abuses which may have contributed to produce this feeling have been borne for centuries, and are not the results of British rule; but it must be remembered that it is only within a very recent period that a native press has existed to call attention to them. Prominent among these is the use of torture by the police, to extort confessions, and the cruel oppression practised in the collection of the revenue—practices denied in Parliament until the report of the Madras Commission rendered denial no longer possible, though even Englishmen have been proved, not only to have been cognizant of, but participators in them. Of late years, too, the Indian Government, relying too much upon the partial enlightenment of the native mind, has interfered with social usages to an extent never ventured before, and which the Hindoos have regarded with much greater jealousy and dislike than had been anticipated. We may instance among these innovations their disregard of the law of adoption, solemnly enjoined by the Vedas, in the case of the childless, as a religious duty, and of which disregard a notable instance was afforded in the case of the Rajah of Sattara; the scrutiny into land titles in the Rohilcund, whence the Bengal army is largely recruited, and which led the fathers and elder brothers of thousands of Sepoys to fear deprivation of the little properties held by the same families for centuries; and the interference with the marriage customs of the Bengalees, which could not fail to arouse ill-feeling among a people, all whose social usages are consecrated not less by the lapse of ages than by the sanction of religion.

It is not a little remarkable that no one has thought of connecting with the Indian mutinies the singular "cake movement," by which they were preceded and accompanied. It originated in the recently annexed kingdom of Oude, and spread rapidly through India. A breathless messenger appeared in a village, bearing a little cake, in size and shape not unlike a gingerbread nut, which he delivered to the head constable, enjoining him to have one made exactly like it, to be immediately forwarded to the next village. Thus the mysterious symbol sped onward, like the fiery cross of the Scottish Highlanders described in the "Lady of the Lake."

Nothing explanatory of the proceeding having yet been elicited, it is not assuming too much to suppose it connected with the manifestations of disaffection which immediately followed. To insure the success of his scheme, the originator, whoever he may be, bethought himself of feigning an order of Government, whose astonished officials were met accordingly with assurances from the village police that the preservation of the old and the making and transmission of the new cakes was enjoined upon them as an express command of the Sirkar, to be obeyed unquestioningly.

The first symptoms of disaffection were exhibited at Berhampore, in the immediate neighbourhood of Calcutta, where the Sepoys objected to the impurity, according to their notions, of the substances used in the manufacture of the new rifle cartridge.

In firing from the Minié rifle it is necessary that the ball end of the cartridge should have an external application of some greasy substance, for the purpose of lubricating the bore of the barrel; but it is not indispensable that this should be composed of tallow, as was the case with those sent out to India, and objected to on religious grounds by the Sepoys. The men of the 19th Regiment had become aware of the objections which had been urged against the new cartridges; and on the occasion of the regiment being ordered to parade for exercise with blank ammunition, they refused, on the evening of the 26th of February, to receive it, on the alleged ground that the paper of which the cartridges were made was of two descriptions, and that they entertained doubts about it, in consequence of the reports in circulation that it was greased with the fat of cows and pigs. The Government immediately resolved to disband the regiment, as a step preferable to coercion, the consequences of which could not be calculated.

The 19th Regiment was in open mutiny, the 34th was in league with it, the 2nd Grenadiers were sympathetic. Not less than 5000 men were in a state of obstinate fanaticism, which any incident might change to fury. Calcutta itself might not be safe from the attack or the example of the mutineers. The capital has for the last two years been left almost unprotected. Formerly there was always a European regiment in the fort, and 1200 artillerymen at Dundum, eight miles off. The transfer of the artillery head-quarters to Meerut left only one regiment in Calcutta, and that was sometimes reduced to a wing. It was barely possible the Sepoys might refuse to obey the order, or display their sympathy in a manner involving a breach of discipline. In that case the fort, if not the town, would be in danger, and the Government acted wisely in providing against the possibility of resistance.

The regiment was marched down to Barrackpore, where the disbandment was carried into effect by Major-General Hearsey, C. B., on the 31st.

Two Queen's regiments, with cavalry and artillery, occupied one side, the native regiments the other, and the mutinous corps were in the midst. A proclamation was read, and they were told they must lay down their arms. They were disposed to resist, but the preparations and firmness of Major-General Hearsey, himself a native of India, thoroughly cowed them. They yielded, piled their arms, and were marched out of cantonments as far as Palta Ghat, and were at once conveyed across the river in steamers ready for the purpose.

The sentence, though inadequate, in the opinion of military men, to the offence, was not without severity. Every native officer lost his commission. Every old Sepoy lost his pension, and, as the Company only receives recruits up to a certain age, his bread.

It speedily became evident that disaffection was not confined to the 19th Regiment, nor to the neighbourhood of Calcutta. The mutineers of Berhampore had scarcely been disbanded when intelligence was received of a mutiny among the Madras troops at Vizieragram. The Madrasees have no caste, and their discontent must therefore proceed from other causes than the cartridge order. The 34th were still sullen; the wavering regiments—notably the 2nd Grenadiers—seemed to have made up their minds to side with the strongest.

Mungal Pandy, a Sepoy of the 34th, while in a state of excitement from the use of intoxicating drugs, armed himself with a sword and loaded musket, and fired at Lieutenant Baugh, the adjutant of the corps, and shot his horse. Lieutenant Baugh, in self-defence, fired his pistol, and missed the man, who thereupon attacked him with his sword, and wounded him in the hand. The sergeant-major of the corps, who went to Lieutenant Baugh's assistance, was also wounded by Mungal Pandy. Major-General Hearsey, on being informed of the occurrence, proceeded to the parade-ground, and, observing the man walking to and fro with his loaded musket, and drawn sword covered with blood, proceeded with some officers and men to secure the Sepoy; but on their approaching him he discharged his musket, and wounded himself. He was then seized, as also the jemadar of the guard, who had refused to go to Lieutenant Baugh's assistance. Both were sentenced to death by native courts-martial, and were hung immediately afterwards. Almost simultaneously with this affair a plot to seize the Mint and plunder the vaults was discovered, and several Sepoys, convicted of tampering with the Mint guard, were sentenced to fourteen years' transportation.

On the 18th April bad symptoms manifested themselves at Umballah. The native troops were ordered to fire what they consider the objectionable cartridges on the following day. The empty European barracks were burnt down at nine in the evening, and the native infantry hospital, a mile distant, three hours after. Notwithstanding these indications of widely spread disaffection, the rulers of India and those at home had no serious misgivings. "The truth is," said the Calcutta correspondent of the *Times,* " we are at this moment passing through one of those periodical storms which every now and then remind us that Government in India 'sits on bayonets.' The Sepoys are restless and dissatisfied. They have no particular grievances, no particular leaders, no particular wants. A war on this side of India would at once remove every symptom of disaffection. But they are idle, and brood, like all Asiatics, over imaginary wrongs and absurd reports, till they are ready for anything, no matter what, that will break the feverish monotony of their lives. Then we have gradually reduced the number of officers, by draining them off for staff employment, till there are not enough left to manage the regiments. Sepoys require nearly as much attention as children. Under such circumstances mutiny, unless stopped by stern and striking punishment, is apt to become epidemic. There is, so far as we know, no real disaffection among the great body of the army. Even the restlessness so conspicuous in places is confined to those places, and will cease the moment it is known the Government will endure no more. The Europeans, the Sikhs, the Irregulars, the Cavalry, and the great body of the Infantry, are not simply obedient, but quite ready to crush the first symptom of disorder among their own comrades." The sequel will show how far this sense of security, and of confidence in Hindoo loyalty, was well founded.

The 34th Native Infantry were disbanded on the 6th of May, with the exception of the three companies which were on detached duty at Chittagong when the disaffection was manifested at head-quarters, and a few native officers who took no part in the mutiny.

The next instance of disobedience of orders occurred at Lucknow, when the men of the 7th Oude Irregulars refused to receive the cartridges served out to them, and left the parade with their muskets; but by the promptitude of Sir Henry Lawrence this movement was at once suppressed. The regular European and native troops at Lucknow, including a battery of eight guns, were immediately called out, the mutineers laid down their arms, and were confined to their lines.

At this time the native force at Meerut consisted of the 3rd Light Cavalry and the 11th and 20th Regiments of Native Infantry. Among the men of the cavalry corps the question of the greased cartridges, which had previously been mooted at Berhampore and other stations, was freely agitated. The result of the movement was, that 85 men of the regiment refusing to handle the cartridges, found themselves tried by court-martial, and sentenced to various terms of imprisonment with hard labour. On the 9th of May their sentences were read out on parade, and the offenders marched off to gaol. Up to this time disaffection had shown itself only through incendiary fires in the lines, hardly a night passing without one or more conflagrations. But on the 10th it appeared at once in all its unsuspected strength. Towards the evening of that day, while many of the Europeans were at church—for it was Sunday—the men of the two native infantry regiments, the 11th and 20th, as if by previous concert, assembled together in armed and tumultuous bodies upon the parade ground. Several officers hurried from their quarters to endeavour to pacify them. What then followed is so well told in the following letter from one of the officers to a friend at Calcutta, that we quote it in extenso :—

"Meerut, May 16th, 1857.

"I must premise by telling you that this is not the first letter I have written you on the terrible catastrophe to which it refers, but the third. Yesterday morning I sat down sleepless, fatigued, and dirty, and wrote you a long account of all that had occurred, and this morning I continued my communication; but on going to the post-office, in order to deposit the letter with my own hand, I learnt that yesterday's down country dâk had been stopped and destroyed a very little distance down the road, and so it is necessary that I should commence all over again. I will now relate over again everything as it occurred on the day before yesterday, giving you mostly a personal narrative, and adding what I have learnt from others, and which I could not have seen. On Sunday, the 10th, between 5 and 6 o'clock in the evening, I was in my bungalow, in rear of the lines of the 11th Native Infantry, where I have resided since my arrival at the station, when, as I was dressing, preparatory to going out for a ride with Colonel Finnis, of the 11th Native Infantry, my attention was attracted to my servants and those in the neighbouring compounds, going down towards the front of our inclosures, and looking steadily into the lines of the 11th, whence a buzzing murmuring noise proceeded, such as I have often heard in cases of fire, or some such alarm. Of this I took little notice, but went down to my gate, still dressing; and the noise still increasing, I returned to the bungalow, put on my uniform, and again went out. I had scarcely got to the gate, when I heard the popping sound of firearms, which I knew at once were loaded with ball cartridge, and a European non-commissioned officer came running with others, towards me from the 11th lines, saying, 'For God's sake, Sir, leave! come to your bungalow, change that dress, and fly!' I walked into my bungalow, and was doffing my uniform, the bullets by this time flying out of the 11th

MASSACRE AT MEERUT.

DEATH OF COLONEL FINNIS

lines into my compound, when the havildar-major of the 11th rushed into the room, terrified and breathless, and exclaimed, ' Fly, sahib—fly at once! the regiments are in open mutiny, and firing on their officers, and Colonel Finnis has just been shot in my arms.' It was evidently becoming serious. I came out, and ordered my horse to be saddled and brought up, my servants still begging of me to fly for my life. I mounted. The lines of the 6th Dragoon Guards (Carabineers) lie to the north of my bungalow, separated by a rugged and barren plain, cut up by nullahs and ravines, upon which, riding out of the back part of my compound, I descended. A Briton does not like actually ' running away' under any circumstances, and I was riding slowly through the uneven ground, when the havildar-major before mentioned exclaimed, ' You, sahib, are mounted and can make haste, ride to the European cavalry lines, and give the alarm.' Good ; I galloped off, crossed the difficult ground all right, got into the cavalry lines and made for the colonel's house, which he had just left, and found him in the barrack lines on horseback, ordering the Dragoons to saddle, arm, and mount without a moment's delay. Here I shall leave the Dragoons and myself, and return to the Native Infantry parade-ground, and the commencement of the mutiny and massacres.

"About 5 o'clock the 20th Native Infantry and the 3rd Light Cavalry rushed from their lines, armed and furious; the former regiment firing off their muskets, approaching the 11th Native Infantry, and calling upon them to arm, come out, and join them. I believe the 11th hesitated at first—cause unknown ; but presently they, too, armed and rushed out, and the mutinous fuel took flame. About this time Colonel Finnis and several other officers of the 11th Native Infantry, came upon the parade, and commenced haranguing the Sepoys, and attempted to pacify them and bring them to order, when the colonel's horse was wounded by a bullet fired by the 20th. On this he saw that the matter was more serious than he had wished to believe; and one of his officers asking him if he should ride off to the brigade-major, ask for aid, and give the alarm, he consented. This is the last time he was seen alive by European eyes; for immediately afterwards he was shot in the back by a Sepoy of the 20th, fell from his horse, and was actually riddled with balls. About this time the other officers of the 11th, seeing that their presence among the mutineers was perfectly useless, and the bullets flying about them in all directions, retreated from the lines, and sought safety mostly in the direction of the Carabineer lines; to which I must now retransfer the narrative. It took us a long time, in my opinion, to get ready, and it was dark before the Dragoons were prepared to start in a body; while by this time flames began to ascend in all directions from the lines, and the officers' bungalows of the 3rd Cavalry, and the 11th and 20th Native Infantry, from public buildings, messhouses, private residences, and, in fact, every edifice or thing that came within reach of the torch and the fury of the mutineers and of the bazaar *canaille,* who, in considerable numbers, I believe, joined in their terrific orgies. On all sides shot up into the heavens great pinnacles of waving fire, of all hues and colours, according to the nature of the fuel that fed them, huge volumes of smoke rolling sullenly off in the sultry night air, and the crackling and roar of the conflagration mingling with the shouts and riot of the mutineers. The entire scene, of which these were but the most prominent external features, and which words cannot describe, I leave to your readers to imagine, if they are fond of the horrible and the tragic. When the Carabineers were mounted we rode off at a brisk trot, through clouds of suffocating dust and darkness, in an easterly direction, and along a narrow road ; not advancing in the direction of the conflagration, but, on the contrary, leaving it behind on our right rear. In this way we proceeded for some two or three miles, to my no small surprise; when suddenly the ' halt' was sounded, and we faced about, retracing our steps, and, verging off to our left, approached the conflagration, and debouched on the left rear of the Native Infantry lines, which, of course, were all in a blaze. Skirting along behind these lines, we turned them at the western end, and wheeling to the left, came upon the 11th parade-ground, where, at a little distance, we found the Horse Artillery, and Her Majesty's 60th Rifles. It appears that the three regiments of mutineers had by this time commenced dropping off to the westward and towards the Delhi road; for here some firing took place between them and the Rifles; and presently the Horse Artillery, coming to the front and unlimbering, opened upon a copse or wood in which they had apparently found cover, with heavy discharges of grape and canister, which tore and rattled among the trees, and all was silent again. The Horse Artillery now limbered up again, and wheeled round, and here I joined them, having lost the Dragoons in the darkness. By this time, however, the moon arose. We 'blessed her useful light,' and the Horse Artillery column, with Rifles at its head, moving across the parade ground, we entered the long street turning from the southward behind the Light Cavalry lines. There it was that the extent and particulars of the conflagration first became visible, and, passing the burning bungalow of the Adjutant of the 11th Native Infantry, we proceeded along the straight road or street, flanked on both sides with flaming and crushing houses in all stages of combustion and ruin, the Rifles occasionally firing volleys as we proceeded. It was by this time past 10 o'clock; and having made the entire circuit of the lines, we passed up to the eastward of them, and, joined by the Dragoons and Rifles, bivouacked for the night. I must now come to the particulars of the brutal outrages and assassinations that marked this infernal outbreak, premising, however, that a sense of delicacy and a regard for the harassed feelings of surviving friends and relatives, prevent me from entering into details, the relation of which could only gratify a mind fond of horrors and atrocities. At the very commencement of the *émeute* the 3rd Light Cavalry, saddling and mounting their horses, galloped off to the gaol, and of course, overpowering all resistance, liberated their 85 comrades, and all the other prisoners, to the number of about 1300, apparently. Returning from this, they joined the mutineers of the 20th Native Infantry, and the work of indiscriminate European massacre began, without regard to rank, age, sex, or employment, furious and merciless. Veterinary Surgeons Philipps and Dawson, of the 3rd Light Cavalry, and the wife of the latter, were massacred, and also Lieutenant M'Nab, of the same regiment, several others of the corps having miraculous escapes, but the surgeon, Christie, being wounded, I fear mortally. Of the officers of the 20th Native Infantry, Captain Taylor commanding, Captain M'Donald, with the wife of the latter, were savagely slain, with, as in the case of the cavalry officers, numerous narrow escapes. Of the 11th Native Infantry poor Finnis was the only officer slain; but Mrs. Chambers, the wife of the adjutant, was pitilessly slaughtered in her own bungalow, which, as I have told you above, we saw burning; and remember, as I have also said above, I refrain from describing details, merely giving the casualties. Among those not in the military employ of the Government, who perished in this indiscriminate massacre, were Mr. Tregear, of the education department, Mrs. Courteney, the mistress of the hotel, and many women and girls whose names I do not know. After all this work was done, and the mutineers had retreated, the remainder of the night passed away in gloom and doubt, and the conflagration, having nothing more to feed upon, was extinguished, as it were, by the rising beams and more powerful light of the sun. I mounted my horse and rode down from the Carabineers lines towards my hospital and the Native Infantry lines, dubious as to the state of affairs, and came to the charred and blackened huts and bungalows, all naked and deserted. On my way down a dhoolee approached and was passing me, when I stopped the bearers and asked what they carried? They answered, 'the Colonel Sahib.' It was poor Finnis's body, which had just been found where he fell, and was being carried towards the churchyard. All sick, to the number of about 40, had fled from the hospital, which was deserted, with the exception of two or three smallpox cases, too bad to move, and who appeared much surprised at my attending to them as if nothing whatever had occurred. All day yesterday the station was under arms, and surrounded and traversed everywhere by patrols mounted and on foot, and the same precautions were of course observed last night; not unnecessarily either, for the carabines of the Dragoons were heard constantly through the night, firing upon marauders and incendiaries, who came prowling towards the lines. In the midst of our own troubles, we are very anxious about the fate of the Europeans at Delhi, whither the mutineers have gone, and as the telegraph wires were cut at the commencement of the outbreak, we know nothing of what is occurring elsewhere, nor of what is known about us. I hope the health of our men will stand the constant duty in this terrible weather, until relief shall come to us, or some move suited to the magnitude of the danger and disaster shall be made by some man of energy and competence, for whom here is an occasion. We have plenty of small arm ammunition, and sharp swords in the hands of as good regimental officers and men as ever sat in saddle or shouldered firelock; and ought to be able to hold our own, if the odds don't rise very much against us. All that we now much dread is fire to our bungalows and barracks, and what we most look to is the descent of the European regiments from the hills to join us. We are not, however, entirely isolated and deserted, for some trumps of zemindars to the southward, hearing of this affair, and that yesterday's dâk containing my letter to you had been stopped and plundered, turned out on horseback, and, with two collector's suwars, took up on the road and brought in a dâk this morning from the southward and Calcutta. These men are to take out the dâk this afternoon, and say they will see it safe on its way down country, so I hope this may reach you safe. I never expected that my letter of yesterday would reach you, but I wrote on the extreme chance, and shall continue to do so as long as there is anything to write about. We take it as a good symptom that we hear nothing from the dâk people of disturbances down country. Two Europeans travelling by carriage dâk to Delhi, one named Mortimer, fell in among the mutineers on the road, a short distance from the station, on the night of the row, and were of course dragged from the carriage and murdered."

Many additional particulars of the outbreak and massacre at Meerut, will be found in the following extract from a letter written by the Rev. T. C. Smyth, M.A., chaplain of the station:—

"All remained quiet till the evening of Sunday, the 10th of May, when I was driving down to church, (distant about a mile from my house,) for the 7 P. M. service, and met on my way two of Her Majesty's 60th Rifles covered with blood and supported by their comrades. On reaching the church I found buggies and carriages driving away in great confusion, and a body of people running and pointing to a column of fire and smoke in the direction of the city. Frequent shots were then heard, and the distant cries of a large mob. My colleague, the Rev. Mr. Rotton, and his wife, came up at the moment; but, finding that the people had all gone back, we abandoned the thought of commencing divine service, and I drove home, about half-past 7 or a quarter to 8, in the direction of the Rifle and Artillery lines, avoiding the most public places of resort. I may mention that a guard of some eight or ten Sepoys at the artillery depôt, or School of Instruction (three of whom were killed shortly afterwards in resisting an officer who came with his party to take their post), saluted me in passing. I reached my house in perfect safety, but found that the Sepoy guard at the Brigadier's (close at hand) had, shortly before, fired a shot, which passed between them while they were standing at the gate of their compound. We went together, just after my return, into the western verandah, and heard a shot in the adjoining road, followed by a cry and the galloping off of a horse with a buggy. This proved to have been the murder of Mr. Phillips (veterinary surgeon of the 3rd Light Cavalry), who was shot and mutilated by five troopers; Dr. Christie (the surgeon of the same regiment), who accompanied him in the buggy, having been sadly disfigured and injured at the same time. He is still living and doing well. By this time the English troops (consisting of the 6th Dragoon Guards, a troop and a battery of Bengal Artillery, with the 1st battalion of the 60th Royal Rifles), had reached the Native Infantry lines, into which they fired with grape and musketry. The inhabitants of the Suddur Bazaar and city committed atrocities far greater than those of the Sepoys, as in the case of Captain M'Donald's wife, whom they pursued some distance and frightfully mutilated (though her children were happily all saved by the ayahs), and of Mrs. Chambers, wife of the Adjutant of the 11th Native Infantry, who was murdered in her garden during Mr. Chambers' absence on duty, her clothes having been set on fire before she was shot and cut to pieces. About 10 o'clock a bungalow, immediately opposite our house, was set on fire by five troopers of the 3rd Light Cavalry, and an attempt (though happily unsuccessful) was made to fire the Brigadier's house. After 11, strong pickets and patrols of the English cavalry, artillery, and infantry were posted on the road near our house, but the firing of houses, &c., continued till close upon day-break, principally caused by the neighbouring villagers, after the guarding of the lines. The loss of property, and alas! of life, has been very dreadful. The part of Meerut in which the insurrection principally raged is a miserable wilderness of ruined houses, and some of the residents (as was the case with Mr. and Mrs. Greathed, the Commissioner of the Division) escaped miraculously from the hands of their pursuers, by hiding themselves in the gardens and outhouses of their burning bungalows, and in some cases by disguising themselves as native servants. Before the European troops arrived on Sunday night at the scene of action, the following were barbarously cut to pieces:—Mr. V. Tregear, inspector of schools; Captain M'Donald, of the 20th Native Infantry, and Mrs. M'Donald; Captain Taylor, Mr. Pattle, Mr. Henderson, all of the same corps; Colonel Finnis, commanding the 11th Native Infantry; Mrs. Chambers, whose murderer was caught on the 15th, tried at once, and hanged on a tree without further delay, his body afterwards being burnt to ashes. In the 3rd Light Cavalry the following were killed:—Mr. Phillips, veterinary surgeon;

Mr. and Mrs. Dawson; Mr. Mac Nab, lately joined, and a little girl of the riding master's, Mr. Langdale; together with several soldiers of the Artillery and 60th Rifles, and women and children of the military, and general residents in the station. Among other instances of frightful butchery, was that of Sergeant Law, his wife and six children, who were living beyond the precincts of cantonments. The state in which the father and three of the infants were found defies description. Happily the mother and three other children, though grievously mangled, crawled about midnight to the Artillery Hospital, and it is hoped will recover. Mr. Rotton and I have buried 31 of the murdered, but there are others whose bodies have not as yet been brought in. The 3rd Light Cavalry (with the exception of some 70 or 80 troopers) and the 20th Native Infantry, went off to Delhi during Sunday night. The 11th Native Infantry, who not only refrained from murdering their officers and burning houses, but protected the ladies and children of the corps, remained in the neighbourhood; 120 of these have returned, and it is thought that many more of them will do so, a proclamation of pardon, under the circumstances, having been sent to them. On Monday night many people (including a large number of women and children) slept in the Artillery School of Instruction, a walled inclosure, well guarded. On Tuesday I returned with my friends to our house, but while we were at dinner I received the news that all the Delhi troops had mutinied, and joined the insurgents. We were consequently ordered, with the ladies and children, back into the depôt, and the troops were at once placed under arms and posted with cannon, so as to command the European lines of the station, the rest being abandoned. The night passed away with no disturbance, except constant shots between the pickets and rioters, the latter consisting of villagers and residents in the city and bazaars."

On the morning of the 11th, a party of the 3rd Light Cavalry, variously stated at from 25 to 250, made their appearance at Delhi. They had come over from Meerut during the night, fully armed, and apparently wild with rage and excitement. They entered the Calcutta gate without opposition from any of the police, and made their way directly towards Deriowgunge, shooting down in their progress all Europeans they met with. Among the first victims were Mr. Simon Fraser, the Governor General's agent; Captain Douglas, his assistant; and Mr. R. Nixon, chief clerk in their office. Notice was immediately sent up to the brigadier, and a regiment (the 54th) with two guns from De Teissier's battery, were sent down. The 54th marched through the Cashmere gate in good order, but on the approach of some of the Sowars, the Sepoys rushed suddenly to the side of the road, leaving their officers in the middle of the road, upon whom the troopers immediately came at a gallop, and, one after the other, shot them down. The officers were, with the exception of Colonel Ripley, unarmed. The colonel shot two of them before he fell; but with this exception, and one said to have been shot by Mr. Fraser, none fell. After butchering all the officers of the 54th, the troopers dismounted, and went among the Sepoys of the 54th, shaking hands with them.

Had the officers been armed with revolvers, they might have shot some of them; but had they done so, it is still a doubtful question whether their own men would not have bayoneted them. The 54th made some show of firing their muskets, but the shots went, of course, over the heads of the troopers, who had evidently full confidence in the reception they were to meet with. Their plans must have been well matured. Meanwhile the people of the city were collecting for mischief; several bungalows at Deriowgunge had been fired; and as the day advanced, the Goojurs of the villages around Delhi became alive to the chances of booty, and were ready for action. The whole city was up in arms, every European residence was searched, the troopers declaring that they did not want property, but life; and when they retired, the rabble rushed in and made a clean sweep, from the roofs to the floor mats.

As soon as the extent of the outbreak was known, it became necessary for the residents to seek some place of safety; and most of them made their way to the Flagstaff Tower, where the gun is fired. A company of the 38th Native Infantry and two guns were stationed here, and a large party of ladies and gentlemen, including the brigadier, brigade major, &c., were here well armed, with

LIEUTENANT WILLOUGHBY BLOWING UP THE MAGAZINE AT DELHI.

the intention of defending themselves against the troopers. The tower is round, and of solid brickwork, and was well adapted for the purpose—better, in fact, than any other building in Delhi. In selecting this spot the brigadier displayed considerable judgment, but he did not know then the extent of the catastrophe; for although the general demeanour of the troops was anything but subordinate, the actual state of the case was unknown. Many of the officers of the 38th still had confidence in their men, and endeavoured to reason with them, when they showed symptoms of insubordination; but, on Colonel Graves haranguing the company stationed at the Flagstaff Tower, it became evident that they were in a state of mutiny, and that the slightest thing would induce them to turn at once against their officers and the other Europeans assembled on the hill. About a quarter to four the magazine in the city exploded; a puff of white smoke, and the report of a gun, preceded the cloud of red dust, which rose like a huge coronet into the air. The explosion that followed was not so great as might have been expected, but the effect was complete. It was soon known that the explosion was not accidental, but the gallant act of Lieutenant Willoughby, Commissary of Ordnance, Delhi, and it is pleasing to be able to add that this brave young man escaped with a severe scorching. About 1500 persons, rebels, are said to have been blown up with the magazine.

On the appearance of the clouds of dust in the air, the company of the 38th made a rush to their arms, which were piled near them. The object they had in view is not clearly defined; but it is supposed that they were influenced by a sudden desire to attack those within the tower. Soon after this, the 38th took possession of two guns sent up to reinforce the party at the tower; and on this becoming known, the brigadier advised all who could leave to do so, intending to follow when the rest had all departed. Conveyances being in waiting, most of the ladies got away, the gentlemen following on horseback; and thus a safe retreat was effected towards Kurnaul for some, while others branched off to Meerut. The mutiny at that place was the signal for all the rogues in the vicinity of that station, including the prisoners in the gaol, who were liberated by the mutineers, to take possession of the road and plunder all passengers, so that all communication between Meerut and Allygurh was entirely cut off for three or four days. It does not appear that the mutineers ever left Delhi, but the communications between Delhi and Agra were stopped in the same way, and the residents at Muttra and Agra were alarmed by reports that the Sepoys were marching down the right bank of the Jumna, direct on the seat of Government.

Immediately on the receipt of this painful and alarming intelligence the Lieutenant-Governor, Mr. Colvin, took the most prompt and decisive measures to suppress the mutiny and to prevent the panic and disaffection from spreading among the native troops cantoned at Agra and the neighbouring stations.

The young Maharajah Sindia of Gwalior no sooner heard of the rising at Delhi than he hastened, with every expression of friendship, to place the whole of his contingent at the disposal of the Lieutenant-Governor of Agra. As a compliment to the Prince, the services of his Highness's Body Guard, consisting of horse artillery and cavalry, with a detail of infantry, were accepted, the political agent and the brigadier commanding the contingent having previously inspected them on parade at the express solicitation of the Prince. The men of this force are a very soldierlike body of fellows. They are of the same caste as the Maharajah, many of them being members of his family; and their assistance, it is thought, may be relied upon. It is said that the King of Delhi sent a deputation of the revolted cavalry to the Rajah of Jhind, asking his assistance against the English. The Rajah was on the parade-ground with his troops at the time, and immediately ordered his soldiers to cut down every man of the messengers. The Rajah of Bhurtpore came forward also at once with the offer of his regiment, and the Rajah of Putteeallah intercepted and sent to the commissioner of his district many seditious letters which had found their way into his territories.

The following is the substance of a letter written by a native who was an eye-witness of the events at Delhi, and addressed to the vakeel of one of the Rajpootana states:—

"Yesterday morning, about 7 o'clock, some regular cavalry arriving from Meerut seized the bridge on the Jumna, killed the tollkeeper, and robbed the till. Leaving a guard at the bridge they proceeded to the Salempore Chowkee, where there was an English gentleman, killed him, and set fire to his house. Then, going under the Delhi King's palace, outside the city wall, they made proposals to the King. The King told them that that was no place for them, but to go into the city. Having entered the Calcutta gate, it was closed. At this time Mr. Simon Fraser, the commissioner, and the magistrate, were in office. Hearing the tumult, they ascended to the top of the river gate of the city, and perceived that troops were coming up along the Meerut road; mounting a buggy, they drove to the city gate, leading to the palace. Finding it closed they dismounted, and getting the wicket of the gate opened to them they proceeded on foot into the citadel. The native governor of the citadel (Killedar) entered after them, and killed them while ascending the steps of the officers' quarters. (Probably of Captain Douglas, commanding Palace Guards.) Thus much the crowd witnessed.

"The mutineers were preceded on their first arrival by 10 or 12 troopers, who, on entering the Rajghat gate of the city, assured everybody that they had come not to trouble or injure the city people in any way, but only to kill the European gentlemen, of whom they had resolved to leave none alive. On this news reaching the ears of the gentlemen they left their respective offices and fled. The mutineers killed all they could catch. Some got hidden among the houses. The greater part rushed to the magazine and closed the gate. About 3 in the afternoon the gentlemen fired a shell from the magazine, which killed and wounded a vast number of the crowd. The report shook the houses as if a magazine had exploded.

"About 10 at night two troops of artillery arrived from Meerut and entered the city, and fired a royal salute of 21 guns. Afterwards the troopers proceeding to the military cantonment (about one and a half mile outside the city), killed a great number of the officers, and their wives and children, and set fire to the houses. All the vagabonds of the city have joined the mutineers, and are ravaging the city. The next day, about 3 in the afternoon, the empire was proclaimed under the King of Delhi, and the Imperial flag hoisted at the Kotwalee (chief police station). The King's chief police officer arrived, with him all the mutineers, horse and foot, and killed all the rest of the Europeans they met or found. Then guns were fired as a salute. The old chief of police fled. The mace-bearers stood aloof. Thousands of rupees' worth of things were pillaged till 12 o'clock in the night.

"There is now no ruler in the city, and no order. Every one has to defend his house. An attack was made on the house of the great banker, Mungnee Ram, but he had assembled so many defenders, that after much fighting the attack was unsuccessful. Other bankers' (names mentioned) were pillaged. The Delhi Bank was entirely pillaged. In short, within these two days, hundreds of thousands of rupees' worth of property has been destroyed and stolen. No one can venture out of his house. The King's officers have the control. The mutineers roam about the city, sacking it on every side. The post is stopped. The electric telegraph wires have been cut. News is closed on all sides. There is not an European face to be seen. Where have they gone, or how many have been killed? Hundreds of corpses are lying under the magazine. The burners of the dead wander about to recognise the looked-for faces and give them funeral rites. I don't know whether I shall live to see the end of all this. Hundreds of wealthy men have become beggars; hundreds of vagabonds have become men of wealth. When an heir to the city arises, then the public market will be reopened and order be restored. For these two days thousands have remained fasting, such of the shops as are left unpillaged being closed."

The events which followed the arrival of the Meerut mutineers at Delhi, are thus related by an officer who escaped the slaughter, and who recounts his sufferings and perils while making his way to Kurnaul.

"Immediately the 54th Native Infantry arrived in the city the men all joined the mutinous cavalry, and cut up all the officers, with the exception of two or three, who managed to escape; the Artillery also turned the guns against us. Nearly all the 74th

Native Infantry followed their example, and many of the officers of that corps were also murdered. A regular slaughter of all Europeans was then commenced in the city—men, women, and children, all shared the same fate. As I told you in my last, I had been ill in bed for a long time, and was to have left for England on the 15th, but God willed it otherwise. Seeing how things were turning, ill as I was, I could not remain quiet, and forthwith volunteered my services to the Brigadier, which he accepted with thanks. I joined the troops, but after a long time it was agreed that we should retire, as all hope of holding Delhi was gone. Our regiment then refused to act, and most of the officers fled to Kurnaul, Meerut, &c., but I, along with a few others, agreed to stay with the troops as long as possible. I placed my little boy in charge of some friends, who took him away in their carriage in safety to Meerut. I then placed Fanny and our doctor's wife in a buggy, and directed them to go as quickly as possible to Kurnaul. Our doctor, who was severely wounded, accompanied them in his gharrie, but unfortunately they were all robbed on the road, and everything taken from them, their gharrie and buggy being broken to pieces and the horses stolen. More about them after. After seeing them off I hastened to our Quarter Guard, where I rallied the men of my own companies, Nos. 3 and 5, and they promised to stand by me. I proposed to the commanding officer to call them together, but he would not permit me to do so. Of course, with this order I could do nothing. By degrees I and Ensign ―― were left to ourselves in the Quarter Guard, when we agreed together to ride away with our colours to a place of security. The Sepoys, however, refused to allow us to take them. ―― then left me alone, and has not since been heard of. Last of all, I persuaded the Sepoys to let me take the regimental colour, and I took it outside, but on calling for my groom I found he had bolted with my horse. You may imagine my horror at this. I went back into the Quarter Guard and replaced the colour, but on again coming out a trooper dismounted and took a deliberate shot at me, but, missing his aim, I walked up to him and blew his brains out. Another man was then taking aim at me, when he was bayoneted by a Sepoy of my company. The firing then became general, and I was compelled to run the gauntlet across the parade ground, and escaped unhurt miraculously, three bullets having passed through my hat, and one through the skirt of my coat. The whole of the houses in cantonments were burnt. Having gone as far as my weak state of health would permit, and being exhausted, I took refuge in a garden under some bushes. About half an hour after, a band of robbers, looking out for plunder, detected me, robbed me of my rings, &c., and only left me my flannel waistcoat and socks. They then tore off the sleeve of my shirt, and with it attempted to strangle me. Imagine the intense agony I must have been in! They left me for dead, as I had become senseless. About one hour after I came to, and managed to stagger on about a mile without shoes, where I secreted myself in a hut until daybreak, when I resumed my dreary journey, and, after travelling about 12 miles, the latter part of which was in the broiling sun, without anything on my head, arrived at Aleepore. I managed to beg a little water, some bread, and a few old native clothes to cover my nakedness, but was refused shelter. Again, I went on and on through the ploughed fields, barefooted, fearing to keep the road, on account of the robbers, and, after being turned from several villages, came to a village where the head man, much against the wishes of his labourers, offered to secrete me. This offer I accepted, and I remained with him for five days, although once the Sirdars came there and wished to murder me, but, seeing my helpless state and how ill I was, they refrained from doing so and went away; and a second time I was forced to flee to the fields and hide myself, as about 50 of the mutinous Sepoys came and searched the village for Europeans; but, after lying the whole day in the sun, my generous friend the Zemindar came and fetched me. On the morning of the sixth day a man came in and gave me such information that I was confident that Fanny, the poor doctor, and his wife were within six or seven miles off. I at once determined at all hazards to go in search of them, and at once started off. I once more gained the high road, and, after making inquiries, found that those I was seeking for had been travelling on foot at night, and were about 10 miles a-head of me. With my feet swollen and in blisters I journeyed on, and at last, to my extreme joy, overtook them. After having been several times stripped and searched by the robbers, they had been taken care of by a Ranee Mungla Dabee for two days. They, poor helpless creatures, like myself had been robbed of all they possessed, the ladies, with the exception of a petticoat and shift, and the poor wounded doctor had his clothes left him, as the blood had so saturated them that they were deemed useless to them. The ladies also had experienced the most distressing and horrible insults. At the same place we also met Major Patterson, who had had two very severe blows on the head with a bludgeon. On the evening of the same day we resumed our march, but as poor Wood was so weak, we only managed to accomplish about three miles, when we put up in a village for the night. The villagers treated us very kindly, gave us quantities of milk, bread, and dhâl, and charpâs to lie on. As soon as the moon rose and we had had about four hours' sleep, we again went on our road; but this time we were more fortunate, as some men offered to carry the doctor in a bed. By this means we got on more quickly, and by the evening we had walked about 20 miles, and put up in a village where the people were very kind indeed, and in the morning conducted us safely on horses, mules, and donkeys, to a place called Lursowlee, about 30 miles from Kurnaul. Here was a police station, and we immediately sent on a man on horseback to Kurnaul to send us a carriage and cavalry escort, which was immediately done; and I thank God we arrived here safe on the night of the 20th."

The following most interesting and affecting letter was written to his sister by a boy of 19, who happily succeeded in effecting his escape from among the mutineers:—

"Meerut, June 1.

"Who would have thought when I last wrote to you all the awful circumstances under which I was again to put pen to paper? However, by the providence of Almighty God, your brother has been spared from the fearful massacre that has taken place at Delhi, and though he is a complete beggar, yet, thank God, he is still alive and well. Oh, my own dearest sister, the escape I have had has been most miraculous—in fact I can hardly realise it, and when one comes to look back upon it, it is scarcely to be believed, yet still here I am and no mistake about it; and as they say there is a slight chance of a letter reaching Bombay in time for this mail, I am writing to you. There is only one other officer of my unfortunate regiment, out of those who were with it at the time of the mutiny, who has escaped to this place, and he, poor fellow, is in hospital with a musket-ball through his thigh—Osborn, our adjutant; but I am glad to say there were three others on leave for a month's shooting in the jungles at the time of the outbreak, and who have consequently escaped—among them my chum Wheatley. You know I myself had only been back from Cawnpore five days when this awful business took place. I have been here now since the 19th of last month, and have not had a single line from my poor mother. All the dawks, you know, are cut off by the insurgents, and though I have written to her several letters, yet I fear none have reached Cawnpore. I was able, however, thank God, to telegraph to them on the 20th, saying I had arrived here safe and well, and got a reply from my father telling what relief I had given them, but since then the wire has been destroyed and there has been no communication at all with Cawnpore. God grant they may be safe and well, and we have reason to suppose that the troops there are quiet.

"There were three native corps at Delhi, besides a battery of six guns, and not a single European soldier. It was about 10 o'clock on the morning of the 11th that we first heard of some mutineers having come over from Meerut, and that our regiment was ordered down to the city, where they were, to cut them up. Of course this time we had not a doubt as to their loyalty. Well, the whole regiment, except my company, No. 1, and our major's, the Grenadiers (who were ordered to wait for two guns and escort them down), at once went off to the city, distant about two miles. On arriving at the Cashmere gate, which leads into a small fortified bastion called the Mainguard, from which there is another egress to the city, they were met by some troopers of the 3rd Cavalry from Meerut, who immediately charged down upon them. Not the slightest effort was made by our men to defend their officers, and they were nearly all shot down at the head of their companies by these troopers. In fact, our poor Colonel was seen to be bayoneted by one of the Sepoys after he had been cut down by a trooper; and then the fact of neither a Sepoy nor a trooper having been killed is enough to convince one of their treachery. Well, soon after our two companies, with the two guns (for whom we had had to wait half an hour), also arrived, and on going through the Cashmere gate into the Mainguard and thence into the city, where all this had taken place, the Sepoys and mutineers all bolted, being frightened at the sight of the guns, and before there was time to open upon them they had all disappeared into the streets. We then went back to the Mainguard, determined to hold that against them till more reinforcements arrived from cantonments, for which we immediately sent. In the meantime we sent out parties to bring in our poor fellows, who were all seen lying about in front of the Mainguard. I myself went out and brought in poor Burrowes. It was a most heart-rending sight, I assure you, to see all our poor chaps, whom we had seen and been with that very morning, talking and laughing together at our coffeeshop, lying dead side by side, and some of them dreadfully mutilated. I had never before seen a dead body, so you may imagine what an awful sight it was to me. The poor Colonel was the only one not killed outright; but he, poor man, was hacked to pieces. We sent him back to cantonments, where he died in the course of the day. At last some companies of the other regiments came up, and we remained here the whole day expecting to be attacked every minute. Lots of women and people who had managed to escape from the city came in to us for shelter, little thinking of the scene that was shortly to be enacted among us. By and by three of our officers, who had escaped being killed by the troopers, also came in, and from them we learnt what I have told you above. All this while we saw fires blazing in the town and heard guns firing, which we afterwards found out were the guns of the magazine, which a few Europeans had been defending against the whole host of the insurgents, and which had at last blown up.

"Well, it must have been about 5 o'clock in the afternoon, when, all of a sudden, the Sepoys who were with us in the Mainguard, and on whom we had been depending to defend us in case of attack, began firing upon us in every direction. A most awful scene, as you may imagine, then ensued, people running in every possible way to try and escape. I, as luck would have it, with a few other fellows, ran up a kind of slope that leads to the officers' quarters, and thence, amidst a storm of bullets, to one of the embrasures of the bastion. It is perfectly miraculous how I escaped being hit; no end of poor fellows were knocked down all about, and all too by their men; it is really awful to think of it. However, on arriving at the embrasure, all at once the idea occurred to me of jumping down into the ditch from the rampart (one would have thought it madness at any other time), and so try and get out by scaling the opposite side ; but just as I was in the act of doing so I heard screams from a lot of unfortunate women who were in the officers' quarters, imploring for help. I immediately, with a few other fellows, who like me were going to escape the same way, ran back to them, and though the attempt appeared hopeless, we determined to see if we could not take them with us. Some of them, poor creatures, were wounded with bullets; however, we made a rope with handkerchiefs, and, some of us jumping down first into the ditch, caught them as they dropped, to break the fall. Then came the difficulty of dragging them up the opposite bank; however, by God's will we succeeded, after nearly half an hour's labour, in getting them up; and why no Sepoys came and shot every one of us while getting across all this time is a perfect mystery. The murdering was going on below all this time, and nothing could have been easier than for two or three of them to come to the rampart and shoot down every one of us. However, as I say, we somehow got over, and, expecting to be pursued every minute, we bent our steps to a house that was on the banks of the river. This we reached in safety, and, getting something to eat and drink from the servants (their master, young Metcalf, had fled in the morning), stopped there till dark, and then, seeing the whole of three cantonments on fire, and as it were a regular battle raging in that direction, we ran down to the river side and made the best of our way along its banks in an opposite direction. It would be too long, my very dearest sister, to tell you of how for three days and nights we wandered in the jungles, sometimes fed and sometimes robbed by the villagers, till at length, wearied and footsore, with shreds of clothes on our backs, we arrived at a village where they put us in a hut and fed us for four days, and moreover took a note from us into Meerut, whence an escort of cavalry was sent out, and we were brought safely in here.

"We started from Delhi with five ladies and four officers besides myself, but afterwards in our wanderings fell in with two sergeants' wives and two little children, with two more officers and a merchant; so altogether, on coming into Meerut, we were a body of 17 souls. Oh, great Heaven, to think of the privations we endured, and the narrow escapes we had! We used to ford streams at night, and then walk on slowly in our dripping clothes, lying down to rest every half-hour, for you must remember that some of the ladies were wounded, and all so fatigued and worn out that they could scarcely move. Of course, had we been by ourselves we would have made a dash for Meerut at once, which is about 40 miles from Delhi,* but having these unfortunate

---

* It is not nearly so much. The distance between the two places is 20 coss, and the coss is usually reckoned by Europeans at two miles, but in that part of India it is not more than one and two-thirds of a mile.

women with us what could we do? Sometimes we heard villagers combining to murder us,* and the whole time were in dread of being pursued and killed by some of the mutineers from Delhi. At one time, when we were attacked by the villagers and robbed of everything we possessed, had we not had them with us we would have fought for it, and sold our lives dearly, instead of quietly giving up our arms as we did, for you must know we had a few blunt swords among us, with one double-barrelled gun. I send you a short account of the insurrection, from which you will see that a great many people escaped to Kurnaul and Umballah, among them the major of my regiment; but, alas! I fear we are the only ones saved. The forces from Kurnaul are fast approaching Delhi, and half the force from here has also gone out. They have been attacked, we hear, by the insurgents, who sallied out of Delhi, and have sent in for more reinforcements. The people here are in a great fright, but I fancy 1000 Europeans can hold their ground against five times that number of natives, and there is not much to fear; however, we are very anxious about them, and are eagerly looking out for a despatch, as firing was heard all last night. We took eight guns from them the day before, but they have no end of them, besides lots of ammunition in the magazines of Delhi. Now I will say good bye, my dear sister. Fond and affectionate love to all. In another week we shall know more about affairs. I have had a few shirts and things given me, otherwise I have not a thing to my back—horses and everything, all gone; in fact, as I said before, a perfect beggar; but I dare say Government may repay us in a measure."

"Jhelum, May 30.

"My letter last time was stopped by the mutiny; so I suppose you will be anxious to hear a full and true account. The first I heard was that the troops at Ferozepore had joined the mutiny, and had tried to take the Old Fort, but that a company or two of Europeans had been sent there in anticipation, who after a hard fight had held their own, but fought only with the butt-ends of their muskets; that they then went off to the station and burnt down the Monumental Church, the Roman Catholic Chapel, and every thatched house, plundering as they burnt; that Mr. Coates and Mr. Hughes, two merchants, alone refused to fly, collected their servants, fortified their houses, and repelled all attacks, Mr. Hughes's son, a boy, killing the only Sepoy shot; that they then pulled down numbers of unthatched houses. Next day they were attacked—the 10th Native Cavalry taking our part—and were disarmed, except some hundred odd, who escaped into the villages, where they are being apprehended. At Umballah and Jullundhur much the same—houses burnt, but no lives lost. At Umballah the deserters were more numerous, but the Patiala Rajah had apprehended many of them. He was the first, as he always has been, to come to our aid, although we did take Budhour from him forcibly so lately. Now we learn that the Europeans took the fort at Agra, and hold their own there; that the Allyghur troops (9th Native Infantry) had mutinied and gone to join the force at Delhi, and that the Commander-in-Chief was still stationary at Umballah, unwilling to move till he had a large force. The Simla and Almora Goorka troops have also mutinied, but it is hoped they are coming round. The troops at Lahore were in vigorous hands. Sir John Lawrence and General Reid, aided by Brigadier Chamberlain, were not men to wait for orders in such an emergency, and have disarmed the troops both there and at Peshawur, only just in time, as we learn, as they

---

* They were, however, neither murdered nor, as it would appear, personally maltreated, although there was ample opportunity for both, during their wanderings, especially after they had been robbed of their arms. With the exception of the Goojurs, who are hereditary marauders, the Zemindars have behaved well to us, which is a great encouragement to good government, for there cannot be a doubt that it is mainly owing to the 30 years' settlement which has secured them against the unlimited exactions of the old revenue system. The uniform fidelity of the native domestic servants, both male and female, has also been very remarkable; and the instances have not been few in which they have protected their masters and mistresses at the hazard of their lives. The poor ayahs have repeatedly carried off the infants intrusted to them amid a shower of blows. These things prove that the people of India are not insensible to just and kind treatment, and indicate that there must have been something wrong in our management of the Sepoys, who in former days yielded to none in attachment to their English officers.

were waiting for the news from Delhi, where it was agreed the mutiny should begin. Half of one of the regiments at Peshawur was at an out-station (Noushera), and was not disarmed, as a few men alone could do nothing; they got the signal from Delhi, but did not know their comrades at Peshawur had been disarmed; so they rose, as agreed upon, and found themselves in a narrow pass between two European cantonments, and a force has started to make a fearful example of them. All the native States are with us, and have sent in their contingents to aid the English, except Maharajah Gholab Singh, who is pouring great supplies of ammunition, corn, &c., into all his forts along our border. Well, the Sepoys, as I learn from really good informants, all believe that we are determined to make them Christians by some means. They believe that all we want to do is to make them eat pigs' fat or bullocks' flesh; and, unfortunately, the cartridges for the new Enfield rifle were greased, and in some places the grease, I believe, really was lard or common bullocks' fat, the native contractor having used these for cheapness. In this frame of mind, which has been going on for several years, they were very suspicious of anything new, and believed at once that the Government really had had the lard put on to cheat them into becoming Christians, and regiment after regiment held meetings to resent this attack on their religion. All the officers who were well acquainted with Hindostanee being selected for staff appointments, only those were left in most regiments who, knowing but little of the language, had but little intercourse with their men, and therefore they learnt nothing of all this, except in one or two corps where some chance linguist remained, and these corps have generally not mutinied, as their officers learnt their complaints and explained the matter to them. It is now believed that all this would have blown over, but the dismissed nobles and grandees of Oude, shorn of all their wealth and rank, seized on this pretext, and sent messengers in the disguise of Fakirs all about, praying the men to stand out for the religion of their fathers, a plan which succeeded too well. Some of the Fakirs, it is said, have been apprehended. The Sepoys of the 14th Native Infantry held a meeting, but luckily had some good officers, and one Lieutenant Smith, a good linguist, and a great friend of theirs; so they agreed not to mutiny, but to resign if they were asked to fire the suspected cartridges. Meanwhile the Government or the authorities had all the new cartridges burnt to reassure the men, but it had unluckily just the opposite tendency. If, they said, there was really nothing in the cartridges, Government would never have burnt them all, but as they were really greased with lard they saw they were found out this time and burnt them, as the only way to get out of the mess. Now they say, such a powerful Government will soon find out some other way, so it is better to fight it out now than to find ourselves cheated into being Christians some day unexpectedly, and then be unable to clear ourselves. The news from the other stations is, perhaps, equally bad. At Moultan they are only restrained from breaking out by Chamberlain's Irregular Cavalry, and at Rawul Pindee they are on the eve of rebellion, it is said. Mooradabad and Barrilly troops are said to be firm, also the 21st at Peshawur. The spark that is said to have fired the train is, that one party of Sepoys did not refuse the cartridges, but tore off the ends with their hands, and would not put them into their mouths, which the officer in command said was unsoldierly, and explained all about the cartridges to them, vowed they were greased with ghee, and told them we did not care if they were of all the religions in the world; but unfortunately few officers left with their regiments are good hands at Hindostanee, and the Sepoys did not understand him at all. They only understood that he was determined they should bite off and not tear off the end of the cartridge, and immediately felt sure that there was something in it, so mutinied. There is a great want of sympathy between the European and the native, which destroys all hopes of comfort, unless you could fall into all their usages. We are all well here. God has hitherto protected us, and we now seem to think all is over. A splendid force is collected in Kurnaul. The native States believe that we must win in the end, and have sent their troops to our aid. We can only trust in God, who is equally able to protect us anywhere. We are in the midst of a mutiny unprecedented in Indian history, and are only a small band of Europeans, fighting and struggling for existence. However, the regiment here is very good, and deserves the title, so common formerly, of the Faithful Sepoy."

The escape of Sir T. Metcalfe was most providential. After being three days in Delhi after the outbreak, he escaped into the jungles, hiding wherever he could, and at length, after ten days, finding his way to Hansee. Several

B

Europeans (said to number 48) were taken to the palace, or, perhaps, went there for protection. These were taken care of by the King of Delhi; but the Sowars of the 3rd Cavalry, whose thirst for European blood had not been quenched, rested not till they were all given up to them, and murdered one by one in cool blood.

We must now return to Meerut. On the evening of the 16th occurred the murder of Captain Fraser, Bengal Sappers and Miners. He was marching down from the head-quarters of his corps at Roorkee to Meerut with a body of his men. On reaching their destination the Sappers fell out among themselves, probably in discussing the propriety of following the mutinous example that had been set them, and when their commanding officer attempted to compose their quarrel, one of their number shot him through the head. They then broke and fled, but were pursued by parties of the Carabineers and 60th, and for the most part killed or captured. Fears being entertained that the Convent at Sirdhana, with its children's school, might be attacked and devastated, a party was sent out from Meerut, which brought in all the nuns and children to a safe asylum at the station.

It remains to mention how the intelligence of the mutiny was received at other stations in the north-west. At Agra, as from its proximity to Delhi might be expected, public excitement at first ran high. But great as was the emergency, Mr. Colvin, the Lieutenant-Governor, proved himself equal to meet it. On the morning of Thursday, the 14th, when the popular ferment was at its height, and the wildest rumours were abroad, Mr. Colvin harangued the whole brigade of the station, the European soldiers as well as the native, on the parade-ground. By all—no less by the two native regiments, the 44th and 67th, than by the European artillery—his address was received with loud applause. Even after he had left the ground the cheering of the Sepoys continued long and loud. The effect of this happy speech was shortly felt throughout the whole of the city, which settled down again into a state of quiescence. At Etawah, a station further down the Jumna, half a dozen of the mutinous 3rd Cavalry were cut to pieces by the police and a small party of the 9th Native Infantry. At Allyghur the 9th Native Infantry arrested a mutinous agent whom they found in their lines, and handed him over to the commanding officer. At Benares, and throughout Bengal, all was quiet.

Two regiments of Native Infantry, the 45th and the 57th, were stationed at Ferozepore, in the Punjaub. Symptoms of disaffection having been manifested, all the Christian women were directed to remove into the entrenched magazine, while the two Native Infantry regiments and 10th Light Cavalry were paraded on their respective grounds with the view of being marched to separate parts of the cantonment. The cavalry regiment took its post under the walls of the new arsenal; the 57th Native Infantry behind the European infantry lines; and the 44th was being marched to the north of Sudder Bazaar, when they came to a halt at the entrance of the said bazaar, and refused to advance a step. They then loaded their muskets and went about to the entrenched magazine. They stood at the north-west bastion, vacillating as to what they were to do. At this moment they received intimation from the company of the 57th on duty within the magazine that there were ropes and ladders in that bastion to scale the walls with. Some parties even threw out these apparati to the mutineers, who immediately, with their assistance, got into the moat and scaled the wall. A company of Her Majesty's 61st Foot were, previous to the marching of the native troops, sent to the entrenched magazine to relieve the company of the 57th on duty there, and, but for this precaution, we should have lost Ferozepore. When the mutineers, to the extent of some 300, got into the magazine, they hurrahed, and made for the gate which affords ingress to the ordnance stores, &c.; they were, however, repulsed by five files of Her Majesty's 61st, who poured a volley into them, which made half a dozen of the mutineers bite the dust. A shot, however, from the mutineers went through the thigh of Colonel Redmond, commanding the Europeans. The mutineers then went round to the east side and thought to take the Europeans in the rear, but they were mistaken, as the gallant 61st repulsed them everywhere, and while the mutineers were retreating over the walls they were knocked down by the Europeans with the butts of their muskets. The Europeans of the garrison were reinforced by two more companies of Her Majesty's 61st, and two guns under the command of Lieutenant Angelo. The company of the 7th Native Infantry in the magazine showing signs of disaffection by having loaded their muskets, Lieutenant Angelo had his two guns charged with grapeshot and turned their muzzles upon the company, who were immediately disarmed by her Majesty's 61st and marched out. The 45th Native Infantry retreated towards the ice-pits, and carrying their dead with them, left them at the Mussulman's graveyard, adjoining our own. At night some 200 of the mutineers returned to the cantonment, and, in gangs of 10 and 20, took lighted torches and set fire to the church, Catholic chapel, two vacant hospitals, Her Majesty's 61st mess house, Captains Salmon, Harvey, Woodcock, Cotton, and Blomfield's bungalows, and several others. They were not even molested in committing the incendiarism, except at the chapel, where a young lad, the son of Mr. Hughes, a merchant, shot one of them. Every one seemed panic-stricken. The next day the mutineers began to plunder some of the officers' houses, when a party of Her Majesty's 61st and 10th Light Cavalry drove them out and shot some of them. Lieut. Prendergast and the sergeant-major of the cavalry were both fired upon and nearly shot; but about seven A.M. the same morning, as the magazines of the 45th and 57th Native Infantry were in danger of falling into the hands of the mutineers, the artillery brought their guns to bear upon the magazines, which were blown up by a couple of shots fired into them. On the same day the 57th Native Infantry were disarmed, and mutineers of the 45th, to the number of 200, sent in the colours of their regiment, and surrendered their arms and themselves. That night a false alarm, at eleven P.M., caused a short fusillade from the entrenched magazine at our imaginary foe. The guns, too, of the magazine sent forth showers of grape shot. The alarm was taken up by the men of the 61st at their lines, and by the detachment of the same corps and artillery posted at the south-west flank of the cantonment. A man of Her Majesty's 61st was shot, he being mistaken for one of the mutineers in the dark. The inhabitants of the Sudder Bazaar removed to the town of Ferozepore, which was fortified by men especially entertained for the purpose by Major Marsden. All the Europeans and their families, excepting Mr. Coates and Mr. Hughes, merchants, who fortified their own houses, went into the entrenched magazine. The Parsee merchants fortified their own places.

At Lucknow the greatest consternation prevailed. The whole of the native troops in Oude were in an undisguised state of mutiny. On hearing of the outbreak the authorities immediately called a council of all the European inhabitants to decide upon what course to adopt. The whole of the ladies were ordered into the fort at Rawul Pindee; meanwhile Her Majesty's 81st Regiment proceeded to the lines of the disaffected, and promptly disarmed them, thus happily depriving at least some portion of them of the means of doing harm. A letter from Lucknow, dated the 17th, says:—

"Our worthy Chief Commissioner is doing all he can to prepare for any outbreak, should such be brewing, of which there is not, however, much apprehension. The Dak Bungalow has been garrisoned by a part of a cavalry corps, and guns placed facing the road. The Muchee Bhowun building is taken possession of by our troops, and Sir Henry personally superintends the mounting of the guns, &c., upon its high walls. The Residency and the adjoining building have been made over to the civil residents, and to a part of her Majesty's 32nd Regiment, the remainder of the corps being located in cantonments. The excitement caused by these changes, and the proceedings at Delhi, is very great."

The disarmed Sepoys, after leaving Lucknow, bent their steps towards Seetapore, hoping to gain over the Sepoys stationed there. On their arrival before the place, however, they found the 41st Native Infantry and the 9th Irregular Infantry drawn up to receive them. They at once beat a retreat, and moved, it is supposed, in the direction of Delhi.

The state of Calcutta on the 19th of May is thus described by the *Phœnix* of that date :—

"We mentioned in yesterday's paper that European sentries had, the night before, been mounted on the quarters of each officer in Fort William. The precaution was not taken before it was required. There are at present six companies of the 25th Regiment of Native Infantry, and a wing of the 47th Madras Native Infantry, on the esplanade between Coolie Bazaar and the Fort. None of those troops have ammunition; but on Sunday night the men of the 25th entered into communication with the Guards from the Barrackpore regiments on duty at the Fort, and composed, we believe, of detachments from the 2nd Guards and 70th Native Infantry. The Guards in the Fort have each ten rounds of ammunition. The men of the 25th asked them for five rounds of this, stating their readiness, if they got it, to storm the Fort during the night time. They were refused, and their treasonous overtures almost immediately made known to the town major by those it was attempted to seduce. Immediately afterwards the bugles sounded, and the Fort was placed in something like a state of siege. The drawbridges were all drawn up, the ladders withdrawn from the ditches, additional guards placed upon the Arsenal, European sentries placed upon all points of the ramparts, with loaded muskets, and armed patrols kept moving through the fortress during the night. All, however, passed off without any attempt on the part of the baffled Sepoys outside. An express appears to have been sent off to Dumdum, for the wing and head-quarters of Her Majesty's 53rd, hitherto stationed at Dumdum, moved into Fort William yesterday morning; the entire of Her Majesty's 53rd, with the women and children of the regiment, are therefore now in Fort William.

"Yesterday evening, and we believe all through the day, sentries with loaded arms were again posted on the ramparts of the Fort. All danger is, we believe, now over, as we have heard that the 25th were disarmed yesterday evening.

"Yesterday, more revolvers, firearms, and ammunition were sold in Calcutta than ever was the case since the days of Job Charnock. There was a regular rush to the establishment of Messrs. Ahmuty and Co., so much so that purchasers were unable to get in on account of the throng. An extensive sale of revolvers of all sizes took place, as well as of other descriptions of weapons, offensive and defensive. The principal purchasers, we understand, were residents of Howrah, who, in self-defence against the possible attacks by Sepoys, had hastened to arm themselves."

The proclamation of martial law in Calcutta, the formation of a militia corps, and the arming of the European crews belonging to the ships in the river, were recommended in Calcutta, and may be taken severally as indications of the alarm which prevailed there.

On the 28th, the 15th Bengal Native Infantry mutinied at Nusseerabad. Suspicion had been entertained of their loyalty for some days, and every precaution was taken for the safety of the station. The Cavalry (1st Bombay Lancers) were nearly all of them under arms every night, and strong bodies of them patrolled the cantonment. The guns were kept limbered up all night and loaded with grape, and a detachment of 250 Europeans of Her Majesty's 83rd, and some European artillery, were sent for from Deesa, about 200 miles south-west of Nusseerabad.

The Bengalees, after a vain attempt to seduce the Lancers to join them, openly mutinied. Our gallant fellows charged them repeatedly, although the rebels had got possession of the guns of the station and outnumbered them eight to one. The odds were, however, too long, and the Lancers were compelled finally to retreat upon Ajmere, thereby securing the safety of the important arsenal at that station. The mutineers having marched in the direction of Delhi, our troops finally returned to, and have re-occupied, Nusseerabad. Major Spottiswood and Cornet Newbury, of the Lancers, fell in the attack; and Captain E. A. Hardy and Lieutenant F. A. E. Loch were amongst the wounded.

The following is an extract of a letter from an officer in the 15th Bengal Native Infantry. It is dated Beaur, May 31:—

"The day after my return reports began to be circulated about the disaffection of our regiment and the 30th Native Infantry, most of them being to the effect that our men were the instigators. We fancied these reports much exaggerated, and imagined that, though our men might follow in a move of the kind, they would not be the first to lead the way. The result shows how much we were mistaken. I used to sleep with a loaded revolver and my sword by my bedside, and should not have been in the least surprised if I had been awoke any night and told that the Sepoys were firing the bungalows, which in other places seems to have been a preliminary step. The excitement seemed to calm down, or at any rate we got easier in our minds, and fancied that the crisis had past. On the night of the 27th I happened to be on duty, and on going round the station at midnight found everything remarkably quiet. Next day, when I was eating my tiffin in my own house, about half-past 3 in the afternoon, my servants rushed in saying that the men had risen. I called for my pony and armed myself, and then went over with W—— to the Colonel's. When he was ready we started for the parade ground, through one of the streets running between the Sepoys' huts and their lines. The men were coming out of their huts and loading their muskets, and I expected they would have popped at us as we passed. On reaching the quarter-guard we found some of the men had already turned out, and by degrees the men of the different companies fell in in front of their respective lines, and were brought up and formed into open column. Soon after we came down and the men fell in, the Colonel sent me with a message to the officer in charge of the guns. He did not know they were in the hands of the rebels. We had heard firing in that direction before, but did not know that the first thing which took place was that a few of the worst men, having induced the native gunners to join them (there were no European artillerymen, but the native ones were considered quite faithful), had possessed themselves of the guns, six in number. I galloped off towards them, and must have been within from 70 to 100 yards, when I began to experience the unpleasant sensation of bullets whizzing past my head, and saw a lot of Sepoys taking potshots at me as I came along. One man put up his hands and warned me off, and I did not require any further hint—the neighbourhood was not the safest. I immediately turned my pony's head, and endeavoured to retreat under cover of a wall which ran in front of the artillery lines. Here I saw more men running up with the kind intention of having a crack at me, so I had to keep along the parade ground right in the line of fire, and had one or two men popping at me from over the wall on my right. My tât (pony) went as fast as ever he could go, and, thanks be to God, carried me back in perfect safety, much to the astonishment of all who saw it. The Colonel then ordered the Grenadiers and Light Company to move off under cover of the bells of arms, and attack the guns, but when they had gone a little way they refused to move further, and man after man deserted and joined the mutineers. At the same time the Colonel told me to take out another company, and extend them in skirmishing order in front of the guns, and to pick off the men at the guns, and, if possible, charge. Fortunately the men would not move; if they had, they would have obeyed orders till told to begin firing, when I should have had a bullet through me and the men would have deserted in a body. As nothing was to be got from them, the companies were recalled. I had forgotten to tell you that the regiment, previous to this, was drawn up in line facing the guns, the guns being about 600 or 700 yards to the left of our lines. In this position we remained upwards of an hour, when, finding the men would do nothing, the Colonel formed open column. The guns, of course, would not open on us, as they knew all the men were going to join them when things were ripe. It was only in active movements the men refused to obey orders; in everything else they were quite subordinate. At one time, when the officers were grouped together somewhat in front of the men, some men came out from the guns and tried to hit us with their muskets, which they could do without injuring the Sepoys. At last sunset began to come on, and it was evident we could not remain much longer, so our Adjutant was sent off to the Brigadier for orders, who told us to retire. The Colonel was determined, if possible, to carry off the colours, which were accordingly brought out of the quarter-guard. When the Colonel gave the order to march, the men refused to go. He then asked who would join in taking off the colours, and the Grenadiers, almost to a man, came forward. The colours were brought to the front, and put under charge of the Grenadiers; very few others came forward, and when the word 'march' was given, a jeer was raised, and a shout, 'You shan't take away the colours.' The men cocked their pieces. I turned round and saw that two men had got the colours, and were running away towards the enemy. The first gun that was fired at us was the signal for the officers to be off. Providentially we were all mounted at the time, so off we started amid showers of bullets towards the cavalry lines. I dodged round the first bell of arms (a small square building detached from all others, in which the arms were kept), and as I passed each bell saw three or four men behind each, who deliberately shot at us as we passed. Either my tât swerved before I came to the Sergeant-Major's bungalow, or else I saw more men in the road; I don't know which. At all events, I had to steer with great difficulty round the outside of the house, which brought me again on the open parade ground. Round the corner, and I was comparatively safe. A moment or two more, and I was safe among the cavalry, who were drawn up in rear of their own lines. Every one of us came in safe, by God's mercy. P——'s charger, a very fine animal, dropped dead directly he had brought his master into safety. The Colonel had an awfully narrow escape; his horse swerved right round at the start, and we thought it was all over with him. The horse received one ball in the forehead, another in the neck, and his knee was grazed by a third, but he brought the Colonel in safe, and is still alive. We now had the explanation of all the firing we had heard going on at the artillery while we were standing under arms. The cavalry had come up and been fired on with grape by the mutineers, and had made several attempts to charge, but could not capture the guns. Newbury, quite a young fellow, charged by himself, was riddled with balls, and then hacked to pieces. Captain Spottiswood was also killed, and two other officers slightly wounded. J—— had his jacket ripped open at the shoulder by a bullet. M——, who cut down a man, had a very narrow escape, and so had several other officers. When we came up they determined to retreat at once. It was just sunset when we left the station. The ladies had been sent on in buggies previously, in case we should have to 'bolt,' so we fell in with them just outside the cantonment. We left by the Ajmeer road, and when we had gone a mile or two struck off to the left, under the hills, making a détour towards Beaur, where it was determined to retire. We went right across country, over fields and rocky hills, for about 10 miles, till we came to the Beaur road, leaving the blazing bungalows of the station behind us. About 2 o'clock we fell in with most of the officers of the 30th who had escaped, and arrived at a bungalow. Here Colonel Penny, commanding the Lancers, who was taken ill on the way from the effects of a fall and over-excitement, died. We could get nothing to eat or drink, and started again at daybreak, and reached this about 11. The journey by road is 32 miles, and our détour must have made it at least 10 miles longer, so you may fancy how tired our horses were. Not a thing has any one saved— I have not even my watch, and my pistol was jerked out of my holster in our flight."

The events at Meerut and Delhi were so little expected in this country—or, if expected in any quarter, all apprehensions on the subject had been sedulously concealed—that we find the leading journal, which, on the announcement of the mutiny at Berhampore, had declared it a mere passing outburst of fanaticism, which would end with the disbandment of the mutinous corps, speaking of them, on the 27th of June, in the following strain:—

"This mutiny has assumed a very serious character. We do not write for the purpose of inspiring alarm or suggesting timid counsels. The moment has arrived for action— sharp, stern, and decisive. An Imperial interest is at stake—nothing less than our dominion in British India. It would be easy enough to point out the errors of omission and commission which have been mainly instrumental in bringing about the present crisis. The course of policy to be adopted for the future is also matter for swift, though serious discussion, but just now it would be idle to waste time either upon recrimination or upon questions of general policy. In the first place the mutiny must be suppressed, and in such a manner as shall impress the minds of the natives with the nature of the power they have defied when its real strength is put forth. If it be true that we are still very much in the dark as to the true feelings and opinions of the natives of India, it is no less true that they know far less of us than we do of them. The disadvantages arising from ignorance may tell upon both sides, but they tell more in our favour than to our prejudice.

The crisis is a most serious one. We do not wish to conceal its true nature from the country, but it is not so serious that it should inspire one moment of hesitation."

In Parliament, also, there was an evident desire to under-rate the magnitude of the blow that had been struck at British domination and influence in the East. At first it was contended that the disaffection was confined to the 19th Regiment; then, when this could be maintained no longer, that it was only the Bengal Army that was disloyal, and that an easy remedy would be found in the free admixture of Sikhs and Ghoorkas with the superstitious Hindoos. But now this "flattering unction" was of no avail; it was undeniable that disaffection to British rule was neither confined to the Bengal Army, nor to the Hindoo Sepoys, nor even to the ranks of the native troops. It had shown itself in the Madras Presidency, where caste is unknown; it pervaded the Mahommedan troops as well as those who bowed to Brahma and Vishnu, and even the Sikhs and Ghoorkas, upon whom so much reliance had been placed, as free from the superstitions of Brahminism; and the shocking events at Delhi had proved that the spirit of discontent actuated civilians as well as military. Two days later, the *Times* returned to the subject, and thus acknowledged the errors and false assumptions upon which its articles had been written prior to the announcement of the outbreak at Meerut:—

"The progress of things speedily sets aside false or insufficient surmises, and the notion that the discontent was confined only to one or two regiments, and arose from trifling and local causes—the greasing of a cartridge or the imbecility of certain officers—is now shown to be inadequate for the explanation of what has occurred. The mutiny has not been confined to one body of troops or one locality. The disturbances, beginning with the Hindoos, have actually ended in placing on the throne of Delhi a Mahomedan Emperor, and the fever has gone on to seize the distant garrisons of what were lately the Sikh States. A movement so universal, and so independent of conditions and circumstances, must have its root in feelings which the prejudices of religion or the neglect of a proper supervision may indeed have strengthened, but which they could hardly have produced."

Not many days had elapsed since the same journal had felicitated the country on the assumed fact that the Mussulman, the Sikh, the Ghoorka, had no share in the prejudices of the Hindoo, and that the Government might always count on the votaries of Islam for support in any tumult arising from the teaching of an idolatrous creed!

Still, the leading journal could find no adequate cause for the disaffection which is now acknowledged to be so widely spread, and could put forward only Hindoo fanaticism and the want of sympathy between the Sepoys and their English officers. "No doubt," says a writer in the *Morning Advertiser*, "native fanaticism and European military hauteur and mismanagement have come into antagonism in the Bengal army, and proved the active cause of the insurrectionary movement. But is there not a more apparent and a more reasonable cause than any that has been put forward, for the insurgent spirit which has broken out in no less than twelve regiments of the Bengal troops? We are cognizant of at least half a dozen assigned causes for the insurgent spirit which has taken possession of the breasts of the soldiery of the native army of Bengal. The confiscations of Sattara and Nagpore, and Oude, and Tanjore, and the Carnatic, not to mention a host of minor states and zemindaries all over the country, are recent events. It cannot be supposed that such a system of spoliation has escaped the notice of the native millions. It is undoubtedly to the fatal policy of spoliation which has been pursued by the Government of India, that we may mainly trace the discontent that has now manifested itself. Although disaffection among the native troops is the form in which this discontent has broken out, the belief in India is, that it is shared very generally by the people themselves. To show that such must be the case, we have only to point to the insurrection in Delhi. In the ancient capital of India, the seat of power of the Mogul Emperors, the native inhabitants received the mutineers with open arms."

These views were not without their exponents in the Indian press. "Whether, in point of fact," observes the *Madras Athenæum,* "these doings do not form a large staple of the conversation of the natives from the Himalayas to Cape Comorin, we leave you to consider. To our thinking, the present condition of India may afford an answer to the question lately propounded—how annexation pays? The people dislike us; our military service has become unpopular; and if we lose our hold on the native army, we have literally nothing to fall back upon. We confess we do not see the faintest prospect of any cure for all this from within. Old doctrines and old principles are as rife in Calcutta and in Leadenhall-street as ever, and old interests as powerful. It is to England, the English Parliament, that we look as the main source of succour and remedy. Our danger is immediate, and our treatment must be the same. The direct responsibility of the Indian Government to Parliament would secure a safeguard to the people against wrongs, either real or imaginary, for which they seem to feel they have now little chance of remedy, and would necessitate a recurrence to those old principles of good faith and fair dealing, from which of late the British Government, in its relation with the natives, has so signally and so grievously departed."

We must now return to India. One of the first acts of the Lieutenant-Governor was to issue proclamations placing under martial law the districts around Meerut and Delhi, to the eastward of the Jumna, warning all landholders and others from joining the insurgents, and announcing that prompt vengeance would overtake all past or future delinquents. The Sirmore battalions were at Boolundshuhur, on the east; the Agra brigades, strengthened by cavalry and artillery from Gwalior, advancing from Muttra on the south; the troops of the Jât Rajahs of Bhurtpore and Ulwar moving up on the west. From the north-west were pouring down the horsemen of the Rajahs of Putteeala and Jheend, while the great road from the hill stations by Kurnaul and Meerut lay open for the march of the Commander-in-Chief. General Anson left Umballa, whither he had repaired in haste from Simla, on the 18th. He brought with him from Kassowlie Her Majesty's 75th Regiment. At Umballa he found the 9th Lancers, the 1st European Fusileers, marched in from Dugshaie, the 4th Light Cavalry, the 5th and 60th Native Infantry, and two troops of (European) Horse Artillery. In Oude Sir Henry Lawrence kept all quiet. The fort at Allahabad, where there is a large magazine, was garrisoned by the European invalids usually stationed in the fort of Chunar. At Calcutta every precaution had been taken to guard against the possibility of a surprise. The 84th Regiment, with the Horse Artillery, were at Barrackpore, and the 53d in Fort William. An Act had been passed empowering all officers in command of brigades and stations to hold general courts-martial, and confirm their sentences without reference to higher authority.

The advanced guard of General Anson reached Kurnaul on the 21st, the main body still remaining for some days at Umballa. The cause of this delay was the absence of heavy artillery at that station, and the consequent necessity of waiting till a siege-train could be brought from the nearest arsenal, which was as far off as Phillour, on the further side of the Sutlej. When the guns arrived, or were nearing his camp, the general advanced, and had reached Kurnaul when he was attacked by cholera, and died at that station on the 27th. The command of the army devolved upon Sir Henry Barnard, who as Major-General had been at the head of the Sirbind Division. Meanwhile Brigadier Halifax, with the advance, had arrived at Paneeput, 56 miles from Delhi, from which place he moved forward on the evening of the 29th.

In the meanwhile the insurgents in that city had been busily engaged in strengthening their position. By the arrival of stragglers from other mutinous regiments, and the disaffected from all parts of India, their numbers had increased to twenty thousand. They had appointed Lall Khan, a Subadar of the 3rd Cavalry, their general in chief, with Buldeô Singh, a Subadar of the 20th Foot, as their second in command. Their first step was to proclaim the King of Delhi Emperor of India; their second to fortify themselves. They had ample means at their disposal for this purpose, a large siege train, and immense stores of powder. The possession of these resources seems to have inspired them with a confidence which gradually increased as they found themselves unmolested. On the 29th ult., they sent out a strong party, with five guns, to guard the bridge over the little river Hindun. They entrenched themselves on the heights near the river with no ordinary skill; but on the following day a detachment of the European force at Meerut, the Carabineers, 60th Rifles, and Artillery, under the command of Brigadier Wilson, took up an advanced position at the village of Ghazee-ood-deen-nuggur. At 4 P.M. the picket gave notice of the approach of the enemy, who opened a fire of five guns. The troop of Horse Artillery crossed the Hindun by a ford on the right, protected by the Carabineers and the Rifles by the bridge. The enemy were driven in by the Rifles and fire of Major Scott's battery, and the Horse Artillery turned their flank and they fled, leaving all the guns and a large supply of intrenching tools. Some took refuge in a village, and were shot down or burnt out. Another party of their force was pursued by the Carabineers. Our loss in killed and wounded did not exceed 44, caused chiefly by the explosion of an ammunition waggon of the enemy's, abandoned near the bridge. Undaunted by this severe check, the rebels returned to the attack on the following day, and were again repulsed.

In the meantime the mutiny continued to spread. The 9th Native Infantry, stationed at Allyghur, the loyalty of which had been commented upon as matter for congratulation, threw off their allegiance unexpectedly, and marched off to Delhi. At Murdaun, the 55th deserted their colours; they were assailed by Europeans and Irregulars, cut to pieces, taken, and dispersed. The 70th Native Regiment at Barrackpore had asked and obtained permission to march against the mutineers, which is regarded by a professional authority (the *United Service Magazine*) as a convenient mode of reaching Delhi at the expense of the Indian Government; the editor speculating in a prophetic mood upon the probable contingency of the attacking force being assailed in flank or rear, at a critical moment, by a volley from the "loyal" 70th.

We are now aware of the full extent of the mutiny and the measures that have been taken for its suppression. No less than sixty-eight regiments have ceased to form part of the Indian army. Most of those have mutinied; some are dispersed; several were promptly disarmed. It is uncertain how many arrived to reinforce the rebels at Delhi; but it is clear that that city was the rallying point of all the mutineers. The throne of the descendants of Aurungzebe, at Delhi, fell into the hands of the British Government when its last occupant died, viz., about the end of the year 1856. The late King of Delhi was a stipendiary prince, but allowed to retain the state ceremonials and trappings of royalty. But when he died, the Government of Calcutta stripped his successor of every external honour, and reduced him to the position of a pensioner of the East India Company.

The measures taken by the Home Government on the receipt of the despatches announcing the state of affairs in Bengal and the north-west, and the death of General Anson, showed a determination to act with promptitude. Sir Colin Campbell, who commanded the Highland Brigade in the Crimea, was appointed to the chief command in India, and 14,000 men received orders to prepare for immediate embarkation. Directions were sent by telegraph that the troops sent out to China should be stopped *in transitu* at Point de Galle, and detained for a still more urgent service. All Indian officers on leave of absence were ordered to return without delay. Sir Colin Campbell's reply, when asked how soon he would be ready to start for India—" To-morrow "—will take rank among the brief but comprehensive sayings of military commanders. It is another instance of that soldierlike promptitude which Sir Colin has never failed to show. A telegraphic message was sent to detain the steamer at Marseilles until his arrival there, and thus not a moment was lost in sending to the scene of our imperilled rule a man who, there is no doubt, will prove himself equal to the emergency.

Among those best acquainted with India there was now no doubt that a serious crisis had arrived, that the one danger to which, in the opinion of Lord Metcalfe, one of the ablest rulers of British India, the stability of our empire there is exposed, had come to pass. The north-west provinces, as well as some parts of Bengal, are in a state resembling more or less that of actual anarchy. Thousands of Sepoys, though not in overt rebellion, are dispersed over the country with arms in their hands. Swarms of marauders are traversing the territories of Hindostan with the power of inflicting serious mischief on native communities or isolated stations of Europeans. Over a considerable portion of British India the ordinary functions of administration must be impaired or suspended. Under such circumstances as these, the leading journal, at last awakening to a full sense of the danger, might well express the opinion that "the open revolt in the Bengal Presidency of five regiments of Native Infantry and of one regiment of Light Cavalry, independently of what may have taken place at Ferozepore, is undoubtedly intelligence as important as any which we have published since the fall of Sebastopol."

Since the article from which the foregoing extract is taken was written, the six regiments of mutineers have been multiplied into sixty-eight, and it is becoming apparent to every one capable of appreciating the gravity of the events that have taken place in India, that the task before us is nothing less than the reconquest of the country.

"India," says the editor of the *Times*, "has now to undergo a second and final subjugation. The nation will do well to consider it as new ground on which everything has to be done over again. And, indeed, where can it be said that the British influence has not been shaken? Do we know enough of Mahomedans and Hindoos and their ways, to say that in any station, from the Indus to Rangoon, the belief in our weakness and our imminent fall has not penetrated? The mutiny has broken out without suspicion on the part of hundreds of officers whose whole lives have been devoted to the superintendence of Asiatics. As the rulers of India have been so completely surprised by the late events, why should not others happen for which they are equally unprepared? They believed in the greased cartridges of Barrackpore up to the moment when the whole army for 1500 miles was in a flame. The same limitation of view, the same undue security, may be found again. Ought Parliament and the people of England to measure their exertions by the reports of Indian officials, when it has been proved that there exists amongst Asiatics an understanding and a power of co-operation which years of service do not enable an European to detect? Therefore, without being alarmists, without believing in the power of any number of Sepoys to resist the charge of European troops, we would urge Government not to fall again into the error of 1854, and to refuse to believe in war until it becomes disaster. With promptitude and a judicious outlay the mutiny can be put down in a few weeks, Delhi recaptured, and the heir of Tamerlane and Aurungzebe conveyed to some safer place of residence. But without vigorous action there is no saying how far the flame may spread. Every day that sees a native army and a native prince affecting to defy us, will cost a month of strictness and vigilance. The Sepoy deserters will have told their tale in more villages, and indoctrinated with the new ideas a thousand localities which formerly worshipped the Company and its delegates. Everything depends on the speedy defeat and the severe punishment of all who have mutinied or fled from their colours. Not only Indian Rajahs, but the Monarchs of Persia and Tartary, of China, Burmah, and Siam, are waiting the result of this blow at English power."

The idea that the greased cartridges were *the* cause of the revolt has now been given up as no longer tenable, though there is little doubt that the impurity, according to Hindoo notions, attempted to be forced upon the Sepoys had something to do in precipitating events. Less causes have brought about bloodshed and destruction, and even revolution, among the nations of the West. A stone thrown by a mischievous idler produced the riots and burnings at Bristol in 1831—a pistol fired at the horse of a Municipal Guard was the simple agency by which a revolution was effected in Paris in 1848. But in both these cases these casual events were but sparks falling upon a long prepared mine of discontent; and so we now find it has been in India. The *Friend of India* for the past four years has urged incessantly that, if the Bengal army were not reformed, "it would reform itself after a fashion that would try the courage rather of soldiers than of statesmen." Men put the misfortune out of their calculations as they would a thunderbolt, an earthquake, or any other catastrophe too great for human effort to avert. The explosion at last has come, and we could not have been less prepared.

"While conquest," says the leading journal, "has been spreading west, east, and north, and while, besides the addition of immense provinces in those directions, we have been withdrawing troops from India to chastise the insolence of Persians and Chinese, we have left the very heart of our Oriental Empire—the Presidency of Bengal—almost denuded of European soldiers. From Calcutta to Delhi, a distance of 900 miles, a march of three months, a dense population, great cities, and important positions are left almost entirely to native troops, dangerously aware of our excessive anxiety to conciliate their attachment. It was necessary to temporize even at Barrackpore until the single European regiment there was reinforced with another from Pegu. While several British regiments have been employed in holding our new acquisitions in the extreme East, a still greater number have been doing the like service in the Punjaub. Thus the real sinew and thews of a great empire have been at its extremities, and the heart has been left to take care of itself. The well-guarded frontier has been treated as a depôt whence troops could be drawn on an emergency, without duly considering that it is the office of an army to prevent attacks rather than put them down, and that a crisis of insurrection is not exactly the time for leaving border provinces less guarded. We should not be surprised to hear that those in command at Lahore and elsewhere, though ever so confident of their position, under present circumstances are not prepared to spare much of their garrisons."

Another of our military mistakes, pointed out by the same journal, is—

"That the armies of India are not supplied with a sufficient strength of officers to furnish, as they now do, servants both for the military and civil departments of the State. Under a Government like that of India, it is highly natural that men inured to military discipline and possessed of military skill should be selected to fill what in any other country would be regarded as purely civil appointments, nor do we doubt that this system is the best that could be adopted for the administration of affairs. But unfortunately an officer, however able, cannot follow two professions at once, and when he is despatched upon staff or political employ, his regiment suffers, though the State may gain. The irregular corps, too, which have now been enrolled in considerable numbers, draw upon the same source for the officers who are to command them. Every new battalion of Sikhs, Bheels, or Beloochees makes its demand upon the regiments of the regular army for its commandant, its lieutenant, and its adjutant, and, when to these draughts are added the abstractions due to furloughs and invaliding, the result assumes a character almost incredible. At the date of our last despatches there were two native regiments in the Bombay Presideney, which, out of a complement of 23 European officers each, had but *six* between them actually present with the corps."

The gravity of the position has caused the warnings and predictions of the late Sir Charles Napier to be recollected, though at the time when they were uttered—during the rule of Lord Dalhousie—they were treated with ridicule, and their gallant author calumniated and insulted. General Tucker has addressed a letter to the *Times*, in which Sir Charles's perception of the coming danger is thus spoken of:—

"We had, not many years ago, the Scinde mutiny—a very formidable business. We had other less important indications of insubordination and ill-will; and, more recently, did not Sir Charles Napier energetically contend that 40,000 Sepoys in the Punjaub were, to a man, ripe for revolt? There was no tangible or precise proof of it, but that the feeling was there, and that a favourable opportunity would at once have evolved it, many besides Sir Charles confidently believed; and I assert that it is upon such a mine, liable at any convenient moment to explode, we have all along been resting. It may be contended that this being so, it was the duty of those entertaining the opinion boldly to proclaim aloud their conviction and to advocate a change; but I presume to dispute the correctness of any such assumption. In Sir Charles Napier's case, the very existence of such a feeling among the Sepoys was authoritatively contradicted and denied by the Governor-General (Lord Dalhousie); and it must be admitted that his Lordship had no proofs before him to warrant, as he thought, Sir Charles's statement, or even to enable him fairly to draw any such inference. By a happy combination of circumstances the mutiny at that time of the 66th Regiment was rendered harmless; and it was doubtless not considered politic to admit that the Sepoy army was so tainted as to be ripe for the wholesale revolt Sir Charles, with an intuitive and just perception, had so wonderfully divined. I believe firmly that he was right in his judgment, but, as I have said, there was no precise evidence, and thus things have gone on until now. Fifteen months ago, when I relinquished the post of Adjutant-General of the Bengal Army, the most entire calm existed; the repose and apparent contentment of the Sepoys were perfect; from Peshawur to Calcutta all was thoroughly quiet; but the truth is, that even then one little cloud, the forerunner of many others, was appearing in the horizon. General Anson anxiously desired to innovate; his predecessor had been harshly charged with supineness and a lethargic apathy; his own he designed should be a reign of a very different description, and he attempted to commence it with a curtailment of the leave or furlough annually granted to the Sepoys—a very hasty and injudicious beginning, and apparently so considered by more than myself, for it was then negatived, though I have since heard that at a later period it was successfully advocated."

The leading journal itself has lately acknowleged the correctness of Sir C. Napier's strictures upon the state of the Indian Army, and the admission is so remarkable, from its former treatment of the deceased General, that we reprint the article in which it occurs, without any abridgment:—

"It has long been set down among the singularities of our race that an Englishman is more than half satisfied when he knows the causes of a disaster. No doubt he is a very reasonable being, and often finds in a sufficient theory a compensation for actual failure. If it be so, our readers will find an immense store of comfort in the shape of Sir Charles Napier's published opinions on the condition of the Indian Army, and some extracts from the more recent official despatches of the Governor-General. Any one who reads the former, unless he resides under the shade of some Director or retired Commander-in-Chief, will only wonder how we have held the empire so long by such a rope of sand as our military system turns out to be. That, no doubt, has been the very reflection that has a thousand times instilled a false security, and stifled the thought of reform. It has gone on in this way for generations; it answers; no other way would answer, for what we can tell. True, there are misgivings, not to say actual dangers. So there were thirty years ago—ay, sixty years. Indeed, there never was a time when there were not people to tell us our empire hung on a thread. Bishop Heber says that had Lord Combermere been forced to raise the siege of Bhurtpore, as Lake had done twenty years before, every man from the Sutlej to the Nerbudda who had a sword, or who could either buy or steal a horse, would have risen against us.

"It so happens that, chiefly owing to the intense jealousy of the Indian Government and the incubus which sits on the pen and the tongue of every Indian functionary, we have not had many means of knowing how the system worked. We have had no men of quick observation, sound judgement, free from professional bias, and able to defy all authorities who passed through India, took notes of all they saw, and gave us the results of the tour. When a man did this, or when opinions did actually transpire, these were set down to disappointment, eccentricity, or malice: and few indeed are the men who are not open to such imputations. In fact, the prophet always was an eccentric, passionate, and rather ill-tempered being. For years it has been known that Sir Charles Napier felt the most grievous dissatisfaction with the state of things in India; and that he had incurred the wrath of its rulers by the freedom of his tongue. But what did this matter? His authority was as dust in the scale compared with the vast reality of an empire which had survived so many hostile predictions, and which it was often said required rather a certain assimilation to the Oriental character than so striking a contrast as the energetic Englishman is apt to become. India is a subject, indeed, on which mere Englishmen—and every one of us who has not seen India is a mere Englishman in the eyes of the more fortunate—have hardly courage to speak. The whole thing is a mystery in our eyes. None of us can divine by what spell or by what law of nature the schoolfellows whom we beat at every possible trial become in a few years collectors or judges with princely incomes, or military officers with extraordinary employments of great responsibility. It was not for us to criticize a state of things in which the least drop of English blood went for so much, where it seemed a positive waste to be clever and strong, and where the only danger was lest, like Gulliver among the Lilliputians, we should occasionally do damage by forgetting the smallness and the frailness of the race we had to deal with. Hence it is that even the British public, ever alive as it is to all misgovernment at home, and quick to hear complaints, was not roused by the known indignation and misgivings of Sir Charles Napier. In fact, what could we do? We have only just renewed and largely modified the charter, with hopes of improvement. As for the army, that we could not reach. These standing armies do indeed stand. The highest military reason is that a thing is so. Why, for example, did we make Delhi a strong fortress, surround it with new bastions, excavate a deep ditch out of the granite rock, leave within it a hundred thousand muskets, two parks of the heaviest artillery in India, and powder enough to blaze away at any enemy for a year, and then place the whole in the sole charge of three native regiments? Why did we not see the absurdity of this course? The answer is, that it always was so in Indian memory. It has been so the whole of this century, and no harm has come of it.

"What is described in these passages from the 'Life of Sir Charles Napier' is the gradual extinction of the British element in the native Indian Army, and the simultaneous elevation of the Hindoo. Had there been a compact by virtue of which we were gradually to surrender our dominion, to relinquish step by step the ground won for us by a succession of conquerors above our own standard, to let the Hindoo acquire the strength, the rank, the self-confidence, the absolute independence, and the contempt of ourselves necessary to qualify him for doing without us, we could not have done otherwise than we have. Here we see the picture of an immense army, of the finest men the country could produce; full of caste and prejudice; well paid; with wives, children, and camp followers; completely officered by their own race; these officers men of years, experience, and dignified character; and everything, in a word, that could make a good native army. We see a long indulgence to native pride and scruples to an extent unknown in our own army at home. On the other hand, we see the British officers of these noble regiments generally reduced to a few youths, learning their profession from the very men they are sent to command and overawe; spending their time in amusements, or, worse, in idleness; or, if they do learn and practise their profession, forthwith transferred to some civil employment. The collection of the revenue, which is said to have drained the judicial department of its best heads, robbed the army also of its ablest hands. Thus in many regiments England has become only a name, as much a name as the puppet we left on the throne of the Mogul and his feudatories. What remained intact, what improved, and grew stronger day by day, was the native organization. There were, indeed, pageants of Mahomedan Royalty, and there were also other men in buckram that stood for the British conqueror. History recorded itself in a few foreign uniforms and idle ceremonies. There was nothing real but the native, and that reality was witnessed with respectful alarm by such men as Sir Charles Napier, with blind indifference by such men as Sir William Gomm, and, we must add with pain, Lord Dalhousie. So Sir Charles protested and prophesied. He knew the breath would be hardly out of his body before the whole rotten fabric would crumble to pieces, but he would not be the Casandra of India, the laughing-stock of Directors and Departments. He would, indeed, have protested in vain. He did protest in vain. His own life and character were a continual protest against the indolence and luxury of the Englishman who plays the soldier to the increasing contempt of the Hindoo. Sir Charles was laughed, at, snubbed, caricatured, and finally beaten from the field, warning his friends to the last of the impending catastrophe. He has, however, done his work. We have his light, and we shall profit by it. We have now to reconquer India, and we shall do it. We have to reconstruct our system, to reorganize our army, and to create a new ideal of the British soldier in India. That we shall do, for we are not a nation to give up our ground once won, or to acquiesce in deterioration. We have lost ground, slipped, and fallen; but we have no doubt India will soon be ours in a sense in which it has never been before."

While the public were anxiously awaiting the arrival of the next mail from India, the distracted affairs of that country became the subject of earnest debate in both Houses of Parliament. On Monday, the 27th, the Marquis of CLANRICARDE, in moving for copies of the correspondence between the Board of Control and the Directors and the Governor-General of India, commented upon the mismanagement of the Indian Government. One bad effect of that misgovernment was, that, during the late Russian war, India, instead of being an auxiliary, was a burthen to us. The late mutiny was partly owing to the annexation of Oude, as well as to the manner in which our Sepoys were officered. It was said that we should disband the Brahmins and Rajpoots in our army, and maintain permanently in India 60,000 British troops. But how, he asked, was such an expense to be defrayed? The only remedy was to totally alter the Government of India, and place it under a Minister of the Crown; and he trusted that by next session Ministers would be able to meet Parliament with a measure prepared for the purpose, and calculated to preserve the noble territory of India to this country. The Duke of ARGYLL said that the papers called for by the noble marquis were already before the Commons, and would be speedily produced in that house. It would be highly imprudent to enter at present into any discussion on Indian affairs, as the subject required full consideration and inquiry. The evil might be greater than is imagined, but he had no doubt that the Indian army would be restored to that fidelity which had distinguished it throughout so many campaigns.

In the House of Commons on the same evening, Mr. DISRAELI rose, pursuant to motion, and moved for—1st. Copy of any minutes or despatch addressed to the Governor-General of India, by his Excellency the Commander-in-Chief, the late Major-General the Hon. G. Anson, dated in or about March, 1856, relative to the state of the Bengal army.—2nd. Copy of a report on the organization of the Bengal army, drawn up by the late Lieutenant-General Sir Charles Napier, and transmitted to his Grace the Duke of Wellington, K.G. He said that nothing was more interesting, and few things more instructive, than to recall the commencement of great events. Street riots in Boston and Paris began the two great revolutions of modern times; and so, when some weeks ago we heard of a Sepoy mutiny, few people read the news, and most persons turned for amusement to more exciting discussions in this house on questions of comparative insignificance. The intelligence of the mutiny was acknowledged to have taken the Government by surprise, and a certain minister—the Chancellor of the Exchequer—had stated as the result of a mature opinion that the revolt was caused by a sudden impulse, occasioned by a superstitious feeling, and that it was only a military mutiny. But it was important to know whether it really was only a military mutiny, or a national revolt. The first question now is, what were the causes of the present crisis in India; and, second, what are the measures which should be adopted under the circumstances? The fiery criticisms of the late Sir C. Napier, and the calmer reflections of Lord Melville, had long since shown that the state of the Bengal army was unsatisfactory. But the mutineers in Bengal were not so much the avengers of their own individual wrongs as the exponents of general discontent, into the vortex of which they had at last been drawn. He conceived that the causes of the discontent were threefold:—1st, the forcible destruction of native authority in India by our Government; 2nd, the disturbance of the settlement of property; and, 3rd, tampering with the religion of the people. Under the first head he classed the annexations of native states on the ground of the failure of heirs, although the Hindoo law sanctioned adoption. He instanced the cases of the Rajahs of Sattara and Berar. The violations of the Hindoo law shook the confidence not only of the princes, but of large and powerful parties. Secondly, our new system as to lands also repealed the Hindoo law of adoption, and alarmed all the India landed proprietors. Inquisitions had also been prosecuted into the titles to landed estates, and he believed that the amount obtained by the Indian

Government by the resumption of estates was not less in Bengal alone than £500,000 a year, while in Bombay, he had been assured, the annual amount was £370,000. The Government had further reduced guaranteed pensions by curtailment and conversion into annuities. The Nabob of Arcot had a pension granted to him of only £4000 a year (a member, £40,000). He (Mr. Disraeli) believed that £4000 a year was the sum, and the descendant of the Nabob of Arcot has now only a pension of £150 a year, which showed that £4000 only had been granted to the once wealthy Nabob of Arcot. All these proceedings had estranged numerous classes from our authority. He now proceeded to the last head—tampering with the religion of the people; and here he hesitated in attributing any part of this cause to missionary efforts. So far from the Hindoo looking with suspicion on the missionary, he was convinced that he was ready to discuss any point of religion. But what the Hindoo did regard with dread and apprehension was the union of missionary enterprise with the power of the Government. He was much misinformed if the Government had not furnished ground for suspicion in relation to native education; but there had been two Acts passed within these few years by the Legislative Council of India which had greatly disquieted the Hindoo mind: one enacted that no man should lose his property on account of changing his religion; the other permitted a Hindoo widow to marry a second husband. Both these Acts had spread the greatest alarm and disturbance among the Hindoos. Mr. Disraeli then adverted to the "startling event" of the annexation of Oude, the consequence of which, he said, was to inspire the Mahommedan princes with apprehension, and to unite them in a common cause with the Hindoos. He had been informed, besides, that in our Bengal regiments there were no fewer than 70,000 natives of Oude, who, in returning to their villages, would find them in the possession of the East India Company, and those who were owners of land would be subject to the hard and severe system of our land revenue. It was after this event that the circulation of symbols in the forms of cakes and lotus flowers throughout the Bengal army proved the existence of a general conspiracy. He thought it was impossible that the Indian Government could have been ignorant that the Bengal troops were in a state of chronic insubordination, and it was their duty solemnly to impress upon the Government at home, and they must have done so, that the time had come when they must seriously consider the state of our Indian army. The greasing of the cartridges Mr. Disraeli dismissed with the remark that nobody believed that to have been the real cause of the outbreak. In the last place, he proceeded to inquire, assuming that the views he had developed were correct, what were the measures which the Government ought to adopt in the emergency. Regarding the revolt as a national one, military measures were not sufficient, and the measures of the Government were inadequate; there should be an expedition up the Indus; our force in India should be doubled. But, further, the population of India should be told that there is a future hope; they should be taught at once that the relations between them and their Sovereign, Queen Victoria, would be drawn nearer; and a royal commission should be sent from the Queen to India to inquire into the grievances of all classes.

Mr. V. SMITH said that no native prince had been concerned in the revolt, nor was there any conspiracy between the native princes. Lord Dalhousie's system as to adoption might be right or wrong, but that subject had no connection whatever with the revolt. As to the alleged disturbance of landed property, a commission had inquired into the enam lands, some of which had been acquired by fraud, and this inquiry may have caused discontent among certain classes. The interference with religion was a matter of immense delicacy; and he had no hesitation in saying that it would be the best policy at once to interfere and prevent the exercise of missionary zeal by our civil and military servants. He coincided with Mr. Disraeli entirely in thinking interference with the religion of the natives of India highly objectionable. On the subject of annexation, he was an enemy to systematic annexation; but the question of Oude was this: the subjects of Oude were kept in subjection by our force, and we made ourselves responsible for everything the King did; Lord Dalhousie, therefore, thought it better to annex the territory, which was done with the least possible injury to the parties concerned. The attempt to connect this annexation with the mutiny had completely failed. He denied that the Government had received any warning of the mutiny, or that there was the slightest indication of any disaffection among the native troops. Lord Dalhousie and Sir W. Gomm had borne testimony to their loyal spirit down to a very late period, and he did not believe that Sir C. Napier had made any representation to the Indian Government founded upon the criticisms he had left behind. It was premature to say what was the real cause of the mutiny; but he thought there must have been some mismanagement at Meerut, and mismanagement at the beginning often leads to serious results in such cases. There had been of late years a severance between the men and their officers in the native regiments, and he was sorry to hear that the latter sometimes spoke of the Sepoys at their mess as "niggers." As to the remedies suggested by Mr. Disraeli, the proposed sending of a royal commission would supersede the Governor-General, which would be a fatal error. Then Mr. Disraeli proposes to connect the name of the Queen with the whole administration of India, but the present system of Indian government had been deliberately opposed by the Legislature; yet it might be advisable, with the sanction of the Governor-General, to send out a commission to inquire into various matters, and, amongst others, into the re-organization of the Indian army, many points connected with which are worthy of consideration.

Sir E. PERRY coincided in the opinion that this was a national and not merely a military revolt. It was caused by the new policy of annexation and by the "resumptive" doctrine, with regard to lands, which invalidated titles of forty years' standing.

Lord J. RUSSELL said, in presence of what had been rightly termed an awful calamity, he could not conceive anything less tending to the advantage of this country or of India than such a discussion, if it was to end either in a vote of censure, or a transfer of India to the Crown. Neither of these measures was proposed in the motion, which was only for the production of papers. Mr. Disraeli, he observed, had never ventured to say that the great mass of the people of India had suffered under oppression. It appeared to him that we had trusted rather too much to Indian troops, and troops of one particular kind, and have had too large an army. He thought that 50,000 Europeans and 100,000 natives would afford a far better security than our present force. The first matter, however, upon which the House of Commons ought to pronounce an opinion was, that the Government ought to be supported; he thought the House ought not to separate without expressing such opinion, and he accordingly moved, by way of amendment, an address to her Majesty "to assure her Majesty that they will support her Majesty in any efforts necessary to suppress the disturbances in India, and in any measures required for the establishment of tranquillity."

Mr. MANGLES dwelt on the commercial good feeling felt towards us by the princes, landowners, and people of India. He entered into details as to the conduct of Lord Dalhousie in regard to the Hindoo law of adoption, and stated the particulars of the case of the Rajah of Sattara. He denied that Government had been warned of the state of the Bengal army, and read from official reports of Sir C. Napier, in which he spoke in warm terms of the native troops. In his General Order of 1853, Sir C. Napier said, "I have never seen a more obedient or a more honourable army."

Mr. DISRAELI replied, and reiterated the opinion that this was a national revolt.

Viscount PALMERSTON expressed his regret that Mr. Disraeli, who held so prominent a position, should have selected a moment of great difficulty for the expression of the opinions which the House had heard. He should not enter. into the question at that late hour; he was satisfied to rest it upon the speeches of Mr. Smith and Mr. Mangles, which would serve as antidotes to those opinions.

General THOMPSON observed that no notice had been taken in the debate, of a breach of military faith and honour towards the soldiers of the Indian native army.

The original motion was then negatived, and Lord John Russell's amendment carried without a division.

In the House of Lords, on Thursday, the 30th, the Earl of ELLENBOROUGH adverted to the Governor-General's Proclamation of the 16th May, declaring that the religion of the natives would not be interfered with. It should be recollected that so far back as the 28th of January last General Hearsey informed the Governor-General that the Sepoys entertained a fear that they would be forced to embrace the Christian faith; and on the 11th February General Hearsey stated that they were dwelling upon a mine, which might explode at any time. Yet it was not until the 27th March that a General Order was made upon the subject, and that General Order was not read to the troops until the disbanding of the 19th regiment. After that came the Proclamation of the 16th May, but it was not issued till after the events at Meerut, and therefore the expected salutary effect could not be produced. He then animadverted upon the manner in which the government of India is conducted, viz., solely through the instrumentality of tedious correspondence between the officials. On the 22nd of January a strong feeling with respect to the greased cartridges was exhibited amongst the Sepoys at Dum-dum, upon which eight different letters were written by one officer to another, and four days elapsed before the Government at Calcutta became acquainted with the ominous event, which took place about eight miles from the Government House; three more letters were written, and two days more elapsed before it was made known at Barrackpore that the objections of the Sepoys were removed, and another delay elapsed before the intelligence was communicated at Dum-dum. Important events occurred at Barrackpore on the 6th February, but the Government was not made acquainted with them until the 10th, the distance between Barrackpore and Calcutta being only 16 miles of as good ground for travelling as any in England. An explanation was asked of General Hearsey, who stated that he had no public means of communicating with the Government; he had no mounted orderly to despatch with his communication, and he sent it therefore by post. That was the way that business was conducted in India in a time of danger. Did any one suppose that if the Marquis Wellesley or Warren Hastings were in India those delays would have taken place? The officer at Dum-dum might have got into his buggy and driven to the Government House in an hour; the officials should have been sent for and consulted; and the Governor-General should have gone at once to Dum-dum; and the whole business should have been done on the evening of the 22nd. If the days between the 22nd and the 29th had been saved, he did not know what might have been the consequences. It was impossible that in times of danger the Indian government could be conducted in the manner indicated by that correspondence, when that government was carried on with difficulty at any time. It showed that the government of India was not in the hands of the Governor-General, but of secretaries and clerks. It was impossible to read the papers and not come to the conclusion that the objection of the Sepoys to the cartridge was a real objection, founded upon religious grounds. He was rejoiced to find that such was the case, because, although a mutiny arising from a cause of that kind destroyed for the present their confidence in them, it did not prevent the revival of that confidence when the Sepoys were brought to a just sense of the real intentions of the Government. Let them take what course they would, it was impossible for them to carry on the government of India until they re-established

c

their confidence in the Sepoys—and their first business should be to re-establish confidence in them after the mutiny was repressed.

Earl GRANVILLE said there was no objection to producing the Proclamation. He denied that the government of India was carried on by clerks and secretaries, and said the Governor-General had paid the promptest attention to all the proceedings. He had seen various letters from India, stating that Lord Canning had risen in the estimation of all Europeans there, and that he had shown himself fully equal to the emergency.

After some observations from the Duke of ARGYLL and Lord PANMURE the subject dropped; but on the following evening, Lord ELLENBOROUGH, whose views, from his former position in India, are deserving of attention, returned to the subject by asking for a copy of any Order in Council issued to provide carriage for the Indian army after the 1st February last; also a return of all means of carriage in the possession of the Indian Commissariat in the north-western provinces and in the Punjaub; also any Order of Council for reducing the number of commissariat animals in the said provinces. He asked for these returns because everything turned on the sufficiency of means for carriage. If in the beginning there had been sufficient land transport to send a few 18-pounders, 5000 men would have been able to knock down so much of the walls of Delhi as would enable them to enter the place. He rejoiced that General Barnard had not attacked Delhi, as he feared an attack must have failed if made. So long as Sir H. Barnard keeps his troops intact, the native states near Delhi will remain faithful. But Sir H. Barnard cannot remain where he is, because when the rains come on he would be imprisoned by the waters in a narrow strip of land, and not merely peril but ruin must ensue. He hoped that Sir H. Barnard, seeing that he could not attack Delhi with a certainty of success, would retreat in time—form a junction with the forces at Meerut, establish himself at Umballa, and keep up a communication with the troops in the Punjaub. He hoped also that he would strike a great blow at the enemy, and obtain a decisive victory at some point on his retirement. He next adverted to the position of Calcutta, and to the want of precaution on the part of the Government, the result being that Calcutta was thrown for protection upon merchants and clerks, who walked about under umbrellas with revolvers in their hands.

Earl GRANVILLE did not object to present the papers called for, but he thought it would do no practical good. He was surprised that the noble earl, in his anxiety to criticise, should discuss points on which we had no clear information. He had received various communications from persons—not so eloquent, perhaps, but with as much knowledge and experience as the noble earl—who were perfectly indignant at the aspersions which he had thrown upon the Government of India. It was stated that the Governor-General had displayed great industry, singular calmness, and real courage on this occasion. He had taken down a list of the telegraphic messages sent by Lord Canning, in consequence of which troops were pouring in; the natives were surprised that a European force could be so speedily collected, and the moral effect was already beginning to be felt.

The Earl of ALBEMARLE had given notice of a question, on behalf of several Indian princes and chiefs now in this country, as to whether it was the intention of the Government to continue the policy of annexing the territories of native rulers, in the event of their dying without natural heirs, as had been done in the case of the Rajah of Sattara, and others. But, on the time coming for him to put the question, he observed that, owing to the present state of affairs in India, he should refrain from doing so. The subject of adoption, however, is so important in Indian politics, and formed so prominent a feature in the debate in the House of Commons, that it is absolutely necessary to the formation of a sound judgment on the conflicting opinions of Mr. Disraeli, on the one side, and Mr. Vernon Smith and Mr. Mangles, on the other, to know what are the rules laid down in the Vedas and the Institutes of Menu. Those great canons of Hindoo jurisprudence are silent upon the point in dispute, namely, whether a stranger may be adopted, as was done by the Rajah of Sattara; but it is to be inferred from the limitations ordained, that the President of the Board of Control, who maintained the negative, laboured under an error. The selection of a stranger's child for adoption is nowhere forbidden; the ceremony is solemnly and imperatively enjoined as a religious duty upon all who are childless, the neglect of which excludes them from heaven; and the grounds of disqualification are so numerous, that many would be debarred from adoption, if their choice was limited to their own family. The child adopted must be a boy, not more than five years of age; he must not be the son of a sister or a daughter, nor have been contracted in marriage, nor had his ears pierced, nor have received the Brahminical thread; he must not be an eldest nor an only son, and his father must be willing to part with him. The considerations arising from these circumstances are strongly in favour of the view taken by Mr. Disraeli.

The following is the return made to the order of the House of Commons, on the right honourable gentleman's motion :—

EXTRACTS "*of such Parts of a Report addressed by Sir Charles Napier, on the 27th day of November*, 1849, *to the Governor-General of India, as relate to the State and Discipline of the Indian Army.*"

" The defence of our Indian Empire is confided to four distinct armies, Queen's, Bengal, Madras, and Bombay, consisting collectively of about 300,000 fighting men, and 400 pieces of field artillery, ready for war, without including those of position, mounted on forts, or lying in our arsenals.

" This is a vast army, and it is in a good state of discipline, complete in its equipments, full of high courage, and a high military spirit reigns through all ranks : it is also necessary to say that this force could be doubled without any injurious pressure on the population, and that every part of India can furnish recruits in abundance; our service is extremely popular, and the troops faithful to a proverb. There are some things which admit of correction, and these may be put right when the Commander-in-Chief is placed on a proper footing, but not till then. I shall consider these matters in another letter. Let it here suffice to say it is my decided opinion that this magnificent army is sufficient to guard India at present, and that the annexation of the Punjaub does not, or at least need not, demand an additional regiment. I shall now proceed to the consideration of the immediate occupation of the Punjaub.

" For this, and indeed for every purpose, I think that Delhi is the proper place for our great magazines. It lies in a central position to supply troops and reinforcements.

" For this reason, also, I think that the head quarters of the artillery should be marched to Delhi or Meerut, as may be hereafter arranged.

" The great principle to follow in India, as regards armed forces, I think is this : to have a large well-organized police to do all those duties for the civil branches of the Government that require armed men ; such as occasional guards for civil servants, escorts of treasure, putting down robbers, arresting men by order of the civil power; in short, a constabulary force that leaves the military to their own duties.

" There is scarcely any illness which the troops suffer from that may not be traced to want of room in barracks.

" I have heard that Lord Hardinge objected to the assembling of the Indian troops, for fear they should conspire. I confess I cannot see the weight of such an opinion. I have never, with an Indian officer who held it, and I certainly do not hold it myself; and few men have had more opportunities of judging of the armies of all three Presidencies than I have. Lord Hardinge saw but the Bengal army, and that only as Governor-General, and for a short time ; I have studied them for nearly eight years, constantly at the head of Bengal and Bombay

Sepoys, and I can see nothing to fear from them, except when ill-used; and even then they are less dangerous than British troops would be in similar circumstances. I see no danger in their being massed, and very great danger in their being spread over a country as they now are; on the contrary, I believe that, by concentrating the Indian army as I propose, its spirit, its devotion, and its powers will all be increased."

The foregoing extracts are a very small portion indeed of the memoir from which they are quoted, the reason for withholding any portion of which, it would be difficult to discover. Sir John Ramsden, in refusing the entire report when asked for by General Wyndham, was anxious to know how the latter knew of its existence, which, he said, was known only to Lord Panmure and one other person. It is said that the other person alluded to was General Vivian, and that it was him who made known the existence of the document, and the nature of its contents, to General Wyndham. The truth is, that the report was published by Sir W. Napier, among the posthumous papers of his brother, a few years ago; of that work 1500 copies were sold, and a new edition is about to be published by Westerton, the anti-Puseyite bookseller of Knightsbridge.

So confident had been the anticipations expressed by the Government and its organs that the mail due on the 29th of July would bring the news of the capture of Delhi and the suppression of the mutiny, and so great and all but universal has been the belief in the prestige of British power, that the telegraphic despatches received on the 30th came upon the public like a thunderclap. Delhi still held out, and the entire Bengal army was in a state of insurrection; while there seems ground to fear that in the other Presidencies the soldiers await the opportunity to be afforded by the withdrawal of the European forces, by which they were overawed, to manifest the same determination to overturn our power. The semi-independent princes give no apparent countenance to the outbreak; and several have shown considerable alacrity in placing their forces at the disposal of the Indian Government. But this forbearance is not to be relied upon, as has been shown by the revolt of troops whose professions of loyalty had been profusely given when the first mutinies occurred, and by the case of the deposed King of Oude. Since his dethronement, and the annexation of his kingdom to the British dominions—the crowning act of the government of Lord Dalhousie—that prince has resided at Calcutta, and his mother, brother, and son are in London, for the purpose of bringing his pecuniary claims and political grievances under the notice of the Home Government. The king and his predecessors on the throne have from time to time lent large sums of money to the East India Company, a considerable balance of which debt remained due when he was deposed, and his capital taken possession of by the Company's troops. Payment is now refused, on the ground that the money in question was lent out of the territorial revenues of Oude, and that the debt was, therefore, extinguished when the territory was annexed to British India. The ingratitude and breach of faith, not to say dishonesty of this mode of evading payment of a just demand has been severely commented upon both in and out of Parliament.

Lord Moira, in 1815, acknowledged having received pecuniary assistance to the extent of £2,000,000, and expressed to the reigning prince "how much he himself and the honourable Company felt themselves obliged and thankful for the liberal aid he had afforded in an hour of extreme need." Lord Amherst, in 1825, conveyed to the sovereign his "cordial thanks for the instance he had given of his friendship by advancing, upon certain conditions, by way of loan, the sum of one crore of rupees (£1,000,000 sterling) in a case of extreme emergency and need; the Burmese war having cost enormous sums of money." Between 1838 and 1842, as Lord Ellenborough has stated, "large sums of money were advanced by the King of Oude to the British Government, at a time when it was in great want of money in connexion with the Affghan war."

The sums were handed to us in addition to the large annual tribute extracted by us as a subsidy for troops stationed by us in Oude, not for the protection of the State against external enemies or internal disaffection, but as a corps de reserve for our own advantage in the hour of danger—an easy and economical means of maintaining a standing army on a war footing with a peace expenditure, so far as the cost to Government was concerned. That the deposed sovereign of Oude is galled and irritated by his deprivation of power, authority, and wealth, every one can readily understand; that he entertained hopes of recovering them by an appeal to a power greater than that of the East India Company, is proved by the mission of his relations to the court of Queen Victoria, by whom they have been received at Buckingham Palace. But that he was in any way connected with the mutinous Sepoys, was scouted by the press as an idea not to be entertained for one moment, though it was known that a third of the Bengal army had been raised in Oude, and that the ex-king's prime minister was in frequent conference with him. "Of political disaffection," said the *Times* " we cannot discover a trace. That the dethroned King of Oude should have been the object of suspicion in current rumours was only natural, but it is allowed on all hands that neither he, nor, in all human probability, any other prince or potentate, has had any share whatever in the creation or encouragement of the discontents referred to." The *Morning Advertiser*, which, throughout, has taken a native view of the revolt, referred to the subject in the following manner, more than a week before the arrival of the last mail :—

"We believe in retribution for national as well as for individual crime; and almost coincident with our last crowning iniquity comes this most fearful revolt. No sooner have we, in the face of the most solemn treaties, dethroned the King whom our policy had ruined, and on the pretexts of a misgovernment for which we were responsible, and of a poverty we ourselves had caused—no sooner, we say, had we consummated this annexation, and began to congratulate ourselves upon the acquisition of this magnificent territory with its 5,000,000 inhabitants, than we find our very existence threatened in the entire peninsula, and that which would have been the buttress of our power, whose forces and treasure would have been poured out like water for our defence, has been converted into an additional danger. No doubt at this moment mutiny reigns in Oude amongst the troops, and discontent amongst its nobles and people, who are grieved and enraged by the exile of their King, the destruction of the Court, and the loss of their nationality. The energy of a Lawrence may dispel the danger for the moment, but only an act of tardy justice and of seasonable penitence can render this beautiful country permanently tranquil."

One of the most significant announcements of the telegraphic despatches received from Marseilles in anticipation of the mail was the intelligence that the ex-King of Oude and his late Prime Minister, Ali Nucky Khan, had been arrested, and confined in Fort William. A fakeer who was sentenced to be hung in Calcutta for tampering with the troops, is said to have made the revelations which have led to this important step. He was a Mohammedan, and a native of Lucknow, and we believe one of the retinue of the ex-King. He was tried by court-martial at the fort on Saturday the 13th of June, and was to have been hanged on Sunday, but the execution of the sentence was postponed in consequence of his revelations. What these amounted to has not been made public, but the prisoner seems to have been of opinion that they were not of sufficient importance to procure his pardon, since he effected his escape on the following day by slipping his hands and feet out of his fetters, which were of full size, and intended for Europeans. How he managed to elude the guard we have not ascertained, but the guard were arrested.

Precisely at three o'clock, A.M., on Monday, the Hon. Company's steam frigate *Semiramis*, made fast to the swinging buoy laid out in the stream off the esplanade, was cast off, steam having been got up some hours previously. She was taken off the ex-King of Oude's residence, Garden Reach, where she was brought to. An hour previous to the steamer casting off, the European troops within the fort were called to arms, and a number of them were immediately afterwards marched down, several field pieces accompanying, to the residence of the ex-King, on reaching which place the troops surrounded the house, and remained under arms till the following morning, when the ex-King was made a prisoner of, and his retainers made to surrender their arms. The former was removed without loss of time in a carriage, in charge of two commissioned officers, to Fort William, and a search immediately after commenced for certain papers of a seditious nature said to have been in his possession. The selection of Fort William as the place of the ex-King's imprisonment is regarded, by old Indian residents, as a step of very doubtful prudence, the fort being the stronghold of the Government arsenal at Calcutta, where 3000 natives are employed in dockyard work and the manufacture of ammunition.

We have given precedence to this event on account of its importance, and the proof it affords of the fallacy of the views promulgated with regard to the outbreak when the mutiny at Berhampore was first announced in this country. We now proceed to relate, in the order of their occurrence, the series of sanguinary outbreaks and massacres which took place during the month of June. Lucknow continued to be a hotbed of disaffection, and the English residents were in daily expectation of such frightful scenes as those which had been enacted at Meerut and Delhi. Every day the Chief Commissioner had been informed that the regiments would certainly rise at night between eight and nine o'clock, and as often the hours passed over without the slightest disturbance. When, therefore, the same story was repeated on the 29th of May, he did not attach extraordinary importance to it, and merely took the ordinary precaution of doubling the sentries and directing every officer to be on the look-out. Nine o'clock struck, and the Chief Commissioner was in the act of remarking that the rumour had proved itself as unfounded as its predecessors, when shots were heard in the 71st Native Infantry lines. He immediately mounted his horse and proceeded to the encampment of the 32nd Queen's, and then moved up to the corner of the Lucknow-road, with two guns and a company of Europeans, to prevent the mutineers from coming down to the city. The remaining six guns remained in position at the encamping ground, guarded by Europeans. Bungalows now began to blaze, and the firing to become hotter. General Handscombe was killed on the spot by a shot from the 71st lines, up to which he had ridden quite close, in the hope that his presence and speech might have the effect of bringing the mutineers to reason. Lieutenant Grant was killed at his picket. The mutineers ran at his men, some of whom turned and fled. A shot from the mutineers then wounded Grant, and the subadar of the guard concealed him under his charpoy. The mutineers then came up, and were told that he had got away. They were not, however, to be deceived, and at last a havildar of the guard, belonging to Grant's own regiment, pointed him out to the mutineers, when he was bayoneted and brutally mutilated. The cantonment soon became one blaze of fire, and it was not deemed prudent to move their guns for fear of the mutineers finding their way into the city; the only means of checking them was by sending detachments of irregular cavalry through the lines. Sharp firing took place frequently between the sowars and the mutineers, without much effect, however, upon either side. Lieutenant Hardinge distinguished himself greatly in these skirmishes, in one of which a mutineer fired at him within a yard, and missing him, charged him with his bayonet, which went through his wrist and entered his chest, where its further progress was stopped by a bullet from Hardinge into the stomach of his assailant, which sickened him of the contest. Lieutenant Chambers, Adjutant of the 13th, had a narrow escape, and was wounded in the leg. This state of affairs lasted until two o'clock in the morning of the 30th, when the fires abated, and two guns were moved up to each of the Residency gates, which were guarded by a havildar's guard from the 13th and some sowars. At four A.M. the rebels had reached the 7th Cavalry lines, at Moodkeepore, which they set on fire, and then returned to the cantonments, where Sir Henry Lawrence had prepared to meet them. Leaving a company of Europeans, six guns, and a squadron of irregulars on the encamping ground, he marched towards them with two guns, the Europeans, some 300 in number, the 7th Light Cavalry, and a handful of each of the irregular cavalry regiments, Daly's, Gall's, and Hardinge's. His force, as he came along the native lines, was increased from the 71st, 13th, and 48th Regiments, who had not joined the insurgents, amounting in all to about 500 men. The 7th Light Cavalry were sent on in advance, but on nearing the rebels, some of them went over to them. The insurgents then retreated, and by the time the artillery had debouched from the lines they were a thousand yards, off, so that they could be only dealt with by round shot. One was sent at them, when they immediately turned and fled, followed as quickly as possible by the artillery and the Europeans.

The companies of the 44th and 67th Native Infantry, stationed at Muttra, rose against their officers, killing one and wounding another, and seized the treasure that was to have been conveyed on the same day to Agra. In consequence of this outbreak, the companies of the same regiments stationed at Agra were disarmed, upon which the greater part of the 44th and some of the 67th left the city, and probably went to Delhi, to swell the ranks of the insurgents there. At Hissar and Hansi, two stations to the north-west of Delhi, the troops, consisting of the Hurreeanah Battalion and the 4th Irregular Cavalry, mutinied, and went off to Delhi. The whole of the Bengal troops at Neemuch broke out into open mutiny on the night of June 3. They began by firing all the officers' bungalows. The Post-office was fired by men of the 1st Bengal Light Infantry, who plundered the treasure chest and destroyed the records. Some European officers were killed, but the political agent and superintendent escaped. Neemuch was left in the hands of mutineers.

A letter from an officer who escaped from this place to Odypore gives the following account of what happened :—

"On the night of the 3rd of June, about eleven, the cantonment was aroused by the report of one of the guns, on which several bungalows broke into flames. One wing of the Gwalior corps, under Macdonald, was in the fort; the other under Rose, in the vacant hospitals. On the alarm, Rose attempted to get his wing into the fort, but the men refused to go, and one fellow fired his musket point blank at Rose's head, but fortunately missed him. After some delay Macdonald came down and got the left wing into the fort: they then made some show of defence, but said, 'If guns are brought against us we must give in.' Shortly after a trooper rode down, and told them to be ready and join them. At length the men told Macdonald and Rose to be off, or their lives would be taken by the cavalry. On this Macdonald, Rose, the adjutant (name unknown), and Durnfort made a bolt to Daroo, and on their way there were joined by the artillery officers, Coates, all the cavalry officers, and several others, in all about fifteen sahibs and five women. The cavalry men were the worst of the mutineers, and spared no Europeans that came across them. The mutineers created Sheik Riadut Ali, subadar of the first cavalry, brigadier of the station, who issued immediate orders in the name of the King of Delhi, and distributed the treasure amongst the Sepoys. Everything was done in form ; a big tent with a flag flying before it was made the headquarters of the brigadier, who appointed the several subadars and jemadars, colonels and majors respectively. A Mussulman subadar, Sheik Kasin, commands the 7th Gwaliors. Lloyd had received a report that an agent from Scindiah had been tampering with the troops, and that it is Gwalior's intention to set up a Raj at Neemuch. Macdonald atempted to take away with him his colours, but they were snatched out of his hand. Abbott, on the afternoon of the 2nd, attempted to *sumjhao* the cavalry, that, as they had sworn to be faithful, they ought to regard their oaths, when they broke out with, 'Why did you break faith at Lahore, and again in Oude, and now you want to take away our religion, but you shan't.' I have neither space nor time to give you all the details ———— told me, but he says that of all the bloody disasters that have taken place, the Neemuch one exceeds all in cruelty. Those houses and things that would not burn they destroyed with hatchets. Old Pestonjee they blew away from a gun, and it is believed they treated some European women in the same way; they have all gone up towards Delhi, and Showers is too late for them."

On the same night the 17th Native Infantry, stationed at Azimghur, mutinied. An escort of 80 Sowars of the 13th Irregular Cavalry brought in on that date seven and a half lacs of treasure from Gorruckpore; it was determined to continue its route to Benares, where the presence of some companies of the 10th Queen's would secure it to the Government. Some days previously the authorities, military and civil, had been occupied in throwing up a breastwork round the kutchery. This, however, was not quickly completed. The escort and treasure moved about six P.M. At nine P.M. all the men in the lines some distance from the kutchery broke out, killed their quartermaster, and wounded the quartermaster-sergeant severely, slightly wounded the havildar-major, and killed the kotwal of the city. The officer on guard at the fort at the kutchery hearing the shots, and having a guard of picked and trusty men, as he thought, turned them out, and desired the golandauzes to make the guns ready for business. They refused this, told him they would not fire or allow the guns to be fired on the regiment, and that all the officers and ladies would be spared; that they wanted the guns to get at the treasure, now some two hours and a half march ahead. Some bungalows were set on fire. About 27 persons reached Ghazeepore in a terrible plight, after having toiled over 44 miles of road. Some men of the same regiment escorted Major Burroughes, the officer in command, to Ghazeepore; he was very much respected by the good men of them. What became of the treasure is at present unknown. Guns were heard during the night in the direction which the escort had taken, but the troopers had promised the Sepoys to cut them to pieces if they came to seize the boxes, and they were to be joined by a reinforcement of 50 more from the same regiment from the Benares side.

At five o'clock on the evening of the 4th the Benares Brigade was ordered out for the purpose of disarming the 37th Regiment, who were known to be disaffected and in correspondence with people in the city. The men were ordered to appear on parade without their arms. Some companies obeyed and did so, but others refused to give up their arms and commenced firing at their officers. This appeared to be the signal, for the rest of the regiment then ran to the bells of arms; the guns, however, began to pour in the grape so sharply upon them, that they were glad to beat a retreat; only a few of the most determined rebels still kept up a fire from the right wing at the officers. The Sikh Regiment all this time remained quiet on parade, passive spectators of the scene, but at this crisis they loaded by order of Colonel Gordon. An ominous change then came over them. The cavalry first turned, and then with the Sikhs poured in a deliberate volley on the officers standing around, three of whom fell. The artillery in return gave them a shower of grape, which sent them flying off the parade. About 100 of the mutineers were killed and 200 wounded; the rest bolted, throwing down their arms. The mutineers of the Sikh regiment tried to capture the guns, and were thrice repulsed with great loss. Only a few men of the irregular cavalry and Sikh regiment stood firm; all the rest mutinied; their discomfiture was complete, thanks to the bravery of 180 European soldiers, who defended the guns, and charged and shot down the mutineers. Eight of these brave soldiers were killed and wounded. The lives of the civilians and their families who had taken refuge in the collector's kutchery were saved by the presence and noble exertions of Soorut Singh, a Sikh prisoner. He went among the Sikhs of the treasury guard, and prevented them from rising after they had heard how the men of their corps had been cut up, and by his influence they were kept at their post until the next morning, when the treasure was removed to cantonments under an escort of Europeans. The portion of the Sikh corps over the treasury remained staunch. The rebels took the road to Allahabad. A letter from Benares, dated June 16th, says :—

"Thank Heaven there is one man of nerve here not afraid to hang a few rascals every evening. I saw a Sikh hung yesterday for shooting at a non-commissioned officer. A gallows stands in front of the Main Guard, from whence the culprit is led at the appointed hour, by the guard under arms, and a grave dug on the flank. No useless parades, prancing, pomp, &c. Benares is ours and likely to remain so, thanks to our brave troops. There is no excitement here, confidence is established, and martial law carried out. I suppose from the position this will be chosen for the formation of a large force. We hold still the fort of Allahabad. The natives about seem very anxious to circulate unfavourable reports."

Another letter states:—

"I have, with deep sorrow, to inform you of the murder of a non-commissioned officer and four privates (Europeans), *en route* to Benares from Chinsurah. They were in a Government bullock cart. They were waylaid and murdered in cold blood by a large party of the disbanded Sepoys, numbers of whom are said to be infesting the country, in the hope of cutting off straggling parties of men travelling."

At Allahabad the mutiny broke out on the 4th inst., when the "loyal" 6th Regiment, which had volunteered to proceed to Delhi against the rebels only a few days before, became the assassins of their own officers, and then marched off to join the mutineers, after burning the church and every bungalow in the place, and plundering the treasury. The whole number slaughtered amounted to 26, and among them we find the names of Captain Birch, the Fort Adjutant; Lieutenant Innes, ex-Engineer; Lieutenant Alexander, 2nd Light Cavalry; Captain Plunkett, 6th Native Infantry; Lieutenants Stewart and Hawes, ditto; Ensigns Scott, Cheek, Dodd, Smith, Way, and Smith (doing duty with the regiment.) The Irregular Cavalry and Ferozepore regiment are said to have remained loyal, and the fort being garrisoned by a few English troops is probably safe. Not an European, however, remains outside the walls, and the last accounts from the city portray the most frightful state of matters there. A correspondent of the *Phœnix* writes:—

"Allahabad is in a most wretched state. All the houses are in a dilapidated state from cannonading. Not a single bungalow has been left untouched, nearly all are burnt down to the ground. Upwards of 3000 prisoners have liberated themselves, and are committing all sorts of outrages. Not a single European or Christian remains outside the fort. It is to be feared that few have escaped. Mr. Archer, the Commissioner's head Clerk, is the only person saved in his and his brother's family. Peeroomull, the great banker, has been plundered, and his house is in a most ruinous state. The Dacoits have obtained their object everywhere by attempts at incendiarism first, and while the people were engaged in quenching the fire the Dacoits made away with the booty. The way from Gopeegunge and Jhousee is occupied by a class of banditti, who have plundered innumerable people, and made some of them return to Mirzapore with a rag only on their backs."

The following is from Allahabad Fort, dated the 13th of June:—

"A party of us went out of the fort this morning to reconnoitre, and fell in with some thousands of the rebels, strongly posted, in arms about a large puckah house. Brasyer and his Sikhs made a good fight of it, but were called upon by our new commanding officer, Colonel Neil, to retire, and to-morrow we storm and take the rascals' position. We sadly want supplies here, and we must have more Europeans. I have not had my sword off for a moment, night or day, since the 6th. Later accounts up to the 15th report all well at Allahabad on that day. A Sikh Sepoy had been murdered in the town. The regiment was let loose on the place and thoroughly avenged itself. On the 15th, at Baroul, half-way between Allahabad and Gopeegunge, three zemindars, who had set themselves up, one as rajah and the other two as naibs, were seized by a detachment of the Madras Fusileers and a party of the 13th Irregular Cavalry, who have done excellent service under Lieutenant Palliser, accompanied by Messrs. Moore and Chapman, and were brought in to Gopeegunge, and hanged. The bridge of boats at Allahabad is in our hands, and defended by five guns."

At Jhansi, near Gwalior, on the Bombay side, the left wing of the 12th Native

Infantry, a detachment of Native Foot Artillery, and the 14th Irregulars, rose against their officers on the 5th. There was an intrenched magazine at this place, defended by two guns, and the few Europeans in the place made good their retreat into it for the time. They were overpowered, however, and the greater part of them were brutally murdered, without distinction of sex or age. Among others, Mr. Skene, Deputy Commissioner, and his family, and Mr. Gordon, 10th Madras Native Infantry, Assistant Commissioner, were killed.

At Gwalior the Contingent mutinied; and, as this consists of seven regiments of infantry, two of cavalry, and five companies of artillery, the defection of this army is most serious. The Maharajah protected our ladies and the officers, who all arrived safely at Agra. The soldiery demanded that they should be given up, but the Prince stood firm and rescued them. Mr. Raikes, one of the judges of the Sudder Adawlut, with much exertion and a vast expense, in which others joined, raised a non-military party of some 60 Europeans mounted; with these he hastened to the aid of some ladies who had collected at Etawah. He returned with his charge all safe. At Jaunpore the cavalry regiment stationed there had mutinied and murdered their commanding officer, Lieut. Mara.

A troop of the 2nd Irregular O de Cavalry, which had gone upon duty against the Mynpoorie and Etawah insurgents, under Captain Fletcher Hayes, has mutinied, and it seems certain that Captain Hayes and Captain Bailey, with Lieutenant Barbar and Mr. Fayror, were all killed. It is supposed that Lieut. Carey succeeded in making his escape.

The mutiny of the Bhurtpore levies, under the command of Captain Nixon, and that of the Malwa Contingent of Mehidpore, were our next disasters. The former troops were supposed to be actuated by the best feeling towards us, forming part of the body guard to his highness the Maharajah of Gwalior. Immediately the news of the Neemuch disturbances reached Captain Nixon, he set out with the Bhurtpore levies, accompanied by Captain Gore Munbee, of the Bombay Engineers, who, though senior in army rank to Captain Nixon, waived all etiquette in the matter, and placed himself under that officer's command. They had only proceeded a couple or three marches, when the men refused to be taken against the mutinous Bengal Sepoys, and set the authority of Captains Nixon and Munbee at defiance. These officers had to fly for their lives, and in doing so had to pass through districts where they were frequently fired upon by the insurgents, and after many hairbreadth escapes were fortunate enough to get safely to Bhurtpore, neither of them having sustained any injury. The infantry and artillery of the Malwa Contingent are said to have remained loyal, the cavalry mutinying on the march to Neemuch and murdering their officers, Lieutenants Brobie and Hunt.

Sirdar Mohun Singh, of Roopur, was hanged on the 5th at Umballa, for countenancing the two mutinous companies of the 5th Native Infantry, lately on duty at that place. Three of the Sepoys were also hanged.

The mutinies at Bareilly, Shahjehanpore, Cawnpore, Jullundur, Hyderabad, Juttogh, and Aurungabad, followed in rapid succession.

At Bareilly all the bungalows were burnt to the ground, and the civilians and officers lost everything they possessed.

The outbreak at Shahjehanpore seems also to have been very bloody, and characterised by circumstances of peculiar atrocity. It occurred on the evening of Sunday, the 8th of June, during divine service, when the church was surrounded, and every man, woman, and child murdered, a detachment of the mutineers being told off to fire the cantonment and slay the people in the bungalows.

At Cawnpore part of Her Majesty's 10th Regiment and a battery of European artillery were fortunately on the spot, and a repetition of the tragedies at Bareilly and Shahjehanpore prevented. There seems, however, to have been several days' fighting, but the mutineers were eventually driven out of the place. Many on our side are said to have fallen.

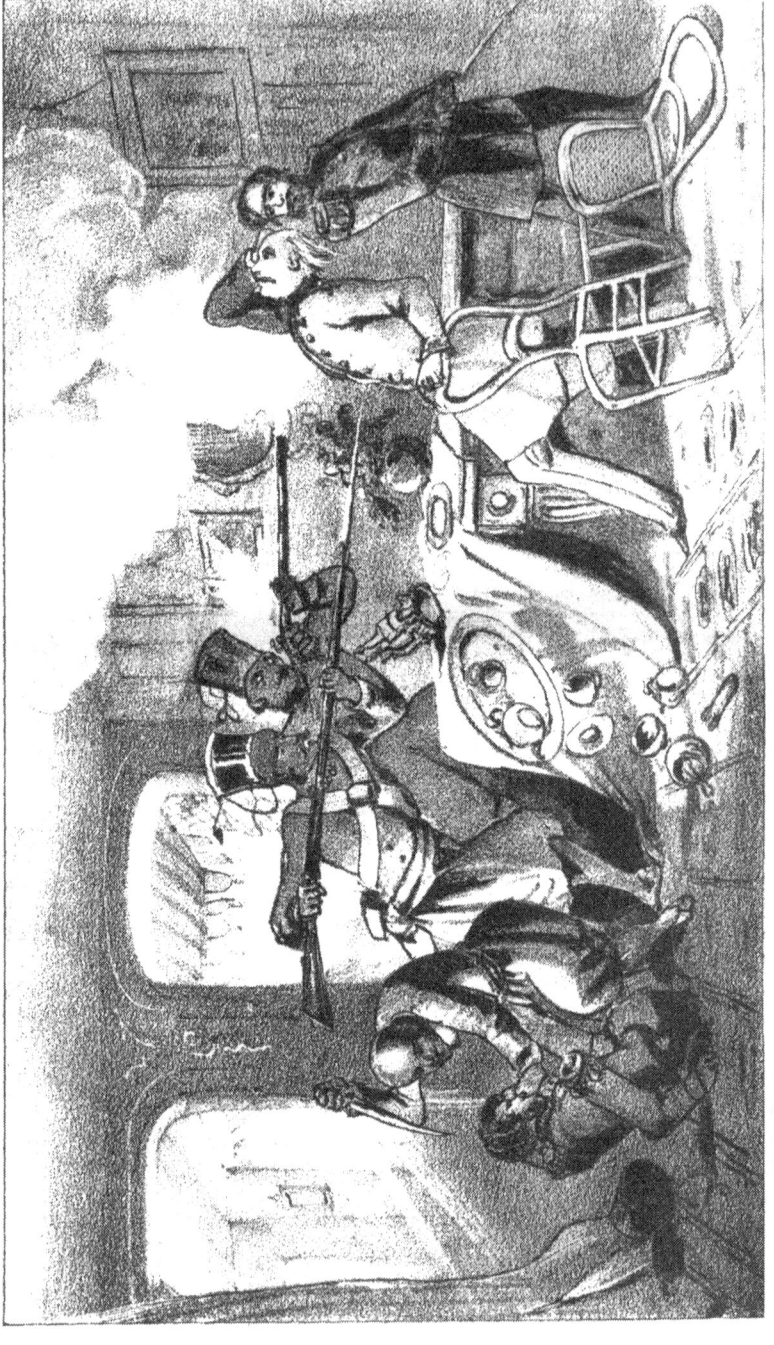

On the night of the 8th a portion of the native troops at Jullundur broke out, and after wounding a few persons and losing 12 of their own number, made off in the direction of Phillour, crossing the Sutlej a few miles above that place. They were pursued by a squadron of cavalry, some European foot and guns, and a body of horsemen belonging to the Allowalla Rajah. The Sikhs belonging to each corps remained staunch. The Native Troop of Artillery behaved throughout in the most admirable manner, firing on the mutineers and maintaining unflinching fidelity. The Allowalla chief rendered most cordial assistance. The bulk of the treasure was brought off in safety by the native guards in charge of it. Forty of the 120 mutineers of the 55th Native Infantry were executed at Peshawur on the 13th. The 64th Native Infantry was ordered in by forced marches to witness the execution.

Major Macmullen, of the 6th Cavalry, was with his regiment at Jullunder, when it mutinied. We hear from a private source that he was standing with his right hand at the moment on his body, when a miscreant advanced and fired a pistol at him; the ball intended for the heart struck the hand. His life was thus providentially saved, but the wound has probably for a time deprived the country of the services of a gallant soldier at a moment when England requires the aid of every one of her sons who is upon the spot. Of Major Smith, Mrs. Macmullen's brother, nothing has been heard; there is naturally a feeling of suspense respecting him, though it is earnestly hoped he is safe. Her brother-in-law, Sir Norman Leslie, has, however, fallen by the assassin's hand, leaving a widow and six children. The following letter, which has been received from Major Macdonald, gives the distressing particulars:—

"Rochnee, June 14th, 1857.—On the evening of the 12th instant, Lieutenant Sir Norman Leslie and Dr. Grant joined me in front of my house as usual, to take tea, and about a quarter to nine o'clock Dr. Grant got up to go to my house to wind up the clock before leaving. On his rising from his chair he said, 'Who can these fellows be?' and at the same instant we heard a rush of feet towards where we were sitting. I had just time to jump up, when I received three sword cuts on the head in quick succession. I seized my chair by the arms and defended myself successfully from three other cuts made at me, and succeeded in giving an ugly poke to my opponent, which appeared to disconcert him, and he at once bolted, followed by the others (three of them in all). I was streaming with blood, and made for the house, followed by Dr. Grant, to stanch my wounds. I found Dr. Grant severely wounded, one deep cut in the arm and a second fearful gash on the hip. We then went back to see after poor Leslie, whom we found stretched on the ground in a dying state; he must have received his death blow, the first cut, and have fallen forward on his face, for he was cut clean through his back into his chest, and breathing through the wound in the lungs; also many cuts on his head; he was quite sensible, and said, as I bent over him, 'Oh, Macdonald, it is very hard to die in this manner,' and added, 'My poor wife and children, what will become of them?' I told him that he had only a few minutes to live, and to make his peace with God, and that all should be done for his poor wife and family that could be done. Under such fearful circumstances he then applied himself to make his peace with God, poor fellow, and breathed his last in about half an hour afterwards."

The tide of revolt next reached the city of Hyderabad. Placards were posted all over the city on the 12th of June, signed by certain Moulavies, calling upon the faithful to enrol themselves, and murder the Feringhees; and at five in the evening three guns from the Horse Artillery, with a detachment of the Cavalry Contingent, went down to the Residency. Each regiment had a company under arms at their barracks at night, which, however, passed without any alarm. The crisis is a dangerous one, and the grand display made at that station by having the whole force out in full marching order, with forty rounds of ammunition per infantry man, and a field service complement for the artillery, is considered to have caused great uneasiness both there and in the city. It is also thought that the Madras Government had committed a very grave error in sending the 1st Native Infantry to Secunderabad. There was a grand display on the morning of the 15th; all the troops, including the 1st, assembled for brigade exercise, with blunt ammunition; the Resident was present, and on the conclusion of the parade he rode up to the 7th Cavalry, and told them it had been reported to him that in the event of a disturbance they had declared to join the city people. He added that he did not believe this report, but that he considered it his duty to inform them of what he had heard, and left them to settle the same with their officers.

On the 14th, the Nusseerabad Battalion at Juttogh received an order to be ready to march at a moment's notice to Phillour, to escort the siege train thence to Umballa. On the order being issued the men on guard at Simla were withdrawn, in order to increase the force of the corps as much as possible, and sixty or seventy spare muskets, with a full allowance of ammunition, were sent to Simla, to enable the "temporaries" stationed there to defend themselves during the absence of the regiment. The Simla people erected a barricade or stockade, planting the guns behind it, and they collected all the European residents of the place at the bank, sending out patrols, and adopting other measures of most decisively military seeming. One of the men on patrol unwisely interfered with and turned back some of the Sepoys who were inoffensively going into Simla on their own business; upon which was immediately spread the report that the guards had been withdrawn from Simla, the Europeans there having no confidence in them. This, with other false reports, soon induced the belief that the Sepoys were being betrayed into a trap for their destruction; and this belief was strengthened by a fresh falsehood, to the effect that the muskets and ammunition sent to Simla had been sent there to be used against the regiment. To these causes of excitement were added some new editions of the cartridge tale; and the whole proved enough to incite them to mutiny. On the 15th, when everything was in readiness for the march towards Phillour, they turned out at about 2 A. M., armed and equipped, and having forty rounds of ammunition in their pouches. Their intention was to march off into Simla. Their European officers, hearing the row, went among them. The first outburst was most determined. Muskets were loaded, with fixed bayonets brought to the charge, but they did not then fire. On several occasions they drew their kocknies to slay their officers; but the well-disposed among them invariably interfered to prevent mischief. Only a few, indeed, were well-disposed; and the men were kept from outrage mainly by the firm and courageous bearing of these few. After the first burst of mutinous feeling had passed, they began to listen to the reproaches and arguments of their officers. Still, to quiet them, their officers had to separate from them the men who had been at the school of musketry at Umballa. Twice did large bodies of them commence to march off towards Simla, but they were persuaded to return.

The Simla people were, naturally enough, in a great fright. One poor lady was killed by a fall from her horse, while endeavouring to escape. Ladies and gentlemen fled in every direction, and in terror and distress. The following morning the Simla guards were replaced. This had a wonderful effect in pacifying the men. They had been led to believe that the English had become their enemies, and this caused great suspicion and much apprehension among them. The confidence which was shown them by their officers, even when in the act of incipient mutiny, gradually divested them of this belief, and showed that they were not mistrusted.

The men on guard at Kussowlie, hearing that the guards had mutinied, robbed the treasury under their guard, and marched in, all loaded, to join their comrades. They were most murderously inclined, and endeavoured to incite the others to an immediate massacre of all the Europeans in the place, and subsequently to a general plunder of the place. These men were eventually induced to give up their arms, and were confined by their own comrades, who were much incensed at their having robbed the Kussowlie treasury. The men seemed as much inclined to assail their native officers as Europeans. Every-

HAULING THE BUDDHA MARBLES AT PITAKATARA

thing was soon afterwards quiet and orderly. For several days subsequently there was a certain degree of alarm prevalent as to their continued quietness; there were only six Europeans amongst 600 natives when the men from Kussowlie joined, and endeavoured to stir up their fellows to mutiny; many of the men turned out in defence of their European officers, rousing them up (it was at 3 A. M.) and warning them of danger.

All was quiet at Simla on the 21st. The Goorkah Regiment was quiet, but, as they had refused to march, it was impossible to place confidence in them. The refusing to march, however, seems to have been the extent of their insubordination. Colonel Mackenzie left Simla on the 16th, after an anxious night on duty at the bank, with 100 European residents of the place, every hour expecting an attack. He arrived at Dugshai on the 18th, and found that officers proceeding to join their corps were ordered to remain for the defence of the hill stations. He accordingly assumed command at Dugshai. An attack was not expected there, but every preparation had been made for such a contingency. The European force at Dugshai consisted of 100 men of the 1st Fusileers, and 17 men of a Queen's regiment, with about 20 officers of the Queen's and Company's service. Nearly all the inhabitants of Simla had taken refuge in the station, but some of them had returned.

Great alarm prevailed at Dacca on the 15th, in consequence of the expected rising of the rabble, and the misconduct of the Sepoys of the 73rd Native Infantry, who refused to allow the artillery officer to take arms from the magazine for the defence of the city.

The mutiny of the 1st Regiment, Nizam's Cavalry, at Aurungabad, took place on the 16th. No Europeans were killed, and General Woodburn's moveable column, which fell in with the mutineers on the 23rd, utterly routed and dispersed them.

The following letter from an officer stationed at Peshawur gives an account of the proceedings there, incidentally noticed in another part of this narrative, and at the same time discloses the beginning of a system of retaliation the frightful consequences of which we shudder to reflect upon:—

"Peshawur, June 14.

"There was no outbreak here, but we have had to disarm three native infantry regiments and one of cavalry, having discovered that they intended to massacre us all on the 22nd (May.) It was done at the same moment to all the regiments, though at different points of the station, a small European force, guns and cavalry, being told off to each. That night the disarmed men began to desert in numbers—a proceeding it was actually necessary to stop lest they should raise the city and neighbourhood; so they were overtaken and brought back, and 13 or 14 hung, *pour encourager les autres*. None have gone since. All their private arms, which every soldier has, were also taken away, guns kept constantly pointed towards their lines, with bodies of Europeans ready to turn out at a moment's notice, and a station flooded with a host of levies brought up from Mooltan by the foresight of Edwardes, who raised them in the last Punjab campaign. One of them offered to polish off all the Sepoys at 6d. (four annas) a-head. The crisis may be said to have been over on the 22nd; but our position then was a most dangerous one, from which the hand of Providence, using as his instrument the best soldiers and politicals in India, has rescued us. Fancy 2000 Europeans in a station with seven regiments, all, with one exception, prepared to rise on us, backed up by a cantonment populated with the greatest scoundrels, a city full of ruffians ready to join the mutineers, and a chain of forts surrounding us, garrisoned by four more regiments, ready to combine and march down upon us! Further on we were encircled by the hills, full of fanatics, thirsting for our blood, and in open concert with the mutineers. To add to our troubles, the country people, knowing what was impending on that day (22nd), would not bring in supplies, nor would the Mooltan levies take service till it was seen how we should fare. The immediate disarming of the regiments above mentioned was imperative, and done accordingly with effect. Confidence was at once restored, and supplies and levies came in the next day. A force of Europeans, with guns, was sent round the fort, one of which, Meerdân, was held by the 55th Native Infantry in open mutiny; they tried to escape when our force appeared, and some got off to Swat; the others were made prisoners, 150 were killed on the spot, 9 tried by drumhead court-martial, and instantly shot, including a native officer of a regiment not in mutiny, who would not act as he was ordered. Others were driven into the hills, and killed by the hill-men, a price of 10 rupees being set on their heads. The colonel of this regiment blew out his brains in disgust at the mutiny. The villains kept their officers in confinement, and told them if they tried to escape they would roast them alive. They did, however, manage to escape. The force then went and disarmed all the other regiments in the forts and quieted the district. Some of the 200 prisoners of the 55th have been tried, and we blew 40 of them away from our guns in the presence of the whole force three days ago, a fearful but necessary example, which has struck terror into their souls. Three sides of a square were formed, 10 guns pointed outwards, the sentence of the court was read, a prisoner bound to each gun, the signal given, and the salvo fired. Such a scene I hope never again to witness—human trunks, heads, legs, arms, &c., flying about in all directions. All met their fate with firmness but two, who would not be tied up; so to save time they were dropped to the ground and their brains blown out by musketry. Trials are going on, and the mutineers will never forget the lesson taught at Peshawur. It is not my business to contrast or compare with scenes elsewhere. I trust and believe we have done what duty demands."

The following communication from Mirzapore is of consequence as showing that the civil portion of the Indian population has made common cause with the military revolters elsewhere than at Delhi. The letter of our informant is dated the 15th:—

"The dour of our magistrate, St. George Tucker, against the village of Gawrah, has been most successful. He and the deputy-magistrate, with 50 Sepoys of the 47th Regiment, arrived at the village early yesterday morning. The steamer with 100 Europeans had not yet reached the ghât, but was in sight. The villagers, on seeing our small force, assembled to the number of some 3000. In the meantime the steamer anchored and landed the English bulldogs, who, to a man, without orders, rushed at the insurgents, fired into them, and killed 30 or 40; the rest took to their heels. The village, which was quite deserted, was burnt to the ground. Mirzapore is perfectly quiet, and all on this side the river. The factories of Comercoly, Pallee, Cutchowa, and Solah are perfectly quiet, and ready to take advantage of a fall of rain to sow. Our assistant magistrate has gone to Gopeegunge to clear and keep the Allahabad road. No news as yet of the arrival of the 'Charles Allen' at Allahabad, or of the garrison there. The murderers of Sir Norman Leslie have been apprehended and hanged. They turned out to be three men of his own regiment, one an old hand, and the two others recruits."

The following is from Major Holmes's Irregulars, Segowlee:—

"June 15.

"We have been very busy making arrangements for the march of the Goorkas, but now they are not to come. We have saved Goruckpore, and have patrols out all over the country. We have sent two detachments to recover Azinghur, one by Allygunge, the other from Goruckpore. That country is one scene of pillage. We hung two Sepoys of the 37th mutineers the night before last. This part of the country is kept in perfect order, but every one now knows that he will be hung for one word of treason. The Legislative Council have passed a law to-day, whereby summary powers over all deserters are given to the local authorities."

We have now got to the end of this terrible list, and feel that any attempt to heighten its significance by comment would be misplaced.

It is with deep gratification that we turn for a moment from the consideration of these painful events to notice the fact that few symptoms of disaffection have appeared as yet in the armies either of Madras or Bombay, which manifest the most perfect loyalty in the presence of this dangerous example; and which repel indignantly every attempt that has been made to seduce them from their allegiance by emissaries from the Bengal troops. A statement found its way into the Calcutta papers some time ago to the effect that the 10th Madras Native Infantry had refused to receive the cartridges in Burmah, but we have looked in vain for any confirmation of the news.

Great excitement continued to prevail in Calcutta and its neighbourhood. A conspiracy for a general rising on the part of the Mussulman population has been discovered, and a regular plan for the capture of the city was found among the papers seized.

Early on the 14th of June, the Government received intelligence from Major-General Hearsey, commanding the Presidency Division, that he had good reason to apprehend a rising of the native troops at Barrackpore, and had, in consequence, taken every precaution to prevent it which he could do with the means at his command, and had sent for the 78th Highlanders from Chinsurah. Orders were instantly issued, in pursuance of which a large European force was concentrated on Barrackpore, and the safety of Dum-Dum amply secured. In the afternoon the whole brigade at Barrackpore were quietly and peaceably disarmed, simultaneously with the entire native force in Calcutta.

When the Sepoy regiments at Barrackpore were disarmed, their huts were also searched for arms, and a large number of tulwars taken away. The arms found in the huts were not, however, all tulwars; some of them were of the most murderous description, as, for instance, swords with serrated blades, two-handed swords, battle-axes, poniards, yataghans, and weapons of various other descriptions.

Many of the disarmed men deserted, considering it *infra dig.* to do duty with ramrods alone. Some of these were captured and punished by being ordered to return to their duty, to desert again whenever they pleased.

The defence of Calcutta had become a subject of great anxiety to the European inhabitants. The Government yielded to pressure, and consented to the enrolment of a corps of volunteer guards, horse and foot, who patrolled the streets, and mounted guard at different points at night, and the vigilance of these volunteers inspired general confidence. The inhabitants, however, still kept themselves armed, and the public buildings, hotels, and other principal places, were garrisoned by sailors belonging to ships in the river.

Sir Patrick Grant, the acting commander-in-chief in Bengal, arrived from Madras on the 17th. What is more important, reinforcements of European troops from Bombay, Madras, and Ceylon arrived also, and were sent up to reinforce the besiegers of Delhi. The troops intended for China were directed by Lord Elgin to proceed to Calcutta, and Captain Jenkins was sent by the Government to Mauritius and the Cape of Good Hope to obtain the assistance of as large a force as can be spared from those colonies. The troops at Calcutta on the 20th consisted of the 53rd Foot in Fort William, of 900 men strong; a wing of the 37th Foot encamped on the glacis, 500 in number; a company of the 3rd battalion Madras Artillery, and No. 2 Horse Field Battery, together with forty men of the Royal Artillery, recently arrived from Ceylon, and the Volunteer Guard, consisting of four troops of cavalry and five companies of infantry; a wing of the 35th Foot, about 350 men were at Barrackpore, and the 78th Highlanders at Chinsurah ready for any duty. The communication with the upper provinces was interrupted, and intelligence of what was taking place in Oude, Delhi, Agra, and the Punjaub could only reach Calcutta *viâ* Bombay.

Delhi is still in the possession of the insurgents. According to the latest authentic accounts, which were to the 16th of June, General Sir Harry Barnard was waiting for reinforcements. Rumours of the capture of the city had indeed been communicated on two occasions to the Bombay Government by their agent at Indore, but these rumours were not confirmed. The Bombay Government received on the evening of the 23rd of June the following electric telegraph message from Colonel Durand from Indore, dated the same day: " There was a very general report of the taking of Delhi, with great loss to the rebels. The superintendent has not received authentic news from Agra." The following electric telegraph message from Indore, from Col. Durand to the Bombay Government, was received on the 24th of June: " News from Neemuch of the 22nd state that Delhi was stormed and taken on the 12th. Such of the mutineers as remained alive took refuge in the palace." Notwithstanding these telegraphic despatches, the city had not been taken on the 16th of June.

The following statement, relating to the Delhi massacres, and derived from native sources, will be found interesting :—

"Three men were sent two months ago, when the Rajah of Kaporthella started for Hurdwar to accompany a professor of music, in the service of the Rajah, to Delhi. They have been servants of the Rajah from childhood. They left Delhi on the 26th of May. I have gathered as follows from one of them who was spokesman.

"They saw no troops from Delhi to Raee; the police-station houses on the road were burnt, as also a tahseel or collection-house, and the villages were being plundered. At Raee there was an advanced guard of the Jheend Rajah's men. At Kussowlee there was a similar party. They then came to Paneeput, but met with no annoyance. Troops, &c., were moving along the road. A number of European Horse Artillery were there; very few native troops. In the evening four Europeans came to search all travellers in the caravansary. A man who had a quarrel on the road with them told them to search two Sikhs with a laden cart. On searching it they found 4000 rupees, a number of weapons, and silver dishes of European gentlemen, evidently plunder from Delhi. The deponents then came to Kurnaul. It was all quiet. The Putteeala Rajah's people were in charge of the road. An European regiment was encamped there. They heard in Kurnaul that the Commander-in-Chief had died there. In the caravansary there were some 50 Europeans, male and female, and about 40 children, who had escaped from Delhi. They then came to Peeplee. There they met the siege train from Phillour. A gun was in difficulty, and people were employed in extricating it. They met some of the European Lancers, about 16 miles on this side. They then reached Shahabad. On arriving at Umballa arrangements were going on for disarming a corps, and at Dourahah Serie they met the Guides Corps. At Lushkuree Khan Ke Serie they met a detachment of Sikh and Punjabee horsemen.

"Now they proceed to state what they saw and heard themselves, for they were in Delhi a month before the outbreak took place. First only five troopers came into Delhi from Meerut. They first went to the house of (name not clear, so I omit it) an agent of the King of Delhi, near the Delhi-gate inside the town. He came out and said he was in the service of the King. They would not listen to him, but cut him down and then murdered his wife and family, and told the people to plunder the house. They then went to the houses in Durya Gunj. Peer Buksh, one of the deponents, saw the troopers go to a pink-coloured house; the owner was an European; they killed him, and plundered and burnt the house. They plundered and burnt all the houses in this suburb, which is chiefly inhabited by clerks, and murdered all who could not escape.

"By this time other troopers and infantry and towns-people joined in the work of destruction. A number of the fugitives took refuge in a building near the mosque of Aurungzebe's daughter, and began to defend it against the insurgents. These were held at bay. They left people all round, and the main body went off to the Bank. There they were joined by more mutineers. They plundered and murdered wherever they found Europeans. The townspeople assisted warmly in the plunder, and the mutineers of the infantry were particularly active. The commissioner, Mr. Fraser, on hearing of the advent of the mutineers, had gone down to cut away the bridge, but was too late. On returning he met the mutineers at this place. The mutineers said to the commissioner's escort, 'Are you on the side of the Europeans or on that of religion.' They said the latter. The commissioner, on hearing this, drove off in his buggy. His escort remained passive. The mutineers followed and cut down the gentleman. He fired one pistol. The mutineers killed people on the road, but being more intent on the magazine, they went to it. After arranging matters for surrounding the place the insurgents and mutineers proceeded to the gaol. One of the sentries shot a man, but when they said they were fighting for religion the guard joined them and 500 convicts were released. They then closed all the gates and went into the Fort. They paid their respects to the King; he made objections, and said he had no army; he at last consented.

"On the second day they went to the magazine, where many Europeans had taken refuge. After some firing on both sides, the natives, such as Lascars, would do nothing, they hid themselves; the Europeans alone carried on the defence; but, seeing they could do nothing against so many, they blew up the wall towards the river; some 200 of the rebels or more were destroyed by this. They however got in and destroyed as many Europeans as they could, and plundered weapons, &c., leaving only the guns and powder. Two native infantry regiments were present. They searched, and everywhere they could find Europeans they slew them. On the third day they went back to the house near the mosque where some Europeans had taken refuge. As they were without water, &c., for several days they called for a Subadar (deponent was present) and five others, and asked them to take their oaths that they would give them water and take them alive to the King; he might kill them if he liked. On this oath the Europeans came out, the mutineers placed water before them, and said 'Lay down your arms and then you get water.' They gave over two guns, all they had. The mutineers gave no water. They seized 11 children, among them infants, eight ladies, and eight gentlemen. They took them to the cattle sheds. One lady, who seemed more self-possessed than the rest, observed that they were not taking them to the Palace; they replied they were taking them *vid* Durya Gunj. Deponent says that he saw all this, and saw them placed in a row and shot. One woman entreated them to give her child water, though they might kill her. A Sepoy took her child and dashed it on the ground; the people looked on in dismay, and feared for Delhi.

"The King's people took some 35 Europeans to the Palace; on the fifth day they tied them to a tree, and shot them. They burnt their bodies.

"On the fifth day notice was given that if any one concealed a European he would be destroyed. People disguised many, and sent them off, but many were killed that day, mostly by people of the city.

"Matters remained pretty quiet for two days. The Durya Gunj Bazaar was turned into an encampment for the mutineers. Shops were plundered in the Chandnee Chouk and Dlereeba Bazaar. The shops were shut for five days. The King went through the city, and told the people to open the shops. At each gate there is a company of native infantry. About 9000 mutineers are assembled. No cavalry have joined, excepting from Meerut. Some 4000 or 5000 new men have been raised, but they are rabble. During the festival of Eed, while at prayers, there was the dust of a kafila of laden animals. An alarm arose—it was the English army; the people all rushed helter-skelter into the city.

"The King refused to go on the throne. The mutineers assured him that a similar massacre had taken place up to Peshawur and down to Calcutta. He agreed, and commenced to give orders. He appointed the following officers—Hukeem, Nussuroola, Mahhoob, Allie, and one other belonging to the mutineers, but deponent knows not his name. His new levies receive 4 annas a-day. Guns are placed on the ramparts of the town. These are pronounced strong. The Sappers and Miners are mounting guns in Selimghur. The mutineers say when the army approaches they will fight, and that the native troops with the army are sure to join them. Many mutineers who tried to get away with plunder were robbed; this has prevented many others from leaving.

"A tailor concealed no less than five Europeans; the deponent thinks many more are concealed.

"The man has been with me, he speaks frankly and without fear. He is able to narrate evidently many a harrowing tale, but I did not wish to hear any. He seemed really to recall with dismay what he had witnessed.

"A. FARRINGTON, Deputy Commissioner.

"Jullundur, June 5."

On the 8th of June, at two o'clock in the morning, General Barnard arrived at Delhi, when the rebels who were encamped outside the Ajmere Gate were attacked and driven from the position which they had occupied. They fled into the town, and the pursuit was so sharp that the gunners threw themselves off their horses, and left the field pieces standing in the sand. The heavy guns remained in position: twenty-six guns in all were captured, and, in addition, large quantities of ammunition and entrenching tools. The outposts were taken possession of. Colonel Chester, Adjutant-General, and Lieut. Russell, 54th, were among the killed. Our loss was about 150, chiefly in the 75th Queen's regiment. The army at the latest date was encamping in cantonments. A message from Major Lake at Jullundur, communicating this information to Sir John Lawrence at Lahore, adds:—"The mutineers had guns in battery round the flagstaff, but we outflanked them on both sides. One column of ours

D

march down the trunk road, and another through cantonments. We work away with heavy guns to-morrow. This has been a brilliant affair. The guns of the mutineers were very well served, and the fire was very heavy. General Reed arrived just as the columns moved off, but did not command on the occasion."

The force under General Barnard consisted of 2 troops of Horse Artillery, 9th Lancers, 1 squadron 4th Lancers, Her Majesty's 75th Foot, 1st Fusiliers, and 6 companies 2nd Fusiliers. These were to be joined by the following troops from Meerut :—6th Carabineers, 60th Rifles, 4 Horse Artillery guns, a horse battery, 2 18-pounders, 120 Artillery recruits, and some Sappers, Sirmoor Battalion. The 60th Native Infantry was at Rohtuk, and a detachment of the 5th Native Infantry, and a portion of the 4th Lancers had reached Saharunpore.

The following despatch has been received from the General, relating the success on the 8th ult. :—

"Delhi Cantonments, June 8.

"Sir,—The forces under my command marched from Alipore at 1 A.M. this morning, and on reaching Baidlee Seraee found the enemy strongly posted in an intrenched position, which I have the satisfaction to inform you we carried after an engagement of about three-quarters of an hour, and proceeded to take up our present position, which we found to be over disputed ground the whole way, and finally a well-defended line of defence from the signal tower to the Hindoo Rao house. Our troops behaved with the greatest gallantry and persevering endurance, and after facing very determined resistance drove the enemy within the walls of Delhi. All this was accomplished by nine o'clock in the morning. Our loss has been comparatively trifling, only one officer being killed; but I regret to say that officer is Col. Chester, adjutant-general to the army, who was esteemed by all for every qualification that could adorn the soldier. I have not been able to ascertain the particulars of our loss, or capture of guns, but I fear I cannot estimate the former under from 40 to 50 killed ; the number of guns taken to be about 16 or 18.

"I do not in this hurried despatch attempt to recommend any one, but I cannot pass over the assistance I received from Brigadier Wilson, whose cool judgment entitles him to an equal share of any merit that may be given to the officer in command. From the Brigadier-General and staff of the army attached to me and from the division-staff, I received every support, and from my personal staff, Captain Barnard and Lieutenant Turnbull, the most daring devotion. The conduct of the Ghoorka Battalion, the Sappers, and other native troops employed, was most praiseworthy. They vied with their European comrades in forward daring; the troops of the native contingents did equally good service, including those of the Jheend Rajah ; and I cannot close this without especial notice of many gentlemen attached to the army in civil capacities, who not only accompanied us into the field, but did every service the extended nature of our position rendered particularly important, in keeping up mutual communications.

"I hope to send you a fuller detail to-morrow. Our siege train is up, and I hope to open on the town without a moment's delay.

"I have, &c.,   H. BARNARD,
"To the Commander-in-Chief.   Major-General, Commanding Field Force."

"Camp Cantonments, Delhi, June 14, 1857.

"You will be anxious to hear how things are going on here. My last letter was to papa from Ghazee-oo-dim-nugger, the other side of Delhi, just after our two actions with the rebels. We left that place on the 4th of June, without seeing anything more of them, and after three days' march joined the force under General Barnard at Allipore, on Sunday, June 7, thus going round the town of Delhi, from the east to the west, crossing the river Junra, at Baghput. Our force now consists of about 5000 fighting men, 4000 of whom are Europeans, namely, the 7th, the 6th (Rifles), Queen's Regiments; 1st and 2nd European Fusileers, Carabineers, and 9th Lancers (Queen's Cavalry), Horse Artillery, Foot Artillery, Regiment of Goorkas and of Guides (native troops), and 200 Sappers (parts of the above regiments only are here). Early on Monday morning, June 8th, we advanced in four columns against the rebels' position, about four miles from Allipore and seven miles from Delhi. They had entrenched themselves very strongly across the Trunk road, their flanks resting on the village, and had constructed several batteries mounting about a dozen heavy guns, and sweeping the ground across

GEN. SIR H. BARNARD'S ATTACK ON THE MUTINEERS BEFORE DELHI.

which we had to advance. Two of our columns, with the advanced guard, marched down the trunk road to attack them in front, and the other two were sent out two or three miles on each side so as to turn their flanks. Owing, however, to the badness of the road, these two did not come up till near the close of the action; the second column of the main body, also, were late in coming up, so that all the fighting fell on the advanced guard and the first column. I was with the latter, having been appointed orderly officer to Major Langton, our chief engineer; and as we kept close to the general and his staff, I had a good opportunity of seeing the whole affair. About sunrise, 4 A. M. in the morning, we came in sight of their position, and they immediately opened a heavy fire of round shot, shell, and grape upon us. The troops were immediately deployed to the right and left, and our Horse Artillery and two 18 pounders opened fire on their batteries; but in consequence of the heavier metal of their pieces, and the accuracy of their fire, our guns could make no impression on them, but rather got the worst of it; so that after about an hour's peppering, the infantry were sent in to take their position at the point of the bayonet, which they did in fine style, cheering as they went on. The rebels could not stand for a moment, but fled on all sides. All our troops now advanced, clearing the village and the orchards, and driving the rebels towards Delhi. Several old officers say they have seldom seen a heavier fire than that we were under for the first hour, during which time we were riding up and down within easy range of all their guns, which were blazing away as hard as they could, and I assure you it was a most curious sensation, seeing and hearing shots of all sorts whizzing past you, the wonder was that you escaped at all, grape especially seemed to hiss on all sides of you without actually hitting. It was during this first half-hour's fire that a round shot killed Colonel Chester (Adjutant-General), and mortally wounded Captain Russell, also slightly wounding another officer (all by one shot.) Colonel Chester was considered one of our best officers, and Russell was a very nice fellow, who came down with us from Missouri. About 7 A.M. we came in sight of the second position of the mutineers, which was on a ridge of hills within a mile of Delhi, which place the ridge shut out from our view: it was on the side (*i. e.* the Allipon side) of the ridge that the Contingent of the troops were before the mutiny. The rebels had got several heavy guns posted here, sweeping all the ground in front; but instead of advancing up directly in front, our troops were divided into two bodies, one of which went up a slanting road to the right, and the other to the left, completely outflanking the rebels, on whom we opened a heavy fire, and they were obliged to abandon all their guns and position, and retire into Delhi. We suffered comparatively little in this second attack; altogether, we made a famous morning's work of it. We are now encamped in the old cantonment on the Allipon side of the ridge, and have got several batteries on the ridge, from which we pound into the town, they returning the fire with wonderful accuracy. The engineers have been hard at work during the week constructing batteries and cover for the guns, always under fire. The ridge is about 500 yards from the walls of Delhi, which lies in the plain beneath. Their shot and shell came whizzing about us during most of the time we were at work; our loss, however, is not much daily—about five killed and wounded on the ridge. They also come out almost every day and attack us in force, but are always driven back with loss. We have now been here just a week. Our loss on the 8th was about 150 killed and wounded, and 100 since. The accounts are still bad, more regiments mutinying every day. As soon, however, as more European troops come up, this state of affairs must end, and the rebels meet with a terrible retribution. General Reed now commands this force, with Barnard second in command. I have been graciously spared hitherto, and am in capital health. We must take Delhi before many days are over, and then there will be a turn in this state of affairs. Tommy Cadell is here, in the 2nd Fusileer Regiment: he is quite well. I saw him this morning. Also A. S. Jones, who you will remember at the Collegiate. He is in the 9th Lancers. I dine with him to-day. Good bye for the present, my dear Will. Best love to dear papa, Charlie, and Lou. Ever your most affectionate brother, EDWARD JONES."

Regarding the internal state of Delhi, much information was furnished in a letter to the Rajah of Jullundur from some one in the city. The Rajah placed the letter at the disposal of the Deputy Commissioner of Jullundur, Mr. Farrington, by whom it was translated. The reports that the King of Delhi had consented to the wishes of the rebels, were confirmed by this document, which also stated that he had nominated a native magistrate, and summoned the principal men of Delhi to attend him, but that they feigned sickness and refused. The city is reported to be in a most distracted state, and to have defied the efforts made by the King to restore order. "The civilization of 53 years," says the news writer, "has been destroyed in three hours; good men have been plundered, scoundrels enriched." The letter also furnishes a hint of the fearful atrocities which have been committed by the Sepoys. "To-day," says the writer, "some fifty odd Europeans who had secreted themselves have been killed; they (the Sepoys) are hunting for more, and if any be found they will be killed." When this letter was written there were six regiments, one battery of artillery, and 500 troopers inside the city. Since that time many other regiments have mutinied and marched to the rebel head-quarters, so that their force must now be considerable, probably not less than 30,000 men. The Delhi Raj has a powerful hold upon the memory of India still : and while the city remains in the hands of the rebels the country will be unsettled from the Himalayas to Cape Comorin. The following proclamation had been posted up in the city, and circulated, in all probability, as far as the emissaries of the insurrection could penetrate:—

"Be it known to all the Hindoos and Mohammedans, the subjects and servants on the part of the officers of the English forces stationed at Delhi and Meerut, that all the Europeans are united in this point—first, to deprive the army of their religion, and then by the force of strong measures to Christianise all the subjects. In fact it is the absolute orders of the Governor-General to serve out cartridges made up with swine and beef fat; if there be 10,000 who resist this, to blow them up; if 50,000, to disband them.

"For this reason we have merely for the sake of the faith concerted with all the subjects, and have not left one infidel of this place alive, and have constituted the Emperor of Delhi upon this engagement, that whichever of the troops will slaughter all their European officers and pledge allegiance to him, shall always receive double salary. Hundreds of canon and immense treasure have come to hand; it is, therefore, requisite that all who find it difficult to become Christians, and all subjects, will unite cordially with the army, take courage, and not leave the seed of these devils in any place.

"All the expenditure that may be incurred by the subjects in furnishing supplies to the army, they will take receipts from the same from the officers of the army, and retain them by themselves; they will receive double price from the Emperor. Whoever will at this time give way to pusillanimity, and allow himself to be overreached by these deceivers, and depend upon their word, will experience the fruits of their submision like the inhabitants of Lucknow. It is therefore necessary that all Hindoos and Mohammedans should be of one mind in this struggle, and make arrangements for their preservation with the advice of some creditable persons. Wherever the arrangement shall be good, and with whomsoever the subjects shall be pleased, these individuals shall be placed in high office in those places.

"And to circulate copies of this day's proclamation in every place, as far as it may be possible, be not understood to be less than a stroke of the sword. That this proclamation be stuck up at a conspicuous place, in order that all Hindoos and Mohammedans may become apprised and be prepared. If the infidels now become mild, it is merely an expedient to save their lives. Whoever will be deluded by their frauds, he will repent. Our reign continues. Thirty rupees to a mounted and ten rupees to a foot soldier, will be the salary of the new servants of Delhi."

The following letter from an officer gives an animated picture of the state of things before Delhi, and shows the feeling which pervades the service:—

"Kussowlie, June 14, 1857.

"The cloud, no bigger than a man's hand, has turned into a hurricane, casting a gloom over the north-west of India. Attendant on its track have been horror and atrocities that were never dreamt of, and for which, if our lives are spared, we hope that a day of retribution will come.

"The alarm about Simla was premature; the regiment seized the guard on arrival, retrieved the treasure, and marched for head-quarters camp. During this disturbance the most stupid confusion reigned: people rushed down Khuds, into the interior; into Kussowlie, Dugshai, anywhere—all, however, quickly down, and 1 believe people are safer here than in most parts of the north-west. So far for our disturbance, caused by a stupid mistake in not sending the Ghoorkas down with or before the Europeans. At Umballa the force was detained for the siege train, which the chief sent for. It marched without the train, which was very slow in making its appearance. Whilst waiting for it at Kurnaul the poor old chief, worn out by heat and the troubles with which he was beset, died of cholera after four hours' illness. His loss will not be very much regretted, for we found he had not much 'go' in him. Sir Harry Barnard assumed command, and pushed on for Delhi.

"The Meerut Brigade in joining the force were attacked twice by the mutineers at the Hindon River, between Meerut and Delhi, at the Suspension Bridge. The latter, about 3000 strong, were all well thrashed, six guns taken, with a lot of ammunition and entrenching tools. They came out again from Delhi, with reinforcements, and, after three hours and a half hard fighting, were again sent flying. The column then pushed on for Raee, and joined the force, the siege train also arriving. On the 8th or 9th the whole force were within five miles of Delhi, and the following morning marched in. They were met by a strong party of the mutineers, who fell back on an entrenched position. Shot, shell, and grape began to fly, but in half an hour the batteries, consisting of thirty guns, were in our possession, and the rascals followed up, up to the city. We were then in possession of cantonments and old Hindoo Rao's house. You may wonder how these fellows contrived to get guns and material together; but must recollect that the magazine was in the town—all the Meerut Artillery practice guns, and worst of all the whole of the sappers from Roorkee had joined the mutineers.

"Whilst all this was going on, they placed the king on the musnud, and sent round proclamations that he was Emperor of Hindostan, &c., &c. The poor old gentleman, in a dreadful stew, went off to the kootal, but was caught and brought back.

"Our latest news from camp is up to the 12th June. The insurgents on that day sallied out in force, and were, after a short tussle, most 'woefully whopped,' and driven in again.

"The force now before Delhi consists of the Artillery, about 500 strong; European Sappers, 150; the siege train, 6th Dragoon Guards, and 9th Lancers, 60th. Rifles; 75th Foot (Bengal Tigers), 1st and 2nd Fusiliers, the Guides from Peshawur, the Jirmont Battalion (Charley Reed's), 9th Irregulars, 4th Lancers, at least some of them; about 1500 Puttela Royal Troops under Captain M'Andrew. In all, about 6000 or 8000 men, but I believe all true and staunch, and well able to thrash four times their number of the rebels. The disaffection appears general amongst the Infantry Troops (Native), but the Irregulars, Sikhs, and Ghoorkas have as yet all proved staunch, and the feeling of the country generally is for us. In the Punjaub and most stations the Sepoys have all been disarmed. At Jullundur, where this was not enforced, the men being trusted, the scoundrels made off, and bodies of them are passing within a few miles of this. Should they make their appearance we could give a very good account of them, but they seem to be in very great fear, and are making for Delhi as fast as they can.

"European troops are coming round from every quarter as fast as possible. Madras, Bombay, the China and Persian regiments, are all doing their best to be in time for the fun. The 84th have reached Cawnpore. 1st Madras Fusiliers, Benares, the 43rd Foot, Ceylon Rifles, 35th Foot, are in Calcutta or on their way, also three more European regiments. Two of these regiments are between Larogehn and Kurrachee, one at Moultan. So that although we are in a mess I am sanguine that in a few months all will be well and matters looking up. The impression seems to be that it is a Mahomedan attempt to overthrow the Government, and that the whole army has been tampered with. The cartridge greased (as they gave out) with pig and cow's fat was to destroy their caste and make the whole army Christians; that the Commander-in-Chief had taken the contract, and agreed to do the thing in one year. My own idea is that the annexation of Oude is mixed up with the business, and that there was a feeling of dissatisfaction prevailing throughout the army consequent on the general service order, and other points bearing indirectly on caste. I am most sanguine that eventually all will be well. The fall of Delhi and the arrival of some twenty or thirty regiments from England will effectually settle the business.

"To-day's post brought letters from Mhow up to the 29th May. All was quiet there, and we trust it will remain so. They were, of course, anxious to see how matters would turn out. If you or yours have any interest with either the Court or Home Government, impress upon them the necessity of sending out very large reinforcements at any cost or any hazard—that is, if they care for the lives of their countrymen, their reputation, or if India is to remain an adjunct to the Crown. Mine is no singular opinion. Every one who watches the tide of events will say the same. We have had a house full for some time now; the gardener, two children, and a Mrs. Macpherson, of the Court, form our party. Poor Chester, the Adjutant-General, was killed at Delhi. Our loss has been rather severe, but that of the enemy very great, for no quarter is given. We are fortified here as at Dugshai. I have laid in lots of supplies, not that they will be needed, I should say.

"First I was ordered down with the force, then directed to stand fast, then re-ordered down, and then told not to move, so here I am. I should like to have seen the Delhi affair. The Governor-General has ordered the whole place to be levelled with the ground. I will not write any more, as there is no certainty of this ever reaching you, our daks having been closed for some time, and open occasionally. Telegraphic communication also interrupted. This will be an entertaining production for the rascals should it fall into their hands.

"The list of those who have escaped will be found in the papers. We expect hourly to hear of the fall of Delhi.

"June 15.—News from the camp up to the 12th, on which date it appears the rebels marched out 7000 strong and attacked our camp. They were well beaten, and, after great carnage, driven back into Delhi. The heavy guns and mortars were at work, and it was expected that the place would fall in a few days. They were fighting amongst themselves, and numbers were anxious to return to us, but how can we trust them now? Sir John Lawrence has raised 50,000 Sikh levies for the Punjaub, so that our regular Sikh Corps may be rendered available. The Gwalior Rajah is collecting Mahrattas; Putteala, Sikh Irregulars, and Bombay troops are by this at Nusseerabad and Mhow. All other mutinies are mere flea bites compared with this one, which extends throughout the Bengal Presidency."

A fakeer, called Sham Doss, endeavoured to raise an insurrection in the territory of our ally the Rajah of Nabah, whose troops are with our army at Delhi. Major Marsden, the Deputy Commissioner of Ferozepore, proceeded against him with a wing of the 10th Light Cavalry and two guns, and some irregular levies of Furreedkota and other places, attacked and dispersed his men, seized the fakeer in a village, in which he had made a stout defence, and hung him.

The following description of the defences of Delhi, from the pen of an Indian officer, will be read with interest :—

"The city is surrounded by a high crenelated wall, in a deep ditch and glacis. At the Cashmeree gate only is there anything of modern fortification; here there is a simple bastion, with properly cut embrasures. It is enclosed, and forms the main guard. The city measures about two miles across, and is some seven or eight miles in circumference. On the east side the walls are washed by the Jumna. The palace is in a commanding position; and though the walls are not calculated to resist heavy artillery, yet the place could scarcely be taken without a breach being made in them, that is, if the garrison showed any skill in its defence. The capture of such a place is a simple matter of time, and its fall might be calculated to an hour; but everything depends upon the plan of defence adopted by the garrison. It is possible that they may risk a battle outside the walls; in which case, after their defeat, they might be followed into the city and into the palace, and so Delhi might be taken by a rush; but as our force is so very small, and such mighty consequences hang upon the success of our attack, the very greatest risk would be incurred by having our men exposed to musketry fire from houses, for a native's fire from a loophole is more than a match for a European in the open. If our force was large, we might afford to make a dash at the place, and it is just possible that events may even justify such a measure; but a regular siege, which cannot well fail, would be preferable. The whole of the western side is one mass of native houses. To scale the walls would be easy, but no object would be gained by pouring our handful of troops into a sea of houses, with streets barricaded; heavy loss would unquestionably follow. This mode of attack would be absurd, and would certainly end in discomfiture. There are two modes of attack, however, which could not well fail, and one or the other must be adopted. The first is to attack the palace at once from the river side, for the water until the end of the month is so very low, and so little more than a stream which is fordable, that it would create no obstacle worth mentioning. The batteries could be erected on the sand, and the camp being across the river would be safe. By shelling the palace and breaking its new wall, an assault could be made, and the fire of our guns would continue till our troops had fairly got in. The shelling would have destroyed all cover, and probably would have driven out the defenders, so that there is little doubt but that the assault would be successful. Having got possession of the palace the city falls at once. There is, however, a chance of the river rising suddenly, when the batteries would be destroyed, so that this attack entirely depends upon the river and the probability of its rise.

"The next and safest mode of attack, and the one that in all likelihood will be the one adopted, is to attack near the Cashmeree gate. The advantage is this, that our left would be protected by the river, a great consideration in a small camp. Our guns would soon render the main guard untenable, and to make a practicable breach in the wall between the Cashmeree gate and the river would be a very simple operation. Our advance would then be made in the open, and with little risk of loss from the fire of musketry from houses, for, owing to the explosion in the magazine, it is probable that from the church to the palace all has been levelled. Our object, then, would be to breach the palace in its north wall, mortars all the time doing their work. To storm the palace would close the proceedings. As the garrison have so few artillerymen, it does not seem likely that their defence is to rest in their guns. They will trust to musketry fire from houses; in all probability, they have undermined all the gates, and their plan will be, to inflict upon us as much loss as they can while gradually falling back, when they will hope to escape with their treasure, dispersing in every direction immediately they leave the walls. It is scarcely to be expected that anything like a vigorous or systematic defence will be shown, and for this very reason it would be most unwise to risk valuable lives, and run the chance of success by the sacrifice of a thousand men, when the same results can be obtained by a moderate delay, with a loss of perhaps not one hundred. Thus, while it is possible that the place may be taken by a *coup de main*, it would be better to do it leisurely and surely, and therefore the public should have no apprehension of failure if they do not hear of its being captured at first sight."

The following extracts from the Bombay correspondent of the *Times* will convey an idea of what is thought of the insurrection in the country where it is raging:—

The North-Western Provinces may be said to have gone, including the whole of Oude, and away across Rajpootana to the Bombay Presidency. At this moment we literally know nothing of Agra, Cawnpore, Lucknow, or even Allahabad. At the latter place some Europeans and Sikhs are in the fort, but they were running short of supplies when the last accounts left, and the Sikhs are doubtful.

In Central India Jhansi and Nowgong are already gone, and fears are entertained of Saugor.

Our Allies from Gwalior and Bhurtpore have been so far faithful that the leaders have not turned against us, but many of the men have. The temptation of plunder is almost irresistible to the Mahratta.

We look southward to Hyderabad in the Deccan with intense anxiety. It contains 60,000 fighting men (Arabs and others), and our adjacent force is one European regiment and five Madras native corps. If our Gwalior and Bhurtpore Rajahs turn, or if Hyderabad rise, or if the mutiny spread to Madras, where are we?

The movement assumes a more Mahomedan character. This renders the complicity of Hyderabad more likely.

In a few weeks the country will be covered with water, and military movements will be rendered almost impossible; but our brave Sepoys, who are such adepts at plunder and murder, and all the released prisoners from our gaols, and all the marauding Pindarees, Mahrattas, and Oude men, will be prosecuting their trade with unabated vigour, spreading wider and wider, and filling up their cup of iniquity. Meanwhile the land will be untilled and unsown, the cold weather will approach with a famine impending, and to meet the exigency the most comprehensive and complete arrangements must be made before the first movement of the campaign. It will not do to send us 20 regiments; it will not do to send us raw recruits. England must bestir herself as when her army and her reputation were in peril during the Russian war. Her militia must return to Gibraltar, to Malta, and to Corfu; and the regiments there must be sent on to us. Her home defence must be trusted to her militia even more than in 1855; and by one grand consummate effort 50,000 more troops must be sent to re-establish British supremacy in India. They must come soon, and all the people here must see our silent, gradual concentration of overwhelming forces and resources and the plain unmistakeable proof that we are thoroughly and sternly in earnest.

What is Scindia doing? This is a question of grave moment, and one not readily to be answered at present. We know that the 7th Infantry Regiment of his Contingent mutinied at Neemuch. We know that the telegraph wire has been cut near Seepree, and all regular communication with Agra, beyond Indore, interrupted; and we have reason to believe that both at Seepree and at Augur the regiments of the Contingent have risen. Indeed, I know that fears are entertained in the best informed quarters that the whole of the contingent (which consists of four companies of artillery, two regiments of cavalry, and seven of infantry) have turned against us, with the exception of three companies which garrison the isolated fort of Asseeghur in this presidency. Then, what will Scindia do? Will he be allured into believing that our power is on the wane, and into declaring against us, or will he, at the head of such troops as may remain faithful, resist the strong temptation, and oppose disloyalty even to the death? Like his fathers before him, he is a sturdy little Mahratta; he is young and active, riding his 50 or 60 miles a day when necessary; and energetic, too, as he showed on one occasion, when his then newly-raised Artillery hesitated to fire upon a body of the old levies who had refused to disband. Scindia jumped off his horse, seized a lighted portfire from the hand of a gunner, and himself discharged the first gun. Such a man, with the command, moreover, of considerable treasures, has the stuff in him to work us much good or ill. Indore, the seat of his rival, Holkar, is perfectly tranquil, and is likely to remain so. The British station of Mhow, in its immediate neighbourhood, is garrisoned in part by the head-quarter wing of the 1st Bengal Cavalry, of which the other wing mutinied at Neemuch. It is, however, safe at present and the approach of the Bombay column from Poonah will probably keep it so.

"With this sketch—hasty indeed, but I think tolerably complete, and I hope, with the aid of a map, intelligible—I quit the Bengal Presidency and turn to those of Madras and Bombay. The chief, perhaps the only danger to be anticipated by the Government of Fort St. George is a rising in the Nizam's country. One regiment of that Sovereign's contingent, as we shall presently see, has shown itself disaffected, and have been punished accordingly, but one only; and the Nizam himself is, in all probability, too much overawed by the powerful force cantoned at Secunderabad, close to his capital, to entertain a thought of revolt. At Kamptee, in Nagpore, a regiment of the newly raised Contingent showed unpleasant symptoms, but the regular Madras troops are there in force, and are thoroughly to be depended upon.

"We have not been without our little alarms either in Bombay, or in Poonah or elsewhere. But no outbreak has taken place (for the Mahomedan riots at Broach some time back, though ending in bloodshed, arose out of a local quarrel between that people and the Parsees), nor did any sensible person doubt the fidelity of the native troops, but only the temper of the loose population of the bazaars. At Poonah, the station was patrolled nightly by parties of the 14th and 12th Lancers. At Sattara, a man employed as a peon or chuprassie in Government employ was apprehended and handed over to the authorities by a party of the 22nd Native Infantry, with whose loyalty he was endeavouring to tamper. He was hanged, 'game' to the last, and uttering passionate bursts of disaffection. A troop of the 14th and a company or two of the 3rd Europeans went down from Poonah to aid the 22nd in case of a rising in this important and so lately independent Mahratta city.

"The whole press of India has been placed by an Act that has recently passed the Legislative Council under a censorship—a step imperatively called for by the indecent and disloyal manifestations of joy at our difficulties which appeared in some of the native prints at Calcutta. Here there has been, to my knowledge, only one instance of the kind, and the writer, a scoundrel of a Parsee, received such a rating from our superintendent of police—an iron functionary equal to the occasion—that he is not likely to offend again."

The article alluded to is one which appeared in the *Parsee Reformer*, edited by a Parsee named Sorabjee Dorabjee. It breathes treason in every line; and the writer points to the ruthless deeds perpetrated at Delhi and Meerut with a ferocity which is only eclipsed by that of the actual assassins. Alluding to the mutinies, the writer blasphemously apostrophizes the Almighty in these words:— "Oh! Lord the English have now seen a specimen of Thy power! To-day they were in a state of high command; to-morrow they wrapped themselves in blood, and began to fly. Notwithstanding that their forces were about three lacs strong in India, they began to yield up life like cowards. Forgetting their palanquins and carriages, they fled to the jungles whithout either boots or hats. Leaving their houses, they asked shelter from the meanest of men; and, abandoning their power, they fell into the hands of marauders." He then again appeals to the Deity, and winds up in the following strain:—"O! Englishmen, you little dreamt that the present King would ever mount the throne of Delhi with all the pomp of Nadir Shah, Baber, or Tamerlane!" If this is not an *Io Pæan* over our anticipated downfall we do not know what is. It ought also to be remembered that the article is written, not by a fanatic Mussulman, not by a high caste Hindoo Sepoy brooding over fancied wrongs, but by a Parsee.

The newspaper press of India is a new power which has sprung up during the last twenty years. The *Parsee Reformer* is not the only one by many which circulates entirely among natives, and is the property of, and conducted by, natives. Those who trace the hand of Russia in the secret spring of every blow struck at our power and prestige in the East ask, if it pays the Russian Government to maintain organs of its policy in Brussels, and Frankfort, and Berlin, would it not pay them much more to have newspapers in their service in India? The advantage to Russia of such an engine of its machinations is obvious; and many circumstances have occurred which lead us to regard that power as not at all unlikely to have stimulated the present outbreak. There are Parsees, Hindoos, and Mahommedans in Moscow and St. Petersburg; there are Russian subjects in India, ostensibly for purposes of trade. A Russian agent was recently in Calcutta, and on the disarmament of the Sepoys and the arrest of the King of Oude, he set out for the north. The north is overrun with the insurgents, travelling unsafe, and the communication stopped. If not bound for Delhi, would he not have chosen another route? Dark warnings dropped by Russian officials during the Paris Conferences, the known intrigues of Russia in Persia, Bokhara, and Afghanistan, and the refusal of the Persians to evacuate Herat, in conformity with the treaty just concluded, all point in the same direction. The Paris correspondent of a morning journal, of August 5th, says:—

"The belief in the influence of Russia in fermenting the Indian revolt is, I find, on the increase. It is, at all events, not so contemptuously pooh-poohed by the Paris journals as it was at first. Nay, they themselves are beginning to publish little morsels of information, showing that, if Russians have not lent a helping hand to the insurgents, they at least are gratified by the success of those insurgents. The *Pays*, the Government organ, published a testimony of this kind the other day. The *Presse*, amongst its miscellaneous news, publishes another to-day. I do not know whether this latter evidence comes from an English source, but, by the terms it is worded in, I should fancy not. I give it, then, as I find it. According to the *Presse*, a number of Russian boyards, assembled at Ems, were invited by one of their party to a dinner, and at this dinner a health was given by the host, which could only apply to the affairs of India, and which was received with immense applause. Its spirit was evidently adverse to England."

The following are extracts from the diary of an officer in Calcutta:—

"We all thought that the last steamer would have taken the news of the fall of Delhi, but still it is in the hands of the rebels, and still is the fate of India in the balance. Every day we hear of more regiments having thrown off their allegiance, and having taken the road to join the head-quarters of the mutineers. Terrible times are these. The Bengal army no longer exists. No trust can be placed in any regiment. One day a corps professes the most devout attachment to the Government, the next day we hear it has murdered all its officers, men, women, and children. Not a day has passed but we have anticipated the fall of Delhi, and the delay to us is unaccountable. Our communications since the outbreak have been very irregular, but now they are entirely cut off, both postal and telegraph. The post, when one does come in, is long overdue. Thank heaven! we have two good men in command, Sir John and Sir Henry Lawrence. They are the saviours of India. The former has kept the Punjab quiet—the latter has stood his ground manfully at Lucknow. We have also another good man in Sir Hugh Wheeler at Cawnpore, and the Governor-General deserves all praise for his conduct in doing all in his power to get reinforcements together and to push them on up country with the greatest expedition possible. I don't know what you will think of all this at home. It must affect nearly every family in England, for there are few who have not relations and friends out here. Men who were here during the time of the Cabul disasters tell me that the panic then was nothing to what at present prevails. Trade is at a standstill. The natives, too, participate in the alarm—those who have to lose and those on the *qui vive* for gain, and there is no want of the latter.

"Goodness knows what has come over the Sepoys, hitherto so obedient, so patient, and so orderly. It is no longer the cartridge question, but a religious war—a call upon all good and true Mahommedans to rise in the name of the Prophet, and slaughter the Feringhee infidels. It is more a revolt of the former sect than of the Hindoos. What hundreds of thousands, in the course of time, must have fallen victims in the name of religion! I suppose all the unfortunate women were murdered in the name of religion. Poor unfortunates! God help them! It is a mercy they are all killed. But I do not suppose all the atrocities were perpetrated by the Sepoys: I imagine they were committed by the scum of the earth, that never comes forth but on such occasions of murder and rapine—whose existence most people are ignorant of. The Sepoys, I suspect, were giving their attention to the plunder that was to be picked up, but that is no excuse for them. Round about Meerut and Delhi there are two or three peculiar castes or tribes, something similar to our gipsies, only holding human life at less value, and which in former days gave constant trouble, but who of late years have lived in peace and quietness, and have contented themselves with picking up stray cattle and things that did not belong to them, but who have now on the first opportunity broken out, and have been guilty of all kinds of depredations. Skinner's Horse was originally raised to keep these people in order about the time of Lord Lake. These men have hitherto been necessary at Meerut, Delhi, and those parts as watchmen. Every one was obliged to keep one; if you did not you would be robbed to a certainty. You will not understand this, but it is necessary to come to India to understand many things—many that are beyond any explanation that I can give at least.

"12th.—Yesterday no news, but plenty of reports. Never was the country in such a state of disorder. The Company's paper is down very low; the new 5 per cent. loan few subscribe to, and the Four per Cents. were yesterday at 20 discount, and I see by the newspaper that at Benares it was at 42 discount. We must have a new loan, and you must give us the money, I suspect. Out of the treasuries alone that have been robbed I should think nearly two millions of money have been taken; and then fancy the expense of the transport of all these Europeans.

"You must be just about receiving the first news of the outbreak, and I hope you have sent off reinforcements from Malta overland. I think steamers ought to be sent to Suez in anticipation of your doing so. Bombay and Madras are not safe now they are denuded of the English troops, and I expect to hear of outbreaks every day. Rebellion is catching, evidently. If you will read the papers you will see that Sir Henry

Lawrence is hanging the fellows at Lucknow as fast as he can. The 37th Native Infantry that has just mutinied at Benares I know very well, having been at Jhelum with them. It was a very good regiment, particularly in Affghanistan, where on several occasions it led the way for the Europeans—for the 44th, for example. The Subadar-Major, the senior native officer of the regiment, was wounded seven times. Is it not odd that he should now forget his duty and turn traitor, after such good and honourable service? I suppose it is all religion, or do you suppose it can be possible that Russia has had anything to say to it? I have no doubt that she stirred up Persia against us, but Persia was too late in breaking out, or the war in the Crimea ceased too abruptly. Persia might now break the treaty and advance upon Candahar. Dost Mahommed would join, and what could we do? The whole country would rise just for the change of the thing, and we should be beaten in detail everywhere. We have not a native regiment to depend on—not one that would stand firm if the day was going against us."

"I cannot help again making mention of the way our countrymen are dressed. My room is rather a cool one. It is a very airy one, and I keep the hot air shut out after the sun has risen, or rather, I close the doors directly it begins to get warm; but the thermometer will stand at 90 and 92. I see the men of the 64th and 84th, and, in fact, all regiments just arrived, are clothed in the tunic, the same as they wear at home. Fancy what the heat must be, fancy the discomfort; and then the cloak and 60 rounds of ammunition! I cannot help feeling for them. The men suffered frightfully out in the Crimea from the weight put on their backs, but what must it be in a much hotter, and more trying climate in every way! It is such absurd folly dressing a man here as he would be at home, when the very sight of a cloth coat gives an unpleasant sensation. I would let them wear the tunic in cold weather, but to put a man in one in June in India is cruel, and not only cruel, but bad policy, for the men must suffer from it, and the first duty of a General is to bring his men fresh into the battle-field; and how can a man be fresh after a march of even ten miles with such oppressive clothing and such a thing as that shako is to wear of a hot day? I would give a man a white smockfrock to wear in cantonments, where he might get it washed, but in the field he should have a coloured one, so as not to require a clean one daily. In the small river steamers the men are being sent up country in (packed like sardines) they still stick to the tunic. I suppose it is in orders from the Horse Guards. I told you in my last of two men being struck down from the sun, proceeding up in the bullock carts. Since then I have heard that others have suffered frightfully, and at a time when the life of every man is of so much consequence; and when is it not? The people at home howl about a murderer being strung up. They can look on and see their soldiers sacrificed with complacency.

"17th, Tuesday.—I went to bed late on Saturday night, and was woke up at 2 on Sunday morning with orders to assemble. On going to parade I found it was feared the troops at Barrackpore were going to break out, and march either on this or Dum-dum. We set out immediately on the Barrackpore road, accompanied by 500 men of the 37th Foot, which had arrived the day before from Ceylon. We marched up the road nine miles, and there halted for the day. On Sunday afternoon the troops at Barrackpore were disarmed, as also all here. They delivered up their arms quietly. At 12 on Sunday night an express reached us from the Governor-General, directing a party to be sent back to Calcutta instanter. I mounted immediately, and cantered in within the hour and went to the fort, where I found a force assembling to march to Garden Reach for the purpose of taking the King of Oude prisoner. It was to be a surprise on our part, and so it proved. We got there at 4 o'clock, surrounded his grounds directly, and had the good fortune to find all at home. We were rather afraid he would get news as to what was going on; but we went down quietly, and the surprise was complete. I was ahead of the party with my men. His Prime Minister and the whole batch, papers and all, were seized.

"All Sunday there was a tremendous panic in Calcutta. Many people went on board the ships, and others had their carriages at their doors to be ready to start at a moment's warning. We have volunteer guards now, cavalry and infantry. They go the rounds at night and look brave. The 37th, in the short march of nine miles, the other night suffered very much, and they had only been but six days on board ship from Ceylon. It was the death of one captain. The men had the small forage cap, fit only for the barrack-square in England—no protection whatever from the sun. They had white jackets on, I was glad to see; but even then the heat was so great that the crossbelt was wet through from perspiration. Stocks, of course."

An evening paper gives the following summary of the rumours circulating in India when the *Colombo* steamer left Bombay:—

"Every subsequent and every detailed piece of news from India is only more and more confirmatory of the very worst anticipations.

"The passengers on board the *Colombo* who have come from India state that Bazaar intelligence outstrips Government intelligence (which is a bad sign, because it shows complicity between the natives in India and the mutineers), and that according to Bazaar intelligence Delhi had fallen.

"When the Madras passengers left, an *émeute* was fully expected in that presidency. The Europeans were under arms.

"The passengers think that the mutiny is not considered in England so serious as it really is. They give some frightful details of atrocities committed by the mutineers. In Delhi six European ladies had taken refuge in a room; one of them, very young and beautiful, concealed herself under a sofa. The other five were subjected to outrage by the mutinous soldiery, and then beheaded. The blood trickled under the sofa, and the young female concealed there betrayed herself by uttering a shriek. She was seized and taken to the harem of the King of Delhi. This is considered a proof that the King is in league with the mutineers.

"One thousand seven hundred armed men were found about the residence of the King of Oude when he was taken prisoner, although, according to treaty, he was not allowed one armed attendant.

"It was reported in Calcutta that if the Queen of Oude had left England she was to be stopped and arrested at Galle. Another report was current that the King of Delhi had taken poison, because he could not agree with the mutineers; another that he had been hanged by the mutineers."

The following letters have been received by the last mail, and are of later date than those which were received on the 31st of July. The first is from an officer of the Madras Native Artillery:—

"Combined Field Force Camp, Residency Compound, Nagpore, June 19.

"These are stirring times. On Saturday, 13th, at midnight, the alarm was sounded at Kamptee, and our troop was ordered to proceed immediately to Seetabuldee on field service, accompanied by two squadrons, 4th Madras Cavalry. We were ready in next to no time, and were on the spot before daybreak. It appeared that at eleven P.M. a trooper of the Nagpore Irregular Cavalry had been caught tampering with certain Sepoys of the Irregular Infantry Regiment, and trying to stir up a mutiny, by telling them 'the standard of Mahomet' was to be raised in the city of Nagpore at midnight; that all Mussulmans of the city were to rise and kill the Feringhee Kafirs (European infidels); and that on a certain signal (a fire balloon) from the city, the Irregular Cavalry were to to murder their officers, and join in the general revolt. He at the same time requested the infantry to join; they refused, and at once made the traitor a prisoner, and ran to report the state of affairs to their commanding officer, Captain Holland (who is still in a very weak state from his rencontre with a tiger). Holland was intreated by his men to fly for his life. All the ladies and families in Seetabuldee were roused, and immediately driven to Kamptee. I must tell you that a small force, consisting of one Madras regiment of infantry, one squadron of Regular Cavalry, and half a battery of Field Artillery, was ordered to proceed from Kamptee, on the 12th, towards Jubbulpore, where there seemed a probability of the Bengal Regiment mutinying. A squadron of the Irregular Cavalry also was to have joined this force on the 14th. About eleven P.M. one of the officers of the Irregular Cavalry rushed into the adjutant's house and told him to fly, as the whole regiment had 'booted and saddled,' in readiness for joining the city people at midnight, and the whole irregular force would join. At that very time a trustworthy native informed Ellis, the deputy commissioner, of what was about to take place. He galloped off to the Residency, and woke Mr. Plowden, who forthwith rode into Kamptee, and gave the alarm to the brigadier and the rest of the force. By some mismanagement the fire balloon did not go up, and the whole conspiracy has been nipped in the bud, most providentially for all at Seetabuldee.

"On our arrival near the Irregular Cavalry lines there, we learned that at two A.M. the whole force had been paraded by the officer commanding the force; the cavalry dis-

SEIZURE OF THE KING OF OUDE.

mounted and deprived of their arms; the battery with guns loaded with grape brought to bear on them, and the Irregular Infantry Regiment in support of the guns. Of what took place at that parade I am not aware, but it was dismissed quietly shortly before our arrival. The man who was caught inciting the Sepoys was brought down to the Residency, and tried at once by drum-head general court martial. We sentenced him to be blown from a gun; the sentence was, however, commuted to transportation for life, and he is now imprisoned in the Hill Fort, Seetabuldee. Five of the principal native officers are confined in irons in the fort also, and are awaiting trial. The native officer who warned the adjutant of danger turns out to be one of the principal ringleaders, but who, at the last moment, feared the consequences. The man we tried was evidently the tool of influential people in the city, and of men possessing rank and wealth; the native officers of Irregular Cavalry are all well-connected native gentlemen. We are now on the alert lest an attempt be made at a rescue of the prisoners.

"It seems that a proclamation has been in circulation at Nagpore and all over India, drawing notice to a prophecy that the reign of the Feringhees in the East would cease on the 23d of June, 1857—exactly 100 years from the battle of Plassey—and the followers of Mahomet once more gain the supremacy. The cartridge question has been taken advantage of to bring about the above prophecy.

"I have got my tent pitched in the Residency Compound, in the troop camp. We expect the rains down in a few days, but as yet all the Europeans in our troop are healthy, and the horses are in excellent condition. Our guns have a support of 100 Madras Infantry, as well as two squadrons of Cavalry, but we are short of officers.

"Three officers and myself go round every night, relieving one another every two hours in visiting the pickets and videttes; so, what with regimental duty and general duty, we have plenty to occupy our time, and we snatch a little rest when we can get it. The Irregular Infantry Regiment and the Horse Battery are, I think, staunch, but in these queer times it is difficult to know whom to trust. It is a great mistake having no European regiment at Kamptee. The country has for some years been gradually denuded of European regiments. Now, the folly of that measure is but too apparent. My revolver is a great comfort, I assure you. I only wish we could have a dash at the insurgents, and treat them to the 'juice of the grape.' The Europeans are very anxious to have a brush with the blackguards. The small hill fort of Seetabuldee is being repaired as quickly as possible, a half-company of Artillery, under Lieutenant Canie, to man the heavy guns, which command all the approaches from the city. A month's provisions have been laid in for the garrison. Half a regiment of infantry support the guns.

"All is tranquil here at present, and a net is gradually being drawn around the principal conspirators in the city. I am writing very hurriedly under great difficulties, as I have much work to do, and the heat is very great; also, in the hurry of departure from Kamptee, I left my writing materials, &c., in my house. The electric telegraph wires have been cut in many places, and the letter dâks are frequently stopped and robbed in the North-west Provinces.

"Nusseerabad and Neemuch are burnt and destroyed. Our house, a pucka (brick) one, they could not touch, but every article of furniture, &c., they took out and destroyed on the lawn—glass, pictures, books, crockery, &c., everything destroyed; the plate, carriage, and horses taken away. . . . George Lawrence is below, doing military duty again as brigadier-general in Rajpootana. He went down to assist Colonel Dixon, who, from fatigue and anxiety, was supposed to be dying. He is now recovering, but the poor brigadier was completely broken down, and has put everything in his hands.

"The fort of Ajmere, with its arsenal, is of great value down here; and here we have been quite successful in dislodging the suspected traitors, and putting in other troops to hold it (which was done without a row), and then getting up European troops from Deesa to hold it. No sooner had they arrived than Mr. Colvin writes to have them sent up to protect Agra—200 Europeans and three guns being all we have to hold Rajpootana in check. George Lawrence has respectfully declined. The Kotah Contingent, 1200 men (cavalry and infantry and two guns), who were under Lawrence's orders, Mr. Colvin ordered away to Agra, and having ordered the commandant, Captain Dennys, to move into Ajmere for its protection, Mr. Colvin then got an order from Calcutta by the telegraph, giving him power over every one in Rajpootana. Had Dennys obeyed Lawrence, Nusseerabad and Neemuch had been saved. . . . General Anson's death saved him from assassination. He was hated by the troops, and they burnt his tents. He was quite unfitted for his post. Horses and gaming appear to have been his pursuits, and as a gentleman said, 'No court pet flunky ought to come to India.' Every one gave a sigh of relief when they heard he was gone. 'Pat Grant' is come over from Madras to head the army till orders come from England. Henry Lawrence (also a brigadier-general) has been named for the appointment, but he cannot be spared from Oude, where he is holding his own with 300 Europeans. A much more difficult position than that at Agra, I fear. God will help him, I have no doubt. He has had one chace after the mutineers, with signal success. George Lawrence has too few troops to follow up the Neemuch mutineers, but was ready to meet them should they come to Ajmere, as they gave out. They, however, have gone the wrong way. I hope they may meet with their reward, for their cruelty was great, and they chased the officers and their wives out of their burning houses all night into the jungles. One poor sergeant's wife whom they attacked, shot down the first man, and was cut down by the second, and her children thrown into the flames."

Under date Benares, June 11, Mr. Gregson gives the following graphic account of the events in that city, and of the state of the surrounding country :—

"On Thursday last, the 4th instant, from an early hour in the morning, the telegraph was occupied almost every hour with the recital of some fresh disaster. In the afternoon tidings came from Azimgurh, a station forty miles distant, that the troops there had risen in mutiny, shot their officers, plundered the treasury, and perpetrated various other outrages. The station had long been watched by the authorities here with suspicion and alarm; and now, when at length the tidings came, they resolved at once to disarm the 37th Native Infantry, which was the most suspected of the regiments here. We had two other regiments, one of native cavalry, and one of Sikh foot, and, though both these also were suspected, still some confidence was entertained that they would remain firm. About half-past five, P.M., we were startled by a rapid discharge of rifles and the boom of cannon. We could not doubt what it meant. The troops had mutinied. Our house is just on the outskirts of the city, and a mile in the opposite direction are the military lines, where the fighting was going on. Now it was fully expected that the mutiny of the troops would be the signal for the instantaneous rise of all the rabble of the city, and the immediate destruction of European property and life. Our only resource was flight. Mr. Heinig and family immediately set off for Rajghat, to Mr. Smith's, our missionary, whose house presents many advantages for a retreat, and is situated on the bank of the river, and quite out of the way the rebels were likely to take. We intended to take the same road, but, after going a little distance, were alarmed by some Sepoys, and fled towards the lines. Mr. Kennedy's house was in our way, and we resolved at once to go there. It was deserted. Mr. Kennedy and his family had fled some time before. We determined to remain here for a little. We were now within about half a mile of the field of conflict, and all this time a ceaseless discharge of rifles and of cannon was kept up. But we knew not who were fighting, and were kept in a state of fearful suspense. We had only about 200 European troops in the station and three cannon, to about 2000 native troops, and had the latter been united, escape seemed impossible. The regularity and rapidity with which the artillery was served, left no doubt that it was still in the hands of skilled men, and so far encouraged the hope that our troops were victorious. Gradually the firing grew more irregular, until it almost ceased—only an occasional shot disturbing the silence that now prevailed. Evening had already set in. From an occasional straggler coming our way we learned that the 37th Native Infantry and the Sikhs had rebelled and been defeated, and had fled. The road was very quiet, and we had only about a fourth or third of a mile to go to reach the Mint, a large building, which had often been talked of as a rendezvous for Europeans in case of tumult, and which was now occupied by a few of our troops. After some hesitation, and not without misgiving, we resolved to go there, and reached in safety, to our great thankfulness and joy. Here many had already assembled, and others were continually arriving. We were only a quarter of a mile now from the battle-field, and we soon learnt that all the 37th Native Infantry had rebelled, all the Sikhs who were on the field, and a considerable portion of the cavalry. The guns had made much havoc of the Sikhs, but nearly all the 37th and cavalry had escaped. On our side one or two officers had been shot dead and three wounded, and one man killed and about five wounded. It was also said that eighty to one hundred Sikhs were left dead on the field.

The night, you may imagine, was a very anxious one. Escorts had to be sent out in all directions to bring in European residents and defend them from the rebel troops lurking about in every corner. The Magazine had to be guarded in one place, and the Mint in another, and the Treasury in a third, and besides this there were 1000 or 1500 native troops in rebellion who might still unite and attack any one of these points in concert, while on our side was only a mere handful of men; and yet I ought not to say so—there was One on our side infinitely greater than all they that were against us, and only to His special interposition can we attribute our safety. Indeed, when I look at the dangers we have escaped, our preservation can only be regarded as a miracle. Our God has, indeed, poured confusion on the councils of our adversaries, and to him alone we would ascribe our safety and deliverance. The outbreak here was immediately followed by complete anarchy throughout the surrounding country. God has very mercifully, and contrary to all expectations, preserved order in the city. No houses have been burnt, and not one plundered; but all round the country is in a state of the greatest confusion.

"Troops are passing here daily. Allahabad is now garrisoned by a small number of European troops, and the fort and magazine are in their hands, but the city has been plundered, and all Europeans without the fort have been murdered. Cawnpore too has received aid. The Europeans there for weeks past have had to entrench themselves, and sleep behind cannon. Oude is in an uproar from one end to the other. Here is the, or, at least, one grand centre of disaffection, and it will be well if Sir H. Lawrence, who has acted with consummate skill and energy, should not at length be overpowered. At Agra all native troops have been disarmed, and as they have a strong fort and one or two English regiments, our friends there may be considered safe. From Delhi nothing can be heard. A telegraph came to Benares only yesterday from the Governor-General, urging our commissioner to send out men on camels, or in any other practicable or impracticable way, to obtain information. At Simla the residents were set adrift—it is feared to starve—after being plundered of everything. While here we have daily to send out escorts twenty, thirty, or forty miles to bring in parties of Europeans who have concealed themselves. Only the night before last about thirty were thus rescued from Jaunpore, 35 miles off. All here had a most narrow escape; Mr. Reuchter, wife, and four children; Mr. Cassar and wife, of the Church Mission, were among them. All have escaped with the loss of all things. Last night another escort went out to bring in about the same number from a place twenty miles distant, and Chunar and Allahabad likewise are the resort of numbers of fugitives. All this will, of course, greatly interfere with the mission work for a long time to come. Happily thus far it has been simply a soldier's question. All the respectable and influential natives stand firmly by the Government, and only a few of the worst characters have joined in plundering. In Benares I believe we are safe. The rebels have no ammunition, no cannon, and not many muskets, and, besides, are destitute of leaders. In addition to that, they are not united, and have no common object to aim at. Most of the disaffected troops disperse and go home, and the only two points towards which any numbers converge are Oude and Delhi. In Benares, too, the measures taken were so vigorous and decisive that the troops fled panic-stricken, and to this time have scarcely recovered their composure. It is not the Sepoys we have now to fear so much as the lawless plundering mob that this state of anarchy must produce. We stay with Dr. Lazarus during the day, and sleep at the Mint, just opposite, at night. Our house is quiet, but being so near the city, and out of cantonments, it is not thought desirable at present to return to it."

Mr. Lawrence, writing from Monghir, on the 16th of June, says:—

"Yesterday there was a very great alarm felt by most parties, natives as well as Europeans, in consequence of a report that the Irregular Cavalry at Deoghur had murdered their officers, and intended coming to Monghir to rob the treasury. The Europeans, who are rather numerous just now, formed themselves into parties, and with loaded guns, pistols, &c., kept watch in turn all night. As our quarter of the station is deserted by Europeans, we thought it right to go to a friend's house in the fort. But I am thankful to say, the night passed quietly, and the native town seems peaceful this morning, but trembling with excitement. Official information has been received by the magistrate, that three officers of the Irregular Cavalry have been murdered, but the men of the regiment deny that they had any hand in the murder. The circumstances, however, look extremely suspicious. These are alarming times, but the Lord can keep his people in peace."

The gravity of the position in which the British Empire in the East now stands cannot be exaggerated. The war with Russia was a trifle in comparison. The case was not overstated by the *Times*, in the observation " that the Army of an immense Empire has revolted, a capital city is in the hands of an enemy instructed by ourselves in the military art, and a few days may bring the news that British power exists only in a few forts or a few cities of the coast." And the writer, now alive to the importance of the interests involved, and a full and clear perception of the extent to which they are imperilled, thus presented to the public the real position of affairs :—

" Delhi, the capital of Mahomedan India, the residence of the heir of the Moguls, the chief arsenal of Upper India, and filled with cannon, shot, and shell, is in the hands of some thousands of Asiatics, many of whom are practised artillerymen. The place possesses warlike stores sufficient to stand a long siege, and it is defended by a wall of considerable strength, considering the artillery we can bring against it; for, according to all accounts, we have only light guns, and are awaiting the arrival of heavier metal before commencing the attack. In the meantime all India is looking out for news from Delhi. Not only throughout Bengal, where it may be said that every soldier is a mutineer at heart, but in the Bombay and Madras Presidencies, the native troops are wavering, inclined to revolt, but afraid to move, and asking each other whether men of their race can really hold the chief city of their country against the foreigners who have till now swept everything before them. All depends upon whether General Barnard will prove himself equal to the occasion. It is an awful stake upon a man almost unknown. It seems to us that in this case courage amounting even to rashness, will be more effective than caution and the most skilful combinations. The capture of Delhi is an affair in which days, even hours, are precious. No one doubts that eventually a British force must take a city garrisoned only by Asiatics, but the capture after a regular siege would be almost as fatal as failure. We cannot afford to make a Sebastopol of the capital of Upper India, although Delhi too is an arsenal, and we are marching to attack it without a siege train. While the troops are making parallels and the General planning scientific attacks, the whole of India would be in a flame. Every discontented Rajah, every unquiet tribe, the Monarchs of the neighbouring regions, and the unfriendly States of Europe might make use of the opportunity to inflict on the country loss and dishonour."

In its anxiety to find the " silver lining" of the cloud now hanging over our Indian Empire, the leading journal had felicitated its readers on the happy idea that had sent the Indian mutineers flocking to Delhi, where they all could be destroyed at a blow, surrounded by General Barnard's army, and taken, as it were, in a trap. Better information led to the opinion that "if Delhi is such a trap, we may possibly pay for it. We have made it ourselves a sort of Indian Sebastopol, strengthened it, and filled it with cannon and ammunition. Why we ever did this with a place of high Mohammedan fame, and then assigned it to the keeping of an exclusively native force, we need not now inquire. We now hear further that several thousand of the defenders are encamped under the guns outside the walls, and, what is worse, that this Sebastopol can be supplied to any extent by the Jumna, which flows under its palace, and which is in the hands of the natives."

It appears that Delhi, when it fell into the possession of the insurgents, contained two complete siege trains, of the heaviest guns in India, 10,000 muskets, 900,000 cartridges, and gunpowder enough to blaze away at any besieging army for twelve months.

SUPPLEMENT.

DELHI had not fallen up to the 27th of June, the date of our latest advices *viâ* Lahore. There had been a good deal of fighting outside the walls, the rebels being defeated on every occasion. The disaffection among the native troops had completed its course, and every standard of the Bengal army was left without a single Sepoy to defend it. At all the Presidencies, business continued to be at a stand; money could scarcely be had on any terms; and the decline in Government securities was uninterrupted. Such were the tidings conveyed by the telegraph on the 12th of August, and the effect on the funds was a depressing one. Many, misled by the confident tone of the Government and its organs, had expected the fall of Delhi, and when it became known that the capital of the Moguls still held out, and that General Barnard had been compelled to restrict his operations to acting on the defensive, Consols experienced an immediate decline.

The letters and journals delivered two days after the receipt of the telegraphic messages tend to confirm the views taken by Mr. Disraeli, and put to flight all the fallacies which have been put forward as to the non-participation of the people of India in the revolt, and the want of organization on the part of the insurgents. The singular cake movement and the lotus mystery might have dispelled the latter delusion; but neither attracted any attention. But every step taken by the insurgents has since tended to prove that they have acted upon preconcerted plans, and are under able leaders, unknown though their names may be to European fame. It has not been the policy of the Indian Government to encourage military genius among its native troops. Premeditation and organization are proved by the facts that the mutineers of Meerut were provided with scaling-ladders wherewith to storm the European entrenchments; that the first step taken by them on reaching Delhi was to secure the bridge of boats; that the mutinies at Bareilly, Shahjehanpore, Cawnpore, and a number of other places occurred almost simultaneously on the news being spread of the seizure of Delhi; that the first step taken by the mutineers, in almost every instance, has been to cut the telegraph wires; and that they have proceeded, after killing or dispersing their European officers, to replace them with those of their own race, whose orders have been willingly and readily obeyed. With respect to the other point—the absence of sympathy with the revolt on the part of the general population, the intelligence now received completely disproves the assumption, which is also destroyed by the despatches of Major-General Hewitt, commanding at Meerut, included in a recent parliamentary paper.

A very few lines sufficed for the statement, that the mutiny had spread to such and such stations, but a long catalogue of horrors follows ere the full tale is told. The telegraph flashed intelligence of the mutiny of the troops at Moradabad, Fyzabad, Seetapore, Saugor, Nowgong, Banda, Futtyghur, Mhow, and Indore; and we proceed briefly to relate the particulars of each, in so far as they are known to us.

It is now evident that an arrangement existed between the troops at Bareilly, Shahjehanpore, Lucknow, and Moradabad, to effect a simultaneous rising. A glance at the map will show the proximity of these stations to each other, and the outbreak occurred at each on the morning of the same day.

The mutiny at Bareilly, of which we have already given a brief account, seems to have been attended with circumstances of peculiar atrocity and treachery.

Only the day before the outbreak, the Sepoys appealed to their officers to recall their wives and families from the hills, where they had been sent for safety, and even to the last moment swore to protect their officers to the death. The 18th and 68th Native Infantry, and the 8th Irregular Cavalry, rose *en masse* on Sunday morning, the 1st of June, a shotted gun being fired as the signal, about eleven o'clock. The men at once rushed upon the officers' lines, and opened a fusillade upon the bungalows. Such officers as were able, immediately got on their horses, and made for the rendezvous previously agreed upon amongst them, the cavalry parade ground. An ineffectual effort was made to bring back the troops to their allegiance, but they opened upon them with grape-shot, and they had to ride for their lives. The country having risen in all directions, it was with extreme difficulty, and only by a ride of seventy miles, that the little band at last found safety at Nynee Tal in the hills, where they had previously sent their families. Here the refugees are congregated in numbers which will probably awe any attempt to attack them, and as the place is of very difficult approach, we may hope they are in safety. The insurgents took possession of the guns, and then set at liberty about 3000 prisoners in the gaol, who laid the station in ruins.

At Moradabad the mutineers gave their officers two hours' grace to make their escape, in which they fortunately succeeded; the whole of the officers (29th Regiment) and the residents, with their families, escaping to Nynee Tal the day after the arrival of the Bareilly refugees. Great fears were entertained that the whole of the British residents at the station of Shahjehanpore had been massacred. We are happy, however, to learn that a good many have escaped.

The rising at Fyzabad occurred on the night of Sunday, the 8th, the 6th Oude Irregular Infantry giving the signal, which was immediately answered by the 22nd Native Infantry. They at once took possession of the battery, and would not allow the officers to approach, but do not seem to have offered them any further violence. Fyzabad is in the very heart of Oude, and is situate upon a branch of the Ganges. We cannot resist the temptation of quoting from a letter on the subject of this affair :—

"The account of the mutiny of the 22nd Regiment beats any romance; they guarded their officers and their bungalows after mutiny, placed sentries over magazines and all public property, sent out pickets to prevent the townspeople and servants from *looting*, held a council of war, in which the cavalry (Fisher's Irregular) proposed to kill the officers, but the 22nd objected, and informed the officers that they would be allowed to leave, and might take with them their private arms and property, but no public property, as all that belonged to the King of Oude. Their officers asked for boats : the rebel Commissary-General, a Ressaldar, was ordered to provide them. He did so, but merely small dingies, so that they could only bring away a bundle each, and then they were presented with 900rs., which the rebels had taken from the treasure chest to give them. When the officers tried to recall them to their duty, they respectfully assured them that they were now under the orders of their native officers, and that the sobadar major of the 22nd Regiment had been appointed to the command of the station, and that each corps had appointed one of its officers to be their chief."

The officers determined to endeavour to escape by boat, and were allowed quietly to embark. What followed is thus related by one of the party :—

"I remember the officers in the two boats; I accompanied Lieutenant Bright, 22nd Native Infantry. Lieutenant Parsons, 6th Oude Irregulars; Lieutenant Cautley, 22nd Native Infantry; Sergeant Busher, 27th Native Infantry, and myself, were in one boat. Colonel Goldney, Lieutenant Currie, Artillery; Lieutenant Ritchie, 22nd Native Infantry; Sergeant Edwards, and Sergeant-Major Matthews, in the second boat; three other boats followed behind; we waited two hours for them, but as they did not come we pushed off. As we were getting into the boat, we saw the Sepoys of the 22nd rushing towards the Treasury; there were about two lacs and 40,000 rupees in Captain Drummond's house (where the treasure had been placed). On reaching a place called Begumgunge, about ten miles below Fyzabad, we met some mutineers encamped. At half-past one these men fired on us. There were 800 or 900 of them. About 100 men fired on us when we were 600 yards off. Colonel Goldney advised our pushing off to the opposite bank of the Gogra. We got on an island among some jhow fields. The mutineers got into dingies and followed us. We made for the main boat from the island. There were about forty or fifty yards of water between us. Major Mills was drowned. The sergeant-major, Lieutenant Bright, and I were taken prisoners, and taken to the camp of the mutineers, who were the men of the 17t and 37th Native Infantry, and the 17th Irregular Cavalry. We were taken before the Subadar commanding the rebels· I do not know his name. He was a Hindoo, and belonged to the 17th Native Infantry· He was an old man, slightly made, about 5 feet 8 inches high, with grey hair; no hair on his face, and dark complexion. He asked us who we were; we replied. He then appealed to the Mussulmans on the Koran, and to the Hindoos on the cow, not to injure us, and told us to go away. Two men of the 17th then stepped out and shot the Sergeant-Major and Lieutenant Bright. I was rescued by an artilleryman, and was hid in a serai at Begumgune and sent off in disguise. While we were talking to the Subadar, some fifteen or sixteen of the Irregular Cavalry, and ten or twelve Sepoys, went after the remainder of our party. We heard firing across the river; the party returned, and reported they had killed Colonel Goldney and six other officers, and that three had escaped. On arriving at Tanda, on the 10th inst., I heard people in the serai saying that six or seven officers had been killed, and two or three were sheltered by some zemindar in Goruckpore district. After this, I came viâ Mattoopoor, Shahgunge, and Juanpore. Captain Reed, Deputy Commissary; Captain A. P. Orr, Assistant Commissary; Mr. E. O. Bradford, ditto, and Captain Thurburn, reached Rajah Mann Sing's house, and he promised shelter and protection. When I was at Mattoopoor, I heard that the above officers were going down in boats, with their families, escorted by some of the Rajah's guard. At Tanda I heard that a Mr. Fitzgerald, clerk in the Deputy-Commissioner's office, and Overseer-Sergeant Hurst, who were escorting the families of some sergeants to Allahabad, viâ Sultanpore, were killed, and the women and children also murdered. I don't know what has become of the officers who were in the boats behind us when we left Fyzabad."

We have reason to believe, however, that a considerable number of the officers have effected their escape from this station, and whatever may have taken place after leaving it, the conduct of the Sepoys at the time seems to have been characterised by the strangest moderation. The following is from Fyzabad, dated 22nd June:—

"We are now with a friendly Rajah at Gopalpore on the river, 25 miles from Goruckpore. He has promised to send us to Dinapore, which is distant 120 miles. I believe we are now quite safe, though we have been in danger, and suffered much discomfort and misery. Our party consists of Captain and Mrs. Reid and two children, Captain and Mrs. Orr and sister and five children, Captain and Mrs. Thurburn and one child, Captain and Mrs. Dawson and four children, Mr. and Mrs. Bradford, Mr. and Mrs. Fitzgerald and child, and Mr. and Mrs. Hurst and child."

A letter from Captain Orr, dated Gopalpore, near Gograh, June 24, mentions that he and his family, with Miss Troup and the rest of his party who escaped from Fyzabad, had reached Gopalpore in safety, and expected to be at Dinapore on the 29th. They were to proceed under the protection of the Rajah of Gopalpore, who has shown himself faithful to the British Government. It is expected that most of the other Fyzabad people will yet turn up. Mrs. Black, Mrs. Goldney, and Mrs. Strahan have been brought in to Allahabad by a native, Ajeet Singh, who saw Lieutenant Grant and the party of 37 Europeans, who accompanied him from his camp near Fyzabad. A letter from Mr. Wynyard, the judge of Goruckpore, reports all quiet at that station on the 24th inst.

We know little of the state of matters at Indore, beyond the fact that the two regiments of the Maharajah Holkar have openly mutinied, and proceeded with the Bengal regiments towards Oojein, on their way, as is supposed, to Delhi. The Maharajah seems to be in no way implicated in this business, but to have acted with the same good faith that has characterised the conduct of the Gwalior Prince. The fidelity and goodwill of Holkar have been ascertained beyond all doubt. By very recent accounts he has sent troops after the mutineers, who had gone off towards Delhi. He had also offered a large reward for the capture of the chief instigator of the rising, and had sent his remaining valuables into the fort at Mhow. A force under Captain Orr is moving up rapidly to his assistance, and Brigadier Stuart's moveable column is by this time well advanced from Aurungabad. It is to be hoped that by these energetic measures the peace of Central India may be re-established and preserved.

Accounts received from Asseerghur, dated the 7th inst., give the following particulars:—The wing of Scindia's Contingent had been moved down into the low country outside the fort of Asseerghur, and the company at Boorhampoor had been disarmed and made prisoners by Captain Birch, with a small party of Bheels. This places the safety of the fort beyond all doubt, as the Bheels are trustworthy men, whose fidelity has never been questioned.

At Mhow the 23rd Bengal Native Infantry have mutinied; the number of Europeans slain is at present unknown, but it is said to be four. The officers are holding a fortified square in the place, where the ladies and all the other Europeans have taken refuge. Captain Hungerford, of the Bengal Artillery, who commands in the Fort of Mhow, is an officer of nerve and experience, and there is little doubt but he will adopt measures, in concert with Colonel Durand and Captain Orr, for the relief and security of his charge.

The following letter gives the details of this rising:—

"Fort Mhow, July 6.

"On the morning of the 1st inst. we received a message from the Resident at Indore that he was attacked by the Maharajah's troops. We sent off a troop of our cavalry, with all our guns, to assist him; but when they had reached within four miles of Indore they got a letter from the Resident, saying that he had been obliged to retire. The guns returned again to Mhow. Then Colonel Platt marched them into the fort, took precautionary measures, and all the ladies and non-combatants came into it. This, I must tell you, happened while I was out; for immediately the guns came in from their march, I was sent out with 30 men on the Indore road as an advanced picket, because we anticipated an attack from Holkar's troops. I was about eight miles from Mhow, and in time, about 7 o'clock, P.M., a fresh batch of 30 men came to relieve those I took out; but we being short of officers, I could not be relieved, and I was told to stop out all night. The first batch retired, leaving me with the fresh men, with whom I conversed, as I liked the men, and I fancied they liked me. About 9 o'clock, P.M., a man came galloping up from the station, and told me I was to bring my picket nearer. Of course we mounted, and away we trotted till we came to the bridge, which is about a mile and a half from our cavalry lines, which are on the extreme right. By the time we reached the bridge, and I had posted my videttes, it was about 10 o'clock. I then sat down and talked to my jemadar, all the men lying down, holding their horses. In about two minutes I heard a shot from the direction of the station, then another, and another, and so on. I took no apparent notice of this, but got up and sauntered away, so as to get to the end nearest the station; my horse, held all ready, as is usual on picket, was at that end. I still continued talking, but now to the havildar and one or two others. All this time the firing at the station was very brisk, and I remarked that they must have been attacked by the Maharajah's forces; and the men replied, 'Yes, it must be so, certainly.' The firing continued about half an hour. It was not a very dark night, when all at once the church, which was situated on the highest and most central position in the station, became illuminated by a bungalow, which had been fired immediately behind it. I was then certain that it was our own troops who had mutinied. I, however, still continued talking to the men, although I knew they (the mutineers) would make for my picket, it being on the only road to Indore. I heard a galloping of horses approaching us, and I called for my horse, mounted, and ordered the men to mount—I had previously ordered them to stand to their horses when the firing began. I posted myself on the bridge, the men drawn up behind me all ready. I did not draw my sword, as, if I had, it would have betrayed an anxiety which I did not wish them to imagine I entertained. The horsemen I had heard came up in single file, and pulled up a little before they reached us, and walked up to me. The first man who came up said that the regiment was drawn up on parade, and that I was to return immediately. I turned round to give the order, and this man passed me. Just as I had moved on at a walk the second man clapped a pistol within a yard of my heart and fired; the ball, however, must have passed under my arm, as I was in the act of ordering the men to march, and had turned round to make them hear me. This was enough. My own guard and the other men called out, 'Kill him, kill him!' when they saw me moving on unhurt. I then put spurs to my horse and went away like the wind. I passed two or three others on the road, and they too fired at me, but they might as well have shot at a flash of lightning. I tried to draw my sword, but it fell from the scabbard, and I had not any pistols with me, so I made the scabbard serve for a sword and galloped on, passing burning bungalows, arrived at the fort, and was, of course, let in and loaded with congratulations, for every one thought I was done for to a certainty. As I galloped along I thought it strange that I met no infantry, but I found the guns had been out and put them to flight, and thus cleared my road. I have lost everything, the servants assisting the Sepoys in the plunder. All I have is the clothes I had on, my scabbard, my horse, saddle and bridle. Others who have saved some things help those who were less fortunate. My house being in a hollow in the cavalry lines, a mile and a-half from the fort, made plundering easy. We are now in a state of siege.

"Major Harris, of ours (the 1st Bengal Cavalry), Colonel Platt, and Captain Fagan, of the 23rd Bengal Native Infantry, are killed. We brought their bodies in on the 2nd and buried them. All the officers are volunteers now, and we go out with the guns when we want to fetch things in, and we mount sentry on the bastions at night to let the artillerymen sleep. Altogether we are earning our pay and are as jolly as possible. General Woodburn's force is coming up, and I think we shall hold our own. It appears that the Maharajah himself (Holkar) was on our side, but it was his troops that rose. They have marched off with our mutineers for Delhi, I believe; however, if they come here we are ready and only too willing to meet them, as they will find to their cost."

The following is the evidence of a Sowar (Nujamooddeen), of two classies belonging to Bhugwandoss's (native jemadar's) establishment, and of one classie of Mahomed Ismael's (native jemadar's) establishment. All four were shut up in the fort with the gentlemen, and on their release thence, on the 10th inst., came to Mahoba and related the occurrences.

"Nagode, June 25.

"For some time since, the gentlemen had been in the habit of passing the nights in the fort, and spending the days at their bungalows. Captain Burgess and his establishment had their tents pitched within the fort, and everything was being put in readiness to retreat into the fort as soon as there should be occasion to do so, which occurred on the evening of the 4th of June. Some few effected their escape from the place altogether; one gentleman (name unknown) reached Burwar Sagar, when, meeting with a native surveyor of the canal establishment, Sahib Rai, he gave him his watch and horse, and procuring a Hindostanee dress escaped on foot. He was scarcely out of sight when two Suwars, who were hotly pursuing him, arrived there, and recognizing the horse, took Sahib Rai and the Thanadar prisoners (bound) back to Jhansi, where they were still when last heard of.

"Lieutenant Turnbull was not so fortunate, as, not having been able to gain the fort, he climbed a large tree. He had, however, been seen, and was shot in the tree.

"From the evening of the 4th until noon of the 8th the gentlemen in the fort kept good their position, the ladies assisting them in cooking for them, sending them refreshments, casting bullets, &c. There were 55 in number altogether (Europeans), inclusive of the ladies and children, and they began to get very much straitened for want of provisions, &c. Behind all the gates they had piled high heaps of stones to strengthen them, and kept up so good a defence that one of the cannon which had been brought too near the gates was abandoned, and it was only by fixing ropes to it in the night time that the mutineers were able to regain possession of it. Lieutenant Powys was the first person killed in the fort. The way he met his death was this:—Two men, brothers, in Captain Burgess's employ (one was his jemadar) declared that they would go out. They were told they would be shot down if they attempted it, but they said they might as well be shot as stay there to be starved, and accordingly commenced undoing the fastenings. One was shot immediately; the other turned on Lieutenant Powys, who happened to be near him, and cut him down with his tulwar. This one also was directly shot by Captain Burgess. The only other person killed inside the fort was Captain Burgess himself, who received a bullet in the head after having, I am told, with his own hand, killed no less than 25. All the natives spoke of his great skill as a marksman.

"The mutineers at last, having forced the Ranee to assist them with guns and elephants, succeeded in effecting an entrance at two of the gates, and they promised the gentlemen that if they laid down their arms and gave themselves up quietly, their lives should be spared. The gentlemen unfortunately trusted to their word and came out. They were tied in a long line between some trees, and after a short consultation had their heads struck off. Such ladies as had children had to see them cut in halves before their own turns came. The Suwars, it appears, bore the principal part in all these atrocities. This took place on the afternoon of the 8th June.

"C. D. KIRCHOFF, Sergeant and A. O."

Concerning the mutiny at Nowgong, we simply know the fact that the headquarters of the 12th Native Infantry and of the 14th Irregular Cavalry stationed there have followed the example of the left wing of each corps which was stationed at Jhansi, but that the officers are safe. The news of the Jhansi mutiny was communicated by last mail, with an account of the bloody tragedy enacted on that occasion in the massacre of all the Europeans in the place. We now learn that besides Mrs. Skene and family, Mrs. Browne, Miss Browne, and Miss Davidson have been killed. Altogether twelve of our countrymen and women were slaughtered in this small station. The only persons known to have escaped are two customs officers, who have reached Agra.

We are as yet without particulars of the mutiny at Saugor, the news of which reached Bombay on the 8th of June, from a correspondent at Kamptee, who was able, however, to state that no atrocities had as yet been committed, all the officers and families, with the European artillery, having taken refuge in the fort. Saugor is the chief station in the districts known as the Saugor and Nerbudda territories, and must have a considerable European population in the shape of writers, conductors, and others, concerning whose safety, after what has transpired at Jhansi, in these same territories, much uneasiness must be felt. It is to be hoped that these men and their families have found refuge in the fort also.

To quell the revolt along the valley of the Nerbudda, which is now general from Mhow to Bundelcund, a light field brigade has been ordered to assemble immediately at Malligaum, under the command of Colonel C. H. Somerset, and the troops are already on their march thither. This force will be composed as follows :—Half troop Horse Artillery (Europeans), a squadron of her Majesty's 14th Light Dragoons, a wing of her Majesty's 86th Foot, 5th Bombay Native Infantry, 3rd Nizam's Cavalry, a detachment of the Poonah Horse, and a detachment of Sappers and Miners.

General Woodburn's moveable column, originally ordered to Mhow, stands fast at Aurungabad, and this arrangement is doubtless a judicious one, in view of the unsettled state of the Nagpore territories, and the doubtful temper of the Nizam's troops. We regret to learn that the General has been compelled to resign the command through severe sickness. Colonel C. S. Stuart is appointed to succeed him. This force is composed as follows :—Two squadrons of her Majesty's 14th Light Dragoons, a battery of European Horse Artillery, 25th Bombay Native Infantry, 24th ditto (one wing), and the Light Infantry battalion from Persia. General Woodburn's column has already crushed the rebellion at Aurungabad, where our readers may remember the 1st Nizam's Cavalry mutinied, and it is hoped that the presence of the force at that station will doubtless overawe effectually any open disaffection in that quarter for the future.

The full importance of the risings of which intelligence has last been received, will be apparent by finding the localities on the map. Indore and Asseeghur are respectively north and south of the Nerbudda, which flows into the Gulf of Cambay, in the Bombay Presidency; Aurungabad is within that division of India, and the nearest point to Bombay which the insurrection has yet reached. Nagpore was the capital of the deposed Rajah of Berar, and marks the present southern limit of the revolt. All is reported quiet throughout the province. As a precautionary measure, the Irregular Cavalry was disarmed on the 23rd of June, quietly. Every effort is being continued in strengthening the defences of the hill at Seebbuldee, and the police of the city and of the cantonments of

Kamptee have been greatly strengthened. At Aurungabad all was quiet. General Woodburn's column was at Ahmednuggur en route to Mhow, where it was expected on the 16th. At Hydrabad all was quiet on the 19th.

The only particulars we have of the mutiny at Banda are contained in a letter from Nagode, dated June 19, of which the following is an extract:—

"We have escaped from Banda to Nagode, and through God's mercy have been miraculously preserved. On Sunday, the 14th, the Nawab's troops mutinied, as well as the Native Infantry. The Mahomedans planted their flag, and wanted to kill us, but the Nawab stood by us, and we got into buggies and on horses, and got off. The place was in a blaze before we had got a mile; it was a fearful scene. We start again to-night for Mirzapore, and hope to reach it safely, but this district is very much disturbed."

Of the whole country of Rohilcund, Futtyghur (Furruckabad) was the last station to rise. The 10th Regiment has unquestionably given in, simply to the force of the dangerous example all around it. The Sepoys of this corps continued for weeks to guard the treasury and maintain discipline, while every station near them was in open mutiny. They do not appear to have offered any violence whatever to their officers, but a most melancholy rumour prevailed in Allahabad on the 23rd as to the fate of the unhappy fugitives after they left the place. We take it from the *Englishman* of the 29th:—"132 Europeans, men, women, and children, in fifty boats, left Futtyghur for this place. They were all the non-military residents of the place. On arrival at Bhitoor the Nana Sahib fired on them with the artillery the Government allowed him to keep. One round shot struck poor Mrs. ———, and killed her on the spot. The boats were then boarded and the inmates landed and dragged to the parade ground at Cawnpore, where they were first fired at, then literally hacked to pieces with tulwars. Report says not one escaped."

From Bhaugulpore, they write:—

"There is no doubt that we are in great danger here; the 5th Irregulars and the Native Infantry are looked upon with great suspicion. The ladies and children have been sent away to the station, and you may fancy how great the occasion was when a lady, who had only been confined a few hours, was put on board the steamer along with the others. Mutiny is spreading daily. The native troops at Berhampore, after what we have seen, cannot well be trusted. A rise is expected; if the re-taking of Delhi becomes generally known, it may be the means of preventing many more regiments from rising. The political agent and the judge, with their families, bolted to the Nawab's palace from Berhampore; and Mr. Spencer, the Berhampore magistrate, writes that the Nawab is doing everything in his power to assist the authorities."

Berhampore is not far from Calcutta; it was there the disaffection of the Sepoys was first manifested. The letter was written, it will be observed, under the impression that Delhi had fallen, rumours to that effect having several times been circulated.

We have already related the circumstances connected with the mutinies at Benares and Allahabad. Colonel Neill, by whose vigour and promptitude the mutinous Sepoys, Sikhs, and Irregular Cavalry were dispersed at the former place, no sooner heard of the outbreak at Allahabad than he set out with the Europeans to crush it. He was just in time to save the fort from falling into the hands of the rebels. He found there discontented and beleaguered troops, deficient supplies, and distracted counsels. The Mahomedan population of Allahabad were "lording it" all over the country, and there were none to put them down. Colonel Neill's presence changed all this very quickly On the day of his arrival the rebels were attacked and dispersed; measures were taken to restore confidence to the well-disposed, and as many of the rebels as were captured were either shot or hanged. Before three days had elapsed, "order reigned in Allahabad," and the indefatigable Neill was preparing to relieve Cawnpore. Carriage was scarce; it was impossible to move. Thus at least ran the reports made to him. He solved the difficulty by simply ignoring the word, and as soon as he could leave Allahabad to take care of itself, he set out at the head, it is stated, of 400 Europeans and 600 Sikhs. He had scarcely left Allahabad when Brigadier-General Havelock arrived there; he had already been joined by the greater portion of the 64th regiment, and on the arrival of a wing of the 78th Highlanders, daily expected, he was preparing to follow Colonel Neill's footsteps at the head of above a thousand Europeans.

The following letter, received after our account of the Benares mutiny was in type, will be read with interest; it is from the wife of Lieut. Tucker, late of the 15th Irregular Cavalry. This gallant young officer was the only one belonging to the 15th Irregular Cavalry whose life was spared. The last accounts brought the tidings that he was safe at Benares, restored to his wife and child, but suffering from fever, consequent upon the perils which for seventeen days he had undergone.

"Benares, June 27.

"I will tell you all about Charlie as it happened, as I know you will like to hear every particular. On the evening of the day I sent off your letters (my birthday, the 14th) one of the coolies I had sent with a letter to Sultanpore, returned with it, and one of our grooms with him, saying that on the 9th the troops at Sultanpore had mutinied, that Colonel Fisher, Captain Gibbings, and others had been killed, but that Charlie had escaped; but the groom did not know where he had gone. You can fancy what a terrible state I was in. Mr. H. Tucker directly sent out in the Sultanpore direction, offering £100 to whoever would bring him in. However, we could hear nothing of him till the following Wednesday evening, when a man brought in a letter from him, saying that he and others were safe under the protection of a native gentleman about 14 miles from Sultanpore. A large party of natives, with elephants, were sent out the next day to bring them in here. They arrived safely yesterday morning. It was at first proposed to send English gentlemen and soldiers for them, and Charlie's brother intended going too; but it was thought that Europeans would have attracted too much attention, and that the people in Oude would rise and cut them off, which most probably would have been the case had they gone, so all the most trustworthy natives were selected instead.

"I will now give you Charlie's own account of his escape. On the Sunday before the mutiny at Sultanpore (which was on the Tuesday morning), Charlie went out some distance to meet the wing of his regiment which he commanded at Seetapore, and which was inclined to mutiny, to see if he could pacify the men; and he apparently did so, and brought them, with the second in command, into Sultanpore on the Monday night late. About 8 o'clock on the Tuesday morning, poor Colonel Fisher, while out, was shot through the body by the native police. Charlie directly went to him, and, after much trouble, persuaded some of the men to get him into a dooly. He said he was dying; but Charlie took out the ball, and gave him some water. He then tried to persuade the regiment to come near their Colonel, but no one would obey any order. They were all under some trees close to our house. A party of them then made a rush at Captain Gibbins, who was on horseback at a little distance, and killed him; and then the men shouted to Charlie to go away.

"He found it was all over then, and so rode off. Three men rode after him about a mile, and then returned. He thinks they must have wished to spare him, as they could easily have done anything they liked; but he was, I believe, a great favourite with the wing he commanded at Seetapore.

"He rode some distance, and then got into a jungle, where he stayed a great part of the day; but he had first gone into a village, with one of his grooms who had got his mare, and who said he would take care of him, but Charlie found out that he meant to betray him; so he rode off.

"Only fancy how dreadful it was for him to be wandering about in the heat of the day, not knowing where to go, and getting people to give him water to drink at wells, and at last drinking it out of little streams, he was so terribly thirsty. At last, about 4 o'clock in the afternoon, he asked a man whom he saw for some water, and also if he could protect him, for he and his horse were both getting knocked up. The man said he would, and took him into his village, and afterwards to his master, who lived in a native fort, and who was the principal person in the place; and there Charlie stayed until the party from here went to fetch him. His escape was most providential, for he did not know the people about there. Soon after he had reached the native's house four others from Sultanpore arrived; but one of them knew the way to the person who took Charlie in. He must be a most noble-hearted native, for when we took Oude it half ruined him. He is to have quantities of presents from Charlie, St. George, Henry, and I believe from government. . . .

"The ladies from Sultanpore all escaped. Only four people were killed there— namely, Colonel Fisher, Captain Gibbings, Mr. Block, and Mr. Strogan; the latter was one of those who were married when we were there. I am very sorry for his wife. Mr. Block was the only other married man of the four. All the houses in Sultanpore were burnt by the mutineers. They stole two or three boxes out of our house first, the groom said, and then burnt it, so we have lost everything, except what I happened to have with me here and the carriage and horses, which had taken away some of the ladies, and the horse that Charlie was riding, which was the Arab that was bought originally for me when we first came to the country. At any other time I should have been dreadfully grieved, but now that Charlie has been spared, when so many have been murdered, I can only feel most thankful to the Providence that has watched over him and all of us in these terrible times."

Meanwhile accounts from Cawnpore are to this extent cheering, that we know that General Wheeler holds out, and intends to do so till relieved. Too much praise cannot be accorded to this gallant officer. With a handful of Europeans he has held a barrack, badly situated for defensive purposes, against thousands of natives, many of them trained by us in the art of war, and armed with guns. He was at one critical period getting short of ammunition; he sallied forth at the head of fifty men, and took a sufficient supply from the enemy to last him for six weeks. Whatever might happen, he would never surrender; indeed, holding only that barrack against the country in open arms against him, he writes with the greatest confidence as to his means of defence. When it is considered that this barrack is crammed with women and children, all of whom have not only to be defended, but to be fed and provided for, and that General Wheeler's resources lie solely in his own nerve and activity, we are confident that the claims of the gallant general to the gratitude of his countrymen will be properly estimated at home. A native who left Cawnpore on the 18th, has written from Allahabad to the effect that Sir Hugh Wheeler was not only holding his ground, but would probably continue to do so, as the insurgents were quarrelling among themselves and many of them had dispersed. This man mentions that the Mahratta chief of Bittore and other rebels had put to death nearly two hundred Europeans, including above one hundred fugitives from, as he says, Nynee Tal, but more likely from Futtygurh. Sir Hugh Wheeler, having been annoyed by a gun brought against him by the insurgents, sent out a party of twenty Europeans to spike it. This they not only succeeded in doing, but killed a good many of the enemy besides.

Equally marvellous has been the position of Sir Henry Lawrence at Lucknow. The whole of Oude has risen. Yet, with 500 Europeans Sir Henry Lawrence maintains his position. With a whole province in arms against him he overawes Lucknow, and keeps the rebels at a distance. They actually dare not attack him. It is perhaps one of the most astonishing feats ever performed. Other men would fail with 5000 Europeans at their beck. It only shows the value of a good head and an undaunted heart. The possession of these has enabled Sir Henry Lawrence to check the enemy in a vital quarter, and to save an incalculable number of lives. There have been a good many mutinies of regiments in the interior, but he had still with him in the cantonments a large remnant of corps that had mutinied, and that were behaving in an orderly and satisfactory manner.

The whole Punjaub remains quiet, thanks to the energetic conduct of the commissioner, and the men in command. Many of the disarmed native regiments have begged the restitution of their weapons, and to be led against Delhi, but it would be madness, after what has transpired, to listen to such prayers.

Intelligence has been received from Peshawur that the 10th Irregular

Cavalry has been disarmed 'at Nowshera. The men of Major Knatchbull's battery have been disarmed at Meean Meer. Major-General Nicholson's movable column was at Jullundur at the date of last advices *viâ* Lahore.

To overawe the Mewar territory, and keep the Gwalior Contingent in check, a considerable force is on the march from Deesa, and must now be in advance of Nusseerabad. It consists as follows:—3 horse artillery guns (Europeans), 500 men her Majesty's 83rd Regiment Foot, 400 men 12th Regiment Bombay Native Infantry, two squadrons 2nd Bombay Light Cavalry.

The following extract from an Agra journal will be read with interest; the points to which we wish to direct particular attention are the evidence it affords of isolation, as shown by the preparations and precautions against the worst, and the doubt which is alluded to of the paper reaching Calcutta or Bombay:—

"It is some time now since we heard anything of or from friends 'far away,' nor have we had an opportunity of communicating our situation to them. Living in the midst of alarms, some anxiety must be felt on our account, which we will endeavour to dissipate by showing how far we are prepared to resist any attack from without, and the precautions taken to prevent any local disturbance by disarming the tag-rag scum, the friends, and arming the wealthy and respectable, the enemies of disorder. And we doubt not but our present issue will find its way even to Bombay and Calcutta. It must be remembered, then, that we have Akhbar's Fort here, and never during nor since the days of the old hero has his citadel been the scene of such rapid and complete preparations to endure a siege or form the lair whence the British Lion, in all the confidence of undaunted courage and unsubdued strength, might leap on the insurgent foe. The walls bristle with cannon, with ammunition in abundance, and handy; in fact, the whole place exhibits a perfect paraphernalia of war. Our old friend Jotee Persaud has again shown himself the best commissariat officer in the world, by laying in, within thirty hours of receiving the order, stores and provisions to last 10,000 men for a month; old buildings have been repaired and rendered somewhat habitable, and accommodation for upwards of 3000 individuals secured. In the search for these habitations, and the consequent clearings and excavations, many strange nooks and subterraneous passages and buildings have been discovered, which will, in more quiet times, form curious objects of research for the antiquarian; among them is a large well, having six ranges of apartments piled one above the other, with steps leading down, the last range reaching the water's edge. The fort, however, is a last refuge, and will at first be used merely as a place of safety for the families of the soldiery, or those requiring special protection, so as to allow them complete freedom of action. However, the European inhabitants, although not in the Fort, are not on that account scattered nor defenceless, but with a prudence taught by the incidents of the mutiny, the largest and strongest buildings in the station have been fixed on by authority as places of rendezvous; of these there are five or six situated in different convenient parts for the residents. Arms and ammunition are provided from the Fort, and those living in the neighbourhood are desired to resort to them in case of any alarm. All men Christians have volunteered to form a garrison for one or other of these posts, the defences of the buildings, which already present a pretty formidable appearance, and the discipline of the men, which being willingly submitted to, already does them credit, are intrusted to military officers. Those capable of riding horses are formed into cavalry corps, of whom some have already seen service on the Allygurh road. A few men have already been dismissed from artillery practice, being pronounced fit to manage cannon."

We come now to the great point of interest—Delhi. The enemy endeavoured on the 17th to erect a battery to annoy our picket at Hindoo Rao's house. They were charged on that evening, driven back, and one of their guns was captured.

The following letter, dated Camp before Delhi, will be found highly interesting:—

" My dear ———,   " June 18 (Waterloo Day), 1857.

" Rather a brisk affair occurred here yesterday. During the day, but particularly in the afternoon, the enemy were observed outside the Lahore gate in large numbers, evidently planning and carrying out some special project. At half-past four o'clock P.M., our troops were turned out to ascertain, if possible, what it might be, and in a very short time they were busily engaged in most laudable musketry practice. Tombs (Major), with his troop of Horse Artillery, was, as usual, on the ground, the Rifles (her

Majesty's 60th) and the Goorkas being the other principal *dramatis personæ*. After a time it was observed that a large Serai, called 'Eed Ghah,' opposite the Ajmere gate, was being occupied by the enemy, and that it had been strengthened from without by the defences which had been constructed during the day.

"It was resolved that the said Serai should be ours; though, I must tell you, that it was an exceedingly strong position, which a few hundred stout-hearted men might hold in face of thousands. It was attacked accordingly, and taken in glorious style. The enemy stood for a time, but their show of resistance was, on the whole, brief. The gates of the place were smashed, the enemy's ammunition (two hackery loads) blown up, and the only gun (a 9-pounder) which they had to bring to the scene of action, spiked, taken, and walked off with *tout de suite*. Their loss was probably considerable. I should think at least 100 were killed; whilst, I rejoice to say, we only lost three or four men in all, exclusive of a small number on the list of wounded.

"In the evening, whilst we were sitting at mess in the open air, General Barnard rode up and asked if Major Tombs was present. On being informed that he was not, the General, without dismounting from his horse, said, that he had come to the Artillery mess publicly to express his opinion of Major Tombs' gallantry in the affair which was just terminated. He said, considering the strong nature of the enemy's position, the resolute manner in which it was attacked, the masterly way in which our troops were handled, and the happy result of the whole engagement, he had never, in the course of his military experience, seen more remarkable bravery, or cooler, better judgment displayed by any officer in the field than by Major Tombs of the Artillery. The word by which the General characterised it was 'glorious.'

"Tombs was slightly wounded on the arm by a musket bullet, and had two horses shot under him, having already, since we left Meerut, lost three chargers in the same way. With such facts, such results, and such praise as I have mentioned, surely the Victoria Cross would be but a well-merited reward to such an officer, who has already his share of medals and ordinary honours.

"The order of the day here as regards the siege seems to be 'delay' till reinforcements arrive. Shortly (within a week, I believe), 1500 European bayonets, two troops of Horse Artillery, and two Sikh Regiments may be expected in this camp. Then for a tragedy, such as the Chandney Chowk has certainly not witnessed since the days of Nadir Shah. If anything escapes destruction may it be the Palace gardens, with the mangoe topes, cascades, and fountains, and the ice pits. *Du reste*, let archæologists and antiquarians write and fight."

Notwithstanding the defeat which they received on the 17th, in their attempt to establish a battery at the Serai, the insurgents made a sortie on the 19th in great force, but were driven in with considerable loss. On the same day the Nusseerabad mutineers, with some (said to be six) guns, contrived to get in the rear of our position and created great confusion. They were driven back, with a heavy loss in killed and wounded and two guns; but our loss was also severe, and when we consider that common precaution would have averted this loss, we feel bound to state that there must be great incompetency somewhere; and the sooner the valuable lives of our brave soldiers are intrusted to other care the better. We find this opinion expressed by an officer on the spot, in a letter which appeared in an Indian journal, the writer adding :—

"If our brave men, the heroes of our country, are to be made targets of after this fashion, we see no policy in delaying the assault. It would surely be better to lose them and gain the city of Delhi, and the punishment of the traitors within it, than to lose them and gain—two guns!"

The English loss in this action consisted of Colonel Yule, her Majesty's 9th Lancers; Captain Alexander, 3rd Native Infantry; Mr. Humphrey, and ten men killed: Colonel Becher, Quarter-Master-General, and several others wounded.

Early on the morning of the 20th, the insurgents opened a warm fire on the English lines with round shot, apparently to cover another sortie, as a somewhat confused and very brief account of the affair in an Indian journal says that they halted as soon as the English began to advance. On the 23rd they again sallied out in great force from the Subjee Mundee side, and fought most desperately the whole day long. They had a strong position in a village and among the garden walls. Their efforts were more determined than on any previous occasion. It is said that their dead, at the close of the day, were counted by hundreds, their aggregate being variously estimated at from 400 to 1000. The gardens and buildings outside the city, in which they had sheltered themselves, and given us much annoyance, have been taken possession of by us; and it is said that, since the above date, they have, in a marked manner, evinced less boldness in their attacks than heretofore. A letter written on the following day says:—

"We have been quiet to-day; how long it will last it is impossible to say. Ever since the day we have arrived here, have the troops been more or less knocked up by exposure to sun and fatigue, &c., but the men, notwithstanding, keep up their truly British spirit, and it is surprising how cheerfully all endure this harassing work, and how manfully, through God's blessing, we have repulsed every one of their desperate attacks. We have now been here sixteen days. A small portion of the reinforcement arrived yesterday, and Brigadier Chamberlain came in, I hear, to-day."

All remained quiet at Delhi during the 24th and 25th. The mutineers made several attacks on our pickets on the 27th, but were repulsed with loss, there being but trifling casualties on our side. It is stated that our artillery did great execution, while the killed on our side did not exceed 12. Lieutenant Harris, of the 2nd Fusiliers, was wounded, and Lieutenant Chalmers, of the Guides, slightly. The rains appeared to have set in. The bridge at Baghput has been broken, and the river has now become swollen by the rains.

General Van Cortlandt, while marching from the north-west upon Jahnsi and Hissar with the Buttiannah Irregular Force, had two engagements with the rebels in the neighbourhood of Sirsa, defeating them in each instance with severe loss.

The following telegraphic despatch, was received through Her Majesty's Consul at Cagliari, August 21, at 7 A M. We publish it *verbatim.*

"Alexandria, August 14, 9 P.M.

"The *Nubia* arrived at Suez to-day. She brings dates from Calcutta to the 21st July; Madras, 25th July; Galle, 28th July; Aden, 8th inst. The telegraphic message from Suez is meagre and confused, and there is not time to receive explanation before the departure of the steamer *Bœotia* for Malta. It is stated that Delhi is not taken, but the date is not given. General Barnard is reported to have died from dysentery. The news given in the *Bombay Times* of the 14th July by last mail, respecting the taking of Cawnpore by the rebels, and the massacre of the Europeans there, is confirmed. The Suez telegraphic message then goes on to say as follows:—'*Simoom* and *Himalaya* arrived at Calcutta with about 1500 of China forces, to proceed at once up country. Only 300 more troops expected, General Hancock's forces.* Rebels beaten on three occasions, and several guns taken, between Allahabad and Cawnpore; the latter retaken from Nana Sahib, whom Havelock is following up the Blittoe† about ten miles. Sir Henry Lawrence died of wounds received in a sortie from Lucknow, where at present all is well. All the troops in Oude mutinied. Agra all quiet; native troops disarmed. Gwalior Contingent mutinied; supposed to have marched on Indore. No political China news given. The *Transit* Government steamer totally lost in the Straits of Sunda; crew and troops all arrived at Suez to-day. This telegraph received from acting Consul-General Green at Alexandria, for the Earl of Clarendon. "'Consul CRAIG.'"

---

* This is probably Havelock. † Probably Bithoor.

PART 2, continuing the Narrative, will appear immediately on receipt of Official Intelligence of the Fall of Delhi.

www.ingramcontent.com/pod-product-compliance
Lightning Source LLC
Chambersburg PA
CBHW031134160426
43193CB00008B/139